MARIONETTE PLAYS
FROM NORTHERN CHINA

MARIONETTE PLAYS
FROM NORTHERN CHINA

TRANSLATED, EDITED, AND WITH AN INTRODUCTION BY

FAN PEN LI CHEN

STATE UNIVERSITY OF NEW YORK PRESS

On the cover: A young male (Wei Tiancai's 魏天才 puppet).
Photo by Fan Pen Li Chen.

Published by State University of New York Press, Albany

Printed in the United States of America

For information, contact State University of New York Press, Albany, NY
www.sunypress.edu

Production, Dana Foote
Marketing, Fran Keneston

Library of Congress Cataloging-in-Publication Data

Names: Chen, Fan-Pen Li, 1953– author.
Title: Marionette plays from northern China / translated, edited, and with an introduction by Fan Pen Li Chen.
Description: Albany : State University of New York Press, [2017] | Includes bibliographical references.
Identifiers: LCCN 2016031493 (print) | LCCN 2016048536 (ebook) | ISBN 9781438464831 (hc : alk. paper) | ISBN 9781438464848 (pb : alk. paper) | ISBN 9781438464855 (e-book)
Subjects: LCSH: Puppet plays, Chinese—China—Shaanxi Sheng—Translations into English.
Classification: LCC PN1978.C5 C43 2017 (print) | LCC PN1978.C5 (ebook) | DDC 895.12/008—dc23
LC record available at https://lccn.loc.gov/2016031493

10 9 8 7 6 5 4 3 2 1

Contents

Illustrations

Acknowledgments

I could never have considered undertaking research about the marionette theater genre in the remote reaches of northeastern Shaanxi if it were not for Yang Fei 杨飞 and his wife, Li Shuwen 李淑文. A famous collector of shadow puppet figures, Yang Fei accompanied me to many otherwise inaccessible villages in Shaanxi when I conducted fieldwork on Chinese shadow theater from 1997 to 1999. Li Shuwen's natal home was in Heyang 合阳, the only location where marionette theater has survived in northern China. Conveniently, Li Shuwen's brother was the deputy county mayor of Heyang during a time when it would not have been easy, or even possible, for foreigners to visit remote regions of China. Yang and Li accompanied me to Heyang, and arranged for me to stay at the home of Li's brother, watch a performance by the official Heyang Marionette Art Troupe 合阳提线木偶艺术团 at a private funeral, and meet with performers such as Dang Wenhui 党文辉 and Wang Hongmin 王红民, and the local researcher Shi Yaozeng 史耀增. Dang Wenhui and Shi Yaozeng were particularly knowledgeable and helpful. Dang provided me with copies of the plays translated in this book, and Shi's articles have been copiously referenced in the introduction.

Thanks to a Faculty Research Assistance Program B grant from SUNY Albany, I was able to return to Heyang to conduct further research in 2004. Aside from Yang Fei and Li Shuwen, I was accompanied by Dang Fengju 党凤菊, a performer hired by a tourist agency in Xi'an, and Ingrid Chen, my younger daughter, who helped with taking photos while I videotaped performances. Dang Fengju took us to Xizhonglei Village 西中雷村 to visit her teacher, Wei Tiancai 魏天才 (1913–?). Convinced that marionette theater originated at their very village, the villagers most graciously put on a show for us after their day of farm work. We also saw members of the former official marionette troupe perform at Maiden Spring 处女泉, a local theme park. I am very grateful for the warmth and generosity shown to me in Heyang.

Translation of most of the plays in this book was accomplished over an extended period of time. I am truly grateful for the generous residence and grant provided by the Institut International de la Marionnette at Charlesville-Mezieres, France, which enabled me to finally complete this manuscript during my fall 2014 sabbatical semester.

I was deeply saddened by the news of Yang Fei's sudden death almost four years ago. He was the only person who thought nothing of accompanying me to remote villages on local buses in the 1990s, and having us stay at the homes of performers and carvers of shadow figures. I also thank him for introducing me to the genre of "post-midnight skits" and the marionette theater of Heyang.

Kimberley Chen and Ingrid Chen have been the most wonderful daughters anyone might want to have. My siblings Sen Pen Pu, Kao Li and Shipen Li have also been very encouraging about my work. I would also like to thank my many friends and colleagues who have been supportive—you know who you are. Donna Albright, my college roommate and lifelong friend, deserves special thanks for editing this manuscript tirelessly and expertly. My gratitude to both her and her husband, Steven Strauss.

1. Dang Fengju 党凤菊 (Heyang Xinyi Oujutuan 合阳新艺偶剧团) performing at Gaojiayuan 高家院 in Xi'an, Shaanxi, with a young female 小旦 puppet. Photo by Fan Pen Li Chen.

2. A young male 小生 puppet performing at Gaojiayuan 高家院 in Xi'an, Shaanxi. Photo by Fan Pen Li Chen.

3. Orchestra directed by Wei Tiancai 魏天才 (1914–?) at a village in Heyang. Photo by Ingrid Chen.

4. Old woman role 老旦 of Heyang Xinyi Oujutuan. Photo by Ingrid Chen.

5. Performance by Wei Tiancai. Photo by Ingrid Chen.

6. Wei Tiancai's trunk of headdresses. Photo by Ingrid Chen.

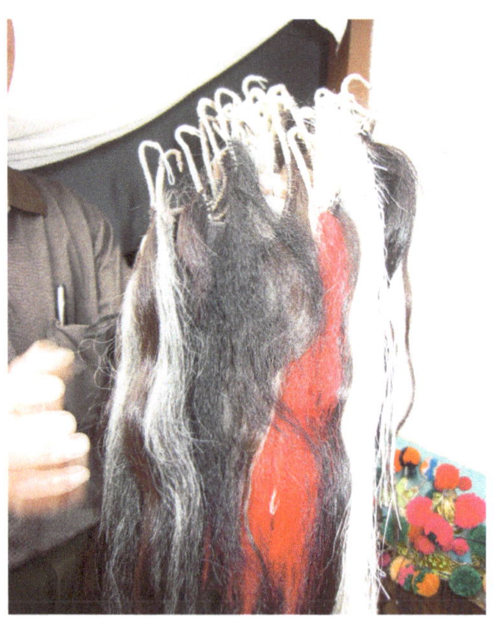

7. Beards for Wei Tiancai's puppets. Photo by Ingrid Chen.

8. Flat headdresses for Wei Tiancai's puppets. Photo by Ingrid Chen.

9. Wei Tiancai's trunk with heads. Photo by Ingrid Chen.

10. Wei Tiancai's son-in-law with some fully dressed puppets. Photo by Ingrid Chen.

11. Monkey King (Sun Wukong 孙悟空) from the Heyang County Marionette Troupe. Photo by Fan Pen Li Chen.

12. Emperor without headgear. Heyang County Marionette Troupe. Photo by Fan Pen Li Chen.

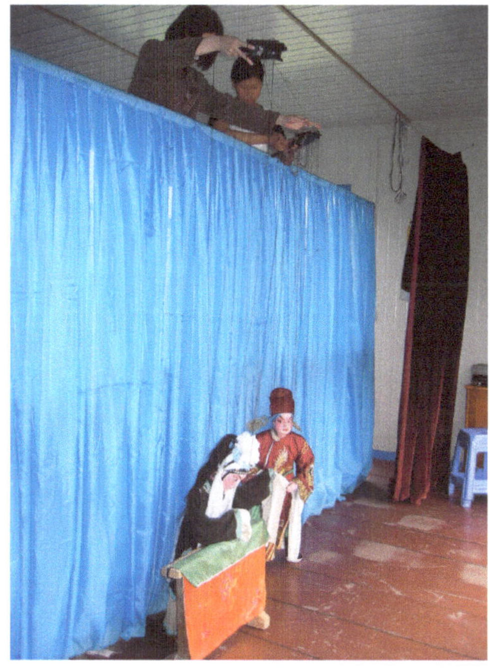

13. Members of the Heyang County Marionette Troupe performing at the Maiden Spring theme park using long strings. Photo by Fan Pen Li Chen.

14. Photo by Mingsheng Ye 叶明生 during 2009 at Nanshun Village 南顺村 of Xinchi Town 新池镇.

15. A female role puppet from the Guojia Troupe 郭家班 at the Fuke 福客 Restaurant on the North Plaza of the Wild Goose Pagoda in Xi'an. Photo by Fan Pen Li Chen.

Introduction

Chinese Puppet Theaters

The traditional string puppet or marionette theater (*tixian mu'ouxi* 提线木偶戏, *xianxi* 线戏) also generally known as puppet theater (*kuileixi* 傀儡戏) is the earliest known form of China's various puppet theaters, including shadow theater (*yingxi* 影戏),[1] glove puppet theater (*budaixi* 布袋戏), rod puppet theater (*zhangtou mu'ouxi* 杖头木偶戏), and iron-rod puppet theater (*tiezhi mu'ouxi* 铁枝木偶戏).[2] Presently in northern China, string puppet theater exists only in Heyang 合阳, Shaanxi. The marionette theater of southern China (particularly in Fujian and Taiwan) has been amply documented (Chen 1986; Jin 2003; *Minsu quyi* 1983, 2002a, 2002b; Ruizendaal 2006; Song 1994; Ye 2004).[3] Only one book and a handful of short articles, however, focus on Heyang puppetry (Heyang xian Wenhua guan n.d.; Huang 1999; Shi 1999).[4]

Possibly due to the similar natures of puppets and statues for representing deities, both are thought to exercise spiritual powers by enacting

---

1. Technically speaking, the Chinese separate the two-dimensional shadow theater, *yingxi* 影戏, from the three-dimensional *mu'ou* 木偶 puppet theaters. For information on Chinese shadow theater, see Fan Pen Chen, *Chinese Shadow Theatre: History, Popular Religion, and Women Warriors*; and Fan Pen Chen, *Visions for the Masses: Chinese Shadow Plays from Shaanxi and Shanxi.*

2. For a survey of Chinese puppet troupes (based on my field trips conducted during 2008 and 2009), see Fan Pen Chen and Bradford Clark, "Survey of Chinese Puppet Theatres."

3. These are selected from among fifty-some bibliographic items I collected concerning string puppetry in Fujian and Taiwan. See the bibliography for a more complete list.

4. These are selected from more than a dozen bibliographic items about the string puppetry of Heyang, Shaanxi. See the bibliography for the others.

specific religious rituals. In Fujian, traditional puppetry has been considered particularly efficacious for representing deities in legendary religious ritual plays (Ye 1999; Ye 2004). However, this formerly vital religious role for puppet theater is all but extinct in northern China and is not mentioned in any published sources. Through fieldwork conducted in Heyang during 2004, I learned from Dang Wenhui 党文辉 (then sixty-eight years old, a former performer and troupe director of Heyang's official marionette troupe) some rituals relating to Lord Guan (Guangong 关公; Guan Yu 关羽),[5] patron saint of Heyang's marionette theater[6] and the most popular local deity. Through Dang, I obtained a rare copy of *Short Version of River Yang*—one of the most popular plays because it featured Lord Guan—which I translated for this book.

History of the Marionette Theater

Puppet theater predates human-actor theater in both India and China. Many scholars have noted string puppetry's influence on human theatrical forms, such as Peking opera (jingju 京剧; Chang 1951, 134–135; Su 1995, 3:13–14; Sun 1965). The geographical origin of puppetry is, however, a controversial topic. Richard Pischel believes India is the home of puppet theater and that gypsies (who migrated from India) spread it to the rest of the world (Pischel 1902). Berthold Laufer connects the Chinese word for puppets—*kuilei* 傀儡—to the Turkish name, *kukla*, for marionettes. Tracing the word to Medieval Greek, he suggests that puppetry spread from Byzantium to the Slavs, who passed it on to Turkish tribes in Central Asia. The word *kukla* is still used in the Slavic, Turkish, and Romani (i.e., gypsy) languages (Laufer 1923, 39). Noting the eleven variant orthographical forms (or characters) for the Chinese word for string puppetry—傀儡 *kuilei*, 窟礧子 *kuleizi*, 魁礧 *kuilei*, 魁櫑 *kuilei*, 窟磊 *kulei*, 魁壘 *kuilei*, 魁擂 *kuilei*, 滙磊 *huilei*, 傀磊子 *kuileizi*, 苟利子 *goulizi*, 加[嘉]礼戏 *jialixi*)—Victor Mair

---

5. For more on the rituals, see the Introduction to the chapter on *Short Version of River Yang*, a play included in this book.

6. When Ye Mingsheng 叶明生 went to Heyang in 2014, members of the Xiangruo Theatrical Society (mentioned below) claim two patron gods, Lord Guan and Prince Zhuang 莊王. According to Wang Hongsheng and Shi Yaozeng, however, Prince Zhuang was traditionally the patron god of human-actor operas (*daxi* 大戏), while only Lord Guan was the marionette theater (known as the *xiaoxi* 小戏 locally) patron god. See Wang Hongsheng and Shi Yaozeng, 200–201.

also concluded that the term ". . . must undoubtedly have been transliterated from a foreign language" (Mair 1983, 18).

Other scholars believe puppet theater originated in the masked dances of exorcistic *nuo* 傩 rituals of the Han (206 BCE–220 CE) and earlier (Dolby 1981, 99; Dong 1983, 36–37; Jiang 1988, 63–68; Sun 1980, 40, 55–57). Still others consider funerary statues symbolizing the dead (and people accompanying the deceased to the underworld) as predecessors of marionettes (Dong 1983, 24–35; Sun 1980, 52–55). In 1978, a large wooden puppet with detachable limbs was found in a Han dynasty tomb in Shandong's Laixi County 莱西县 (Ye 2004, 3–4). Earliest use of the word *kuilei* 傀儡 occurs in a source from the end of the Han (Ying Shao's 应绍 [ca. 178 CE] *Fengsu tong* 风俗通) (quoted in Sun 1952, 4), although this source was not recorded until the sixth century (Dolby 1981, 97). According to this and later sources, by the end of the Han, puppets were used during funerals, but also to entertain guests at private parties. Foreign puppetry influences may, consequently, have co-existed with those of Chinese provenance even before the Tang period.

During the Northern Qi dynasty (550–557) of the Northern and Southern Dynasties period, Baldy Guo (Guo Tu 郭秃)—a renowned clown puppet character, also known as Master Guo (Guo Lang 郭郎 or Guo Gong 郭公)—came to represent puppetry itself. According to the Northern Qi scholar, Yan Zhitui 颜之推 (531–ca. 591), a certain Guo, bald due to illness, habitually entertained others by clowning around. Puppets were fashioned in his likeness and called Baldy Guo (Yan Zhitui 1993, 17:305). The Tang dynasty musicologist, Duan Anjie 段安节 (fl. 894), notes in his *Yuefu zalu* 乐府杂录 that marionette song-and-dance shows were always led by a bald clown puppet known as Guo Lang (Duan Anjie 1982,1:62). The relationship between Guo Lang and puppetry in Central Asia deserves further investigation. There is a striking resemblance between bald Guo Lang and the prominent Turkish shadow puppet figure Karagös (a clown figure of gypsy origin, also famously bald). However, a form of string puppetry may already have existed in China that was deeply affected by foreign influences arriving during the Northern Qi (550–577) and Tang (618–907) dynasties. Incidentally, Guo Lang is generally considered to have survived in Heyang's marionette theater as the ever-popular bald clown Lai Baozi 赖包子 (excerpts of whose comical monologues have been translated in this book).

A plethora of different puppet theater forms thrived as secular, commercial entertainment in the Song dynasty capitals. But unlike shadow theater and human-actor operas, marionette theater was apparently performed mainly to entertain the gods and exorcise evil spirits in rural areas (since the Yuan (1206–1368; see Wang Hao 汪颢, *Lintian xulu* 林田叙录, quoted in Jiang 1992, 51) and Ming dynasties (1368–1644; Zhu Yu 1975 reprint, 40). Marionette theater continued to serve these religious functions through the Qing (1644–1911) and the Republican period (1911–1949), particularly in Fujian and Taiwan. Considered a more ancient theatrical form, in many areas it is still revered and given precedence. The marionette stage is given the more exalted location (i.e., to the left of any human actors' operatic troupe), (Liu 1986, 322) and commences its performances first (Ye 2004, 119).

Heyang and Its Marionette Theater

Heyang is about 200 kilometers northeast of Xi'an (five hours, by train, from this capital of Shaanxi Province when I traveled there in 1999 and 2004). It is situated in the cradle of Chinese civilization, within the ancient State of Qin 秦 that unified China in 221 BCE. Part of this region, Hechuan 洽川, has extensive river marshland along the Yellow River, reputedly the location of the first poem in the *Book of Odes* (*shijing* 诗经).[7] Besides claiming to be the birthplace of Chinese marionette theater,[8] Heyang boasts two ancient rituals related to *nuo*: Dancing Play 跳戏[9] and Beating Gongs and Drums (*shangluogu* 上锣鼓).[10]

---

7. This verse starts with the stanza: "*Guanguan* chirp the ospreys/ On the river isle/ The beautiful young lady/ Is sought after by gentlemen" 关关雎鸠 在河之州 窈窕淑女 君子好逑.

8. A long tradition of marionette theater also exists in Zhaoyi 朝邑, Dali 大荔, and Chengcheng 澄城 in Shaanxi, Ruicheng 芮城 in Shanxi, and Lingbao 灵宝 in Henan (*Zhongguo xiqu zhi* weiyuan hui 1995, 105). It is a Heyang researcher who insists that marionette theater originated in Heyang (Shi 1998, 93–101).

9. Considered a living fossil of ancient drama, this simple dramatic form emphasizes martial arts postures. See "Heyang tiaoxi jiqi shehui huanjing" 合阳跳戏及其社会环境 in Shi 1998, 111–127. Also see Holm, 2003.

10. This unusual exorcist ritual consists of male villagers beating gongs and drums, almost completely in the nude, during the cold First Month. See "Huanghe panshang xiangren nuo de yicun—Shaanxi Heyang Donglei cun de shang luogu" 黄河畔上乡人傩的遗存—陕西合阳东雷村的上锣鼓; "Ye shuo shang luogu de 'man'" 也說上锣鼓的 '蛮'; "Weibei nongmin de gangyang zhi mei—Qiantan 'shang luogu' zhong de luoti 渭北农民的刚阳之美一浅谈 '上锣鼓' 中的裸体'; "Wo shi zheyang jinxing 'shang luogu' de tianye diaocha de" 我是这样进行 '上锣鼓' 的田野调查的 in Shi 1998, 140–164 and 247–254.

Heyang's string puppet/marionette theater was traditionally known as *xianhou* 线吼, *xianhu* 线胡, or *xianhou* 线猴, and formally labeled String Opera (*xianx i* 线戏) in 1957.[11] It is now also called the Heyang Operatic Tradition (*heqiang* 合腔) (Shi 2008, 78–80).[12] Performers use strings to manipulate the puppets, combined with singing, music, and dialogue. The facial features of Heyang's traditional marionette puppets[13] resemble those of Tang dynasty figures, providing some support for locals' claim that their marionettes originated during the Tang.

Thirty-six troupes existed in Heyang before 1949. According to Dang Wenhui 党文辉, former director of Heyang County's official marionette theater, all the local troupes' trunks were confiscated by the government sometime after 1949. A troupe formerly named Morning Light Marionette Troupe of Heyang (*heyangxian chenguang xianjushe* 合阳县晨光线剧社) became the official troupe when it changed its name to The Red Marionette Troupe (*hongxian jutuan* 红线剧团) and performed revolutionary plays. In 1973, this troupe was renamed again as the Heyang Marionette Art Troupe (*heyang tixian mu'ou yishutuan* 合阳提线木偶艺术团), and dominated the local puppet theater scene until early this millennium.

In 2004, I was told that only three troupes survive in Heyang: the official county troupe (the Heyang Marionette Art Troupe); a private troupe (New Artistic Marionette Troupe [*xinyi xian'outuan* 新艺线偶团]); and amateur

11. See Zhongguo Xiquzhi Weiyuanhui 1995, 105. It is also referred to as the minor theater (*xiaoxi* 小戏) in Heyang, versus the major theater (*daxi* 大戏), the human-actor theater.

12. The *qiang*, or musical style, is what distinguishes various traditions of traditional Chinese drama or opera.

13. The official troupe changed its stage setup and style of puppets to resemble the more modern configurations created by the famous official marionette troupe in Quanzhou 泉州, Fujian (the most renowned string puppet troupe in China). Twenty Heyang students were sent there to study puppetry for a three-year period—first in 1961, and then again in 1979. See Wang Hongsheng and Shi Yaozeng, 79–80. The use of long strings by Heyang's government-sponsored troupe is a result of Quanzhou influence (although the traditional short strings continued to be used). The newer style of facial features, with larger eyes and more prominent noses, also came to dominate the local scene. The number of strings also increased for many puppets. Wang Hongmin 王红民, director of the official troupe in Heyang when I visited, had a puppet (manipulated by thirty-four strings) take off his robe himself in a playlet titled, "Zhou Ren Decides to Return Home" 周仁回府.

village performers at Xizhonglei Cun 西中雷村.[14] Tourism has become an important factor in keeping many of the traditional arts alive, including the marionette theater. The official troupe was still, by far, the most formal and elaborate. It received 160 awards between 1986 and 1994,[15] but was already in decline by 2004. Selected for training based on their voices and appearance, most of the fifteen troupe members were attractive females, in their mid-thirties by 2004. Although an official troupe, support (if any) from the county had become minimal, and its performances were mainly hired by locals. The troupe had to seek its own sources of income, so it performed at individual events (e.g., weddings, funerals, birthday celebrations of the aged, and the building of new houses) and communal events (e.g., festival celebrations and temple fairs). Aside from these traditional venues, the troupe also participated in commercial fairs and exhibitions and other tourist venues (e.g., Maiden Spring 處女泉,[16] a Yellow River marshland theme park at Hechuan 合川). Two to four puppeteers (hired from the official troupe by this private park) regularly performed, for free, short excerpts on their own elaborate, permanent stage, three to four times daily. The troupe also performed on request, for thirty *yuan* per excerpt or playlet.[17] Apparently, fifteen years ago it was an honor to be a member of

14. In 2009, Guo Cuicheng 郭崔成, a member of Guo Family Troupe 郭家班 at Guojia Slope 郭家坡 in Lujing Town of Heyang County, performed regularly at the tourist venue of Fuke 福客 Restaurant (at the North Plaza of the Big Goose Pagoda 雁塔北广场 of Xi'an 西安, Shaanxi). Guo Cuicheng claimed to be a descendant of Baldy Guo 郭秃. See the chapter on "Lai Baozi" for more information on Baldy Guo. The local Heyang cultural bureau also discovered (since I last visited in 2004) a troupe named Xiangruo Theatrical Society (*xiangruo jushe* 向若剧社) at Nanxun Village 南顺村 of Xinchi Town 新池镇 in Heyang, which boasted having twenty members. Ye Mingsheng visited them and shared his photos with me.

15. In 1987, it received first place representing Weinan 渭南 region and Shaanxi Province at a Beijing art festival. From 1992–1994, it was selected three years in a row as the most progressive performing arts troupe in the province (*sheng xianjin yishu tuanti* 省先进艺术团体).

16. This spring is characterized by small, individual waterholes of spouting sand and water that are able to keep one afloat when stepped on. Traditionally, brides in this region were sent to bathe in this spring before marriage, hence its name.

17. Tourists could also play with the marionettes or take a picture with them for 2 *yuan* each (about 25 cents U.S. then). The park charged a 30-*yuan* entrance fee. A 10-*yuan* fee was charged for "swimming/sporting" in the spring, the main attraction of the park. The performers were paid a salary of 2,000 *yuan* per month.

the official marionette troupe. Today, troupe members are so poorly paid that this is no longer the case.[18]

The private troupe was a small and simple setup, directed by a middle-aged female performer named Dang Fengju 黨凤菊. Dang was native to Heyang and hired to perform short excerpts of marionette plays, and one shadow play, for 10 *yuan* per person (for a 10–15 minute-show, at a traditional Xi'an mansion converted into a tourist attraction in 2004).[19] Four other performers (primarily musicians) accompany Dang; two of them sing, and one of them manipulates marionettes as well. The performers learned the short shadow play recently to add variety to their show. The performance took place in a tastefully decorated room (with a small stage and chairs near the mansion's gate), and the performers slept on boards behind the stage. Dang also sold VCDs (one of her own performance, and others by the official Heyang county troupe and a local shadow theater troupe).[20]

Villagers at Majiazhuang xiang Xizhonglei cun 马家庄乡西中雷村 formed what they called Self-Entertainment Group (*zileban* 自乐班). Believing that the marionette theater originated in their small village, the villagers proudly boasted twelve members who continued to perform (as singers and/or puppeteers, or musicians). Usually, three to eight performers were recruited when a marionette show was required, either by one family, or the village as a whole. The performers were given gifts (wine, cigarettes, candies, steamed buns) and partook of the banquet that invariably accompanied such events, but they received no cash payments.

Shows by this amateur group would typically start between 6 and 7 pm, and last until around 10 pm. A main play was usually performed first, followed by a light-hearted 10-minute short play that ended the show. When I visited in 2004, the star of the village was the ninety-two-year-old master puppeteer Wei Tiancai 魏天才 (1914–), whose index finger was callused

18. By 2009, the official county troupe, which was no longer supported by the government, had only sixteen members and was strapped financially.

19. This mansion was known as the Gao 高 residence. Its address was Beiyuanmen yihao minju Gaofu 北院门一号民居高府. It was located close to the grand mosque in Xi'an 西安. When I went to Xi'an again in 2009, no one was performing at the Gao residence. Dang Fengju was performing at Maiden Spring instead of the official troupe, which was there during 2004.

20. The VCDs cost about 100 *yuan* each. According to Dang, profits were split 30 percent to the tour guides who brought the tourists, and 70 percent to the establishment. It was not clear how much Dang's own percentage was.

and deformed from manipulating strings since he was fifteen. Modest and affable, Wei (who directed the orchestra) also sang and manipulated a puppet for me for about eight minutes, to the delight of the villagers. The village did not have any puppets, so Dang Fengju brought a few of her own. Dang also made a detour to her home village to collect her portable stage when she accompanied me to Wei's place. Normally, the villagers would arrange to borrow, when needed, Wei Tiancai's old set of puppets[21] (which belonged to Wei's only daughter and her husband in a different village).[22]

The entire repertoire of the Heyang marionette theater boasted more than five hundred titles, of which two hundred-some were supposed to have survived. However, the performance was unlike the shadow theater in Shaanxi in that the repertoire of the Wanwanqiang 碗碗腔 shadow theater tradition benefited from the creation of its most famous ten plays by the *juren* 举人 (holder of the prestigious Select, or Second Degree) Li Fanggui 李芳桂.[23] During the Qianlong reign (1736–1796), Heyang's marionette plays tended to be comparatively less intellectual. Numerous high-ranking scholars did, however, leave their mark on this tradition. One source considers two late Ming (1368–1644) scholars, Ning Hong 宁宏 and Li Guan 李灌 (1601–1676), as particularly involved and influential in the earliest known history of this tradition.[24] Both of them retired to the countryside after the fall of the Ming dynasty, and performed marionette plays as a form of self-expression thereafter.

Ning Hong was the son of Ning Shimo 宁时镆, who obtained his *jinshi* 进士 degree (the most prestigious Presented Scholar, or Third Degree) in 1589, although Ning Hong himself was apparently a respected scholar without a degree. The father and son rewrote and created numerous plays, but only a Clapper Opera and a marionette play have survived. *Pavilion of the Immortals in Exile* (translated in this collection) was the marionette play

21. This set of puppets consists of four trunks of old puppets and props. The puppets are carved, painted, and outfitted in traditional style with Tang dynasty features.

22. When I visited Xi'an in 2009, I was told that this collection had already been sold. Fortunately, I had been permitted to take photos of most of it in 2004.

23. Li Fanggui's plays are so refined and intriguing that some of them have been adapted by the marionette theater.

24. Huang 1999, 69. Li Guan may have been influential in drawing puppetry away from religion. He was supposed to have resided in Nanxun Village 南顺村 of Xinchi Town 新池镇, where he established a Xiangruo Theatrical Troupe 向若剧社. A puppetry troupe of the same name has been revived at the village (see Fig. 1.13 and Fig. 1.14).

attributed to them.[25] Li Guan was a *juren*, credited with rewriting many plays and authoring one play. Having received his degree at the end of the Ming dynasty, but dissatisfied with the ensuing Qing (1644–1911) government, Li Guan retired to the countryside and associated frequently with marionette theater performers. He sang sorrowful lyrics most expressively when performing with them, rewrote many of the popular plays of his day, and authored a play titled *Tale of the Black Mountain* 黑山记 about contemporary events. Unfortunately, this play was banned and lost due to its anti-Manchu sentiments.[26] Tradition also remembers contributions, during the mid-Ming, by a certain village school master (*mou shushi* 某塾师), the scholars Wang Bopeng 汪伯彭 and his brother Wang Yi 王异, and a member of a Qin 秦 family.[27]

Ten figures who have contributed to the creation (or rewriting) of marionette plays are remembered from the Qing dynasty.[28] Most were learned scholars, although the majority of them wrote only one marionette play. They include two *jinshi* (Xu Pan'gui 许攀桂, who received his degree in 1661, and Cui Wenyu 崔问余, who received his degree in 1801); a *juren*, who was also a magistrate (Lei Yu 雷豫, who received his degree in 1714); a Licentiate Wang (Wang Xiucai 王秀才, holder of the First Degree, mid-Qing); an anti-Manchu scholar (Xu Baigong 徐拔贡, early Qing); a certain secretary (*mou shuli* 某书吏, late Qing); an eremite (Luoyi Chushi 洛邑处士, late Qing); a certain Wang Wenzhi 王文志 (late Qing); and two marionette performers, Chen Lai 陈来 (late Qing) and Du Jinhu 杜晋虎 (mid to late Qing). Chen Lai was the only author of a play not known to have received extensive education. He was a performer who wrote a short, "extra" playlet, known as *shaoxi* 捎戏,[29] about a contemporary flooding

25. Ibid. The play was more likely written by Ning Hong, with minimal (if any) participation by his father, since the Ming dynasty fell 55 years after the father obtained his *jinshi* degree.

26. Huang 1999, 70–72.

27. This local scholar or squire supposedly created the marionette play version of *Romance of the Western Chamber* (*Xixiangji* 西厢记) by adding episodes on quelling foreign incursions and eliminating Chinese traitors (after attempts at invasions by "barbarians" to the north during the Jingtai [1450–1457] and Tianshun [1457–1465] reigns). Huang 1999, 60–61.

28. Huang 1999, 75–76, 90–92, 103–106.

29. These are short, extra plays, usually light-hearted and based on daily life or contemporary events. Before the Qing dynasty, they were performed prior to the main plays and were called *shaoxi* 梢戏 ("tip" plays). Since the Republican Period, they have been performed after the main plays and are called *shaoxi* 捎戏 ("extra" plays). Huang 1999, 146.

event. The most important playwright of this tradition appears to have been Du Jinhu.

Also known as Du Jinhu 杜进虎,[30] this marionette performer has been attributed the authorship of not only *Pavilion of the Immortals in Exile* (translated in this book), but also just about all the most renowned and popular pieces of this theatrical tradition during its heyday[31] (when more than seventy troupes performed within Heyang County).[32] Du is also known to have written, edited, and rewritten more than one hundred plays![33] Hailing from an educated background, Du Jinhu's misfortune in his pursuit of the standard career in civil service was a blessing in disguise for Heyang's marionette theater. According to oral tradition, he was disqualified from taking further civil service examinations when, during one of the tests, he made the mistake of writing a character used for one of the reigning emperor's names.[34] He was so disheartened by the experience that he befriended marionette performers, joined their troupes, and became an expert of its plays.

Although theatrical performers were considered of low social status, and the theater in general was condemned by orthodox Confucians, this seems not to have been the case in Heyang. As we have seen, many of the playwrights were scholars. According to Dang Wenhui 党文辉 (former director of the official marionette theater of Heyang County), his father Dang Shengkun 党生坤 was an educated man, who was told by his own father to become a marionette performer for some unknown reason. Aside from being a performer, Dang Shengkun transcribed more than two hundred plays (recited from memory by old performers). In 1953, when the Cultural Bureau of Northwestern China (*xibei daqu wenhuaju* 西北大区文化) began collecting traditional play scripts, Dang Shengkun donated

30. Zhongguo xiquzhi 1995, 106.

31. The above gazetteer on the performing arts makes this attribution (which differs from Huang's book, which attributes *Pavilion of the Immortals in Exile* to Ning Hong and his father). It lists the following as the most popular plays of this tradition, and attributes all but the last two titles to Du: *The Hundred Treasure Hairpin* 百宝钗; *Romance of the Western Chamber* 西厢记; *Nangzai Fills the Trunk* 囊哉装箱; *Pavilion of the Immortals in Exile* 谪仙楼; *Pavilion of Mandarin Ducks* 鸳鸯楼; *The Gold Bowl Hairpin* 金碗钗; either *The Double Bowl Hairpin* 双碗钗 or *The Golden Phoenix Hairpin* 金凤钗; and *The Butterfly Bracelet* 蝴蝶环). Ibid.

32. Ibid. and Huang 1999, 147.

33. Huang 1999, 106.

34. Considered highly irreverent, this was a punishable offense.

all his transcriptions. Thirty-five marionette plays (selected from the plays collected) were "published internally" in three volumes in 1962 by the Cultural Bureau of Shaanxi Province (*Shaanxi sheng Wenhua ju* 陕西省文化局).[35] During the upheaval of the Cultural Revolution (1966–1976), all the hand-copied play scripts, marionette puppets, and other performance paraphernalia collected by the government were lost. Even the published plays have become very rare.

When I interviewed Huang Shengwen 黄笙闻 from the Provincial Research Institute for the Arts (*sheng yishu yanjiu suo* 省艺術研究所) in Xi'an, I asked him about the possibility of obtaining photocopies of extant marionette plays. He contacted his superior and reported that they needed to know which ones I wanted, that the plays may be difficult to locate, and that the cost may be considerable due to the issue of cultural heritage and legacy. Such institutes generally charge for photocopies of materials by the page, with negotiable rates. At first I thought this was an attempt to negotiate a higher rate, but it occurred to me that perhaps the Institute no longer had the play scripts. However, I was subsequently able to obtain photocopies of five plays from Dang Wenhui when I interviewed him in Heyang. Dang possessed parts of the three published volumes of marionette plays (from which he selected five of the most popular and had them photocopied for me). He also presented me with a printed booklet containing the lyrics for a few short "Extra Playlets" (*shaoxi* 捎戏)[36] and excerpts from main plays.

The latter item—the booklet, *Collected Heyang Marionette Arias* (*Heyang xian'ouxi changduan* 合阳线偶戏唱段集锦)[37]—is forty-two pages in length, and was compiled to help people follow an audiotape of select plays and arias recorded by the official Heyang Marionette Troupe. The troupe did not give me a copy of the audio recording, but did present me with a copy of a newer VCD recording lacking scripts. This VCD (titled *A Treasure of China—The Heyang Music Marionette Theatre of Shaanxi* [*zhonghua yijue—shaanxi heyangxian heqiang tixian mu'ouxi* 中华一绝 - 陕西合阳县合腔提线木偶戏]) includes the complete version of "Baldy's Wedding Night" (translated in this book). The selections about the clown, Lai Baozi, and

35. The entire set consisted of seventy volumes.

36. These are also known as Post-Midnight Plays (*houbanye xi* 后半夜戏), and ribald plays (*saoxi* 骚戏). See the Introduction to "Baldy's Wedding Night" for more information on such plays.

37. Li Keming, 1999.

the perennial favorite "Peddling Notions" (translated in this book) are also from the booklet.[38]

Besides the above "Extra Playlets," I have also translated for this book the five traditionally most popular plays (which Dang copied for me from the three volumes printed by the Provincial Cultural Bureau in 1962). They include three fictional renditions of historical characters: *Empress Lü Usurps the Throne*; *Yang Wenguang*; and *Short Version of River Yang*. The tale about Empress Lü of the Han dynasty (206 BCE–220 CE) is a one-sided presentation, with some attempt to preserve historical fact (at least in spirit). The stories about Yang Wenguang of the Song dynasty and the Wanli Emperor of the Ming dynasty (1368–1644) in the other two plays, however, are nearly totally divorced from history. *Yang Wenguang* closely follows the tradition of women warrior stories, while *River Yang* casts the Wanli Emperor (and other characters) as reincarnations of the main characters from *Romance of the Three Kingdoms* (the famous novel about the Three Kingdoms period [220–280]). An important work for the worship of Guan Yu 关羽, *River Yang* is unique to Heyang. *The White Undershirt* and *Pavilion of the Immortals in Exile* are fictional romances with no connection to known historical characters. The former was based on a Ming dynasty *chuanqi* 传奇 drama, *Tale of the Hairpin and Bracelet* (*chaichuanji* 钗钏记), while the latter (similar to *Short Version of River Yang*) is the only tale of its kind and exists only in Heyang string puppet theater.

When I began translating these plays, I soon discovered that three of them had missing and torn pages. I then asked Yang Fei 楊飞, my collector friend (whose wife Li Shuwen 李淑文is native to Heyang), for assistance. Yang and Li accompanied me to Heyang during 1998 and 2004, and were my main contacts for all the performers and sources there. Yang knew a retiree at the Xi'an provincial research institute whom he felt could

38. This form of marionette play used to be performed in Dali 大荔 and other nearby counties. The troupe's addition of *Heqiang* (Heyang musical style) in its title might have been intended as a political statement. Traditionally, the marionette theater of the region has been known as String Opera or String Music Opera (*xianqiangxi* 线腔戏). The term *Heqiang* seems to have been created to help support the Heyang government's insistence that marionette theater in that region originated at Heyang. See Shi Yaozeng 史耀增, "String Opera Should Be Called Heyang Opera" (*xianqiang yinggai jiao heqiang* 线腔应该叫合腔), 1999.2–3: 59–60; and his "The Home of the Chinese Marionettes is in Heyang" (*xianqing de laojia zai heyang* 线腔的老家在合阳), in *Zoujin gu Xin* 1998), 93–101. Shi Yaozeng is a very knowledgeable retired senior researcher of the Heyang Cultural Bureau.

help, but he lacked that person's telephone number. Cai Yuanli 蔡源莉, my researcher friend in Beijing, located the Xi'an researcher's phone number so Yang could contact him. According to the Xi'an researcher, the printed volumes of the plays were difficult to locate because, during the Cultural Revolution, copies of the entire *Traditional Plays of Shaanxi Province* (*Shaannxi sheng chuantong jumu* 陕西省传统剧目)—including the three-volume set of marionette plays—had been piled up in the Institute's courtyard for anyone to take. No record was made as to who took what. Yang eventually obtained for me all the requested missing pages. Someday, perhaps, I will learn the location of a complete copy of the series.[39]

39. I hoped to learn from Yang Fei where he managed to find them, but unfortunately he passed away in 2012. Yang Fei was one of the most famous collectors of shadow figures in Shaanxi.

16. Clown role with movable mouth and eyes (Wei Tiancai's puppet). This puppet can be used for all the male protagonists in this section. Photo by Ingrid Chen.

Part I

Post-Midnight Skits

Post-Midnight plays (*houbanye xi* 后半夜戏), also known as extra or additional plays (*shaoxi* 捎戏) or ribald plays (*saoxi* 骚戏), are comical skits traditionally performed after midnight, when women, children, and elderly men have left. Their performance is no longer restricted to post-midnight viewing. These plays are known for their bawdy content and treatment of topics from daily life, with a clown and a young female in the lead roles. Post-Midnight plays are found in a variety of theatrical media (including marionette theater, shadow theater, and human-actor minor operas (*xiaoxi* 小戏).[1] They may be related to lascivious skits, part of ancient religious masked *nuo* 傩 performances.[2]

Although "Lai Baozi," the first selection, is an excerpt from a play (rather than a complete skit of its own), such comical excerpts are frequently performed as stand-alone skits. Sexual content in the Post-Midnight skits may have originally been employed to promote fertility. Under Confucianism traditionally and Communism in contemporary times, however, "lewd plays" were condemned. Consequently, few Post-Midnight Plays have ever been transcribed, and those that I found and collected have been entirely purged of explicit sexual content. "Baldy's Wedding Night," the second selection translated here, was bowdlerized (not surprisingly) by the government troupe that performed it. An unscripted version of the play by a private troupe in rural Heyang would probably have been studded with hilarious sexual innuendos and double entendres. "Peddling Notions," the third skit included here, is likely the most popular skit of this type at present.

1. For translations of Post-Midnight shadow plays, see Fan Pen Chen, *Visions for the Masses*, and "*All Three Fear Their Wives* (*Sanpaqi* 三怕妻): A Post-Midnight Play."

2. See the introduction of Fan Pen Chen, "*All Three Fear Their Wives* (*Sanpaqi* 三怕妻): A Post-Midnight Play," for more information on this genre.

Lai Baozi (赖包子)

Introduction

Lai Baozi is a character peculiar to the marionette theater of Heyang 合阳. The locals consider him a descendant of Baldy Guo (Guo Tu 郭秃), a renowned clown puppet character also known as Master Guo (Guo Lang 郭郎 and Guo Gong 郭公), who came to represent puppetry itself (from the Northern Qi dynasty (550–557) of the Northern and Southern Dynasties period onward). As mentioned in the Introduction to this book, Duan Anjie 段安节 (ca. 894) noted that marionette song-and-dance shows performed during the Tang were always led by a bald clown puppet known as Guo Lang.

Playing the roles of numerous lesser characters, Lai Baozi emerged as a beloved clown in many Heyang marionette plays. Below, the excerpts from one play and two skits describe the humorous exploits of Lai Baozi. The first selection shows Lai Baozi as a messenger in the play *Loyalty, Filial Piety and Virtue* (*zhongxiaoxian* 忠孝贤). The second selection is an extended monologue by Lai Baozi, as the servant of an official in the skit "Visiting Turtle Mountain" (*youguishan* 游龟山), who relates to investigators the events leading to his master's demise. The reference to Lai Baozi's pigtail may indicate that this tale was created during the Qing dynasty. In the last selection, Lai Baozi tries to wriggle out of the consequences for his theft in "Stealing Turnips" (*wamanqing* 挖蔓菁).

Basically a lowly clown figure, Lai Baozi may cheat and steal, but he is not an evil character. His misdemeanors are lessened by his foolish nature and his anxious desire to impress others. Despite his attempts at self-aggrandizement, Lai Baozi inevitably fails to garner respect. In the first selection, he is a pompous, but very lowly civil servant. In the second excerpt, he relies on the status of his master to lord it over an old man, but ends up being sorely punished for his actions. The tale itself and the language used in this second skit, however, prevent us from being sympathetic to Lai Baozi; not only does he deserve his punishment, but his descriptions of his own sorry condition are more comical than sorrowful. In the third selection, Lai Baozi is a clever little rogue. He weasels out of being punished for theft by expounding on the ridiculous topic of farting. But despite his attempts to sound erudite, the topic itself and the content of his exposition reveal him as the ultimate clown that he is.

Lai Baozi as the Messenger in *Loyalty, Filial Piety and Virtue*[1]

MESSENGER: Doo, doo . . . stop! (*Sings.*)

> I, the messenger, am by nature quick-tempered,
> Sticking a flag around my neck, I represent the authority.
> From the beginning of the year to the end, I receive a salary,
> Just for making announcements for the government.

I'm a messenger from the capital. My lord, the Prize Candidate,[2] just received an official appointment at the capital. He just ordered me to return home to report the good news and deliver the certificate. Now that I'm on my way, I'll have to give this horse of mine a few more whips. Everyone, duck from my path! I, a messenger from the capital, am coming through. . . .

END OF EXCERPT

Lai Baozi as a Servant in "Visiting the Turtle Mountain"

SERVANT: It was like this, venerable ones. On that certain day, me and my lord, we went to Turtle Mountain to visit, and up there we met this old fella. He said that he was selling something. My lord asked him what he was selling. The old one said he was selling a curio-fish (*qiyu* 奇鱼). My lord said "I don't see you pulling a donkey" (*qilü* 骑驴), and the

1. See Li Keming, 9–12, for the play scripts.

2. That is, he is the top scholar of the highest level of the civil service examinations. Although this messenger works for the government, the person he is reporting for happens to be a relative of his.

old guy said he was selling a curious type of fish. My lord said he'd never seen a curio-fish before, so he said to us, "Boys, bring it over and let me take a look." I brought him the fish, and my lord took a look at it. Aiya! It was a fish with the head of a boy and the body of a fish! It was really awesome, really, really neat. My lord said, "Boys, let's buy this fish and put it in our own pond. Wouldn't it be a great sight for all the other officials to see when they come to visit?" I said, "Yeah, yeah, let's buy it!" My lord asked the old one, "How much do you want for this fish?" The old one said, "I don't dare ask for a lot of money from an official—three thousand copper cash will do." My lord said, "What are you talking about? So you don't dare ask for more from an official, three thousand cash will do. If I were a commoner, would you have asked for a hundred thousand or even a million?" I said, "Would you have asked for ten thousand or even a million?" You see, I was chanting along with my lord. My lord then said, "I won't cheat you, I'll give you three hundred copper cash. But I didn't bring any money with me; come to the prefecture to collect the money another day." The old guy replied, "For three hundred cash, I wouldn't even let someone look at the fish, let alone buy it!" My lord said, "What are you talking about? It's not that you won't let someone look at the fish, you just don't want to accept credit." My lord then threw the fish on the ground, and that tiger-like dog[3] of mine pounced on it and began to gulp it down. When the old guy approached to pick up his fish, his hands were devoured by that tiger-like dog of mine. The stupid old one then began to yell and curse until he got my lord so mad that my lord ordered me to give him forty hearty strokes with the leather whip. Then out of the blue appeared this son of the magistrate of Jiangxia 江夏 County called Tian Yuchuan 田玉川. Half of him must have been made out of red bricks and he clobbered all of us, even though there were more than ten of us. He smashed my head, my pigtail came all undone and loose, my arms were twisted and broken, and one of my embroidered shoes went totally missing. Even my lord got beaten to a pulp. When he returned to the prefect, he, uh . . . gulp, gulp . . . swallowed his last breath and kicked the bucket!

END OF EXCERPT

3. This is a ferocious breed of dog known as *saihuquan* 赛虎犬, literally, tiger-like dog.

Lai Baozi in "Stealing Turnips"

LAI BAOZI: Aiya! Run! (*Sings.*)

I was just digging for turnips out in the field,
When all of a sudden I hear yelling all around me.
Basket in my hand and shovel on my shoulder,
I head for home in a great huff and puff.
Turning around, I close the gate behind me,
And shut that old man right outside the door.

OLD MAN: Thief, open the door!

LAI BAOZI: Only someone dumber than me would open it.

OLD MAN: How are the turnips you dug from my field?

LAI BAOZI: They are so soft, so sweet, and so yummy!

OLD MAN: Let's go to the main street and reason it out.

LAI BAOZI: We can reason it out across this gate—there's no need to go to the main street.

OLD MAN: You stole my turnips. What right do you have to do that?

LAI BAOZI: If I don't have 80 to 100 percent right to do it, I wouldn't have dared to dig your turnips.

OLD MAN: You're a bunch of farts!

LAI BAOZI: What are you talking about, you old thing! A bunch of farts you said—do you really understand the meaning of fart?

OLD MAN: What kind of meaning can there be for fart?

LAI BAOZI: There's a lot to the meaning of fart.

OLD MAN: You tell me!

LAI BAOZI: Listen to me, old one. (*Sings.*)

Fart is none other than the *qi* 气[4] of the five grains,
Without release, it expands; when released, it is loud.
Fart is a tiger. When it comes out, no one dares to block it,
So great, it is capable of conquering the city of Tongguan 潼关
and the Prefecture of Xi'an 西安.
When three thousand tartars arrived to the rescue,
One fart wiped out two thousand and five hundred of them.
Another count was made when they passed through Lintong 临潼,
Nine hundred of them had lost their jawbones.

4. Energy.

Old Man: What happened to their jawbones?

Lai Baozi: What happened to them? They were blown away by the fart!

Old Man: What a powerful fart!

Lai Baozi: The big fart sounds like "dongr, dongr"[5]—just like when the eight tiger-generals of the Yang family entered Youzhou 幽州. The small fart sounds like "nair, nair"—just like when the First Emperor of the Qin was entrapped in the City of Wengzhou 瓮州. Some people fart standing up. When people fart standing up, the fart puffs up their pants and flies away. Some people fart sitting down. When people fart sitting down, the fart blows up dirt and dust. People avoid a fart when they smell it. But dogs delight in it. Don't ever speak of fart henceforth. I can't help but become incensed whenever I speak of it!

END OF EXCERPT

5. This represents the sound of war drums.

"Baldy's Wedding Night" 禿子鬧房

Introduction

This version of "Baldy's Wedding Night" (*tuzi naofang* 禿子鬧房) is the one performed by the government-sponsored Marionette Troupe of Heyang County.[1] Due to the evolving nature of unscripted performances characterizing Post-Midnight skits, the origin of this version of "Baldy" is difficult to ascertain. But judging from the use of a fake queue (pigtail), this skit originated no later than the Qing dynasty (when Chinese men were ordered by the ruling Manchus to wear queues). The reference to Qigong is of more recent origin and suggests input possibly as late as the 1980s.[2]

In order to illustrate the tremendous disparities among different versions of such originally orally transmitted skits, I append an excerpt from another version of "Baldy's Wedding Night." The text for this excerpt was included in the same source as for the more complete version,[3] but the shorter version seems to have lost its appeal and is no longer performed by the troupe. The arias in the excerpt use literary allusions and similes that seem sophisticated, but are not necessarily the most appropriate. The characters in the popular longer version speak most convincingly in the colloquial language and dialect of the audience. The excerpt focuses entirely on Baldy's discovery that his wife is bald, and his reaction to that revelation. Although only an excerpt, the fact that the bride sits in the nuptial chamber, with bald head bared for all to see, seems to indicate that the complete version it came from was not interested in the ingenious and gradual development seen in the full

1. See Li Keming, 12–15, for the play script.

2. I would like to thank the anonymous reviewer who contributed this and other cultural insights to this study when this translation was published as "Baldy's Wedding Night: A Post-Midnight Marionette Play" in *Chinoperl Papers*.

3. See Li Keming, 33–34.

version.[4] The fact that such skits have traditionally been transmitted orally, without the aid of scripts, underscores the drastic disparity between the two versions. Indeed, both the full version and the excerpt translated here are rare examples of the same story in this genre that have actually gotten into print.[5] "Baldy's Wedding Night" replicates a battle between the sexes, conveniently situated during their wedding night. In the complete version, the bald-headed couple (each of whom believes the other party has a nice full head of hair) attempt to outwit each other. Many traditional societies feel no inhibitions when it comes to making fun of the physical defects of their fellow human beings. "Baldy's Wedding Night" is a typical Post-Midnight skit in that it first builds up to a vehement dispute, but then ends in marital harmony. Humor is created through sexual connotation, exaggeration, ingenious language, and irony. Many among the audience might have picked up the sexual connotation associated with baldness. The shining bald head is often compared to a penis, and "little monk" (monks have shaven heads) is a common designation for the penis. When the husband flies into a rage and compares his wife's shiny bald head to a gourd and a blown-up balloon, the audience already knows that he himself is also bald. Verbal abuse is accompanied by physical action. When he throws a hammer at her, she responds by hurling a brick from their brick bed (*kang* 炕) at him. While domestic quarrels and intra-spousal violence are accepted, the sanctity of arranged marriages is never questioned. Although the wife is not an admirable paragon of virtue in this battle of the sexes, she is the smarter and more sensible party. She accepts her own baldness, sees through her husband's trickery, and resorts to even more drastic violence when he tries to put her down. A vainglorious clown, the husband is conceited, deceitful, and irascible. Despite these shortcomings, he is nevertheless ultimately a likable comical character. One moment swelling with arrogance, and the next abjectly accepting his defeat (to the point of suggesting that her act of violence toward him was a sign of love), he is truly the vanquished husband whom young men in the audience could both identify with and feel superior to. Like his audience, Baldy is a commoner; for many of the henpecked young men, Baldy's comical hypocrisy and his bride's exaggerated violence conceivably made audience members feel better about their own shortcomings and domestic squabbles.

4. The performer credited for the excerpt was an older man (born in 1959, began to learn the art in 1973), while the performer credited for the full version is much younger (born in 1972, joined the marionette troupe in 1988). See Li Keming, 33 and 12.

5. See Fan Pen Chen, "*All Three Fear Their Wives,*" 206–214, for a translation of an example of a transcription (made without scholarly input) of a Post-Midnight shadow play.

Cast of "Baldy's Wedding Night"

Egg Flower (Danhua 蛋花[6]): the bride.
Rabbit Boy (Tuwa 兔娃[7]): the bridegroom.

Egg Flower: I'm the bride, and my name is Egg Flower. On top of my head, I've got no hair. What I am wearing is a wig. Tonight is the night when candles will blaze in the nuptial chamber. I'm going to expose the brilliance of my top to him. If he still loves me, I'll love him too. If he rejects me, I won't go easy on him!

Rabbit Boy: If you were to ask me who I am, I can't really explain it all in just a few words. I was bald since I was a baby, so I was called Baldy. Baldy, Baldy—the more I was called that, the worse it was. When it came to trying to arrange a marriage for me with such a name—that was quite a problem. That frustrated my mom and dad so badly that there was nothing else to do but change my name to Rabbit Boy.[8] I was very fortunate to have had an extremely capable matchmaker—she got me a most beautiful girl.[9] I'll do my thing when she's dreaming tonight. When the "rice has been cooked" and the "wood has been made into a boat,"[10] she'll have no option but to "marry a rooster stick with the rooster; marry a dog stick with the dog"! Dear wife! Dear wife!

Egg Flower: What are you calling me for?

Rabbit Boy: Please come over to take off your clothes and go to sleep.

Egg Flower: Do you love me or not?

Rabbit Boy: I brought you over in a bridal palanquin. How can I not love you?

---

6. The egg part of her name suggests her most prominent physical feature (her baldness).

7. His name, Tuwa 兔娃, sounds very similar to *tuwa* 禿娃, bald boy/child, the only difference being that the former *tu* is in the fourth tone, while the latter *tu* is in the first tone.

8. "Rabbit" (*tuzi* 兔子, *tu zaizi* 兔崽子) was once used in Beijing as a curse word to intimate that the person referred to was a catamite. I am not aware of it being used this way in this region and doubt that Rabbit Boy's parents would have named him so if it were the case.

9. Up to this point, every single line that he has spoken has rhymed within the same rhyme-category (*sha* 啥, *ya* 牙, etc.). From here the rhyme-category changes and the use of rhyme is slightly less insistent. I have not tried to make the translation rhyme. The entire speech, with the exception of his calling out to his wife at the end, is rhythmic and syncopated. The first rhyme-category of this speech appears several times in the arias below, but other rhyme-categories are used only once, and at most for only six lines.

10. The deed (sexual act) has been done and is irreversible.

EGG FLOWER: If I take off my clothes, would you still love me?
RABBIT BOY: The more you take off, the more I'll love you.
EGG FLOWER: How about my socks and shoes?
RABBIT BOY: Off with them.
EGG FLOWER: How about the hair on my head?
RABBIT BOY: Off with it too! Wait a minute . . . no, no! Hair grows on your flesh, how can you take it off?
EGG FLOWER: Of course you can take it off. I do it all the time at my natal home!
RABBIT BOY: What? You take it off all the time?
EGG FLOWER: Don't you believe me? Take a look!
RABBIT BOY: Ah! You, you . . . so it turns out you're a baldy!
EGG FLOWER: Didn't you just say the more I take off, the more you'll love me?
RABBIT BOY: How mad this makes me! (*Sings.*[11])

Seeing her bald head makes my lungs with anger explode,
So shiny and bright, it dazzles one's eyes.
I'd say it was a gourd, but there's no trellis,[12]
On second look, it's just like an over-inflated balloon about to pop.
As my anger rises, I pick up this hammer to give her a knock . . .

EGG FLOWER: (*Sings.*)

With one snag, I've seized hold of these chicken claws of yours.
If there's no hair on my head, what's wrong with that?
It enabled me to walk the straight and narrow.[13]

RABBIT BOY: (*Sings.*)

To flash a bald head in front of others, how shameful!
It's just like a pig's bladder with a face painted on it.

EGG FLOWER: (*Sings.*)

---

11. The arias are composed of couplets. The even lines always rhyme, but the odd lines often rhyme with them.

12. In China, gourds are grown on trellises and scaffolds rather than on the ground.

13. The assumption is that no one tried to seduce her because she was bald.

You're just like a dog biting a mason–obviously looking to be
chiseled.[14]
Let me pull apart this brick bed of ours and smash you with a
brick!

Rabbit Boy: Aiya! My good mother—please forgive me!

Egg Flower: Don't you worry. Since I'm already married to you, I can't bear to realy hit you. As for that brick just now. . . .

Rabbit Boy: You're absolutely right. That brick just now was actually your way of cherishing me, loving me, teaching me. From now on, I'll also cherish you, love you.

Egg Flower: Let me tell you—this world is full of hairless baldies! (*Sings.*)

Are baldies really not as good as you?
Are baldies supposed to be teased?
Are female baldies never to get married?
Are male baldies never to take a wife?

Rabbit Boy: Dear wife! My dear virtuous wife! You've really hit it right on this cockscomb of mine. It's all the fault of this thing! (*Sings.*)

It was this tail of mine which was so full of itself,[15]
That it looked down upon your baldheadedness.
The prime criminal and number one cause of disaster is naught
but it,
I will have to pull it out completely, roots and all!

Egg Flower: Are you going to pull all your hair out?

Rabbit Boy: If I pull it all out, we'll really be able to respect each other and love each other.

Egg Flower: Hair grows on your flesh. Can you pull it all out?

Rabbit Boy: I have practiced Qigong[16] and can pull it all out in an instant!

Egg Flower: Aren't you afraid of the pain?

---

14. A dog who tries to bite a mason is obviously asking to be hit by the mason.

15. The "tail" could be a double entendre for penis/bald head here.

16. A form of breathing and Kungfu exercises that may give the perfected practitioner special powers.

RABBIT BOY: For the sake of our marriage, to suffer a little pain is worth it. Come, grab hold of my pigtail. Now pull!

EGG FLOWER: Ah! So it turns out that you're also a baldy!

RABBIT BOY: No, I wasn't a baldy before—it's only now that I am one.

EGG FLOWER: So, you were pretending before, and now you're still trying to fool me?

RABBIT BOY: No, no, no. It was the true power I attained through practicing *qigong*!

EGG FLOWER: I've also attained true power through practice.

RABBIT BOY: What type of true power?

EGG FLOWER: I can cut off a person's head and then stick it back on.

RABBIT BOY: I don't think that's possible!

EGG FLOWER: Today I am going to try it on you.

RABBIT BOY: Ah! You . . . you want to kill me!

EGG FLOWER: I'm just trying to imitate you!

RABBIT BOY: You're too polite, too polite!

EGG FLOWER: (*Sings.*)

> Wearing a red robe, the black crow teases the turtle for being black,[17]
> The male baldy taunts me, a female baldy.
> Step by step, you laid a trap for me,
> Move by move, you tried to hoodwink me.
> I wonder what else is hidden in that noggin of yours?
> Tonight, I, this old lady of yours will. . . .

RABBIT BOY: What—what are you going to do?

EGG FLOWER: I'll take the kitchen knife and split open that watermelon![18]

RABBIT BOY: Ah—you won't dare! You won't dare to do it! (*Sings.*)

> In no way will you dare to do something like this!

EGG FLOWER: (*Sings.*)

> I'll open it to take a look at what kind of a melon it is!

---

17. Just like a crow that disguises its black color and laughs at the turtle for being black, he pretends not to be bald and ridicules her for her baldness.

18. That is, his head.

Rabbit Boy: (*Sings.*)

Let me . . . let me frankly tell you the truth,
Ever since I was a mere baby I was a baldy.
How I regret trying to trick you,
I will love you for the rest of my life without further delay.

Egg Flower: (*Sings.*)

Do these words come from your true heart?

Rabbit Boy: (*Sings.*)

If I am fooling let lightning strike me dead!

Egg Flower: Get up! Do get up!
Rabbit Boy: Do you believe me, my dear wife?
Egg Flower: I've finally straightened you out by holding you flat upside the blade of the chopper!
Rabbit Boy: I'm terribly fond of you too!
Egg Flower: Do you think I'm pretty?
Rabbit Boy: I think even your bald head is pretty.
Egg Flower: Then we can enter the nuptial chamber!
Rabbit Boy: And sleep together on one single pillow.
Egg Flower: Not yet. Put your hands on my shoulders first.
Rabbit Boy: Together let's twist and entwine!

END OF PLAY

Excerpt from an Older Version of "Baldy's Wedding Night"

Rabbit Boy: (*Sings.*)

Even old Dong Zhuo 董卓 got to fool around with Diaochan 貂蝉,[19]
How much more so should it be with Tuwa who is merely eighteen?

---

19. In *Romance of the Three Kingdoms* (*Sanguo yanyi* 三国演义), both the elderly Dong Zhuo and his adopted son, the young Lü Bu 吕布, were enamored with beautiful Diaochan. She had been presented as a gift to Dong precisely to arouse the jealousy of Lü, who ends up killing Dong.

Like the oil peddler who was able to win over the top courtesan,[20]
I, too, intend to be a turtle which manages to transform itself into a frog.[21]
My fake pigtail is fully two and a half feet long,
My black cap is adorned with a bright red bow.
Wearing a red robe underneath my black gown,
I have on my feet a pair of cloud-pattern shoes.
From outside the bedroom door, I see that lovely wife of mine,
Erectly sits she, beneath the burning oil lamp.
Her silhouette resembling precisely a beauty in a painting,
With her eyes closed, she awaits for none other than yours truly.
Swaggering confidently, I enter the room. . . . Wake up, dear wife!

EGG FLOWER: Who dares to yell for me?
RABBIT BOY: (*Sings.*)

Seeing her baldhead, my lungs explode from anger!
So brightly it shines that it dazzles one's eyes.
You'd say that it's a gourd but one doesn't see a trellis,
On second look, it looks more like an over-inflated balloon, about to pop.
Secretly, how I curse the match-maker—
With sweet talk and trickery, how you've deceived me!
Did I kill a child of yours,
Or pilfer from your house?
Should I see you at this very moment,

---

20. This refers to the Ming short story "The Oil Peddler Wins the Top Courtesan" (*mai youlang duzhan huakui* 卖油郎独占花魁), published by Feng Menglong 冯梦龙 (1574–1646) as story number three in his *Eternal Words to Awaken the World* (*Xingshi hengyan* 醒世恆言).

21. A turtle is a derogatory term used to refer to cuckolds and male brothel workers.

I would for sure extract that tongue of yours.
This wedding night of mine is truly a letdown,
My whole body feels weak, ready to collapse.

END OF EXCERPT

17. Village girl (Wei Tiancai's puppet). Photo by Ingrid Chen.

18. Heyang County Marionette Troupe performing "Peddler" using short strings. Photo by Fan Pen Li Chen.

"Peddling Notions" 卖杂货

Introduction

A perennial favorite "extra playlet" or "post-midnight playlet" in Shaanxi and Henan,[1] I have personally seen "Peddling Notions" performed in Shaanxi's shadow, rod, and string puppet theaters. Judging from the peddler's claim that he hails from Jiangzhou 绛州, this playlet probably originated (at the latest) during the Qing dynasty. The place name Jiangzhou (presently known as Xinjiangxian 新绛县 in Shanxi) was used from antiquity through the Qing dynasty. This light-hearted skit portrays the flirtations between a village girl and a young itinerant peddler, which turn into mutual teasing and quarreling. In this "battle of the sexes," the girl is ultimately the winner. She uses her attractiveness to get a good bargain, and then short-changes the peddler with a "bad" coin (slipped in with good currency). The village girl attempts to sweet-talk the peddler out of demanding a new coin by promising him tea and a pipe at her home *the following year*. When he resists, she scares him off by threatening a beating by her father and a trip to the magistrate.

Cast of "Peddling Notions"[2]

Peddler 货郎: a young man
Village Girl 村姑: a young woman

1. This play was also popular during the Republican period in the city of Sanmenxia 三门峡市 in Henan. See Sanmenxia shi wenhuaju, ed., 82.

2. The script for this play is found in Li Keming, 2–4.

PEDDLER: (*Calls.*) Selling notions! (*Sings.*)

I, the peddler, hail from Jiangzhou 绛州,[3]
Shouldering the poles of my trunks, I enter the village.
(*Calls.*) Selling notions!

VILLAGE GIRL: (*Sings.*)

Suddenly, I hear a *notions* peddler outside the door,
So it is none other than the notions fellow from Jiangzhou.

PEDDLER: (*Sings.*)

My wares are numerous; I have so many different things,
Let me open the trunk lids, so you can pick whatever you want.
First, I have embroidery needles; second, I have flower-patterned kerchiefs.
Third, I have rouge; fourth, I have peach-colored powder.
Fifth, I have caltrop-shaped mirrors;[4] sixth, I have hairpins.
Seventh, I have rings, bracelets, earrings, and necklaces; eighth, I have crepe silk handkerchiefs.
Ninth, I have wigs; tenth, I have colored threads.
All sorts of things, a variety of them, I have them all!

VILLAGE GIRL: (*Sings.*)

I only want a set of matching boxes of rouge and powder.

PEDDLER: (*Sings.*)

I only want fifty copper cash from you.

VILLAGE GIRL: (*Sings.*)

Fifty copper cash is too much,
I will give you five and twenty.

---

3. Jiangzhou lies in southwestern Shanxi, across the Yellow River, northeast of Heyang in Shaanxi.

4. The mirror in caltrop style has eighteen petals and a sequence of concentric circular patterns. See Antonia Finnane, "Folding Fans and Early Modern Mirrors," 399.

Peddler: (*Sings.*)

You sure know how to drive a bargain, dear miss,
Let's just say that I brought them over for you.
If you get the money, I'll get the merchandise,
And we'll consider this business of ours done.

Village Girl: (*Sings.*)

Here's five, here's ten,
Here's fifteen, twenty, and five extra.
I place the money on top of your trunk,
Now you hand over those boxes of yours.

Peddler: (*Sings.*)

Don't you walk away yet, my dear miss,
I need to count this copper cash of yours.

Village Girl: (*Sings.*)

Count, count, go ahead and count,
Short of one, I'll give you ten.

Peddler: (*Sings.*)

Here's one, here's ten,
Here's fifteen, twenty, and ah—five extra.
There is in fact nothing wrong with the number,
But there's an old thin coin that I can't use.

Village Girl: (*Sings.*)

Of course you can use it, peddler brother dear,
Please listen to what I have to say to you.
Come back to this gate at my house next year,
I'll make you tea and offer you a pipe.

Peddler: (*Sings.*)

This little miss is so prettily dressed up,
And her cute face as round as an egg.

Her hairdo is truly ever so nicely done,
With a flower on each side fluttering so.
She looks just like a beautiful painting,
The more I look, the more smitten I feel.

VILLAGE GIRL: (*Sings.*)

This peddler sure is an oddball,
Are you here to stare at me instead of peddling?

PEDDLER: (*Sings.*)

Don't you call me an oddball!
Listen, I'll tell you what's odd.
What are your Da[5] and your Ma doing right now?
Who told you to come out to buy make-up on your own?

VILLAGE GIRL: (*Sings.*)

My Da and my Ma are as busy as ants on fire,
They are getting ready to marry me off on the twenty-fourth or -fifth.

PEDDLER: (*Sings.*)

Your family can't be as busy as mine,
My family is really rushing around these days.
All the tradesmen are around to decorate the bridal room,
On the twenty-fourth or -fifth I'm marrying this cutsie-youtsie woman right here.

VILLAGE GIRL: Ah! Off you go! (*Sings.*)

What the peddler says is flirtatious and naughty,
So angry and frustrated am I.
I'll go home and tell my Ma,
My Ma will then tell my Da.

---

5. In Shaanxi, people informally call their father "da," with the second tone.

My Da will come out to beat you up:
He'll hit you with a stick, tie you up with a rope,
And drag you to the gate of the yamen.[6]
They'll beat you first and then lock you up,
We'll see if you'll regret it or not!

Peddler: (*Sings.*)

Hearing this, I, the peddler, realize that my situation is not good,
Let me pick up my carrying pole and disappear really fast!

END OF PLAY

6. Office and court of the local official.

Part II

Historical Fiction

Presented chronologically, the three plays selected for this section are either fictional histories or historical fiction. *Empress Lü Usurps the Throne* follows historical facts somewhat closely (to such an extent that it might be considered a fictional historical play). *Yang Wenguang* and *Short Version of River Yang,* however, both give only a passing nod to history (insofar as each contains the name of at least one historical character and is situated within a specific dynasty); they are so thoroughly products of the authors' imaginations that they are more properly viewed as historical fiction. Empress Lü (241–180 BCE) of the Han dynasty was an empress as well as the first historical female ruler in Chinese history. She came to be depicted as a *femme fatale* in popular traditions. Yang Wenguang (999–1074) was a Song dynasty general of the Yang family, made famous through a fictional saga about the predominantly female warriors of the Yang family. This play, however, centers on five fictional sons of Yang Wenguang, and bears no relationship to other tales in that saga. *Short Version of River Yang* contains another completely fictitious tale that was probably considered sacred because it featured Lord Guan, the most revered deity of that locality. Situated during the Ming dynasty (1368–1644), *Short Version of River Yang* centers on reincarnations of characters from the Three Kingdoms Period (220–265) who became widely known through the Yuan dynasty popular novel, *Romance of the Three Kingdoms*. Although the historical figure Liu Bei (161–223) is cast as the reincarnation of the Wanli emperor (1563–1620) of the Ming dynasty, the play is otherwise a completely fictional creation.

19. Empress Lü and two princes (Wei Tiancai's puppets). Photo by Ingrid Chen.

20. Middle-aged man of integrity (Wei Tiancai's puppet). This puppet can be used for Minister Wang Ling. Photo by Ingrid Chen.

21. Photo by Mingsheng Ye 叶明生 during 2009 at Nanshun Village 南顺村 of Xinchi Town 新池镇. Liu Ying and Consort Yan in *Empress Lü Usurps the Throne*.

Empress Lü Usurps the Throne 吕后篡位

(a.k.a., *Chen Ping Preserves the State* 陈平保国)

Empress Lü 吕后 (241–180 BCE) (named Lü Zhi 吕雉; styled E'xu 娥姁, and also known as Han Gaohou 汉高后 and Lü Taihou 吕太后) was the first female ruler in Chinese history and one of the most controversial characters in Chinese history. While her abilities as a sovereign are affirmed in historical records, and she had plausible reasons for some of the atrocities she committed, in popular tradition, Empress Lü has been cast as a power-hungry, lascivious, and evil queen. Her reputation seems to be based on two main factors: she overstepped her gender role and ruled in a patriarchal society; and her natal family became powerful but lost factional struggles after her death. Losers are almost always portrayed negatively in Chinese history. In this string puppet play, in which the characters are simplistically portrayed as either all good or all bad, Empress Lü is a narrow-minded, lascivious, ruthless, and willful character. The play conflates some historical facts and makes mistakes in others, but is consistent in its creation of an evil character (in simple but logical fashion) reflecting perceived history, if not actual facts.

Historically, Empress Lü married below her station. Her father was impressed by the future emperor (but former peasant) Liu Bang's (Emperor Gaozu; r. 202–195 BCE) physiognomy, and married her to him. She suffered greatly before Liu Bang succeeded in becoming emperor, and was of immense assistance to her husband in stabilizing the realm, including helping him eliminate the powerful generals Han Xin 韩信 and Peng Yue 彭越. But during his later years, Emperor Gaozu favored a much younger and prettier wife, Consort Qi 戚姬. Desiring for her son, Liu Feng 刘奉, to displace Empress Lü's son, Liu Ying 刘盈, as the heir apparent, Consort Qi "wept day and night," pleading with the emperor. Because the emperor was favorably disposed toward both Consort Qi and her son, she almost succeeded. Empress Lü, however, garnered support for her son from the ministers, and ultimately prevented any change in succession to the throne.

A year after Emperor Gaozu's death, Empress Lü had Consort Qi's son murdered with poisoned wine. Empress Lü's subsequent retaliation against Consort Qi represents one of the cruelest reprisals known among imperial family members in Chinese history. She had Consort Qi's limbs chopped off, eyes gouged out, ears sliced off, forced her to drink a potion that made her mute, and had her thrown into a latrine to die a slow death. Naming the limbless "creature" a "human swine," she had her son, Emperor Hui 惠帝 (r. 195–188 BCE) view "it" several days later. Emperor Hui was so disgusted and disheartened by his mother's barbarity that he fell sick and thereafter ceased to participate in state affairs. As a result, Empress Lü dominated court politics for almost fifteen years, until her own death.[1]

After her son, Emperor Hui, died in 188 BCE, Empress Lü arranged for his two young sons to be named emperors consecutively, while she in fact ruled. Soon after her death, an opposing faction led by Chen Ping 陈平[2] and others organized a successful *coup d'état* against the reigning emperor and members of the Lü family (then headed by Lü Chan 吕产), claiming the latter was planning to place himself on the throne. Fan Kang 樊康, son of Empress Lü's younger sister, was then killed along with his mother. The victors legitimized the coup by naming it the "Lü Chan Disturbance" (*lü shi zhiluan* 吕氏之乱) and installed Emperor Gaozu's fourth son, Liu Heng 刘恒, as Emperor Wen 文帝 (r.180–157). His mother was surnamed Bo 薄.

Although ruthless in meting out revenge, Empress Lü was in fact a remarkable ruler. Even the historian Sima Qian 司马迁 concludes,

> Kao-hou (Gaohou 高后; Empress Lü), as a female ruler, announced [she would issue] the imperial decrees and managed to govern without going out of her chambers, and the world was peaceful, punishments and penalties were rarely employed, and those who had committed offenses then became rare. The people devoted themselves to planting and harvesting, and [as a result] clothing and food became increasingly abundant.[3]

1. See Watson 1961, 322–340, for Empress Lü's biography.

2. He was the chief plotter in the overthrow of the Lü family. See Watson 1961, 152–163, for his biography.

3. Sima Qian, "Records on Empress Lü" (*Lühou benji* 吕后本纪). This translation is taken from William H. Nienhauser, Jr., ed., *The Grand Scribe's Records*, 137. The *History of the Former Han Dynasty* (*qian Hanshu* 前汉书) arrives at a similar conclusion concerning her ability to govern. The translator notes that the historian's comments to "Gaohou ji 高后纪" in *Han shu* are essentially the same.

She would have been remembered much more positively if she were an emperor (rather than an empress), or if her kinsmen had not been annihilated by the faction that won the political struggle. But then her tale might not have been chosen as the topic for a play.

The play itself is much more simplistic and unsophisticated, replete with childlike squabbling and narrow-mindedness on the part of the villainous protagonist. Empress Lü feels slighted and resents Consort Qi because the latter did not come out of her residence to properly greet the empress when she visited. After the emperor dies, Empress Lü sends her own son away and poisons Consort Qi's son. The infuriated Consort Qi then accuses Empress Lü of killing the general, Peng Yue, because he refused to submit to her attempts to seduce him. So Empress Lü has her executed and her corpse nailed to a wall to rot into a "human swine."

The playwright obviously has heard of the term "human swine" but did not read the historical records to know the details concerning its origin. Indeed, the plot belongs to the popular tradition of denouncing the empress,[4] without familiarity with actual history. The four fictional historical tales Empress Lü's son gives to his mother (about the disastrous fates of conniving queens) are a case in point. Examples of misinformation (due to transmission of the story through traditions independent of historical sources) also exist. They include naming Liu Heng's mother Consort Yan 闫妃 (rather than Consort Bo), and calling Lü Chan Empress Lü's brother (rather than her nephew).

But most of the deviations from historical fact seem deliberate, in order to tighten the plot structure while maintaining the historical stance of the characters. With the exception of Fan Kang, all the characters historically against the Lü family appear as good characters and join forces at certain times (though, in fact, did not do so historically). Wang Ling 王凌's presence in the play, before and after Lü Chan's ascension to the throne, provides still another example. In the histories, Wang Ling was already banished from court before the "Lü Chan Disturbance" because he disagreed with enfeoffment of Empress Lü's kinsmen.[5] But as a staunch opponent to the Lü's, he is conveniently paired with Chen Ping in the final annihilation of Lü Chan.

Fan Kang's joining forces with Chen Ping in this play could have been the result of misinformation, since Fan Kang was, in fact, executed along

4. A shadow play in Xiaoyi 孝义, Shanxi, and a marionette play in Quanzhou 泉州, Fujian are examples. See Shanxisheng xiju yanjiusuo Lüliangshi xiju chuangzuo yanjiushi, ed., *The Great Western Han* (*da xihan* 大西汉); a.k.a., *Chen Ping Rejects an Edict* (*Chen Ping dingben* 陈平顶本), 1–36; and Quanzhou defang xiqu yanjiushe ed., Vol. 11: *Empress Lü Executes Han* (*Lühou zhan Hen* 吕后斩韩), 260–301.

5. See Watson 1961, 163–164, for the biography of the historical Wang Ling.

with the Lüs as a cousin of Lü Chan. But this bending of historical fact might also have been deliberate. In the play, Chen Ping needs a general related to Lü Chan, so the assassin can get close to the usurper and hack him down with ease. Changes of historical facts for the cohesion and convenience of the plot also abound, but they tend to be in keeping with the spirit of the history. Examples include making Liu Heng into the third of three sons, Prince Hui's committing suicide, and Empress Lü's ascension to the throne. Even the ending is probably a concession to history insofar as a character as heinous as Empress Lü is only banished to the "cold palace" in the play. Normally, such a character would have been executed to satisfy the expectations of the audience. But in real history, Empress Lü did die peacefully.

Ultimately, however, the play aims to portray the story of an evil queen. As such, pure fabrication of events is necessary. The allegations concerning Empress Lü's narrow-mindedness, her squabbles with Consort Qi, her alleged lasciviousness, her attempt to kill Consort Yan and her baby, and Prince Hui's advice to them to seek refuge at Chen Ping's are all aimed at fashioning the Empress into an absolute *femme fatale.*

Cast of *Empress Lü Usurps the Throne*[6]

LIU BANG 刘邦 (r. 206–194 BCE): Emperor Gao 高皇.[7] Founding emperor of the Han dynasty (206 BCE–221 CE).

CHEN PING 陈平: an aged minister, a general who helped Liu Bang found the dynasty. In this play, he has the title of Prince[8] and is referred to as an "older brother" of Liu Bang.

WANG LING 王陵: a minister.

LIU YING 刘盈: Eldest Prince;[9] Prince Hui 惠王; historically, he reigned as Emperor Hui 惠帝 (194–187 BCE). Son of Empress Lü.

---

6. The script for this play is found in Shaanxisheng Wenhuaju, ed., *Heyang xianxi* in *Shaanxisheng chuantong jumu, xianxi,* 347–381. This play script originally belonged to the Heyang Marionette Troupe (*heyang xianxi she* 合阳线戏社).

7. The play script says Gaohuang 高皇, although the proper term should probably have been Gaodi 高帝. He is commonly referred to as Gaozu 高祖.

8. Although the title *wang* 王 is usually translated as "king" in modern usage, the position is in fact more akin to that of a prince or even a duke rather than a king, given the existence and power of the emperor.

9. Although referred to as the Eldest Prince in this play, historically, he was the Crown Prince and in fact ruled as emperor from 195 BCE until he died in 188 BCE.

Liu Feng 刘奉: Second Prince; also known as Ruyi 如意; Prince Zhao 赵王. Younger brother of Liu Ying. Son of Consort Qi 戚妃.

Fan Kang 樊康: a general; his mother is a sister of Empress Lü, making him a nephew of both Empress Lü and her brother, Lü Chan. In this play, Fan Kang's father is referred to as an "older brother" of Chen Ping.

Lü Chan 吕产: Empress Lü's brother; also known as Maternal Uncle of the State 国舅.[10]

Empress Lü 吕后: Empress of Liu Bang; addressed as Mother of the State 国母 in this play. Historically, she reigned from 187 to 179 BCE, after the death of her son.

Qi Jinlian 戚金莲: Consort Qi. A younger wife of Liu Bang. Queen of the Eastern Palace.

Yan Fei 阎妃: Consort Yan. Another consort of Liu Bang. Queen of the Western Palace.

Prince: Young Prince, youngest son of Liu Bang; son of Consort Yan. Historically, he reigned as Emperor Wen 文帝 (179–156 BCE). In this play, he appears as the Crown Prince.

Eunuchs: referred to as Palace Officers

Palace Maids

Guards

Servant

Soldiers

Scene 1: "An Evil Plot"

(*Chen Ping and Lü Chan enter and stand in attendance; four eunuchs lead Liu Bang onstage.*)

Liu Bang: (*Recites.*)

On my head, I carry a gold-storing treasury,
Below my feet, I step on a granary for ten thousand years.

We are Liu Bang, Emperor Gao of the Han dynasty. We had to annihilate the Qin 秦 and the Chu 楚[11] before the empire was reunited. We made the mistake of executing three princes and have

10. Historically, he was Empress Lü's nephew, the son of her brother.

11. The Qin was the previous dynasty. The Chu 楚 was a powerful region in the southern part of the area of Chinese civilization during that time. Xiang Yu 项羽, the King of Chu, almost defeated Liu Bang 刘邦 and became the emperor.

contracted an illness from ghostly terror.[12] A treacherous scoundrel presently monopolizes the power in the imperial court. We now commence the morning audience at court. Our dear Minister Chen!

CHEN PING: Present!

LIU BANG: You are getting on with age, our dear elderly minister. It pains us to see you prostrating yourself at our court morning and night. Henceforth, you will never have to attend court audiences again. Go back to your residence and rest yourself!

CHEN PING: Your minister obeys the imperial edict. (*Exits.*)

LIU BANG: Imperial Relative Lü! There is a vacancy in the provincial post at Taiyuan 太原. We would like to ask you to go there and guard the area. How do you feel about doing this?

LÜ CHAN: Your minister was already thinking about doing so, but did not dare to leave the capital without your Majesty's decree.

LIU BANG: You and we concur in our decisions—you are indeed a loyal subject. We will bestow upon you an army of three thousand for you to guard Taiyuan. You will leave immediately. You can take the edict and leave the court.

LÜ CHAN: Your minister obeys the edict. Ha, ha! Hey, hey! What a muddle-headed Emperor! (*Exits.*)

LIU BANG: Ah, ah, ah!

EUNUCH: What's wrong, your Majesty?

LIU BANG: What a treacherous scoundrel that was! He left the court but made us, the Emperor, so infuriated that our soul floated out of our body. We feel our illness getting worse. Palace Officer, get us a carriage to the Palace of Eternal Trust (*changxin gong* 长信宫) to convalesce. (*Sings.*)

We are furious that the evildoer scoundrel
Victimizes and coerces our civil and military ministers.
Outwardly, we, the Emperor made him an official of Taiyuan,
Inwardly, we in fact put him in exile away from the capital. (*Exits.*)

12. Three of his most able generals were awarded fiefs and became titled princes after they assisted Liu Bang to become emperor. They remained powerful militarily, however. Perceiving them as threats to the throne, Liu Bang supposedly eliminated them with the help of Empress Lü. According to legend, the ghosts of these victimized generals haunted Liu Bang and caused his eventual death.

Scene 2: "Visiting the Sick"

(*The Head Eunuch and a Palace Maid lead Empress Lü onto the stage.*)
Empress Lü: (*Sings.*)

My Emperor received the mandate and presides over the dragon court,[13]
The three palaces and six courts of his harem have all received entitlements.
The glamour and wealth are too plentiful to describe,
And I alone am the presiding empress, in full glory.

I am Empress Lü. My lord his Majesty has contracted an illness from ghostly terror and is convalescing at the Palace of Eternal Trust. I'll have to pay him a visit and look in on him. Palace Officer, arrange a carriage for me to go to the Palace of Eternal Trust! (*Sings.*)

My lord his Majesty has contracted an illness from ghostly terror,
And made me, the Empress, ever so worried.
The palace officers hurriedly arranged for a carriage,
So that I may pay him a visit at the Palace of Eternal Trust.
(*They exit.*)

Scene 3: "Assuming the Post"

(*Lü Chan enters with a soldier.*)
Lü Chan: (*Sings.*)

Obeying the imperial edict, I dare not tarry;
Guarding the City of Taiyuan, I am more than willing.
I have been loyal, only for the sake of my elder sister,[14]
I have been filial, only for the sake of my parents.

I am the Imperial Brother-in-Law, Lü Chan. The muddle-headed emperor made the mistake of exiling me to guard Taiyuan. Once I reach there, I'm

13. Emperors were viewed as having received the Mandate of Heaven, which gave them the right to rule. The dragon is a symbol of the emperor.

14. In this play, he is Empress Lü's younger brother. Historically, he was her brother's son.

going to gather soldiers and train warriors to snatch his empire. We have just left the capital. Let me give my order: Generals—let's go to Taiyuan! (*Sings.*)

> I announce the order from atop my horse,
> Let's all embark on our trip to the City of Taiyuan. (*They exit.*)

Scene 4: "Entrustment"

(*Qi Jinlian helps Liu Bang on stage, followed by a palace maid.*)
LIU BANG: (*Sings.*)

> We made the mistake of executing the three princes and contracted this illness.
> Recalling how they accompanied me in the battles of Hongcheng 鸿城,[15]
> —That grand combat of the great heroes—
> It was because of them that we procured the empire.
> We are Emperor Gao of the Han.

QI JINLIAN: I am the consort, Qi Jinlian.
LIU BANG: We executed the three princes by mistake and have contracted this serious illness. It is more likely that we will return to the world of darkness than stay in this world of light.
QI JINLIAN: How does your Majesty feel?
LIU BANG: We feel worse and worse!
QI JINLIAN: Please try to feel better. The lads[16] are still so young—what would the empire depend upon should anything happen to you?
LIU BANG: If King Yama wants my life, there's nothing I can do. Consort wife, we feel so weak and tired. We would like to take a nap on your lap, what do you think?
QI JINLIAN: Your consort is willing to be with your Majesty.

---

15. Hongcheng probably refers to Pengcheng 彭城, where Liu Bang suffered defeat originally but eventually emerged victorious.

16. In this play, the sons are frequently referred to as *yuanjia* 冤家, a person to whom one owes a debt from a previous incarnation. This appellation is usually used to refer informally to spouses, but in this play, it is used by the Emperor and his queens to refer to their sons. I translate the term as "lad" to reflect the informality and the somewhat inappropriate nature of the term that reflects the immaturity of, and lack of respect for, the Emperor's sons.

Liu Bang: Don't disturb me then! (*He naps. The head eunuch and a palace maid lead Empress Lü on stage.*)

Empress Lü: Lead the carriage! (*Recites.*)

Having left Weiyang Palace 未央宫,[17]
I proceed to pay a visit to the sick.

Eunuch: I report to Mother of the State—we have arrived at the gate of the Palace of Eternal Trust.

Empress Lü: Stop the carriage. (*Descends.*)

Palace Maid: I, Xue'er 学儿,[18] prostrate myself to Mother of the State!

Empress Lü: Palace Maid—report to your Lady Qi that I've come to visit his ailing Majesty. Tell her to come out of the palace to greet me.

Palace Maid: I obey the edict. I report to Lady Qi—Mother of the State has come to visit his Majesty. She wants you to go out to greet her.

Qi Jinlian: Tell her that although I really should be there to welcome her personally, his Majesty is taking a nap on my lap and I can't move right now. We are members of the same family—tell her to come in on her own.

Palace Maid: Yes. I'll report to Mother of the State—my Lady Qi said that although she really should come out here to welcome you personally, his Majesty is taking a nap on her lap and she can't move right now. Mother of the State, you are of the same family—she said for you to go in on your own.

Empress Lü: Wait a minute—what an evil consort! Have you no sense of respect? If you don't come out to welcome me, how insulting it would be for me to enter the palace by myself. Palace Officer, take the carriage back to Weiyang Palace. (*They exit.*)

Palace Maid: I report to Lady Qi—Mother of the State has returned to Weiyang Palace.

Qi Jinlian: Heavens! Oh no! (*Liu Bang wakes up in a start.*)

Liu Bang: Why are you crying, dear Consort?

Qi Jinlian: I'm not crying.

Liu Bang: There are clearly traces of tears on your face. Why lie to us? You must have been tired of taking care of such a sick person for so long. Wasn't it so?

17. The name of her own residence.

18. Xue'er literally means "learner." All the palace maids and eunuchs refer to themselves as Xue'er in this play.

QI JINLIAN: (*Weeps.*) Your Majesty wouldn't have known—Mother of the State came to visit your Majesty. I wasn't able to move because your Majesty was taking a nap on my lap. She got so angry that she turned the carriage around and returned to her palace. She is not a good person and will invariably harm me and my son. What am I to do?

LIU BANG: While we are alive, we will take care of you.

QI JINLIAN: Now that you are alive, you can take care of us. But should you leave, upon whom can we, mother and son, depend?

LIU BANG: Don't cry anymore. We have an idea. Palace Maid, summon the Eldest Prince and the Second Prince to the palace here to discuss official matters with us.

PALACE MAID: His Majesty has issued an edict for the Eldest Prince and the Second Prince to come to the palace to discuss official matters.

LIU YING AND LIU FENG: (*Off stage.*) We accept the edict. (*They enter together and kowtow.*) Our reverent Father, the Emperor, we brothers prostrate ourselves to you!

LIU BANG: Rise and sit down.

LIU YING AND LIU FENG: Auntie,[19] we brothers greet you!

QI JINLIAN: There's no need for formalities. You can sit down.

LIU YING AND LIU FENG: Thank you. May we inquire of our Father the Emperor as to the state of the dragon's illness?

LIU BANG: We feel worse and worse.

LIU YING AND LIU FENG: You must take good care of yourself. We brothers are so young—upon whom will the empire depend should anything happen to you?

LIU BANG: This is fate—your Father can't do anything more for you.

LIU YING: Our Father the Emperor has summoned us here. What instructions would Father like to impart?

LIU BANG: We wouldn't call them instructions. Liu Ying, come over to our bed.

LIU YING: What would Father like to say?

LIU BANG: Listen to what we want to entrust to you! (*Sings.*)

> We call for our son, Liu Ying, to come forward,
> So that your Father, the Emperor, can entrust you with the empire.
> Should we, your Father the Emperor, pass away,

19. Technically speaking, all the children of the head of the household belonged to the formal wife. Hence, the children call the concubines "aunties."

The civil and military officials will support your ascension to the throne.
The Eastern and Western Palaces[20] you should take good care of,
And your two imperial younger brothers, you should treat kindly.
Your Mother has a tendency to be rather narrow minded,
Do not listen to her, no matter what.
Discuss state matters with the ministers at the court,
Visit and inquire after her health only after the court sessions.
Be sure to remember all the words your Father entrusts to you,
And not let them fly by your ears like idle gossip.

Liu Ying: (*Sings.*)

After hearing my Father's words, my liver and entrails burst from grief,
I, your son, Liu Ying, am not a disobedient, unfilial child.
Should you, heaven forbid, my Father the Emperor, pass away,
The heavy burden of ten thousand catties, I am willing to carry.

Liu Bang: Good! Stand aside for a moment. Come over here, Liu Feng.
Liu Feng: Here I am. What does my Father, the Emperor, wish to say?
Liu Bang: My dear son! (*Sings.*)

Seeing the lad, my heart is shattered from love and grief,
For your mother and you, your Father is so extremely worried.
Should we, your Father the Emperor, pass away,
We intend to have your elder brother ascend the throne.
Do not contend with him to occupy the throne yourself,
Lest foreign states attack us with swords and arrows.
It is difficult to separate Bo Yi 伯夷 from Shu Qi 叔齐,[21]

---

20. These refer to Consort Qi and Consort Yan.

21. Bo Yi and Shu Qi were the eldest and third sons of the king of the state of Guzhu 孤竹 around the end of the Shang dynasty (1766–1050 BCE). The king designated Shu Qi as the heir; but after he died, Shu Qi insisted that Bo Yi should be the new king. Bo Yi, however, declined as it was the wish of their father for Shu Qi to rule. The two brothers subsequently served as ministers under King Wen 文王 and King Wu 武王 of the state of Zhou. When King Wu rebelled against the Shang, Bo Yi and Shu Qi retreated to Mount Shouyang and died there.

These ancients have left their names at Mount Shouyang 首阳山.
Filial and friendly brothers are admired by the people,
Your Father will be content even in the Underworld.

Liu Feng: My suffering Father, the Emperor! (*Sings.*)

Having heard my Father's words, tears fill my face,
I feel as if scalding oil sears over my entire abdomen.
The words of my Father, the Emperor, I will definitely heed.
I would not end up creating a scandal for all under Heaven.

Liu Bang: Good! Stand over there for a moment. (*Sings.*)

Our son Liu Ying is filial, our son Liu Feng is sagacious,
Now we, the Emperor, can rest in peace.
Just as we, the Emperor, are entrusting our sons. . . .

(*Off stage in mid-air*: Return to your post!)

Suddenly, we hear a voice mid-air.
We see Ying Bu 英布, Han Xin 韩信, and Peng Yue 彭越[22] here to pay us an audience,
We, the Emperor and ministers are arriving at the Gate of the Ghosts (*guimen guan* 鬼门关).

(*Liu Bang dies.*)
Liu Ying and Liu Feng: (*Weeping.*) Oh no, our Father the Emperor, who died so untimely! (*They exit.*)

Scene 5: "Devising a Scheme"

(*The Head Eunuch and a Palace Maid lead Empress Lü on stage.*)
Empress Lü: I am so furious! (*Sings.*)

22. Ying Bu (?–195 BCE), Han Xin (?–196 BCE), and Peng Yue (?–196 BCE) were the three most able generals who helped Liu Bang establish the Han dynasty (206 BCE–220 CE). Although Liu Bang bestowed upon them the title of prince, they were all charged with rebellion and executed by the emperor and Empress Lü within three years of the founding of the dynasty. Empress Lü was directly responsible for the demise of Han Xin and Peng Yue.

I am so furious with that Qi Jinlian,
Who had no respect for my seniority.
If she should ever land in my hands in the future,
I will ensure the demise of the evil consort!

(*Liu Feng and Liu Ying enter together.*)

Liu Ying and Liu Feng: (*Kneeling.*) Mother of the State! We have bad news!

Empress Lü: What happened?

Liu Ying and Liu Feng: Our Father the Emperor has passed away!

Empress Lü: (*Weeps.*) The Emperor who died so untimely! Ah well! Since the Emperor is already dead, crying will not do any good. I know what to do. Liu Ying, your Father the Emperor has died. I, your Mother, bestow upon you, my son, the title of Prince Hui.[23]

Liu Ying: I, Prince Hui, give thanks for the favor!

Empress Lü: Liu Feng, I, Mother of the State, bestow upon you, my son, the title of Prince Zhao.[24]

Liu Feng: I, Prince Zhao, give thanks for the favor!

Empress Lü: You brothers should proceed immediately to set up the spirit tablet for your Father's funeral!

Liu Ying and Liu Feng: Your sons understand. Our Father, the Emperor, who died so untimely! (*They exit.*)

Empress Lü: I'm secretly delighted by the Emperor's death. Let me take advantage of this opportunity to do harm to Qi Jinlian. Wait a minute! If Liu Feng ever finds out that I killed his mother, he would never forgive me. (*She thinks.*) I've got it! Let me make a bottle of poisoned wine and kill Liu Feng before I victimize the evil consort. Wait a minute! My son studies with Liu Feng. What if I end up poisoning him instead? I've got it! Let me have my son perform a sacrifice at the imperial mausoleum. So this will be the scheme. Palace Maid, summon the Eldest Prince here to discuss an official matter.

Palace Maid: Mother of the State has issued an edict—the Eldest Prince should come to the palace.

Liu Ying: (*Offstage.*) I accept the edict. (*Enters.*) I greet Mother of the State.

Empress Lü: You may rise.

Liu Ying: Thank you, Mother of the State, for the imperial favor.

Empress Lü: Sit down.

---

23. Historically, he was already Prince Hui. He should have been titled "Emperor Hui."

24. Historically, he was already Prince Zhao.

Liu Ying: Thanks for offering the seat. May I ask Mother of the State why your son has been summoned to the palace? What admonitions does Mother wish to impart?

Empress Lü: Your Father, the Emperor, has already passed away, what admonitions are there? Your Mother would like to ask you to go outside the city to perform a sacrifice at the imperial mausoleum. How would you feel about it?

Liu Ying: If that's the case, Palace Officer, let Liu Feng know about it.

Empress Lü: Come back. Your Mother just asked you to perform an imperial sacrifice. Why do you have to tell Liu Feng everything? This is so infuriating!

Liu Ying: What is this about? Why was Mother of the State infuriated when my younger brother was mentioned? Oh well! Mother of the State, my imperial Mother!

Empress Lü: Ai!

Liu Ying: Please don't be angry, Mother of the State. Your son won't take Liu Feng with him.

Empress Lü: So you won't take Liu Feng with you?

Liu Ying: Right, I won't.

Empress Lü: Since you won't take Liu Feng with you, Mother is not angry anymore. Proceed immediately to perform the sacrifice and return immediately lest I worry about you. You can leave right now.

Liu Ying: May I, your son, entrust something before I leave the palace?

Empress Lü: Hmm! Sit down and speak!

Liu Ying: (*Sings.*)

I ask the Mother of State to listen to me carefully,
And remember the words of your son in your heart.
Liu Feng is presently studying at the Azure Palace (*qinggong* 青宫),
I implore that you, Mother, will take good care of him.

Empress Lü: My dear son! Don't you worry—you just go ahead with performing the sacrifice at the imperial mausoleum. I, Mother of the State, will take care of the lad just right.

Liu Ying: (*Sings.*)

I make my bow and exit the palace court
To lead the civil and military officials to the mausoleum. (*Exits.*)

Empress Lü: (*Sings.*)

My son did not know what was really going on,
The moment the evil consort was mentioned,[25] I became furious.
Let me first concoct here the poisoned wine,
Then I'll send for a eunuch to execute my order.
You are to send this poisoned wine to the Azure Palace immediately,
And tell Liu Feng to drink a few cups of it.
You can tell him that on account of the cold weather,
I have had this bottle of wine sent to him.
Tell him to study once he finished drinking,
There's no need for him to visit and inquire after my health.
(*The eunuch exits.*)

(*Speaks.*) I am so delighted! (*Sings.*)

I have dispatched a eunuch to send the poisoned wine,
Which will ensure delivery of the lad to the City of Wronged Deaths (*wangsi cheng* 枉死城). (*Exits.*)

Scene 6: "Cruel Death"

(*Liu Feng enters with two guards.*)
Liu Feng: (*Sings.*)

I am so angry with my Elder Brother the Prince,
You should not have gone to the imperial sacrifice on your own.
Certainly you are a blood-related son of our Father the Emperor,
But I, Liu Feng, am not an adopted son either.

(*Speaks.*) This was really wrong of my Elder Brother the Prince! Why didn't he tell me about performing a sacrifice at the imperial mausoleum? When he comes back, I'm going to make him speechless with shame.
(*A eunuch enters with wine.*)
Eunuch: (*Recites.*)

With orders from Mother of the State,
I am here to deliver the poisoned wine.

---

25. The "evil consort" refers to Consort Qi. Although she was not mentioned earlier, she came to Empress Lü's mind through association with her son.

(*Speaks.*) I have arrived at the gate of Azure Palace. (*Entering.*) Reverent Prince, I, Xue'er, kowtow to you!

LIU FENG: Which palace are you from? What are you here for?

EUNUCH: I was sent by Mother of the State at the Empress's Palace. On account of the cold weather, she has asked me to bring you a bottle of warm wine.

LIU FENG: Leave the wine and report back to Mother of the State that after I drink the wine I will go to inquire after her health.

EUNUCH: Dear Prince! Mother of the State sends clear instructions that after you, the Prince, have finished drinking the wine, you should study hard. There's no need for you to inquire after her health.

LIU FENG: If that is the case, you can leave the wine and report back to Mother of the State.

EUNUCH: Xue'er obeys your command. Hmm, hmm, hmm! (*Exits.*)

LIU FENG: What do you make of this? My Mom always told me that Mother of the State, the Empress, is full of ill intentions and that I should be wary of her. But look at how she sends over a bottle of warm wine when the weather is cold. It would seem that she is, in fact, kind hearted and that my Mom has accused her wrongly. Let me enjoy the wine by myself.

GUARDS: Wait a minute, Prince! There's something curious about this wine. Why do you have to drink it?

LIU FENG: Get out of here! How dare you, you barbarian slaves! I, the Prince, was just about to enjoy some wine. How dare you dampen our[26] fun? You should be beheaded for this!

GUARDS: If such is the case, please forgive us for being so forward!

LIU FENG: Yes, you were too forward. Why don't you stand over there?

GUARDS: Yes, yes, yes! We won't interfere with your drinking.

LIU FENG: Let me enjoy the wine by myself. (*Drinks.*) Aiya, what good wine!

GUARDS: If the wine is good, drink a few more cups.

LIU FENG: Ai!

GUARDS: Prince—what happened?

LIU FENG: Why does this wine feel like burning coal when it reaches the stomach?

GUARDS: Maybe it's poisoned! Vomit, Prince!

---

26. It is inappropriate, but he does use the royal "we" (*gu* 孤; literally, the Orphaned One, a term used by an emperor to refer to himself) here.

Liu Feng: Ah, ah, ah! How come I can't vomit?
Guards: There's nothing we can do if you can't vomit!
Liu Feng: Yes, yes, yes! Now I understand. (*Sings.*)

> Yes, yes, yes—it is now all very clear,
> I have been deceived by the evil consort.[27]
> I cry for my Empress Mother, whom your son will never see again,[28]
> How would you know that your son is returning to the Underworld?
> The Auntie[29] and my imperial younger brother know nothing of this,
> My Elder Brother, the Prince, left the city and has not yet returned.
> While I speak, I can feel my *hun* 魂 and *po* 魄 souls dissipate,[30]
> My three souls[31] are dispersing and returning to the Underworld. (*Dies.*)

Guards: Prince, Prince! Oh no, he's dead! He wouldn't listen to us—we wonder if he regrets it now.
Guard B: Blaming him won't do any good. We should report this to Consort Qi. (*They exit. Offstage:* We report to Consort Qi, respectfully—Mother of the State, the Empress, sent over a bottle of warm wine to our Prince on account of the cold weather. But our Prince was not used to drinking. The wine flooded his heart and lungs and killed him.)
Qi Jinlian: (*Offstage: Aiya! Oh no! She enters weeping.*) Oh no, my poor, poor son! (*Sings.*)

> Seeing my hapless son dead,
> Gave me, the Queen, a great shock.
> Now that you're dead, you have no cares,
> But who will now take care of your Mom?

---

27. Although Empress Lü is not a consort, the term "evil consort" (*jianfei* 奸妃) is a standard term. It also reflects Liu Feng's desire to lower her status.

28. Just as he reduces Empress Lü's status in the previous line, he now elevates his mother's status inappropriately.

29. He is referring to Consort Yan here.

30. The Chinese believed in the existence of several different souls within each body. The *hun* and the *po* are the main ones—the former being the spiritual or *yang* component of the soul, and latter being the material or *yin* component. See Thompson 1979, 11.

31. See footnote 30.

(*Weeps.*) I cry and call out to Liu Feng—how did I, your Mom, warn you at my palace? That lowborn Empress Lü is full of evil intentions, and I told you to be wary of her. Now you have been killed by her scheme. Let me ask you if you now regret not having listened to your Mom? (*Sings.*)

I embrace the corpse and call out to Liu Feng,
But you are dead and unable to respond to Mom.
Again and again, you did not heed Mom's warnings,
At Azure Palace, you stayed and studied.
Empress Lü has truly intrigued to cause your murder,
Poor mother and child, who are now totally separated.

(*Empress Lü enters and pretends to weep.*)

EMPRESS LÜ: I call out to Liu Feng—what illness did you contract, my dear son, that you should die this way? This will kill me, Mother of the State, with grief!

QI JINLIAN: Who is this person that is embracing my son's corpse and weeping?

EMPRESS LÜ: My Imperial Sister! It is I.

QI JINLIAN: So it's Empress Lü!

EMPRESS LÜ: Let me ask you—what illness did this son of mine[32] contract that he should die this way?

QI JINLIAN: You're asking me? How could you not know about my son's death?

EMPRESS LÜ: My Imperial Sister—how would I know about the lad's death?

QI JINLIAN: Empress Lü! Oh you cruel-hearted, evil consort! (*Sings.*)

How dare you argue about it, you evil consort?
I, the Queen, have something to say—you listen to me.
When the Emperor contracted an illness from ghostly terror,
It got worse so he returned to the Palace of Eternal Trust.
It was on my lap that he did take a nap,
Who would have known that you would arrive then?
I, the Queen, was unable to come out to greet you,
But you, evil consort, harbored a grudge in your heart.
Secretly you poisoned wine to take my son's life,
Even if people would endure you, Heaven will not.

32. The formal wife has a claim to all the children of her husband's concubines.

Empress Lü: (*Sings.*)

You have no respect for me or for hierarchy,
I, Mother of the State, amount to nothing in your mind.
So I poisoned the wine to take your son's life,
I'd like to see the punishment you will mete out to me.

Qi Jinlian: (*Sings.*)

So you blame me for not having greeted you,
And hence caused my son to lose his life.
When Chen Xi 陈豨 raised rebellion and created havoc,[33]
The Emperor led an army and a military expedition.
For a full month, he did not return to the court,
You, evil consort, were unwilling to live by yourself.
Xiao He 萧何 was too old by then and no longer of use,[34]
At night time, he was but unable to please you.
Chen Ping and Peng Yue were both very handsome,
But neither of them stayed behind at the imperial court.
Accompanying his Majesty, Chen Ping was at the front,
General Peng, however, was guarding the City of Tongguan 潼关城.
Disregarding any sense of shame, you, evil consort—
You traveled to Tongguan privately, on your own initiative.
When the general heard that you had arrived,
He hurriedly kowtowed and inquired of the Emperor's situation.
But with your own hand you grabbed the general's arm,
And secretly brought him back to your Weiyang Palace.
A hundred ways you tried to seduce him with honeyed words and flirting,
But the stubborn general was unwilling to submit to you.
When the Emperor eventually returned and came back to the court,

33. Chen Xi (?–195 BCE) rebelled in 195 BCE, supposedly under the instigation of Han Xin. The emperor led an army and defeated him himself.

34. Xiao He (257–193 BCE) was one of Emperor Gao's most trusted advisors. He was instrumental in aiding the emperor in founding and stabilizing the empire, including strategizing the annihilation of Han Xin, Ying Bu, etc.

You schemed and caused the death of the hapless general.
When I was unable to greet you at the palace gate the other day,
You similarly retaliated by causing my son's death.
I only wish I could have you fried in boiling oil!

EMPRESS LÜ: (*Sings.*)

Hearing the evil consort revile me so loudly,
I, the Empress, am totally filled with shame.
Those events in the past, who dares to mention them?
Who would have thought that the evil consort remembers them all?

(*Speaks.*) What an evil consort! If you revile the Mother of State anymore, I'll make sure that you'll end up dead!

QI JINLIAN: (*Weeps.*) I cry and call out to Liu Feng—don't leave so fast, your Mom is following right behind you! (*Sings.*)

Now that Empress Dowager Lü has been reviled by me,
There's no way that she will allow your Mom to remain alive.
Just wait a minute for me at the Gate of the Deceased,
We mother and son can travel together as a pair of ghosts.

(*Speaks.*) Empress Lü, you shameless, evil consort! (*Sings.*)

Pointing to the evil consort, I yell at her loudly,
Let me see the torture and punishment you will mete out to me!

EMPRESS LÜ: Leave! What an evil consort! How dare you yell and scream at me! Summon a guard into the palace!

GUARDS: (*Enters.*) Mother of the State, we are at your service.

EMPRESS LÜ: Execute Qi Jinlian!

GUARD: Watch my broadsword! (*Qi dies.*)

EMPRESS LÜ: The way the evil consort yelled and screamed at Mother of the State, being killed with one hack is too light a punishment. Guard, nail the evil consort to the southern wall[35] and let it rot into a human swine 人彘! (*The Guards nail Qi's corpse.*)

---

35. The south facing wall is probably selected so that the flesh would rot more readily.

Guards: We have nailed the corpse to the southern wall to let it rot into a human swine.

Empress Lü: You can all leave the palace! (*They exit.*) Let me take a look at the human swine. Qi Jinlian—you evil consort—how dare you yell and scream at Mother of the State! You deserved to die. It's time for my son to return. Let me wait for him.

Liu Ying: (*Enters.*) I am walking. I, Liu Ying, just returned from performing a sacrifice at the imperial mausoleum. I went to inquire after my Mother's health, but was told that she went to the Azure Palace. Aiya! Doesn't she care that the civil and military officials would laugh at her? I'll have to look in on her. Empress Mother, Mother of the State, your son is here to inquire after your health.

Empress Lü: Dispense with the formalities. So you're back, my son.

Liu Ying: Yes. I, your son, am back.

Empress Lü: I'm glad you're back, so I won't have to worry about you.

Liu Ying: May I inquire, Mother of the State, as to why you are here at the Azure Palace rather than at your own Weiyang Palace?

Empress Lü: I, your Mom, came here to look at the sights.

Liu Ying: The best sights are at the imperial garden of the Palace of the Retirees (*yanglao gong* 养老宫). The Azure Palace is where we brothers study, what sights are here for you to see?

Empress Lü: I, your Mom, came here to see the human swine!

Liu Ying: What is a human swine?

Empress Lü: How can you, the head of a state, not know what a human swine is?

Liu Ying: Your son truly has never seen one before.

Empress Lü: It's nailed to that wall there right now. You can go and take a look!

Liu Ying: Alright. Let me see what this human swine is. (*Looks.*) Oh no! My Aunt who has been killed wrongly! (*Sings.*)

Seeing the dead corpse of my Aunt,
I, Prince Hui, am dumb struck by shock.
What crime did you commit just now,
To have your corpse nailed to the wall and your flesh rotting?

(*Speaks.*) Mother of the State, why did my Aunt die like this? Where was my Imperial Younger Brother?

Empress Lü: The lad is sleeping in that room.

LIU YING: Aiya! What an ignorant Younger Brother! How can you sleep when your Mother was killed like that? Let me call for him. Liu Feng, my Imperial Younger Brother! (*Looks.*) Oh no! My Imperial Younger Brother! (*Sings.*)

Both Aunt and Younger Brother have entered the Underworld,
Causing me, Prince Hui, to pine most grievously.
I, your Elder Brother, was not at the imperial palace,
The deaths of you, mother and son, are very mysterious.

(*Speaks.*) Mother of the State, how did my Imperial Younger Brother die?

EMPRESS LÜ: I, your Mom, was afraid that he would snatch the empire from you. I had the mother and son killed so that your throne would be safe and secure for a long time!

LIU YING: (*Weeps.*) I yell and denounce Emperor Hui of the Han.[36] What you have committed today are acts against Heaven and Earth. How will you be able to secure your throne for long? (*Sings.*)

What you have done today is most unrighteous,
The weighty azure Heaven cannot be deceived.
Today I committed a most heinous immoral act,
I fear that even if people condone it, Heaven will not.

EMPRESS LÜ: Don't weep anymore, my son. Your Mom killed the mother and son for you!

LIU YING: My muddle-headed Mother of the State! (*Sings.*)

Your son went to the imperial mausoleum to perform a sacrifice today,
And that mother and son died at your hands, my Mom.
For your lad, you have schemed and worked very hard,
You feared that he would contend with me for the throne.
When the foreign countries hear of this, they will revile me for it,
How will your son be able to stand proud and erect in the world?
I have some comparable tales from history I'd like to tell you, Mom,
I ask that you, Imperial Mother of the State, will listen with patience.
In the past, Daji 妲己 eliminated the loyal and upright from her husband's court,

---

36. He denounces himself here and refers to himself as the Emperor.

And caused Consort Huang 黄贵妃 to fall to her death from
the Jade Pavilion (*yulou* 玉楼).
By forcing the lady to become a female martyr,
She caused the Huang family to rebel at Xiqi 西歧.
From there King Wu 武王 led an army to invade Zhou 纣,
Fire burnt the muddle-headed ruler and Daji was executed.[37]
There was also the woman called Liji 丽姬 of yesteryear,
Who, in order to obtain the throne for her beloved son,
Conceived for him a "Strategy of the Bees" (*mifeng ji* 蜜蜂计)
in the garden.
Her son, Shensheng 身生, regretted her actions, but it was too late.
Chong'er 重耳 led an army and arrived in revenge,
With a broadsword, he hacked the prince to death and killed Liji.[38]
There was also the greedy, lowborn Consort Zou Rongchun 邹容春,
Who caused the loyal and upright ministers to leave the court.
Yue Yi 乐毅 led an army and invaded the State of Qi 齐,
Making an example of Duke Min 湣王, he also hacked Consort
Zou 邹妃 to pieces.[39]
Aijiang 哀姜 and Qingfu 庆父 fomented turmoil,
But midway they met up with Gao Xi 高傒

37. Daji was the favorite queen of King Zhou (he was called king rather than emperor because a feudal system existed at the time), who was the last ruler of the Shang dynasty. Historical sources from this period justified King Wu's rebellion by blaming King Zhou's downfall on his fondness for wine and women, of which Daji was identified as the main culprit. Popular literature, such as *Investiture of the Gods* (*Fengshen yanyi* 封神演义) eventually developed Daji into a heinous figure responsible for the downfall of the dynasty.

38. "Strategy of the Bees" refers to a scheme devised by Consort Liji of Duke Xian 献公 in chapter 27 of *Romance of the Warring States* (*Lieguozhi* 列国志) to incriminate Shensheng, her stepson and heir to the state. In order to prove to the Duke that Shensheng was amorously inclined toward her, Liji put honey in her hair to attract bees and asked Shensheng to brush away the bees for her. The unknowing Duke observing from a distance was thus convinced by Liji and eventually had Shensheng executed. This incident is not found in the historical source on Liji's schemes. See Watson 1989, 22–24.

39. Another story derived from events during the Warring States period, the Peking/Beijing Opera, *The Golden Terrace* (*Huangjin tai* 黄金台) has Consort Zou, the evil consort of Duke Min of the State of Qi, accuse the heir of flirting with her. The Duke orders the Crown Prince executed, but the latter manages to escape and eventually regains the throne after Yue Yi of the State of Yan 燕国 attacks the State of Qi and kills Duke Min and Consort Zou.

Who exterminated the evil-doer and the slut.[40]
These are tales of those who harmed others to benefit themselves.

EMPRESS LÜ: My dear son! All the stories you just told are about bad women. How can they compare with your Mom, a most sagacious being!
LIU YING: (*Sings.*)

Just because Auntie did not come out to greet you,
You had her corpse nailed to a wall to rot into mud.
How and why did Peng Yue die?
Your son risks being unfilial by asking the question.

EMPRESS LÜ: My dear son! You should never mention these again!
LIU YING: (*Sings.*)

I have more questions at the tip of my tongue,
But I do not dare ask anymore from now on.

EMPRESS LÜ: What happened? Did you contract some illness from performing the sacrifice at the imperial mausoleum that you should be saying crazy things here? Ai! This is not a good place to stay, let me go back to my Weiyang Palace. (*Exits.*)
LIU YING: (*Weeps and looks at the corpse.*) You are my Auntie! (*Turns around and looks.*) You are my Imperial Younger Brother! Ah—my Auntie and Imperial Younger Brother, who died wrongful deaths! (*Sings.*)

Mother of the State has returned to Weiyang Palace,
Leaving me here all alone, and so full of grief.
I cry for my Auntie whom I won't see again,
I cry for Imperial Younger Brother who has gone to the Underworld.
Now that you have both returned to the Yellow Spring,

40. Aijiang was the wife of the Duke Zhuang 庄公 of the State of Lu 鲁. When the Duke died in 662 BCE, Aijiang engaged in an adulterous affair with Qingfu, a younger brother of the deceased Duke. The couple initially put the son of Aijiang's sister, another consort of the deceased, on the throne, but subsequently had the new duke assassinated and plotted to have Qingfu enthroned. Historically, Gao Xi did not kill them. Qingfu was forced to commit suicide, and Aijiang was summoned back to the State of Qi 齐 and killed by her brother or cousin, Duke Huan 桓公, for her unacceptable behavior.

What am I, Liu Ying, going to do?
With a loud wail, I cry and fall to the ground,
I, Prince Hui, am becoming crazy from all this.[41] (*Falls.*)

Eunuch: (*Helps him up.*) What happened, Prince?

Liu Ying: I'm fine. Take the corpses of Lady Qi of the Eastern Palace and the Second Prince and bury them in the golden well. (*The eunuch carries the corpses offstage.*) I just realized that I've offended Mother of the State with crazy and harsh words. I'd better go to her palace and apologize! (*Sings.*)

I cry for Auntie whose life is no more,
I cry for Imperial Younger Brother with whom I can't reunite again. (*Exits.*)

Scene 7: "Getting Rid of a Potential Danger"

(*A eunuch leads Empress Lü on stage.*)

Empress Lü: (*Recites.*)

When a budding sprout is deprived of its root,
It's totally destroyed and will never grow again.
When one does not eliminate the root of a sprout,
It will chill one's spirit when it does grow up.

I am Empress Lü. I have gotten rid of the mother and son of the Eastern Palace. Now, Consort Yan of the Western Palace also has a son who will invariably contend for my son's throne when he grows up. (*Liu Ying enters secretly and listens.*) Palace Officer! Be sure to take sulphur and saltpeter to the Western Palace tonight to burn it down. (*The eunuch exits. She sings.*)

I've dispatched the Palace Officer to set a fire
To burn Consort Yan and turn the Western Palace into ashes.
Lest she eventually contends for the throne,
Burning her should not contravene the laws of Heaven. (*Exits.*)

41. The disease he claims to have contracted is *oufengji* 呕疯疾, literally, vomit-insanity-illness.

Scene 8: "Revealing the Secret"

Liu Ying: (*Enters.*) What a muddle-headed Mother of the State! (*Sings.*)

> Mother of the State has concocted another evil idea,
> She was not content with merely murdering the Eastern Palace.[42]
> I should not stand around and stay here any longer,
> Let me go and warn the Auntie all about it. (*Exits.*)

Scene 9: "Saving Yan"

(*Consort Yan enters carrying her son, followed by a palace maid.*)
Consort Yan: (*Sings.*)

> The Emperor has passed away, the Dragon has returned to Heaven,
> Prince Hui has ascended the throne; he is kind and sagacious in nature.
> Full of ennui, I sit at the court of the Western Palace,
> My eyelids twitch and my flesh shivers; I feel so agitated.
> I am Consort Yan of the Western Palace.

Liu Ying: (*Enters.*) Auntie, I have bad news!
Consort Yan: Why are you so flustered, Prince Hui?[43]
Liu Ying: Mother of the State has conceived of some evil ideas. She has already murdered the mother and son of the Eastern Palace and is sending a eunuch to come and burn the Western Palace.
Consort Yan: What should I do, Prince Hui?
Liu Ying: Auntie, I think you'll be safe if you take your son to Chen Ping's residence.
Consort Yan: Thank you, Prince Hui, for your kindness. We, mother and son, prostrate ourselves to you!
Liu Ying: Please get up, Auntie! You'll kill me, your son, with such excessive formality!
Consort Yan: (*Sings.*)

---

42. The Eastern Palace stands for Consort Qi.

43. He really should be called "Emperor Hui," but I retain the title in the original.

We, mother and son, both prostrate ourselves in the Western Palace,
So touched and grateful are we to Prince Hui for his kindness.
Mother of the State has conceived of an evil plot,
We are indebted to you for coming here to leak the news.

Liu Ying: Please rise, Auntie! (*Sings.*)

Please lower your voice when you speak, dear Auntie,
What is spoken inside the walls can be heard outside.
You, mother and son, should escape from the Western Palace,
And secure yourselves at the residence of Minister Chen Ping.
If my Mom should ever change her mind about things,
I, your child, will move you back to the Western Palace.
Without an imperial edict telling you to leave,
Stay at the Chen residence until you die and never be known.
What I have told you, please remember carefully,
Do not let them fly by your ears like idle gossip.

Consort Yan: Ah, the gracious and righteous Prince Hui! (*Sings.*)

Today you saved the lives of this mother and son,
We can't repay your kindness even if we tried to with our lives.
Hurriedly, I leave without a moment of hesitation,
Carrying in my bosom the delicate little one.
With tears in my eyes, I escape from the Western Palace,
And will stay at the residence of the Imperial Elder Brother Chen.[44] (*Exits.*)

Liu Ying: Auntie, leave quickly! (*Sings.*)

Auntie and my Imperial Younger Brother have left the Western Palace,
I am so despondent that my liver and entrails seem to rot in pain.
If the foreign states would know, they would certainly revile us,

44. She might be referring to him as an imperial elder brother because of his age and closeness to the deceased emperor.

And my people would definitely blame me, Liu Ying.
I'm so angry that Mother of the State acted so immorally,
She has absolutely no regard for the love between blood relatives.

(*Speaks rapidly.*) I, Liu Ying, think to myself. Before my Father the Emperor passed away, he summoned me to his bed and entrusted me several times. He said, "Liu Ying, our son! Ah, our son! Should I, your Father the Emperor, pass away, you will have to take good care of the Eastern and Western Palaces and your two imperial younger brothers." At the time, I agreed to it readily. But now, under my good care, they have all ended up at the Terrace of Home-Viewing (*wangxiang tai* 望乡台).[45] When I die and meet with my Father the Emperor in the Underworld, he will invariably say, "Liu Ying, my son, so you are also here. What did I, your Father, ask you to do? So you took such good care of them that some died while others had to escape for their lives!" Mother of the State victimized the Eastern and Western Palaces cruelly all because of my throne, to ensure the longevity of my reign. But now that it has come to this, I see no way out but to die myself. What a muddle-headed Mother of State you are! (*Sings.*)

I can't be an Emperor anymore; I am unable to rule the people,
I have earned infamy for thousands of years to come.
All the actions you did on my behalf have in fact ruined me,
How can I wish for peace in the future after this?
Covering my face with my dragon robe and sleeve,
I will ram my head against the pillar and die at the Western Palace. (*He hits a pillar and dies.*)

EUNUCH: (*Enters and recites.*)

Receiving an order from Mother of the State,
I have come here to burn the Western Palace.

(*Speaks.*) I am the Xue'er, Wang Cheng 王成. I have an edict from Mother of the State to come and burn the Western Palace. I will go straight into the palace. Why is it so quiet here? Ai! There's a person lying there. Let me see who it is? (*Looks.*) Aiya! Oh no! I report to Mother of the State—the Eldest Prince died from ramming his head against a pillar in the Western Palace!

---

45. This terrace is in purgatory.

Empress Lü: (*Enters.*) Let me take a look! (*Embraces the corpse.*) Liu Ying, oh no! My son who pains your Mother's heart! (*Sings.*)

I see that my lad has lost his life,
Embracing his corpse, I call for Liu Ying.
When did I ever upset you, my dear son?
You should have talked to your Mom about it.
For you, your Mom has murdered people,
But now you have abandoned me and all is lost.
Now that you're dead, you will have no more worries,
But who will take care of your Mom in the future?

(*Speaks rapidly.*) I cry for the Heavens! Oh Heavens! I, Empress Lü, have never done anything unrighteous since I was born, how could you have allowed my son to die this way? How I can die of grief! But the lad is already dead; crying will not do any good. Palace Officer, take the Eldest Prince's corpse to the golden well and bury it there. (*The eunuch carries the corpse off stage.*) The way I see it, the imperial court can't exist without an emperor. Palace Officer, tell the civil and military officials to attend an audience with their heads bowed to support my ascension to the throne. (*They exit.*)

Scene 10: "Contention"

(*A eunuch leads Empress Lü, garbed in imperial robe, on stage. She is seated.*)
Empress Lü: (*Recites.*)

The emperor has passed away, the dragon has returned to Heaven,
The civil and military officials support my ascension to the throne.

(*Speaks.*) I am Empress Lü. The Emperor has passed away, and my Imperial Son is also dead. I have therefore been asked to take charge of the administrative businesses in the imperial court. Palace Official, rush this edict to Taiyuan and tell your Lord, the Imperial Maternal Uncle,[46] to come back to the court to ascend the throne.

46. That is, her brother, although historically, Lü Chan was a son of her brother.

Eunuch: I obey the edict! (*Exits.*)

Empress Lü: I think I should discuss this matter with the ministers. Palace Officer, summon Wang Ling to the court.

Eunuch: The Empress Dowager has issued an edict to summon his Excellency Wang to the court.

Wang Ling: (*Offstage.*) I accept the edict. (*Enters.*) I, your minister Wang Ling, prostrate myself to the Empress Dowager!

Empress Lü: Are you Minister Wang Ling prostrating there?

Wang Ling: Yes, your minister is he.

Empress Lü: Observe—the Emperor has passed away, and Emperor Hui is also dead. Ever since Pan Gu 盘古[47] created the world, has a woman ever ruled?

Wang Ling: Since there's no ruler in the state, it is but natural for the Empress Dowager to assume the throne.

Empress Lü: What are you talking about? That it is but natural? When foreign states arrive to pay tribute to us at court, it would be somewhat inconvenient. I would like to take off my dragon robe and give up the throne. What do you think that about this?

Wang Ling: To whom does the Empress Dowager intend to give the throne?

Empress Lü: I would like to give the throne to your Lord, the Imperial Maternal Uncle, Lü Chan!

Wang Ling: Wait, wait, wait a minute! You cannot do this, Empress Dowager! His Lordship the Imperial Maternal Uncle is of a different surname from the imperial clan. I'm afraid that the civil and military officials will not agree to let a minister usurp the imperial throne.

Empress Lü: I have decided to take off my dragon robe and give up the throne to another. Let the minister who refuses to comply report his name to me!

Wang Ling: I, Wang Ling, for one, refuse to comply!

Empress Lü: Leave our presence! What a treacherous scoundrel! I am giving up my throne for the good of the state. How dare you voice dissension! You should be executed. . . .

Wang Ling: Empress Dowager! I, your minister, recognize the crime I have committed.

Empress Lü: Well! Considering that you were a loyal subject, I will excuse you this time. You are relieved of your official post and title. Leave

47. According to Chinese mythology, Pan Gu created the universe.

your official hat on the dragon table. Go right now! (*Wang Ling doffs his hat and exits.*) Ai! We got rid of one! Palace Official, summon Chen Ping to the court.

Eunuch: The Empress Dowager issued an edict summoning Prince Chen to the court to discuss official business.

Chen Ping: (*Off stage.*) I accept the decree! (*Enters.*) I prostrate myself to the Empress Dowager.

Empress Lü: Please rise, Imperial Elder Brother. Palace Official, help him get seated.

Chen Ping: Thank you for offering the seat. Please allow me to inquire, Empress Dowager, as to the military business you have summoned this old minister to the court to discuss?

Empress Lü: Imperial Elder Brother Chen, who does not understand the situation! (*Sings.*)

Ever since the Emperor passed away and his dragon life ceased,
The civil and military officials supported my ascension to the throne.
Since the creation of the universe by Pan Gu until the present time,
Have there been cases of women presiding over governance of the state?

Chen Ping: (*Sings.*)

Ever since Yao 尧, Shun 舜, Yu 禹, Tang 汤, Jie 桀, and Zhou 纣,
Women have ruled the realm whenever the states were in turmoil.
It is but natural for the Empress Dowager to ascend the throne,
You can govern the people and bring peace to the hundred surnames.[48]

Empress Lü: (*Sings.*)

When foreign princes come to our court to pay tribute,
They will laugh at the fact that our court is dominated by a woman.
I would like to take off my dragon robe and give the throne to another,
Do you think this would be acceptable or not?

48. The "hundred surnames" refers to commoners.

Chen Ping: (*Sings.*)

To which person do you intend to give the throne?
Pray tell me, Empress Dowager, let your minister know.

Empress Lü: (*Sings.*)

I'll give the throne to Lü Chan, His Lordship the Imperial Maternal Uncle,
I intend to move him back to the capital to preside over the dragon court.

Chen Ping: (*Sings.*)

His Lordship the Imperial Maternal Uncle is not of the imperial clan,
It is not right for a minister to usurp the position of a throne.

Empress Lü: (*Sings.*)

He is an imperial relative and the Maternal Uncle of the state,
It is appropriate for him to accept the property of the Han dynasty.

Chen Ping: (*Sings.*)

Considering how numerous the descendants of the Han are,
Who do you think will support his ascension to the throne?

Empress Lü: (*Sings.*)

I am going to bestow upon him the Sword of Execution (*zhansha jian* 斩杀剑),
Anyone who disobeys him will end up eating green duckweeds.[49]

Chen Ping: (*Sings.*)

The court has the nine board ministers and four prime ministers,
How would a treacherous faction be allowed to preside over the imperial court?

49. This seems an unusual way of referring to an execution.

Empress Lü: (*Sings.*)

So, you, the Imperial Elder Brother, must be the one desiring the throne!

Chen Ping: (*Sings.*)

I, the minister, will not ascend the throne, but neither will he!

Empress Lü: (*Sings.*)

I will give him the throne, yes I will, indeed I will!

Chen Ping: (*Sings.*)

I won't let you, no I won't, indeed I won't!

Empress Lü: (*Sings.*)

The state belongs to my family; I am the one to give it away,
What business is it of yours, you of the Chen family?

Chen Ping: (*Sings.*)

The state of the Han was created by many loyal subjects,
I, of the Chen family, deserve seventy to eighty percent of the credit.

Empress Lü: (*Sings.*)

When Earth takes advantage of Heaven,[50] the rains will not be regular;

Chen Ping: (*Sings.*)

When Heaven takes advantage of Earth, the seedlings will not grow.

Empress Lü: (*Sings.*)

When a subject takes advantage of a ruler, he should be executed;

50. Here Earth refers to the subject, while Heaven refers to the ruler.

CHEN PING: (*Sings.*)

When a ruler takes advantage of a subject, the latter will escape abroad.

EMPRESS LÜ: (*Sings.*)

When a son takes advantage of a father, the son will be short-lived;

CHEN PING: (*Sings.*)

When a father takes advantage of a son, two gates will be established.[51]

EMPRESS LÜ: (*Sings.*)

When a wife takes advantage of a husband, the ethical relationship is upset;

CHEN PING: (*Sings.*)

People like you are rare in this mortal world of ours.

EMPRESS LÜ: (*Sings.*)

The old Emperor bestowed upon you too high a position,
You defy me, the female ruler, and have no regard for me.

CHEN PING: (*Sings.*)

My high position is due to my enormous merit and service,
It has nothing to do with favors from you, Empress Dowager.

EMPRESS LÜ: (*Sings.*)

Based on the laws of the state, you should be executed;

---

51. That is, the family will be separated into two households.

Chen Ping: (*Sings.*)

The old Emperor had decreed that I am never to be executed.

Empress Lü: (*Sings.*)

Loudly, I call and summon the executioners (*two guards enter quietly*),
I want you to execute Chen Ping at the Wu Gate 午门.

Chen Ping: (*Sings.*)

Loudly, I yell to halt the executioners,
Which one of you dares to approach me?

Guards: We dare not.
Chen Ping: Why are you still here? (*The guards exit.*)
Empress Lü: (*Sings.*)

The old Emperor has passed away; laws are no longer obeyed,
Even at the imperial court, old Chen Ping rebels against me.
Holding the jade imperial seal, I come down to hit him. (*She strikes.*)

Chen Ping: (*Sings.*)

I use the bronze hammer bestowed upon me by the Emperor to protect me.

Empress Lü: Ah, you treacherous scoundrel! (*Sings.*)

I, Empress Lü, lower my head in grief,
At my court, there is a treacherous minister.
I cry to the Emperor, who died so untimely,
And to Liu Ying, who returned to the Underworld.
Lowering my head I return to my residential palace,
I await my brother to find a way to release the anger. (*Exits.*)

Chen Ping: (*Sings.*)

Seeing that the evil consort has left the golden court,
I, Chen Ping, feel furious within my heart.
I order a colonel to summon my palanquin without delay (*two colonels enter, exit, and re-enter. Chen sits.*)
Writing a letter, I will bring Fan Kang to the capital.

(*Speaks.*) The verandahs are very quiet right now. (*The colonels exit.*) Let me take a brush in my hand. (*Sings.*)

I write, I prostrate myself to you, I prostrate myself to you, to you I prostrate myself,
I prostrate myself to you, Fan Kang, please read this letter carefully.
In our court, a treacherous scoundrel is raising a rebellion,
With the intention of usurping the throne of the state of Han.
I, your Younger Paternal Uncle,[52] respectfully present you with a letter,
First thing tomorrow morning, march your army to the capital of Chang'an 长安.
Should you arrive one step too late,
A minister will meet with demise at our court.
Having written the letter, I wrap and hide it hurriedly,
And summon a servant to come and listen to me. (*A servant enters.*)

(*Speaks.*) Servant, give this letter to the horse courier and order him to travel day and night to Lord Fan at the Prefect of Hanzhong 汉中. Tell him to dispatch his army immediately. Do it right away! (*The servant exits. Chen sings.*)

A letter I have dispatched to Hanzhong,
And I await the arrival of Fan Kang's army. (*Exits.*)

Scene 11: "Relieved of the Post"

WANG LING: (*Enters and sings.*)

I am so infuriated by Empress Dowager Lü,
Favoring and trusting the treacherous faction which will usurp the throne.

52. Given the difference in their surnames, they are obviously not really related. This appellation shows intimacy and the fact that Chen Ping is a generation older than Fan Kang.

At the imperial court, I memorialized[53] concerning it and
opposed the move,
I've been relieved of my official post and title, and must return
to my native home.

(*Speaks.*) I am old Wang Ling. After Empress Lü ascended the throne, she wanted to give the throne to her brother. When I memorialized at the court against it, she relieved me of my official post and title, so I must return to my native home as a commoner. Upon traveling past the Chen residence, I was asked to stay there and wait to see what happens next. I feel so aggrieved. Let me take a walk in the countryside to relieve myself of my misery. (*Sings.*)

When I, Wang Ling, came to join the Han in the past,
I served the Emperor, just as one who slept with a tiger.
Execution was the punishment for anyone who forgot to respond,
It would be much better and easier for me to return home. (*Exits.*)

Scene 12: "Mobilizing the Army"

(*Fan Kang enters with soldiers.*)
Fan Kang: (*Recites.*)

Pursuant to an imperial edict, I guard the territory of Hanzhong,
And lead a fiercely brave army of one million soldiers.
Whenever arms are raised within the confines of any state,
I[54] would ride my horse and proceed on an expedition.

(*Speaks.*) I am Fan Kang, son of the great general, Fan Kuai 樊哙.[55]

---

53. "Memorialize" refers to making a report at the imperial court.

54. I believe the *mojiang* 末将 (the most minor general) is a misprint for *benjiang* 本将 (I, the general) in the play script.

55. Fan Kuai (?–189 BCE) was one of the generals who helped Liu Bang found the Han dynasty. He is credited with helping to save Liu's life at the famous Banquet of Hongmen (*hangmen yan* 鸿门宴) when Xiang Yu, the Hegemon King of Chu, almost had Liu killed. After Liu Bang became the emperor, Fan Kuai was instrumental in crushing several revolts. Historically, he married Lü Xu 吕媭, Empress Lü's sister, and effected the annihilation of Han Xin as a henchman of the Empress. He died of natural cause, and his son succeeded him as the Marquis of Wuyang (*Wuyang hou* 舞阳侯).

Soldier: Prince Chen has sent a letter from his residence.

Fan Kang: There's no need for me to meet the messenger. Just bring me the letter.

Soldier: Here is the letter.

Fan Kang: Let me take a look at this. I wonder what happened in Chang'an that Uncle should want me to mobilize my army? Tell all the troop leaders to light their lanterns and torches, and march towards Chang'an tonight. (*They exit and re-enter. Sings.*)

In the Prefecture of Hanzhong, I mobilize my army,
The soldiers and cavalry resemble tigers enjoying themselves.
I wonder which minister is monopolizing power in the court,
That Uncle has written for me to take the army there.
Urging on the warring horse, I tarry not a single moment,
And have now arrived just outside the City of Chang'an.

Soldier: We have arrived at the City of Chang'an.

Fan Kang: Fire the cannon three times and enter the city! (*Sings.*)

Suddenly I hear a report from a junior colonel,
Urging the horse on, we enter the City of Chang'an. (*They exit.*)

Servant: (*Off stage.*) I report to the Prince: Lord Fan's army has arrived.

Chen Ping: (*Off stage.*) How delightful! Considering his position, we should go through the ceremony of opening the main gate for him. But the imperial family needs the army urgently. Just open the middle gate and let me go greet him.

(*Chen Ping enters. Fan Kang enters with soldiers and colonels.*)

Fan Kang: My dear Uncle! Please allow your child to prostrate himself to you. (*The servant enters quietly.*)

Chen Ping: There's no need. Have a seat. Servant, see to wine and a banquet.

Servant: The banquet is ready.

Chen Ping: Let's partake of the banquet. Please drink some wine, General!

Fan Kang: If you please, Uncle!

Chen Ping: I didn't know when you arrived from the fort. Please forgive me for not going out of the city to welcome you.

Fan Kang: There was no need. May I ask, Uncle, what the affair is at Chang'an? Your letter expressed so much urgency that half of my soldiers and horses died from rushing here.

Chen Ping: My dear child! We are in the midst of turmoil right now. When we regain peace, Uncle will make up for all your losses.

Fan Kang: Loyalty to the state is but my duty—why talk about things like that? Please explain to your child what the problem is.

Chen Ping: Leave us, all guards and soldiers. (*The soldiers and colonels exit.*) Fan Kang, if you please! (*Sings.*)

Today I have a banquet prepared at my residence,
In order to explain the affair at the imperial court.
A treacherous faction has appeared within the Han dynasty,
Of one who fully intends to usurp the throne of our emperor.
The Empress Dowager is giving up the throne for him to assume,
This was why Uncle wrote for you to mobilize your army.

Fan Kang: Uncle, what treacherous scoundrel is monopolizing the power at the court? Could you make it clear to me? Let your child kill the rebel scoundrel of a usurper!

Chen Ping: (*Sings.*)

The way I see it, General, you won't dare to do it,
You won't be able to save the empire of the Han.

Fan Kang: How can you say that I won't dare to do it?

Chen Ping: Aiya! Yes! I don't think you'll dare to do it!

Fan Kang: I'm willing to swear to Heaven that I will do it.

Chen Ping: Uncle is to hear it!

Fan Kang: (*Sings.*)

I, Fan Kang, take my armory and kowtow below the verandah,
I ask all the passing gods and spirits to examine my intentions.
Whether he be an imperial relative or my maternal uncle,
If he tries to usurp the throne of the Han, I will invariably kill him!
Should I renege on this promise to protect the throne of the Han,
Let me die in a battlefield from being trampled by war horses!

Chen Ping: (*Sings.*)

Now that I've seen you, the General, swear to fealty,
I, your Uncle, finally feel ever so relieved.

The usurper is none other than Lü Chan, your maternal uncle,
He fully intends to usurp the throne and become an emperor.

FAN KANG: (*Sings.*)

Now that Uncle has explained it all to me,
I grind to pieces my teeth of steel and my hair sticks up against my headgear from anger.[56]
Let alone the fact that my maternal uncle is a relative of mine,
I would not have condoned the crime even if he were my own parent.

(*Speaks.*) Uncle, when is the treacherous scoundrel planning to ascend the throne?

CHEN PING: The coronation is at noon.

FAN KANG: What time is it now?

CHEN PING: The watch drum has just struck five[57]—it is still dark.

FAN KANG: It's still early then. Let me go home and inquire after my Mom's health.

CHEN PING: This won't do! Your mother and your maternal uncle were born of the same mother. For the love of her brother, she will invariably dissuade you from killing him. You can't go home.

FAN KANG: Where should I wait for you then?

CHEN PING: Wait for me at the Ten League Pavilion 十里亭.[58]

FAN KANG: I'm on my way then! (*Exits.*)

CHEN PING: Ai! Now that I've aroused his killer instinct, this is going to be exciting. (*Thinks.*) Aiya, oh no! It just occurred to me that he is but a young man. What if he is pulled back by his love for his uncle and can't kill the scoundrel? What would happen then? Servant, tell Lord Wang to hide a weapon on himself and follow me to the Ten League Pavilion to welcome the new emperor. (*They exit.*)

---

56. The text says *yaosui gangya nuchongkou* 咬碎钢牙怒冲寇, which I have changed to *yaosui gangya nuchongguan* 咬碎钢牙怒冲冠 since *nufa chongguan* 怒发冲冠 is a famous line from Yue Fei's 岳飞 (1103–1142) lyric, "*manjianghong*" 满江红, and the *guan* rhymes with the line after the following line, *shengshen fumu bu rongkuan* 生身父母不容宽.

57. The fifth watch is around 4:00 a.m.

58. This pavilion is apparently ten *li* 里 from the capital. A *li* is generally recognized to be 360 paces, or about 1,890 feet.

Scene 13: "Assassination of the Treacherous"

(*Lü Chan enters with soldiers.*)
Lü Chan: (*Sings.*)

> I have worn the imperial headgear and dragon robe for an entire night,
> For the throne, I have exhausted all my energy and endeavors.
> The imperial edict from my older sister, I read carefully,
> From the Lü family, I am to emerge, as a veritable dragon.
> The fortuneteller calculated the coronation to take place at noon,
> Whether I succeed, the attempt will be made, and I can die content.
> Riding on my horse, I raise my head, and watch with my eyes.

(*Fan Kang enters with soldiers.*)
Fan Kang: I prostrate myself to Maternal Uncle.
Lü Chan: (Sings.)

> I see before me, my nephew, Fan Kang.

Fan Kang: You have returned, Maternal Uncle. Please accept a kowtow from your nephew.
Lü Chan: Is it Fan Kang in front of my horse?
Fan Kang: Yes, it is.
Lü Chan: Why have you returned to Chang'an suddenly and are not guarding the Prefecture of Hanzhong?
Fan Kang: When I heard that Maternal Uncle is going to ascend the throne, I left the fort in order to protect you, the future emperor.
Lü Chan: What? You've come to protect me, the future emperor?
Fan Kang: Yes! I will make sure that Maternal Uncle will ascend the throne.
Lü Chan: Good, good, good! When Maternal Uncle ascends the throne, you'll kill whomever I tell you to. I intend to eliminate all the potential scoundrels in the court. Remember my words and follow my horse. March, the entire army! (*Sings.*)

> Riding on my horse, I am full of smiles,
> My nephew has left his fort to protect my coronation.
> Right now, my army and I are proceeding forward;

(*Chen Ping and Wang Ling enter.*)
CHEN PING AND WANG LING: We prostrate ourselves to the new emperor!
LÜ CHAN: (*Sings.*)

I see prostrated before me, Chen Ping and Wang Ling.

(*Speaks.*) Are you Chen Ping and Wang Ling before me?
CHEN PING AND WANG LING: Yes.
LÜ CHAN: All the civil and military officials in the court consented to our ascension to the throne except for the two of you, you treacherous scoundrels. You deserve to be executed for your crime.
CHEN PING AND WANG LING: Please cease your anger, our new emperor! If all the officials consented, how dare we not consent? We have both come to welcome the new emperor to the throne!
LÜ CHAN: Oh good, good, good! Stand up! You may stand up!
CHEN PING AND WANG LING: We thank the new emperor for your imperial favor.
LÜ CHAN: Listen to the edict then! (*Sings.*)

Proclaiming an edict, we hear hailing three times.

FAN KANG: (*Sings.*)

After stirring my desire to kill, then we may move forward. (*He kills Lü Chan and they all exit.*)

Scene 14: "Enthroning the Emperor"

(*Chen Ping, Wang Ling, and Fan Kang enter. Chen Ping tries to kill Fan Kang.*)
FAN KANG: Uncle, what are you doing?
WANG LING: The Prince thought you were someone else.
CHEN PING: Ai, ai, ai! I got so confused from all the fighting that I'm fighting my own side. (*Looks at Fan Kang.*) What did you do with the treacherous scoundrel?
FAN KANG: I went to the Ten League Pavilion and hacked the scoundrel down with one strike!
CHEN PING: You killed well! You killed well!

Fan Kang: The imperial court must not be without an emperor for a single day. Let me support the ascension of you, Uncle, to the throne.

Chen Ping: This will not do! This will not do! The Han still has a descendant!

Fan Kang: Uncle, who else of the Han is still around?

Chen Ping: Consort Yan of the Western Palace has a son who is hiding in my residence right now. Isn't he a descendant of the Han?

Fan Kang: If that's the case, you should have the authority to designate the emperor and preserve the state.

Chen Ping: Fan Kang, do you think I, your Uncle, have the authority to designate the emperor?

Fan Kang: Yes.

Chen Ping: Wang Ling, do you think, I, the Prince, can preserve the state?

Wang Ling: The Prince's support for the foundation of the Han Empire right now demonstrates that he is a loyal subject who is preserving the state.

Chen Ping: Fine, then! Tell the civil and military officials to attend the audience to establish the young Prince as the Emperor. (*They exit.*)

Scene 15: "Imprisoning Lü"

(*Wang Ling and Fan Kang stand in audience. Chen Ping enters holding the Crown Prince and sits.*)

Chen Ping: (*Recites.*)

The entire imperial court is filled with an aura of peace,
Once again the imperial family of the Han presides over the
state.
In one voice, the court hails thrice, applauding His Majesty,[59]
And wishing that he will live for a hundred million years.

59. The emperor was referred to as *wansui* 万岁, one who will live for ten thousand years. People typically hail "*wansui, wansui, wanwansui*!" 万岁万岁万万岁, literally, "ten thousand years, ten thousand years, ten thousand of ten thousand [i.e., a hundred million] years!"

(*Speaks.*) The new Emperor ascends the throne. The reign will be renamed and he will be known as Emperor Wen.

MINISTERS: We, the civil and military officials, prostrate ourselves. (*They prostrate themselves.*)

CHEN PING: Listen to the enffeoffments. Wang Ling will be Governor of Jiumen (*jiumen tidu* 九门提督). Fan Kang will receive the title of Grand Marshal of the Cavalries (*binma dayuanshuai* 兵马大元帅). An amnesty is proclaimed for all under Heaven. You may all rise. Summon a warrior to the court.

GUARD: (*Enters.*) I prostrate myself to the new emperor!

CHEN PING: Guard, tie Empress Lü up and bring her here!

(*The guard brings Empress Lü on stage.*)

GUARD: Kneel!

EMPRESS LÜ: Get out of here! Why should I kneel to him?

GUARD: She refuses to kneel!

CHEN PING: Stand down there! What an evil consort! How dare you refuse to kneel to the new emperor?

EMPRESS LÜ: I have not committed a crime. Why have you tied me up?

CHEN PING: You murdered the mother and son of the Eastern Palace. How can you claim to be innocent? Young Emperor, enumerate the crimes of the evil consort.

CROWN PRINCE:[60] Imperial Uncle, ever since the creation of the world by Pan Gu until this dynasty of ours, when has there ever been a case of a child indicting a parent?

CHEN PING: The new Emperor who has just ascended the throne is an ethical and wise ruler.

EMPRESS LÜ: I think he is an unethical and muddle-headed ruler!

CHEN PING: How dare you, evil consort, continue to argue? Guard! Imprison the evil consort in the Cold Palace (*linggong* 冷宫)[61] and let her torture herself to death. Escort her down! (*The guard escorts Empress Lü offstage.*) Now that peace prevails at the court, a banquet

60. The play script refers to him as the Crown Prince, although technically he should be referred to as the emperor at this point. He was never named an heir apparent in history.

61. A deserted and neglected part of the harem.

has been prepared at the Temple of Light and Prosperity (*guanglu si* 光禄寺)[62] to celebrate the occasion with all the ministers. (*They exit.*)

END OF PLAY

62. This is a building within the palace compound.

22. Warrior without headgear (Wei Tiancai's puppet). Photo by Fan Pen Li Chen.

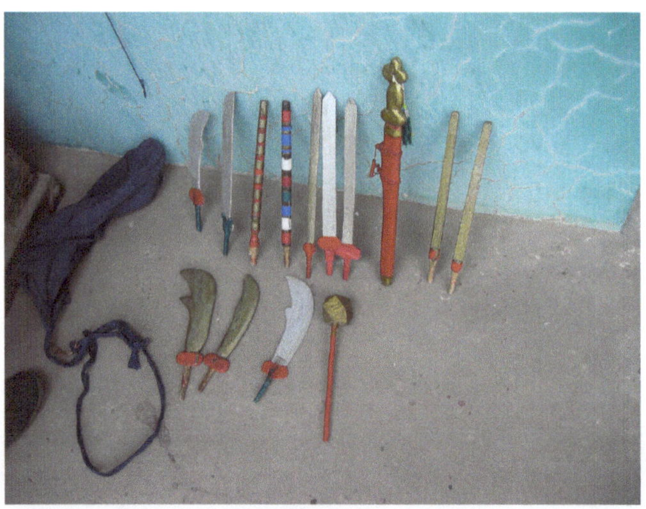

23. Weapons (Wei Tiancai's puppet). Photo by Ingrid Chen.

Yang Wenguang 杨文广

(a.k.a., *Yang Wenguang's Military Expedition to the West* 杨文广征西)

Introduction

A historical character who gained greater fame through fiction, Yang Wenguang (999–1074) was a descendant of the renowned Northern Song (960–1127) generals of the Yang family (*yangjiajiang* 杨家将). His father was Yang Yanzhao 杨延昭 (958–1014), and his grandfather was Yang Ye 杨业 (?–986).[1] In the novel *Romance of the Family of the Yang Generals* (*yangjiajiang yanyi* 杨家将演义), and in various performing arts, however, Yang Wenguang is cast as the son of a fictional character, Yang Zongbao 杨宗保, who in turn is cast as a son of Yang Yanzhao.[2] Hence, in these fictional tales, Yang Wenguang is the grandson of his historical father.

The historical Yang Wenguang had four sons, of whom the most remarkable was his youngest Yang Huaiyu 杨怀玉. The puppet play translated below instead attributes five sons to Yang Wenguang and assigns the character Huan 环 to each of their names (probably because the characters for Huai and Huan resemble each other). Aside from this tenuous connection, however, not a modicum of historicity can be found in the play.

1. For more information on the generals of the Song dynasty, see He Guanhuan, 2011.

2. For more information on this novel and renowned women warriors in Chinese novels, including those of the Yang family, see Fan Pen Chen, "Female Warriors, Magic and the Supernatural in Traditional Chinese Novels." For information on a string puppet play from western Fujian about the romance between Yang Zongbao and his barbarian/foreign princess warrior wife, Mu Guiying 穆桂英, see Fan Pen Chen, "Baishazhen Shuizhu'yangcun Tiangonghui de luantan kuileixi, *Mu Guiying zhaoqin*."

The tale seems to have developed so independently of history and even the popular fictional traditions on the Yang family generals elsewhere, that it may be the only version of its kind about Yang Wenguang. In fact, the story centers more on the sons Yang Wenguang than on the title character himself.

With the exception of Yang Wenguang, all the characters seem to have been newly created. However, the play shows familiarity with the popular traditions of the Yang family saga, and maintains the same relationships between the newly created characters and their ancestors portrayed elsewhere. Hence, the newly created fictional character Hu Jiqing 呼继青 (purportedly a descendant of the great historical general Hu Yanzan 呼延赞 (?–1000) is the husband of Yang Wenguang's daughter. This relationship may have been inferred from the novel *Complete Tale of the Hu Family* (*shuo Hu quanzhuan* 说呼全传), in which Hu Yanqing 呼延庆 (son of Hu Yanzan) was a sworn brother of Yang Wenguang.

Similarly, the earlier fictional tradition (reflecting an inveterate enmity between the Yang and Di 狄 families and portraying the latter negatively) has also been maintained. The enemy of Yang Wenguang in this story is a fictional character named Di Yanfeng 狄彦风 (cast as a descendant of the historical character Di Qing 狄青 (1008–1057), a great general and civil minister). Historically, Yang Wenguang served under Di Qing when the latter suppressed the rebellion of an indigenous group in Guangxi. No animosity between them has ever been recorded. In the popular literary and performing arts traditions, however, Di Qing is an evil minister who tries to murder Yang Zongbao (and resembles the notorious minister Pan Remei 潘仁美, mentioned twice in this play as "the treacherous minister of yesteryear").

Simple in structure and thematically predictable (particularly in the marriage between Yang's warrior son and a foreign princess), the play is nevertheless unusual in its emphasis—demonstrated through its lengthy discussion—on the conflict between loyalty to an unjust emperor and the right to rebel in such circumstances. Yang's main wife is an ideal Confucian who valiantly upholds the concept of loyalty. But ultimately rebellion is shown to be the more correct path. Despite the significant role of Confucian scholars in the writing of Heyang's play scripts, and the apparent recognition of the importance of Confucian ideals, the popularity of military romance (applauding the right to rebel in this play and in *River Yang*) clearly reveals its audiences' preference. Violence is applauded and regarded as entertaining and satisfying (e.g., when the colonel who executed Di Jiqing returns to stage holding the villain's head). Yang's youngest son (played by a clown who insists on rebelling) and his impetuous mother (who refuses to tie him up to be executed) are the play's most memorable and likable characters.

Cast of *Yang Wenguang*[3]

EMPEROR: Zhao Shu 赵曙, also known as Emperor Yingzong 英宗 (r. 1064–1068) of the Song dynasty
YANG WENGUANG 杨文广: the marshal
LADY YANG 杨夫人: Yang Wenguang's first/formal wife
CONCUBINE WANG 王妾: Yang Wenguang's second wife
CONCUBINE MEI 梅妾: Yang Wenguang's third wife
YANG HUANFENG 杨环风: Yang Wenguang's eldest son
YANG HUANQING 杨环青: Yang Wenguang's second son
YANG HUANLONG 杨环龙: Yang Wenguang's third son
YANG HUANZHEN 杨环真: Yang Wenguang's fourth son
YANG HUANHU 杨环虎: Yang Wenguang's fifth son; played as a clown role
DI YANFENG 狄彦风: officer in charge of escorting provisions; Yang Wenguang's enemy
HU JIQING 呼继青: Yang Wenguang's son-in-law
YANG MANTANG 杨满堂: Yang Wenguang's daughter
EIGHTH PRINCE 八王: the emperor's younger brother
GAO WANG 高旺: a warrior with knowledge of magical arts; Yang Mantang's adopted brother
BARBARIAN KING 番王: a foreign king named Tianshou 天寿 who raised arms against Chinese sovereignty somewhere west of China
BARBARIAN GIRL 番女: also known as Princess Hundred Flowers 百花公主, she is the daughter of the ruler of a foreign state by the name of Xiaohanguo 肖韩国
GOD DINGJIA 丁甲神: the spirit conjured up by Princess Hundred Flowers to help destroy the barbarian king's magic
PALACE ATTENDANT 侍臣
COLONEL 校尉
SOLDIER 小卒
WARRIOR ATTENDANT 家将

Scene 1: "Leaving for the Military Expedition"

(*Yang Wenguang, Di Yanfeng, and two court ministers enter, followed by a eunuch who leads the emperor on stage.*)

3. The script for this play is found in Shaanxisheng Wenhuaju, ed., *Heyang xianxi* in *Shaanxisheng chuantong jumu, xianxi*, 311–346. The original play script belonged to the Heyang Marionette Troupe 合阳线戏社.

The Emperor: We are Emperor Yingzong, the fifth Son of Heaven of the great Song dynasty. Ever since we ascended the throne, peace has prevailed. But just now a galloping horse arrives with the report that a Western barbarian by the name of Tianshou has raised a rebellion.[4] We'll have to dispatch a general to pacify him during our morning audience. Ministers Di and Yang, listen to our edict: the Western Barbarian Tianshou has raised a rebellion. Our dear Minister Yang will be the commanding general for our army. Our dear Minister Di will take charge of transporting the provisions. Minister Yang's third son, Huanlong, will lead the vanguard. You will command a great army of a hundred and fifty thousand to destroy the Western Barbarians. Take our edict and leave the court. (*Di and Yang exit.*)
(*Sings.*)

Our dear ministers have departed the golden court with visible anger,
Causing us, the emperor, to worry within our palace.
'Tis a calamity from Heaven that the bandits rebelled without cause,
We, the emperor, issued an edict that our dear Minister Yang
will command our army.

Scene 2: "Bidding Farewell"

(*Enter Lady Yang, Concubine Wang, Concubine Mei, and their sons, Huanfeng, Huanqing, and Huanhu.*)
Lady Yang: (*Sings.*)

My lord occupies a prominent position within the imperial court,
It is he who helps to secure the brocade-like rivers and
mountains of the Song emperor.

Concubine Wang: (*Sings.*)

It was my misfortune that my parents lost their lives early,
I married into an official household, but as a concubine.

4. That is to say, the leader of a foreign tribe has decided to wrest Chinese control from that region. The Western Barbarians usually refer to the various nomadic tribes in northwestern China and central Asia. When at peace, the tribes traditionally submitted to the Chinese emperor as tributary states. Historically speaking, however, the Western "Barbarians" were so powerful during the Song dynasty that the Chinese paid a reverse tribute to maintain peace.

Concubine Mei: (*Sings.*)

A daughter of the Mei family, I'm the second concubine but am well respected,
I'm ever so grateful that my two elder sisters[5] treat me with great kindness.

Yang Huanfeng: (*Sings.*)

I'm so angry that the Western Barbarian bandit rebelled without cause,
Having accepted the seal as commanding general, my old father will have to leave the imperial court.

Yang Huanqing: (*Sings.*)

As vanguard, my third brother will lead the army in the front,
We only hope that our father will return in victory.

Yang Huanhu: (*Sings.*)

I was born with an ugly face, but was pitied by the emperor;
Each day I study military skills under our father and brother.

Yang Wenguang: (*Enters and sings.*)

Having finished the imperial audience, I leave the golden court bursting with anger,
I cannot stand Di Yanfeng, that treacherous traitor.

Everyone Our lord has returned!
Yang Wenguang: Yes, I'm back.
The Wives: Let's pay our respects.
Yang Wenguang: Ladies, there's no need for formalities. Please seat yourselves.
The Sons: Your sons pay our respects.
Yang Wenguang: Stand to the side.
The Wives: May we ask our lord why you look so worried after the imperial audience? Were you angry with another minister?

5. In an ideal polygamous family, the wives existed harmoniously as "sisters."

YANG WENGUANG: My ladies, you wouldn't have known, but the Western Barbarian Tianshou has rebelled. The emperor commanded me to lead the pacification expedition against him. Our third son Huanlong will head the vanguard, and Di Yanfeng will be in charge of the provisions. How can I not worry?

THE WIVES: We and the treacherous bandit don't get along. What if he backstabs us? What shall we do?

YANG WENGUANG: We're dealing with an important national affair. I don't think he'll dare to do that.

THE WIVES: Our lord should be wary nevertheless.

YANG WENGUANG: Of course. There's no need for you to remind me of that. (*The warrior attendant enters.*)

LADY YANG: Warrior attendant, see to a feast!

WARRIOR ATTENDANT: A banquet will be prepared.

LADY YANG: Go. (*He exits.*)

YANG WENGUANG: My lady, what is the banquet for?

LADY YANG: Our lord is embarking upon a military expedition. The banquet is a farewell party.

YANG WENGUANG: My lady is too considerate—you trouble yourself too much.

LADY YANG: My lord, please have some wine. (*Sings.*)

> I told the warrior attendant to quickly prepare a banquet,
> Because my lord will leave the court and embark upon a military expedition.
> Huanlong my son, you are young and inexperienced,
> Do be careful and beware that you don't fall into a trap.

CONCUBINE WANG: (*Weeps.*) Ah, my lord! (*Sings.*)

> Hearing that my lord is embarking upon an expedition, tears fill my face;
> Now that you are commander of a great army, this is no ordinary matter.
> We only hope that you will defeat the bandit and return victorious,
> Only then will our family be able to enjoy peace.

CONCUBINE MEI: (*Weeps.*) My lord, please have some wine! (*Sings.*)

> The whole family at the inner hall bids you farewell,
> I, this daughter of the Mei family, have a few unsavory words.

Treacherous villains have frequently been known to suppress the provisions,
Di Yanfeng and our family harbor an irresolvable enmity.

Yang Huanfeng: (*Weeps.*) Ah, my dear old dad! (*Sings.*)

I, Yang Huanfeng, step forward and pour the wine personally,
Receiving the commanding seal, my old dad will annihilate the barbarians.
Even though I, your son, have deeply felt filial intentions,
Without an imperial edict, in no way can I join the fight.

Yang Huanqing: (*Weeps.*) Ah, my dear old daddy! (*Sings.*)

I, Yang Huanqing, step forward hurriedly in order to bid you farewell,
Lifting the golden cup, I kneel down quickly before my aged father.
I only hope that during this trip you will destroy the barbarian dogs;
Returning victorious, the whole clan can then show gratitude to the azure Heaven.

Yang Huanhu: Please drink some wine, dear old one! (*Sings.*)

I, Yang Huanhu, step forward and pour the wine personally,
Hurriedly, I pull up my gown and kneel in front of the old one.
Di Yanfeng is truly a danger within the imperial court,
I truly fear that he will memorialize to the throne against us.

Yang Wenguang: Don't worry! (*Sings.*)

The entire family gathers at the inner hall with tears all over their faces,
Making me, the old one, feel as if my heart has been pierced by an arrow.
To suppress the provisions for the fighting army, I expect he will not dare.
After I leave, I want everyone in the family to ease your fears.

Warrior Attendant: (*Enters.*) The soldiers and horses are all ready to leave. They await my lord to mount the horse and lead them on their way.

Yang Wenguang: Bring my horse and wait for me. (*Sings.*)

Suddenly I hear cannon firing and a multitude shouting,
Bidding farewell to my family, I leave my residence and mount my carved saddle.

The Wives: We bid farewell to our lord!
Yang Wenguang: Go back.
The Sons: We bid farewell to our dad.
Yang Wenguang: (*Weeps.*) Go, go, go back! (*He exits.*)
Lady Yang: (*Sings.*)

Seeing my lord ride away, my tears fall. (*She exits.*)

Concubine Wang: (*Sings.*)

This has caused members of the entire family to worry to no end. (*She exits.*)

Concubine Mei: (*Sings.*)

We only hope that once gone, he will return victorious. (*She exits.*)

Yang Huanfeng: (*Sings.*)

The entire family will then burn incense to thank the azure Heaven. (*He exits.*)

Yang Huanqing: (*Sings.*)

I will have to dispatch the warrior attendant to seek news frequently. (*He exits.*)

Yang Huanhu: (*Sings.*)

And hope for news that our old father will return victorious and meritorious. (*He exits.*)

Scene 3: "Seeking News"

Di Yanfeng: (*Enters and sings.*)

My sorrowful eyebrows are tightly locked, they can't relax;
Anxiety and hatred fill my chest.
When will I be able to destroy Yang Wenguang
So that I can kill the muddle-headed emperor and execute my designs to attain the dragon bed.[6]

(*Speaks.*) I, the old one, am Di Yanfeng, a descendant of Di Qing 狄青. I am a minister at the Song court. I would like to usurp the throne but with Yang Wenguang at the same court, I have been too terrified to act. Now that the Western Barbarian bandits have rebelled, Yang Wenguang has been ordered to lead the military expedition to pacify them, and I've been given the task of providing provisions for them. I'm going to suppress transport of the provisions. It is commonly said, "An army without food will dissipate on its own." What worry do I have that the fellow won't end up dead? Colonels, find out when the Yang father and son are leaving with their army and report to me right away. (*Sings.*)

I dispatch my men to find out news,
And hope that the fellow will die at the borderland. (*He exits.*)

Scene 4: "Defeating the Barbarians"

(*Yang Wenguang leads his son Huanlong, a soldier, and a colonel on stage.*)
Yang Wenguang: (*Sings.*)

Before the expedition proceeds, the cannon fires thrice,
Men and horses fill the capital Bianjing 汴京 like a rising tide.
Huanlong at the front opens the pathway,
Which warrior dares to dally?
Just as we gallop forth,
I suddenly hear a soldier making a report.

Soldier: I report—we are approaching the camp of the barbarians.
Yang Wenguang: Charge into the bandit's camp! (*Yang Wenguang fights with the barbarian king, who loses and exits.*)
Soldier: The barbarian bandit has escaped.

6. The dragon represents the emperor.

YANG WENGUANG: Don't chase after the defeated army. Tell the warriors that we'll have a feast.

SOLDIER: But there's no more food for the army.

YANG WENGUANG: How can there be no food?

SOLDIER: The provisions have not arrived yet.

YANG WENGUANG: Go borrow some grains from the locals. We'll return them as soon as the provisions arrive.

SOLDIER: This region has suffered drought for the last three years. There's been so little harvest of the six grains that the commoners can barely feed themselves. Where can we borrow any food?

YANG WENGUANG: Brothers, lower your voices. Don't let the barbarian soldiers hear this. This national calamity has been caused all because His Majesty employed a disloyal subject. Pity those lives of yours! Please be patient for a little longer. Stand there. Ah, Di Yanfeng, what a treacherous traitor you are! (*Sings.*)

Hearing the report from the three armies,
Without food, I, the commander shiver from fright.
I hate this Di Yanfeng who practices evil administration,
Causing a calamity and the deaths of our warriors. (*The barbarian king leads his soldiers on stage.*)

BARBARIAN KING: Surround them!

YANG WENGUANG: Huanlong, look how we're surrounded by barbarian soldiers on all sides. There's a road in the southwestern corner. Fight your way out of there. Go to Bianliang 汴梁[7] to get reinforcements.

YANG HUANLONG: (*Weeps.*) My muddle-headed old daddy! (*Sings.*)

Before I speak, my tears unwittingly surge like a spring,
My old daddy, please be patient and listen to me.
The eight tigers of the Yang family came forth to join the Song dynasty,
With their seven spears and one broad sword, they established peace for it.
When their army went to Mt. Lianglang 两狼山, they entered a trap.[8]

---

7. This is the full name of the capital, while Bianjing literally means Capital Bian.

8. Literally, a tiger's mouth.

They fought valiantly but were completely surrounded by barbarian forces.
One of them was dispatched to get reinforcements from Guazhou 瓜州,
But he was tricked by the villain Pan 潘[9] to dismount and was shot to death.
How can I, your son, now bear to part with you, my dear daddy?
Our parting today is truly similar to the pouring of water—it is utterly irretrievable. (*Huanlong fights the Barbarian King, who is defeated and chased off stage by Huanlong. The Barbarian King then re-enters.*)

Barbarian King: What a good fight! What a good battle! Yang Wenguang fights valiantly! Let me use sorcery. (*He fights.*)

Barbarian Soldier: We've captured Yang Wenguang.

Barbarian King: Don't hurt him. Hang him up at the camp and beat him with split wood. We'll see if he won't surrender then. (*Sings.*)

I depend on sorcery and magic spells to win my battles,
I fear neither spears nor swords—only fire intimidates me. (*He exits.*)

Scene 5: "Fabricating a Rumor"

Di Yanfeng: (*Enters and sings.*)

Following the imperial edict, I left the capital—but then suppressed the provisions;
I heard that it caused the entrapment of that fellow at the border.
Without food, more than half of the warriors were starved to death,
The soldiers report that the fellow was captured by the Western Barbarians.

I am old Di Yanfeng. The soldiers report that the barbarians have captured Yang Wenguang. I'll have to return to the court secretly, and say that the old one feared fighting and surrendered to the barbarians. His Majesty will undoubtedly be greatly incensed and will confiscate his properties

9. This is probably Pan Renmei who was mentioned in the introduction to this book.

and execute his entire clan. So this is my plan. Colonel, let's ride back to the court. (*Sings.*)

I will now return to the court and memorialize to the emperor,
And cause his entire clan to meet their demise at the Yellow Springs.[10]

Scene 6: "Persuading Marriage"

BARBARIAN GIRL: (*Sings.*)

Born and raised on barbarian land,
I grew up in a totally different world.
When bored, I ride the horse and shoot arrows,
My sole hobby is plucking strings of the lute.

I am Princess Hundred Flowers. My father is the king of the country of Xiaohan 肖韩国, and I am his only child. He is presently ill and bedridden. If anything should happen to him, who will inherit the kingdom from him? I had my fortune told last night, and discovered that I am to meet my future husband today. So I have brought some barbarian soldiers with me to ride and hunt on the grassland. As I speak, I see a big horse approaching with a young warrior. He must be a defeated warrior of the Song dynasty. Soldiers, set a trap to stop that horse. Capture that southern barbarian of the Song alive.[11] (*Sings.*)

I examine him from my horse,
What a romantic, handsome young man! (*She exits.*)

YANG HUANLONG: (*Enters and sings.*)

I, Yang Huanlong, shiver from fright on my horse,
I fear that the life of my old daddy will be in jeopardy.

10. The Yellow Springs refer to the Underworld.

11. Barbarians to the south were called *man* 蛮. While the Chinese called the northern and northwestern foreigners *fan* 番 barbarians, the latter reciprocated by referring to the Chinese as *man* barbarians in traditional fiction and drama.

I truly hate that Di Yanfeng, who is a national disaster,
He is exactly like that villain Pan Renmei 潘仁美 of yesteryear.
Today I will return to the imperial court and seek an audience,
I will have the treacherous traitor killed and avenge ourselves.
As I urge on my horse, I suddenly hear yelling,
And tartar soldiers emerge from nowhere to stop my horse.

Barbarian Soldier: (*Enters.*) We've captured the southern barbarian of the Song.

Barbarian Girl: (*Enters.*) Don't hurt him. Tie him up and take him to the main camp. What a warrior! (*Sings.*)

Today my wishes have finally come true,
I have fortunately procured a wonderful man. (*She exits.*)

(*The Barbarian Girl re-enters with a soldier guarding Huanlong.*)

Barbarian Girl: (*Sings.*)

The two of us will be strung together in the embroidered tent,
And be husband and wife until we reach a hundred years of age.
How come he enters the tent and remains standing,
Let me question him and gather all the details.

Barbarian Soldier: He won't kneel.

Barbarian Girl: Stand over there. What a southern barbarian of the Song! How dare you stand and not kneel at the sight of the princess?

Yang Huanlong: Woman of a barbarian state. Ugly maid! Now that you've captured this young lord as yours, you can hack if you intend to kill me, you can open your mouth if you intend to eat me. How would I kneel to you?

Barbarian Girl: So you won't kneel. Well, you don't have to kneel! I won't blame you. Tell me, where do you live? What's your name?

Yang Huanlong: Since you ask, little girl, listen to me—

Barbarian Girl: He's indeed some warrior!

Yang Huanlong: (*Sings.*)

Since you've asked, little girl, listen to what I say,
Listen to me, your young lord, tell you about my home.
I live in Huotang 火塘 at the prefecture of Cizhou 磁州,
My ancestor was known as the King of the Fire Mountain.

My father's name is Yang Wenguang,
He begot us five brothers, known as the five tigers.

BARBARIAN GIRL: Why did you come here?
YANG HUANLONG: (*Sings.*)

Because the Western Barbarian bandits rebelled,
We, father and son, led an army and left the court.
The treacherous villain Di Yanfeng suppressed our provisions,
My father ordered me to get reinforcements from Bianliang.
I, young lord of the Yang family, have now fallen into your trap,
Quickly, let me pass through this barbarian state of yours.

BARBARIAN GIRL: Listen to me, young warrior! (*Sings.*)

Please don't be stubborn, my dear warrior,
The two of us can imitate the mandarin ducks right here.
I will entrust the administration of my state to you,
I beseech you to stay here and marry into my family.[12]

YANG HUANLONG: (*Sings.*)

Don't speak utter nonsense, you little girl,
Listen carefully to what I have to say.
The Yang family produced loyal and upright warriors for generations,
How could I fear death and surrender myself to you?

BARBARIAN GIRL: My dear warrior! (*Sings.*)

Please don't feel flustered, ah dear warrior,
I have something to say; we can talk it out.
If you are willing to enter the damask bed curtains right here,
I will guarantee that your clan will never be endangered.

YANG HUANLONG: Rubbish! (*Sings.*)

How can a small state like yours attract a great warrior?
How can a fish pond harbor a dragon?

---

12. This form of marriage, *zhaodongchuang* 招东床, entails the man marrying into the woman's family rather than the usual patrilocal and patrilineal situation.

How can a weed infested slope grow miracle mushrooms?
How would a phoenix land on a chicken fence?
Don't even think about having this young lord submit to you,
Even the slave of my slave will not submit to your mother.

Barbarian Girl: Oh suckling boy! (*Sings.*)

The boy doesn't know when he is being flattered,
Each word he uttered, he said to hurt me.
Angrily, I called for a barbarian warrior,
Take him away, chop off his head, and let him die.

(*Speaks.*) Take him away and execute him. (*Yang Huanlong exits.*) Barbarian soldier, come back. Let me whisper to you. (*She whispers to the soldier.*) Remember well what I just said.
Barbarian Soldier: I'll release him in a while.
Barbarian Girl: Great! (*Sings.*)

I truly love his handsome appearance,
But he obstinately refuses to marry into our family.
Men of the imperial court tend to be rude and stubborn,
I'll have to use a good scheme to succeed in this.

Scene 7: "Fearing Indictment"

Yang Huanhu: (*Enters and sings.*)

When I, Yang Huanhu, heard this, my three souls floated away,
I'll have to step up and hurry myself ever so much.
That Di Yanfeng at the court was a beast in human form,
I'll have to report everything to our Daniang 大娘, Eldest Mom.[13]

(*Speaks.*) Mother—please hurry up and come here!
Lady Yang: (*Enters*) Coming! Is it Huanhu?
Yang Huanhu: Yes.

13. *Daniang* refers to the first and formal wife of his father. Given the fact that neither the father nor his parents are around, she is in charge of the household. The concubines, secondary wives, are sometimes addressed as "aunts" or "second moms" by the sons.

LADY YANG: Why are you so flustered?
YANG HUANHU: My dear mother! We're really in for it now!
LADY YANG: What happened?
YANG HUANHU: You know how old daddy led the expedition against the rebels. Now Di Yanfeng has returned to the court and is accusing father of being a traitor and surrendering to the barbarians. His Majesty is greatly incensed. He gave the treacherous villain men and horses to arrest us and confiscate our home.
LADY YANG: I'm shocked to . . . (*She falls.*)
YANG HUANHU: Mother has fainted from the shock. Mother, please wake up.
LADY YANG: (*Sings.*)

Hearing this, I was so scared that my soul floated away,
My body falls over right in the inner hall.
Slowly I raise my head and examine with my eyes,
So Huanhu is the person standing right next to me.

(*Weeps.*) Di Yanfeng—what a traitor you are! (*Sings.*)

Suddenly a calamity befalls us from Heaven,
I'm incensed that the treacherous villain is so evil.
We of the Yang family have been loyal warriors for generations,
I ask Heaven why it takes no heed of it? (*Yelling is heard back stage.*)

(*Speaks.*) I'm scared to death! (*Sings.*)

The men and horses sound like crashing waves.

(*Speaks.*) Ah, my dear Huanhu! (*Sings.*)

Follow me while I meet the villain and his soldiers! (*They exit.*)

Scene 8: "Confiscating the Residence"

(*Di Yanfeng enters with a colonel.*)
DI YANFENG: (*Sings.*)

Bearing an edict issued by His Imperial Majesty,
I lead men and horses to confiscate the Yang residence.
The men and horses are just making a turn,
Suddenly, a colonel approaches to report to me.

Colonel: We've arrived at the gate of the residence.

Di Yanfeng: Let's charge into the residence.

Yang Huanhu: Are you asking for death? There are three feet of sacred ground at our residence. Where do you think you're rushing to? Mother, do you want to come here?

Lady Yang: (*Enters.*) Is this His Excellency Di?

Di Yanfeng: Yes.

Lady Yang: You treacherous villain! You charge into my residence without a single word of announcement—what kind of crime is this?

Di Yanfeng: You old slut! Your husband feared fighting—he became a traitor and surrendered to the barbarians. His Majesty ordered me to arrest you and confiscate your home. Since you claim to be loyal subjects, why aren't you offering yourself to be tied?

Lady Yang: As for this . . .

Di Yanfeng: What are you saying?

Yang Huanhu: Mother, go ahead and curse the villain. Your child is behind you!

Lady Yang: (*Weeps.*) Di Yanfeng, you treacherous traitor! (*Sings.*)

Angrily, I curse at the treacherous villain,
Furiously, I call the bandit a veritable robber.
You are basically a slandering sycophantic courtier of the Song court,
You are worse than fowl, beasts, jackals, and wolves.
I don't know how your parents begot you and raised you,
You are worse than pigs, dogs, cattle, and sheep.
I can yell and scream, but it would all be in vain,
If I resist the imperial edict, I'd be considered disrespectful to the emperor.

(*Weeps.*) Oh, what I'd like to do to you, you villain! (*Sings.*)

Retreat right now so that I can have everyone in my household tied up.

Yang Huanhu: At least you've said your fill!
Lady Yang: (*Sings.*)

Our family will go together to the execution ground. (*She exits.*)

Yang Huanhu: Leave! Leave! What do you think you're doing, you treacherous villain? I won't have anything to do with you!
Di Yanfeng: Colonels, surround the gate. Don't let a single person escape. (*They exit.*)

Scene 9: "Forced into Rebellion"

Lady Yang: (*Enters and sings.*)

Returning to my residence, I lower my head and think,
I resent that my lord has made a mistake in handling this matter.
Following the imperial edict, he left the capital but then lost his direction,
Having been defeated in one battle, how could he resort to surrendering?

(*Speaks.*) My two younger sisters, come here quickly! (*Enter Concubines Wang and Mei.*)
Wang and Mei: What does eldest sister want to tell us?
Lady Yang: (*Sings.*)

Come forward, my two younger sisters, and listen to me,
How could you have known that our family has been struck by a calamity?

Wang and Mei: Struck by what calamity?
Lady Yang: (*Weeps.*) My ignorant dear sisters! (*Sings.*)

Our lord surrendered to the barbarians and caused a great calamity,
Di Yanfeng brought soldiers fiercer than tigers and wolves.
Surrounding our residence, they will not spare us easily,
Our entire family will now meet our demise on this very day.

Concubine Wang: (*Weeps.*) I'm scared to death! (*Sings.*)

Hearing this, tears of blood pour down my cheeks,
Who would have expected a disaster to occur right at our home?
That Di Yanfeng is too wild and insolent in his behavior,
And I also denounce that unreasonable, muddle-headed dog of an emperor!

Concubine Mei: (*Weeps.*) What a treacherous villain! (*Sings.*)

My two elder sisters weep so loudly and woefully,
That even a man made of stone or iron would have grieved.
Turning to them, I plead for the sisters to please listen to me,
Should we as a family just wait here for our deaths?
I dispatch our son Huanhu to go relay to the warrior attendant,
That we'll all charge out in our saddles to seek the muddle-headed emperor.

Lady Yang: (*Weeps.*) My dear younger sister! We shouldn't rebel! (*Sings.*)

Don't speak nonsense, my dear younger sister,
We of the Yang family have been loyal and upright for generations.
To resist the imperial order signifies an act of rebellion,
How can we endure the defamation of our name for ten thousand generations?

Concubine Mei: My dear eldest sister! (*Sings.*)

My dear eldest sister, please do not shed any more tears,
Please listen to me, your younger sister, speak my heart.
The Yang family has indeed been loyal and upright for generations,
Our lord could not possibly have surrendered to the barbarians.
The muddle-headed emperor did not protect the good in handling this matter,
We'll face their broad swords and spears outside the imperial court.

(*Speaks.*) Let's rebel!

Lady Yang: (*Weeps.*) My dear younger sister, we shouldn't rebel! (*Sings.*)

My dear sister's words lack propriety,
Confused and unclear of the situation, you speak nonsense.
That treacherous villain has memorialized to the throne that we are traitors,
It is but natural that we should gather and tie ourselves up.

Huanhu: My dear Eldest Mom and Second Moms—(*Sings.*)

I, Yang Huanhu, step forward,
Eldest Mom and Second Moms, please listen to your child.
We have seen no evidence that our father has in fact surrendered,
This was totally based only on Di Yanfeng's memorial.
I think it would be better for the entire family to rebel together,
We'll fight our way to the throne hall and avenge the wrong.

Lady Yang: My dear child! We must not rebel! (*Yelling is heard off stage; Yang Huanfeng and Yang Huanqing enter.*)
Yang Huanfeng: (*Sings.*)

My ears suddenly hear people yelling,
The brothers' hearts feel as if on fire.

Yang Huanqing: (*Sings.*)

One wonders which nation has raised a rebellion,
And they're brave enough to raise a racket in front of our residence.

Yang Huanfeng: (*Sings.*)

Entering the residence, I pay obeisance to my mother,
And inquire of the Eldest Mother how you are faring.

Lady Yang: (*Weeps.*) My dear sons, Huanfeng and Huanqing. We're in deep trouble!
Yang Huanfeng: What happened?
Lady Yang: (*Sings.*)

Di Yanfeng returned to the court from the borderland,
He said that your father surrendered to the Western Barbarians.

His Majesty listened to the memorial the villain presented,
And angrily issued an edict right there and then.
Today our entire clan is to be executed together,
Di Yanfeng received an order to arrest us and confiscate our estate.

Yang Huanfeng: (*Sings.*)

Hearing my mother relating it all to me,
I, the hero, am incensed within.
Turning around, I call for my brothers,
Open our armory and prepare the broad swords and bows.
On my lone horse, I'll trample the city of Bianjing,
I'll fight my way to the throne hall and set the wrong straight.

(*Speaks.*) Let's rebel!
Lady Yang: (*Weeps.*) My dear son, you should not rebel! (*Sings.*)

My son's words show ignorance,
Ministers and subjects must not disobey Heaven.[14]
That treacherous villain has memorialized to the throne that we are traitors,
It is but natural that we should gather and tie ourselves up.
Let him scheme and try to defend himself,
In Heaven, justice will naturally eventually prevail.

Yang Huanhu: My dear eldest brother and second brother! (*Sings.*)

Eldest brother and second brother, let me beseech you,
Our Eldest Mother is tired of living.
She is willing to become a condemned criminal at the execution ground,
I am not willing to follow her to the Yellow Springs.

Yang Huanfeng: I am so mad! (*Sings.*)

Hearing my brother, fire rises from within my heart,
To have the entire clan die together, this I don't agree to.

14. The emperor is the Son of Heaven. Here Heaven also refers to the emperor.

I'll ask my mother to please let this son of hers fight my way out,
I'll fight my way to the golden court and avenge the wrong.

(*Speaks.*) Let's rebel!
Lady Yang: You little knave! (*Weeps.*) How dare you, you knave! (*Sings.*)

The little knave's words are unreasonable,
Disobeying your mother is a non-filial act.
All the labor in raising you is forgotten in one day,
What use is there in having all you knaves?
I will personally tie you up with this rope of the law.

Yang Huanfeng: Stop! You can't tie up your son for what happened today!
Lady Yang: My dear son! (*Sings.*)

Why don't you hit your mother a few times and stop me from breathing?

(*Speaks.*) Aiya, my son! Why don't you go ahead and hit me, your mother?
Yang Huanfeng: I, your son, don't dare.
Lady Yang: (*Weeps.*) I'm so mad I can die! (*Sings.*)

No one heeds my words of reason,
These knaves of mine force me to the edge.
I try to think and think, but I can't think of a way,
Better die right now and make an earlier exit.

Yang Huanfeng: (*Weeps.*) Mother, you can't do that! (*Sings.*)

I besiege you, mother, not to abandon your life,
Your son is willing to go face the execution.

Lady Yang: My dear filial son! (*Sings.*)

My son's words show an understanding of principle,
I now step forward to loosen my dear son's robe.
Taking this rope of the law, I will now tie you up,
Our whole clan can now await for blood to stain our clothes.

Yang Huanhu: Don't you act crazy now!

Lady Yang: Come here, Huanqing.

Yang Huanhu: Second Elder Brother, stand up for yourself!

Lady Yang: Your elder brother just allowed himself to be tied. Let me, your mother, tie you up too.

Yang Huanqing: Stop! You tied up your own son for what happened today. But don't you feel badly about tying up someone else's son?

Lady Yang: I . . .

Yang Huanqing: You what?

Yang Huanhu: You can't get my second eldest brother, can you? You're really stuck now, aren't you! My dear Eldest Mom—why don't you say something? Actually, it's best that you die anyway. If you die, then I'll get to live! Why are you pretending that you're dying?

Lady Yang: (*Weeps.*) I'll die from anger! (*Sings.*)

> The little knave is so utterly impertinent,
> I'm stuck for words; I can't answer him.
> I can only say that all the sons are the same to me,
> But the little knave won't let me tie him up.

(*Speaks.*) Come here, Ms. Wang. (*Sings.*)

> I ask Ms. Wang why she doesn't give her son a beating,
> Could it be that both of you, mother and son, refuse to obey the law?

Concubine Wang: Don't be angry, Elder Sister! Let me tie him up. Come here, Huanqing.

Yang Huanqing: Here's your son.

Concubine Wang: You little knave, you! (Weeps.) How dare you disobey us, you knave! (*Sings.*)

> The little knave's words are too insolent,
> How dare you refute Eldest Mother to her face?
> You are totally ignorant of the laws of the land,
> I'll take the rope of law and tie you up myself.
> We can't let future generations condemn us,
> We have to let the treacherous villain come after us.

Yang Huanhu: That was quick!

Lady Yang: Come here, Huanhu!

Yang Huanhu: Ah, my good mother. Are you coming after me now? What did you just say? Please don't come this way . . .

LADY YANG: Your eldest and second eldest brothers have both succumbed to being tied up. Let me tie you up, too.

YANG HUANHU: Why don't you give me the rope? I'll tie myself up and save you the trouble.

LADY YANG: My dear filial son!

YANG HUANHU: Ai, Eldest Mother! How come that heart of yours is so cruel? How many brothers do we have in this family? Even if a few of us die, half of us are gone. Who will be there to burn mock money for you after you die? Why are you so anxious to dig up the seedlings and eradicate the roots?

LADY YANG: Quit the jabbering. Submit yourself immediately!

YANG HUANHU: I'm not going to let you tie *me* up! I'd better make a run for it!

LADY YANG: Come back, Huanhu! Turn back! (*Yelling off stage. She weeps.*) I can die from the fright! (*Sings.*)

The sounds of men and horses are certainly frightening,
The blood of our entire clan will dye the yellow sand.
Utterly loyal, I fear not that we may be sliced a thousand times,
Let me go to the garden to take Huanzhen. (*They exit.*)

YANG HUANZHEN: (*Enters and sings.*)

After much thought, one must be loyal and filial during one's life,
For the sake of the Song state, the Yang family has frequently toiled.
My old father has gone on an expedition despite his advanced age,
We don't know when he will return singing the songs of victory.

(*Speaks.*) I am the fourth son, Yang Huanzhen.

YANG HUANHU: (*Enters.*) Fourth Elder Brother, guess who's here?

YANG HUANZHEN: Are you Huanhu?

YANG HUANHU: What did you think I was? An eggplant?

YANG HUANZHEN: Why do you look so upset?

YANG HUANHU: You know that our dad led a military expedition to the West. But that Di Yanfeng has returned to the court secretly and accused our dad of being a traitor who surrendered to the barbarians. His Majesty was so mad that he ordered the treacherous villain to confiscate our estate and round up the members of our entire clan. Eldest Mother tied up Eldest and Second Eldest Brothers. She wanted to tie me up, too! But I ran away. I expect that they're coming to the garden to get you next!

Yang Huanzhen: I'm furious! (*Sings.*)

Hearing Huanhu tell me the news,
I, a great hero, feel as if my heart is on fire.
Lifting my face, I can't help but yell at Heaven,
How can we, the Yang family, deserve this tragic fate?

Yang Huanhu: What good will your complaints to Heaven do?

Yang Huanzhen: So, what's your plan?

Yang Huanhu: The way I see it, we'd be better off if we rebelled. First, let's meet with our brother-in-law and abduct everyone from the execution ground.

Yang Huanzhen: Huanhu, do you think we should rebel?

Yang Huanhu: If we don't rebel now, it'll be too late!

Yang Huanzhen: So we should rebel! Let's do it! (*They exit and he sings off stage*).

Angrily, I give orders to Huanhu,
Open the armory and prepare the spears and swords. (*They re-enter.*)

Yang Huanhu: Please mount your horse, Fourth Elder Brother.

Yang Huanzhen: Bring the horse.

Yang Huanhu: Fourth Elder Brother rode away. Let me mount this black horse of mine. (*He exits and re-enters.*)

Yang Huanzhen: (*Sings.*)

Intending to rebel, we leave our home for the Hu residence,
We'll meet up with our brother-in-law and start a battle. (*They exit.*)

Scene 10: "Joining the Rebellion"

(*Enter Huyan Jiqing and Yang Mantang.*)

Hu[15] Jiqing: (*Sings.*)

---

15. Although the full family name is Huyan, this rare last name is usually changed to Hu in novels and operas.

In the past, my ancestor Huyan Zan 呼延贊 helped to preserve the state,
Receiving imperial favor, my official position is high.

YANG MANTANG: (*Sings.*)

The twelve[16] led a military expedition to the West, fiercer than eagles and hawks they were.
They strove and toiled only to preserve the river and mountains of the Song state.

HU JIQING: I am a descendant of Huyan Zan. My name is Huyan Jiqing.
YANG MANTANG: I am none other than Yang Mantang. Greetings, My Lord!
HU JIQING: There's no need for formalities, My Lady. Please take a seat. (*Yang Huanzhen and Yang Huanhu enter.*)
YANG HUANHU: Dismount, Fourth Elder Brother. Go inside. Let's go in. The couple has nothing better to do right now. Hiya, brother-in-law—guess who's here?
HU JIQING: Is this Huanhu?
YANG HUANHU: Who did you think it was?
HU JIQING: Why do you look so flustered?
YANG HUANHU: It's all because my father led a military expedition to the West. Di Yanfeng returned to the court and accused him of being a traitor and surrendering to the barbarians. His Majesty got so angry that he ordered the treacherous villain to confiscate our estate and arrest members of our family. Our Eldest Mother had just about everyone in the family tied up. She ran after me to the garden to try to tie me up, too. She said she was going to tie up the relatives as well!
YANG MANTANG: (*Weeps.*) Oh no! (*Sings.*)

Hearing the detailed report presented to me by Huanhu,
I'm filled with hatred for that murderous bandit Di Yanfeng.
Without reason, he performs evil and lords over the imperial court,
Causing the lives of my entire family to end up in the Underworld.

---

16. The twelve refers to the twelve women warriors of the Yang family who went into battle after most of its men died. This happened before Yang Mantang's time, but she claims this illustrious heritage as a female member of the Yang clan.

(*Speaks.*) Ah, my dear lord! (*Sings.*)

> I turn around and call out to My Lord,
> Please think of a way to rescue my family from disaster.

Hu Jiqing: Don't get flustered, My Lady. Let me memorialize to the throne and rescue all the lives of your family.

Yang Huanhu: Go ahead! By the time you return from the court, our whole family will be at the Home-Viewing Terrace in the Underworld.

Hu Jiqing: So, what's your plan?

Yang Huanhu: I suggest that you gather your soldiers at your residence. We'll abduct everyone at the execution ground and then memorialize to the throne.

Hu Jiqing: The Hu family has always been loyal and upright. We're not going to be known as rebels.

Yang Huanhu: These words really stab! Now, kid of the Hu family—if you're loyal and upright, what am I supposed to be?

Hu Jiqing: We're both loyal subjects.

Yang Huanhu: If we're both loyal, then why don't you rebel when I do it?

Hu Jiqing: The Hu family won't rebel.

Yang Huanhu: Are you really not going to rebel? Let me take care of you!

Hu Jiqing: If I don't rebel, who dares to do it?

Yang Huanhu: Who says no one at the Hu family dares to rebel? Elder Sister, he won't rebel because his heart is distant from us. Are you going to force me, in turn, to disown you?

Yang Mantang: Brother, do you think we should rebel?

Yang Huanhu: If we don't rebel within three days, we'll be too late.

Yang Mantang: So we'll rebel! (*Sings.*)

> Seeing Huanhu yelling at the top of his voice,
> I can't help but feel black blood surging within me.
> I open my mouth and address My Lord,
> If you won't rebel, I'll go there and fight myself.
> Angrily, I changed my attire and outfit,
> In order to save my family from imprisonment.
> I order my entire household to join the rebellion,
> So that my own family won't have to endure the steel blade.
> (*She exits.*)

HU JIQING: Come back, Huanhu. Have some stewed pig's trotters.

YANG HUANHU: If you won't rebel, I won't force you. What are you delaying me for?

HU JIQING: You can't succeed if I won't join you.

YANG HUANHU: Hey! What do I see here? Oh! It's the commander's platform of the Hu residence. It's no use arguing with you. Let me climb onto the platform and make an announcement. Listen, soldiers of the Hu residence—the Hus and Yangs are close relatives. The Yang family has been convicted and is willing to die out of loyalty. The Hu family is now blabbering gibberish. Hu tells me that being executed is no fun, so he'll let me rebel by myself and live for a couple more days.

SOLDIERS: (*Off stage.*) What's your plan?

YANG HUANHU: I have no plans of my own. I'm waiting for the Hu family to decide if the Hus and Yangs will rebel together.

HU JIQING: Huanhu, ah! We shouldn't rebel!

YANG HUANHU: Get away from me! Watch that stupid mouth of yours! You've made a worthless thing out of my sister for years! (*He exits.*)

HU JIQING: They're all rebelling. I'd better go along with it. I, Lord Hu, am joining the rebellion.

YANG HUANHU: (*Off stage.*) We've got enough soldiers! (*Hu exits.*)

Scene 11: "Abducting the Prisoners at the Execution Ground"

DI YANFENG: (*Off stage.*) Colonels, escort the Yang family to the execution ground.

LADY YANG: (*Sings off stage.*)

Being tied up, my heart and liver will rot from regret.

(*She enters under the escort of a colonel. She weeps.*) How I shall die from regret! (*Sings.*)

Being tied up, my heart and liver will rot from regret,
I weep and ask, where are you, that dear old husband of mine?
Loyal to the state, he must not have surrendered to the barbarian dogs.
This is all created by the treacherous villain who memorialized a lie.
At our residence, I should have listened to my sons and rebelled,

We should have fought our way to the muddle-headed emperor and cleared up the injustice.
I made the mistake myself—whom can I blame?
I shouldn't have tied up the family and entered the depth of the dragon pool.
I was too stubborn in not heeding the words of my sons,
I will now end up as a headless ghost and die a wrongful death.
I now regret it all, but it is already too late,
This is why it is better to regret sooner than later.

COLONEL: Go to the scaffold. (*A colonel escorts Concubine Wang on stage.*)
CONCUBINE WANG: (*Weeps.*) Oh, Heaven without open eyes! (*Sings.*)

Entering the execution ground, I cannot help but blame Heaven.
What has the Yang family done to deserve this evil injustice?
I hate that Di Yanfeng, with a human face but the heart of a beast.
I hate the fact that that dog of a muddle-headed emperor got the issue upside down.
Without considering how we preserved the state as securely as if forged by copper and iron,
He condemned us loyal subjects to death. Truly pitiable is our lot.
Thinking of this, I become so incensed that black blood boils from within.
The dragon is without love, the tiger is without virtue[17]—what more is there to say?

COLONEL: Go to the scaffold. (*A colonel escorts Concubine Mei onto the stage.*)
CONCUBINE MEI: (*Weeps.*) Ah, my son, whom I'll never see again! (*Sings.*)

Entering the execution ground, my tears flow all over my face.
I cry for Huanzhen and Huanhu—where are the two of you?
I can only hope that you two brothers will rebel together,

17. The dragon typically symbolizes the emperor. The tiger here seems to refer to Di Yanfeng.

Fight your way to the imperial court and voice the injustice personally.
After I die, my soul will travel to the Senluo Court 森罗殿of the Underworld,
There I will tell the King of the Underworld the injustices we have suffered.
At that meeting, I'll get the iron tally and have the villain summoned.
I'll have the treacherous villain sliced a thousand times to avenge us.

COLONEL: Go to the scaffold. (*A colonel escorts Yang Huanfeng on stage.*)
YANG HUANFENG: (*Weeps.*) My old daddy whom I'll never see again! (*Sings.*)

Entering the execution ground, my liver and entrails burst unwittingly,
I weep and call for my old daddy—where are you?
My father must think that we brothers are practicing shooting arrows at willow leaves.
Who would have expected our entire clan to be harmed by the villain?

COLONEL: Go to the scaffold. (*A colonel escorts Yang Huanqing on stage.*)
YANG HUANQING: (*Weeps.*) My old daddy, whom I'll never see again! (*Sings.*)

I, Yang Huanqing, enter the execution ground and look up,
I see the entire clan tied up, the sight is truly pitiable.
They are all tied to the scaffold with their hair loose and disheveled,
This is the unspeakable end of loyal and upright subjects!

COLONEL: Line up all the Yangs!
DI YANFENG: (*Enters.*) Take them from the scaffold and execute them!
CROWD: (*Enter.*) Let's abduct the prisoners at the execution ground! (*Yang Huanhu rescues the family, and they exit.*)
COLONEL: I report—the Hus and Yangs have abducted the prisoners.
DI YANFENG: Surround them and kill them!
COLONEL: They are such skilled warriors—we really can't take them.

Di Yanfeng: Lock the four city gates. Don't let a single person escape. (*He exits.*)

(*The Hus and Yangs enter with their soldiers.*)

Crowd: Aiya, mother! Look, the treacherous villain has ordered all four gates locked. We can't escape even if we could fly!

Lady Yang: (*Weeps.*) Now that it has come to this, we are truly at the end of our rope. Follow me to Nanqing Palace 南清宫.[18] I'll ask for help from the Eighth Prince. (*Sings.*)

Because of the abduction at the execution ground, we broke the law severely.
The treacherous villain issued an order and had the four gates closed.
We of the two families can't escape even if we had wings.
Let's go visit the Eighth Prince and explain to him the injustice. (*They exit.*)

Scene 12: "Rescued"

Eighth Prince: (*Enters and sings.*)

The dragon sons and grandsons control the imperial court,
Which civil and military official dares to disobey?
Although I do not occupy the highest position,
I get to relax and enjoy peaceful tranquility.

Eunuch (*Enters*): I report to the prince. The three ladies of the Yang family have brought all the warriors of the Hu and Yang families and request to enter our palace.

Eighth Prince: Whatever for?

Eunuch: I, your slave, don't know.

Eighth Prince: Pass along my edict. The warriors of the Yang and Hu families should retire to the quarters for the troops. The three ladies of the Yang family can enter the palace.

Eunuch: Warriors of the Yang and Hu families should retire to the quarters for the troops. The three ladies of the Yang family can enter the palace. (*Lady Yang leads Concubine Wang and Concubine Mei on stage.*)

---

18. The Eighth Prince is usually known as the Virtuous Eighth Prince 八德王, and his palace is named Nanjing Palace 南进宫.

LADY YANG: I receive the edict. Please save us, dear Prince!
EIGHTH PRINCE: Ladies, please rise.
LADY YANG: Thank you, dear Prince for the imperial favor![19]
EIGHTH PRINCE: Palace attendants, see to their seats.
LADY YANG: Thank you for allowing us to be seated.
EIGHTH PRINCE: May I ask you ladies what has transpired?
LADY YANG: (*Weeps.*) Allow me to explain, my dear Prince. (*Sings.*)

Before I speak, tears fill my entire face,
Please take heart and listen, my lord Prince.
The Yang family has encountered a clan-exterminating calamity,
I request that you, the Prince, take charge of the whole affair.

EIGHTH PRINCE: What kind of calamity occurred?
LADY YANG: (*Sings.*)

When the Western Barbarian bandit rebelled without cause,
My lord obeyed the imperial edict and led the army.
At the court, His Majesty selected the wrong person—
Di Yanfeng was dispatched to transport the provisions, and created problems.
Secretly he returned to the court and memorialized to the throne.
He accused my lord of being a traitor who surrendered to the barbarians.
The dragon ears of His Majesty were gullible, and he believed the memorial.
Di Yanfeng then came and confiscated our entire estate and arrested our clan.
Two of my sons who refused to be tied met up with relatives,
Together they entered the dragon pool and abducted us from the execution ground.
The treacherous villain then hurriedly locked all four city gates.
At the end of our rope, as a last resort, we have come to you for help.
I ask you, my dear Prince—pity our two families,
Even if we die, we will be grateful to you at the court of the Underworld.

---

19. Anxious to ingratiate herself to the prince, some of the language used by Lady Yang may have been more appropriate for an emperor than for a prince.

Eighth Prince: I am so incensed! (*Sings.*)

After hearing my lady relate the entire story from beginning to end,
I am so angry at Di Yanfeng, that evil traitor and slanderer.
Since no one knows whether the surrender to the barbarians is true or false,
Why did you secretly memorialize to the throne the false accusation?
I ask my ladies to relax your sorrowful knitted eyebrows,
I, the Prince, will take complete charge of this matter.
I will order my palace attendants to fetch my golden imperial court pass.
Let me, the prince, go to the palace and memorialize to the throne. (*He exits.*)

Lady Yang: (*Sings.*)

Angrily, the Prince left for the golden throne in a huff,
When this is resolved, we will know who is loyal and who is treacherous.
Yang Huanhu, that little knave, is careless but courageous,
If it weren't for him, the lives of our entire family would have been gone. (*They all exit.*)

Scene 13: "Meeting"

(*The Barbarian Girl and Yang Huanlong enter.*)
Barbarian Girl: (*Sings.*)

Sitting next to my husband[20] day and night,
Like fish in water, our love and care for each other are intense.
We are the best couple to have ever existed, but
I notice that he seems to be unhappy these days.

Yang Huanlong: (*Sings.*)

Thinking of the past, my abdomen bursts from anger,
My own flesh and blood and I are now at two corners of the world.

20. The term she used, *fuma* 驸马, is the title given to the husband of a princess.

I wonder if fortune or misfortune has fallen upon my aged
father,
Neither loyal nor filial, I am an utter disgrace.

BARBARIAN GIRL: Please come here, my dear husband. Greetings. (*She bows.*)

YANG HUANLONG: There's no need for formalities, my dear Princess. Please sit down.

BARBARIAN GIRL: Aiya, my dear husband! My father has passed away—shall I give the throne to you?

YANG HUANLONG: Ai!

BARBARIAN GIRL: You seem so unhappy. I think it'll be good for us to take a stroll on the grassland. How do you feel about it?

YANG HUANLONG: It's entirely up to you, my Princess.

BARBARIAN GIRL: In that case, tartar soldiers[21]—bring our horses over!

BARBARIAN SOLDIER: (*Enters.*) Please mount the horse, Princess.

BARBARIAN GIRL: Bring me the horse.

BARBARIAN SOLDIER: Please mount the horse, Prince.

YANG HUANLONG: Bring me the horse.

BARBARIAN GIRL: (*To the soldier.*) Stay here. (*To Yang Huanlong.*) Please go ahead, dear husband. (*Sings.*)

I ask my husband not to knit his eyebrows any more,
Let me give you in detail my words of reassurance.
I'll pick an auspicious date and make you the ruler of Hanguo,
And then I'll dispatch someone to find out the fate of your family.

YANG HUANLONG: (*Sings.*)

Although living in luxury, I feel as if I'm sitting and sleeping on
needles,
Not knowing if members of my family are dead or alive.
Neither do I know if fortune or misfortune has befallen my
father,
Nor how that dog of an evil villain is turning the court upside
down?
I have to spur on my horse to pass through this barbarian land.

---

21. She called them "barbarian soldiers" literally.

Barbarian Girl: Where are you going, husband?
Yang Huanlong: (*Sings.*)

With the kind princess following so closely, how can I escape?
I have to give her credit for being so sagacious and kind.
Husband and wife, we'll ride together and stroll around the grassland.

(*The Eighth Prince enters with the Yang family warriors and soldiers.*)
Eighth Prince: (*Sings.*)

Fortunately, His Majesty decided to issue an edict
For me to take some men to go to the borderland.
I look up while riding my horse,
I'm spirited, and my horse is strong.
The soldiers carry bells,
The warriors carry eight-foot spears behind their saddles.
The horses and men proceed along happily.

Yang Huanlong: I, Huanlong, pay my respects to the Prince.
Eighth Prince: (*Sings.*)

I see the third son of the Yang family.

(*Speaks.*) Huanlong is here. Let's stop for a moment. Are you really Huanlong? You went on a military expedition to the West with your father. How come you're now dressed like a barbarian?
Yang Huanlong: (*Weeps.*) Oh Prince, you wouldn't have known! (*Sings.*)

Before I speak, my tears stream down unwittingly,
I besiege that my Prince will listen to all the details.
Receiving the imperial edict, we, father and son, led the warriors and soldiers
Against the barbarian bandits, most of whom we killed in one battle.
Di Yanfeng, that dog of a treacherous villain, suppressed the provisions,
My father the commander dispatched me to gallop back to Bianliang.
When I traveled to the state of Xiaohan, however, I was blocked by barbarian soldiers,

A girl named Hundred Flowers besieged me to marry into her family.
Each day I think of my whole family and am worried sick,
Unable to drink the tea and eat the meals, I grieve secretly.
Seeing how depressed I am, how my eyebrows are perpetually knitted,
She came riding with me on the grassland to relieve my misery.
I'm so happy to have gotten the chance to run into you and your army,
May I inquire as to where you're headed with all the horses and men?

EIGHTH PRINCE: (*Sings.*)

It was all on account of the fact that there was no news of you and your father,
Di Yanfeng submitted a memorial and brought tragedy upon your entire clan.
But your brothers Huanzhen and Huanhu refused to be tied up,
Together with Hu Jiqing, they abducted your imprisoned family at the execution ground.
That treacherous villain Di gave the order and had all four city gates locked.
Your family went to my residence, the Nanqing Palace, and hid there temporarily.
I subsequently went to the imperial court and offered my guarantee for them.
Because of that, I now travel beyond the borders with horses and men.
If we win, the two families will receive official titles and meritorious awards,
If we lose, the two families will die and perish together.

YANG HUANLONG: My wise and virtuous Princess![22] (*Sings.*)

Hearing these words, my tears stream down unwittingly,
I besiege my dear Princess to please think on my behalf.

---

22. He is referring to Barbarian Girl here.

Look at how my entire clan has been entrapped and ensnared,
If you rescue my family, I will be forever indebted to you.

Barbarian Girl: (*Sings.*)

Hearing my husband relate to me the entire tale from the beginning to the end,
I can't help but turn my body around, completely overcome by sorrow.
I tell my husband and the Prince to go ahead with their army,
My barbarian soldiers and I will follow you and provide assistance.

Yang Huanlong: Let's go! (*The Barbarian Girl exits.*) My dear Prince, the barbarians rely solely on magic to win. It's really difficult to defeat them.

Yang Mantang: Dear Prince, I have an adopted brother by the name of Gao Wang. He's thoroughly skilled in Daoist magic and is presently guarding Yazhi Prefecture 雅志府. Let me bring him, and we'll win for sure.

Eighth Prince: Go right away! (*Yang Mantang exits.*) Huanlong, you are familiar with the way here—you can lead. Let's go! (*Sings.*)

I am so glad that I have five superior warriors,
Causing me, the Prince, to overflow with joy while riding.
Yang Huanfeng here is stronger than a horse,
Yang Huanqing here is more militarily skilled than anyone else.
Yang Huanlong here is husband to a princess who controls Hanguo,
Yang Huanzheng here is good at using two firework-tipped spears.[23]
Yang Huanhu here is most heroic when it comes to personal duals,
Playing tricks on battlefields, he is a hard one to deal with.
If it weren't for the fact that he ran away so quickly, the entire Yang clan would have been annihilated.
Truly we have five tigers here who will preserve the emperor of the Song dynasty. (*They exit.*)

23. These *huaqiang* 花枪, literally, flower-tipped spears, probably refer to *lihuaqiang* 梨花枪—pear-flower spear—a type of weapon with a firework-like explosive device that can be shot from the tip of the spear.

YANG MANTANG: (*Enters and sings.*)

Finally today our wishes have come true,
Half way there, we run into Yang Huanlong.
He tells us about the secret behind barbarian warfare,
They use magic to harm, and will be hard to defeat.
The Prince issues a command in the army,
I will go to Yazhi Prefecture to fetch my adopted brother, Gao.
For the sake of saving the lives of my parents,
We will manifest the loyalty and filial piety of the Yang clan.
(*She exits.*)

Scene 14: "Defeating the Barbarians"

(*Off stage.*) Surround them and kill them all! (*The Yang warriors defeat the barbarian king, who exits. The warriors follow him off stage; the barbarian king enters again.*)

BARBARIAN KING: What a good battle! The Yang brothers are such good warriors! If they come again, I'll use magic on them and win. (*He uses magic and captures the Yang brothers.*)

YANG HUANZHEN: (*Enters.*) Oh, no! (*Sings.*)

This battle scares me to death,
I can't even use my firework-tipped spears; I have them in vain.
I see the sorcerer pursuing and chasing after me,
I really don't expect to survive. (*He exits.*)

(*Enter Gao Wang and Yang Mantang.*)

GAO WANG: (*Sings.*)

My adopted younger sister Yang told me all about it,
She also says that barbarians reply on magical tricks.
Remembering how in the past I lived on Mount Black Wind,
Younger Sister Yang and I fought at the borderland twelve times.
The firework-tipped spears of the Yang family were truly formidable,
I had to use my magical "black wind" to defend myself.[24]
A wind reaches my ears and I hear yelling and screaming.

---

24. This part is not clear. It seems to suggest that Gao Wang and Yang Mantang met during a series of battles in which neither won; they probably decided to call it a truce and adopted each other as siblings then.

(*Speaks.*) Younger Sister, go back. (*Yang Mantang exits; he sings.*)

Riding on my "black wind" (*Rides on wind.*)
I see the sorcerer chasing after the warriors.
They do look like the four Yang brothers,
I ride on the "black wind" without any further ado.
I have to rescue the young men from certain death.
A barbarian soldier arrives and looks up at me,
Here we go—have a taste of this whip of mine. (*He exits.*)

Barbarian Girl: (*Enters and sings.*)

Today my wishes have finally come true,
I will follow my husband back to the central plain.[25]
I suddenly hear sounds of yelling and screaming,
I see a black wind that has covered the sky.
A sorcerer is chasing the warriors from behind,
Twelve feet in height, he is truly fierce.
Not fearing piercing and hacking by spears and swords,
I think he is only afraid of being burned by fire.

(*Speaks.*) God Dingjia 丁甲神, where are you?
God Dingjia: (*Enters.*) At your service, Officer of Ritual Arts 法官.[26]
Barbarian Girl: Burn the sorcerer with fire. I will thank you with paper horses and yellow money!
God Dingjia: I obey the commands of the Ritual. (*A fire burns.*)
Barbarian Girl: You have accomplished much—you can now return! (*God Dingjia exits; so does the Barbarian Girl.*)
(*Gao Wang enters with the Barbarian King and kills the latter.*)
Soldier: The barbarian bandit has fallen from his horse!
Gao Wang: Open the prisons and free the Yang family warriors. Let me return to Yazhi Prefecture. (*He exits.*)
Eighth Prince: (*Enters and sings.*)

I am so happy that Heaven granted my wish and we won the war,
My dear Minister Yang can be considered most loyal and wise.

---

25. That is, China.

26. In modern Chinese, the term *faguan* refers to a judge, an official in charge of the law; but here the *fa* refers to *fashu* 法术, supernatural, magical, ritual arts.

Di Yanfeng is truly a national calamity at the imperial court,
When I return to court, I will definitely get rid of that traitor and slanderer. (*He exits.*)

Scene 15: "Celebratory Banquet"

Emperor: (*Enters and sings.*)

Just now the palace attendant reported to us
That the Yang family has attained great merit.

Palace Attendant: (*Enters.*) I report to Your Majesty. The Eighth Prince has returned victorious. He has brought the heroes of the Yang and Hu families.

Emperor: Tell the Eighth Prince to return to his palace to rest and the heroes of the Hu and Yang families to come to the throne hall. (*Yang Wenguang leads the others on stage.*)

Yang Wenguang: We receive the edict. I, Yang Wenguang, kowtow to Your Majesty the emperor!

Emperor: My dear minister, so you've returned to the court.

Yang Wenguang: Yes, I've returned to the court.

Emperor: You have remained loyal. Listen to the edict of awards: Minister Yang will be granted the title of Duke of Pacifying the West 平西国公. Minister Hu's rank will be increased by three levels. The five sons of the Yang family will receive the title of Five Tiger Generals. The Hundred Flower Girl achieved merit through surrendering to our state—she will be granted the title of the Marquise of Subjugation 投顺侯. You can all rise! Summon a colonel to the court.

Palace Attendant: Summon a colonel to the court.

Colonel: (*Enters.*) At your service, Your Majesty!

Emperor: Tie up Di Yanfeng and bring him here. (*The colonel escorts Di Yanfeng on stage.*)

Di Yanfeng: Please spare my life, Your Majesty!

Emperor: What a treacherous villain! You've almost caused the death of my dear Minister Yang here. How can I spare you? Colonel—take the treacherous villain away and bring his head! (*The colonel exits with Di Yanfeng and returns.*)

Colonel: I present the head.

Emperor: Take it away. You ministers have toiled for our state. We've had a banquet prepared for you at the Guanglu Temple 光禄寺[27] to help celebrate your achievements. (*They exit.*)

END OF PLAY

27. This temple is presumably within the palace grounds.

24. Emperor without headdress with a minister (Wei Tiancai's puppets). Photo by Fan Pen Li Chen.

25. Guan Gong (Wei Tiancai's puppet). Photo by Fan Pen Li Chen.

Short Version of River Yang 小阳河

(a.k.a., *The Four Saints Return to Heaven* 四圣归天)

Introduction

A story found only in this local theatrical tradition,[1] *River Yang* seems to have been considered a particularly sacred play in this region because Lord Guan (Guangong 关公; Guan Yu 关羽), patron saint of the Heyang marionette theater, appears in this play. According to Dang Wenhui 党文辉, he is the most popular and most revered of the local deities. Through the puppet that represents him in the play, Lord Guan was ritually invited to the show and worshipped with due ceremony before the performance. The sponsor of the performance would provide a welcoming ritual, which included setting off firecrackers,[2] burning incense, and a yellow piece of paper known as the "yellow petition horse" (*huangbiao ma* 黄表马) (representing the petition-bearing spiritual messenger to the deity). Unlike the heads of the other male puppets, Lord Guan's head is placed in the trunk reserved for the heads of the female roles,[3] and performers are not allowed to sit on that particular trunk. Ye Mingsheng's local informants at Nanshun

1. Huang 1999, 169. Many plays are shared, often in variant forms, among the various theatrical traditions.

2. Ye Mingsheng's 叶明生 informants at Xiangruo Theatrical Society 向若剧社 in Nanshun Village 南顺村 said that an explosive blast would be set off whenever Lord Guan appeared on stage. In southern China, such blasts could be used to accompany the entry of all deities, but in this region, this custom was reserved only for the highly revered Lord Guan.

3. He was probably placed there to protect the "women." To show his trustworthiness and integrity, he slept on a table outside the room of Liu Bei's wives when he was entrusted with protecting them in chapter 26 of *Romance of the Three Kingdoms*.

Village added that, unlike the puppet heads of other characters, which are distinguished by role types, the head for Lord Guan could be used only to represent him.[4] Indeed, he is so loved and revered that the episode "Fleeing City Mai 走麦城" (in which Lord Guan dies) is never performed in Heyang.

The other title of the play, *The Four Saints Return to Heaven*, suggests that *River Yang* probably represents only the core of a longer version. In *River Yang*, only two (rather than all four) reincarnations of the deified sworn brothers of the Kingdom of Shu of the Three Kingdoms Period (220–265) "return to Heaven."[5] Lord Guan is a god in this play; he appears as himself and not as a reincarnation. Zhang Fei 张飞, Zhao Yun 赵云, and Liu Bei 刘备 all appear as reincarnations, but only Zhang and Zhao die and "return to Heaven." Reenacting a typical story of enmity between a maligned loyal military family and an evil disloyal civil minister, the short version of *River Yang* casts several of its protagonists as reincarnations of some of the most famous historical characters popularized by the novel *Sanguo yanyi* 三国演义 (Romance of the Three Kingdoms). The three sworn brothers of the Peach Orchard, Liu Bei (Eldest Brother), Guan Yu (Second Brother), and Zhang Fei (Third Brother), are respectively now the Wanli 万历 Emperor, Deity Lord Guan, and General Yang Sifan 杨四藩. Zhao Yun, who joined the three later, but came to be recognized as their Fourth Brother in *Romance of the Three Kingdoms*, is reincarnated as General Xu Feng 许奉. This link to a loyal general in his past existence explains his denunciations of the treachery of his own father, Xu Zan 许赞, before he dies. He dutifully fights at his father's behest, but ultimately regards his father and brothers as traitors. The convoluted story and representation of figures from the Three Kingdoms Period also suggest a local re-interpretation of the greater pan-Chinese historical and literary traditions.

The fact that what is translated below is not a complete version probably explains some of the unusual features of the way the story unfolds. For instance, Yang Bo 杨博, the supposedly "good" general, is initially presented as the first one to engender animosity. He purposely departs furtively, without raising the flags or firing the cannons, and takes with him three days of provisions so he can later accuse his enemy Xu Long 许龙 for arriving late with supplies. He almost summarily executes both Xu Long and his brother, Xu Jiao 许蛟, prefect of the county. It is only Yang Bo's fear of

4. In rod puppetry, the puppet for Lord Guan could also be used to play Zhao Kuangyin 赵匡胤, Shan Xiongxin 单雄信, and other red-faced characters.

5. Many of the warrior heroes and heroines in pseudo-historical plays of this type are reincarnations of deities as mortals. Their deaths are therefore considered to be a return to Heaven.

the power of their father, Xu Zan, at the imperial court, and concern for the safety of the Yang family at the capital that ultimately saves their lives. But although Yang Bo seems to be at fault for trying to eliminate Xu Long and Xu Jiao for no clear reason, we learn (through Xu Feng at the end of the play) about Xu Zan's past treachery, which earned the inveterate hatred of the "upright and loyal" Yang Bo for this chief minister and his sons.

This conflict between the military and civilian ministers probably reflects the court's perpetual fear of successful generals whose military power could threaten the court itself, and the unfair treatment dealt to many a general after his usefulness ended. In many a shadow theater and puppet play, a civilian minister, rather than the emperor himself, is blamed for the victimization of such a loyal and meritorious general (whose family then rebels to punish the minister and regain the emperor's favor). The rebellion eventually forces the emperor to accept and enfeoff the rebels, and brings about the execution or demotion of the evil minister (if not killed by the rebels already). The popularity of this motif, and the conviction of the righteousness of the rebels, allow peasants to imagine receiving rewards through joining rebellions. The sometimes unjust and irrational behavior of Yang Bo and his grandson, Yang Baotong 杨宝童, may consequently be overlooked, and their victory at the play's end is both expected and celebrated.

Typical of military romances, a foreign warrior princess is instrumental to the success of the Chinese forces against Tianliang 天凉, the barbarian state to be pacified in *River Yang*. However, unlike other military romances (in which the foreign princess typically falls so madly in love with a handsome young Chinese general that she betrays her own state and father), in *River Yang*, the "barbarian" princess, Liu Qiulan 刘秋兰, turns out to be the sister of one of the Yang family's warriors. The orphaned daughter of an official of the borderland city of Guihua cheng 規化城 (literally, City that has been Transformed/Sinified), Liu Qiulan was abducted by "barbarians" and raised by their king. She plans the annihilation of her own camp and ensures the victory of the Chinese. As a sensitive and filial daughter, however, she nevertheless weeps over the impending death of the "father" who raised her. She is the most powerful warrior in this play, and is instrumental in the death of Xu Feng through her military skillfulness and acuity. In a conventional military romance, Liu Qiulan would have married the handsome Chinese warrior she defeats; in *River Yang*, however, the defeated warrior, Xu Feng, is fated to return to Heaven (as a member of a disloyal family) and dies without a romantic interlude. Liu Qiulan will, in the end, marry the young Yang Baotong by imperial decree. Thus, as expected, all the rebels receive titles, and the powerful warrior princess marries a general of the righteous Yang family.

As usual, the emperor is portrayed as muddle-headed, but here his ineptness is attributed to his youth. The fact that he is the reincarnation of Liu Bei and sincerely desires to meet his "Third Brother" (whose death he causes) also provides an unconventional twist to the tale, and makes him a more sympathetic character. Hence, *River Yang* is a mélange of conventional motifs, superimposed by an unusual reincarnation scheme that ensures the appearance and continuation of the tale of Lord Guan, the most popular deity of the region. Indeed, this play may have been created to be performed at festivals and celebrations conducted at Lord Guan's numerous shrines. While the creator of this story has managed to weave together the two strands of civilian-military conflict and reincarnation motifs fairly ingeniously, the end result contains several unconventional elements: a general commits suicide for hitting the emperor by mistake; the barbarian princess is in fact Chinese; and she does not fall in love with her Chinese adversary (who, in this case, is the son of the evil chief minister, and although a righteous warrior himself, is destined to die). The fact that *River Yang* was once one of the most popular plays demonstrates the audience's preference for the military over civilian officials, and the subjectivity of "righteousness." Those deemed "righteous" can get away with practically any kind of unjust and irrational behavior.

Cast of *Short Version of River Yang*[6]

EMPEROR: Zhu Yijun 朱翊钧,[7] the Wanli 万历 Emperor (r. 1573–1620). He is a young emperor in this play.
YANG BO 杨博: an old general[8]

6. In shadow and marionette plays, the addition of *xiao* 小 (little) to the title of a play indicates that it is a short version of that play. This play was narrated by Wei Runsheng 魏潤生, from memory. The script for this play is printed in Shaanxisheng Wenhuaju, ed., *Shaanxi sheng chuantong jumu, xianxi*, 线戏 1157–1229.

7. The play script uses Zhu Yijun to refer to the Wanli Emperor throughout.

8. Yang Bo seems to be the same figure as the Yang Bo 杨波, who helps preserve infant Emperor Wanli's throne in the Beijing/Peking operas, *Da baoguo* 大保国 (Greatly Protecting the State), *Tan huangling* 探皇陵 (Visiting the Imperial Mausoleum), and *Er jingong* 二进宫 (Second Entrance to the Palace). These three plays are collectively known as *Da Tan Er* 大探二 (from the first characters of each of the three plays). The evil minister of *River Yang*, Xu Zan, is not mentioned in those plays, but is in another Peking opera play featuring Yang Bo, *Yulin jun* 御林郡 (Imperial Forest Commandery). The ultimate source for these Peking opera plays is thought to be a *guci* 鼓词 (drum ballad) named *Xianglian pa* 香莲帕 (Fragrant Lotus Kerchief). I thank David Rolston for bringing up the idea that the Yang Bos of *River Yang* and these Peking opera plays are probably connected. See Goodrich, 1525–1528 for a biography of the historical Yang Bo.

Xu Long 许龙: president of the Board of Revenue and Population; eldest son of Xu Zan; an enemy of Yang Bo
Liu Qiulan 刘秋兰: a woman warrior; Liu Yong's sister abducted by barbarians
Yang Sifan 杨四藩: Yang Bo's fourth son, also known as the Fourth Young Lord; a warrior
Liu Yong 刘勇: one of Yang Bo's main warriors
Xu Jiao 许蛟: Xu Zan's second son; Xu Long's brother
Barbarian King: the king of Tianliang 天凉
Soul of Guan Yu 关羽: a renowned historical warrior of legendary status
Soul of Guan Ping 关平: a son of Guan Yu; also a great warrior
Eunuchs
Barbarian Soldiers
Soldiers
Colonels
Soul of Zhou Cang 周倉: a friend of Guan Yu; also a great warrior
Lady Yang 杨老夫人: Yang Bo's wife
Madam Wang 王氏: Yang Sifan's wife
Yang Baotong 杨宝童: Yang Sifan's thirteen-year-old son
Zhang Jin 张进: prime minister; friend of the Yang family
Xu Zan 许赞: an eminent minister;[9] father of Xu Long, Xu Jiao, and Xu Feng
Cui Shou 崔寿: Xu Zan's son-in-law; a warrior
Xu Feng 许奉: Xu Zan's third son; a general
Warrior Attendant 家将: a warrior attached to the Yang family
Edict Messenger

Scene 1: "Embarking on a Military Expedition"

(*Four eunuchs enter. The head eunuch leads Zhu Yijun to his throne.*)

Emperor: We are the Wanli Emperor of the great Ming dynasty. We have just received an emergency report that brigands in the River Yang region have rebelled.[10] We'll have to dispatch a general to chastise them. Palace Attendant Minister! (The head eunuch responds.) Issue this imperial edict: Yang Bo will be the commander-in-chief; Yang Sifan and Liu

9. See Goodrich, 608–609, for a biography of the historical Xu Zan.

10. The River Yang region seems to have been an area north of China that was, perhaps, a nomadic state that attempted to declare independence. The Chinese would have considered such behavior rebellious and called the defiant locals "robbers" and "brigands."

Yong will head the vanguard. Xu Long of the Board of Revenue and Population will be in charge of transporting the provisions. An army of a hundred thousand will proceed to the River Yang region to pacify the rebels. (*Sings.*)

The imperial edict is dispatched from the court like a toppling mountain,
We order Yang Bo to take the seal of command and set out the weapons.
Xu Long of the Board of Revenue and Populations will transport the provisions,
This expedition will ensure that the brigands will die in the wilderness. (*They exit.*)

(*Four extras lead Yang Bo onto the stage.*)
Yang Bo: (*Sings.*)

I resent the fact that the Wanli Emperor is too young to know better,
How can I, a hoary aged minister, go out to fight?
Returning home, I can't help but feel flames issuing out of the seven apertures,[11]
Sitting in the inner hall, frustrated, I am totally consumed by anger.

(*Speaks.*) I am General Yang Bo, a minister of the Ming dynasty. Brigands of the northern country have rebelled. The Emperor has issued an edict ordering me to lead a military expedition against them. Xu Long of the Board of Revenue and Population will be in charge of transporting provisions. This villain and I don't see eye to eye. It's commonly said, "The first to act will win; the second to act will suffer." Colonels! (*An extra answers.*) Dispatch my command: tell your Fourth Young Lord to lead the vanguard. Liu Yong will follow him and set up the camps. The warriors will proceed with their soldiers with three days' supply of food. Don't raise the flags or fire the cannons.[12] Set out for the River Yang region right away. (*Sings.*)

---

11. The eyes, ears, nose, and mouth.

12. Rituals that announce the departure of the expedition.

An order issued in my military tent resembles the roaring of a tiger,
Any villain crossing my path will be sliced and stabbed ten thousand times! (*They exit.*)

Scene 2: "Pacifying the Barbarians"

(*Four barbarian soldiers lead Liu Qiulan onto the stage.*)
Liu Qiulan: (*Sings.*)

Unfortunately, both my father and mother died early,
Leaving behind my brother and me, siblings of the same mother.
During the Qingming 清明 Festival,[13] brother and I went to their graves,
Barbarians from Tianliang abducted me and took me to their lair.
Impressed by my flower-and-moon vying beauty, their king, Li Hao 李好,
Adopted me as foster daughter and had me trained in military skills.
This morning I heard a report from a little barbarian soldier,
The good news he brought has helped me relax my knitted eyebrows.

(*She sits and speaks.*) I am Qiulan of the Liu family. Hailing from Guihua City of China, my father was a minister under the Longqing 隆庆 Emperor (r. 1567–1572). But he died and ascended to Heaven unexpectedly and left behind my brother and me. During a Qingming Festival, we went to visit the cemetery, and I was abducted by soldiers from Tianliang and thus came to this northern country. The king adopted me as his daughter and had me trained in the military arts. Because I'm good at using the iron pitchfork, the barbarians call me Princess Iron Pitchfork. The soldiers just reported that the father and son of the Yang family are arriving with an army. I also heard that my brother is in their camp. I'll have to write a short letter and have it sent there. We'll kill the barbarians[14] through coordination within and without.

13. A festival during which the Chinese worship at their family's graves.

14. Although she has been adopted by a barbarian king and is a barbarian princess, she identifies herself with the Chinese and is loyal to the Chinese state. She will now help the Chinese army against her adopted barbarian kinsmen.

Barbarian Soldier! (*Barbarian Soldier A responds.*) Here is a short letter. Deliver it to the Yang camp. I, the princess, want a reply from them.

BARBARIAN SOLDIER A: What do you want a reply for?

LIU QIULAN: This is a two-way battle declaration. Go immediately! (*Barbarian Soldier A responds and exits.*) I am so happy! (*Sings.*)

I can't help but clap and laugh concerning this event,
My short letter will invariably ensure the end of their lives.
Thinking of my older brother, tears flow down my cheeks,
The affection of siblings ended in one day, and we've lived on two ends of the Earth.
The incident that happened this very day occurred by pure chance,
I'll make sure that none of them will escape with their lives.

BARBARIAN SOLDIER A: (*Enters.*) I report—here is the reply letter.

LIU QIULAN: Attention!

BARBARIAN SOLDIER: Yes. Attention troops!

LIU QIULAN: (*Looks at the letter.*) So they've agreed to fight tomorrow night and will use fire as the signal. Barbarian soldiers! Go collect firewood in the countryside and make piles of it around our camp. When the Yang army approaches, we'll light them as a signal. Be careful! (*Sings.*)

The northern barbarian brigands have fallen for my trap,
Tonight I'll use fire and burn the entire camp.
The two-way battle declaration did stipulate using fire as a signal,
This clever ruse is truly the result of my immense talent and intelligence. (*They exit. Four soldiers pushing carts of grain enter with Xu Long.*)

XU LONG: (*Sings.*)

My brother in the River Yang region dispatched an emergency report,
I immediately memorialized to the throne concerning the matter.
Yang Bo as the commander-in-chief will proceed to exterminate the rebels,
I have been ordered to go there and transport the provisions.

(*Speaks.*) I am Xu Long, President of the Board of Revenue and Population.

Messenger: (*Enters.*) I report—the father and son of the Yang family left three days ago without raising the flags or firing the cannons. (*Exits.*)

Xu Long: Oh no! The old one must have planned to undermine me by not firing the cannons to indicate his departure. Soldiers! (*Four soldiers respond.*) Start moving the grain carts right away. Travel night and day, and rush them over to River Yang. (*Sings.*)

The old one, Yang Bo, is proud by nature,
I'm only afraid that I, Xu Long, will lose my life.
I hurriedly order the provisions carts to proceed immediately,
And make the trip by traveling both night and day. (*He exits.*)
(*Four extras enter with Yang Bo.*)

Yang Bo: (*Sings.*)

The northern barbarian brigands are just like jackals and wolves,
Without reason they've captured River Yang and acted without restraint.
When Xu Long is mentioned, however, I grind my teeth until they shatter,
If he should ever land in my hands, I'll have him sliced ten thousand times.

Soldier: (*Enters.*) I report—the grain provisions officer has arrived.

Yang Bo: Tell him to come in.

Soldier: Yes, sir. Grain provisions officer—please come in. (*He exits.*)

Xu Long: (*Enters.*) Your Highness the marshal, I, the grain provisions officer, respectfully seek an audience with you.

Yang Bo: When I mobilized the army, why did you withhold the provisions?

Xu Long: The commander-in-chief did not raise the flags and fire the cannons. Your humble officer had absolutely no knowledge of it.

Yang Bo: You are full of rubbish! There's been a saying since antiquity, "The grains and hay should travel before the army is mobilized." You obviously withheld the provisions with the intention of creating problems for me. Soldier! (*A soldier responds.*) Take him away and have him beheaded!

Soldier A: Yes, sir! (*He escorts Xu Long off stage.*)

Xu Jiao: (*Enters.*) Your Highness the commander-in-chief, Xu Jiao kowtows to you. (*He kowtows.*)

YANG BO: What do you want?

XU JIAO: What crime did the provisions officer commit? Why is he tied to the stake to be executed?

YANG BO: He's to be executed because he withheld the provisions.

XU JIAO: It's bad luck to execute the provisions officer before you fight the barbarians.

YANG BO: Stop! It is commonly said that official posts have their hierarchies, and each has its own yamen. How dare you charge into my official gate without invitation? Soldier! (*Soldier B responds.*) Take him away and have him beheaded!

SOLDIER B: Yes, sir. (*He escorts Xu Jiao off stage.*)

YANG SIFAN: (*Enters.*) Hold off the knives! Your Highness, my father—I, Sifan, respectfully seek an audience with you.

YANG BO: What do you want?

YANG SIFAN: What crimes did the Xu brothers commit that they are tied to the stakes to be executed?

YANG BO: One for withholding the provisions, the other for transgressing into my yamen.

YANG SIFAN: Father! We, father and son, haven't fought the barbarians. It will be all right if we win. But should we lose, with the villain Xu Zan wielding ultimate power at the court and us serving as officials there, who will guarantee the safety of the lives of our entire family?

YANG BO: My son has a point. Rise! (*Yang Sifan rises.*) Soldiers! Untie the Xu brothers. Give each of them twenty lashes and then chase them out of my gate! (*Soldier A and B respond off stage and then enter.*) Sifan, listen to my orders!

YANG SIFAN: Yes, sir!

YANG BO: You and Liu Yong will ambush the enemy camp and stronghold tonight. Lean over, my son. (*He whispers.*) Remember what I told you.

YANG SIFAN: I won't forget. (*He exits.*)

YANG BO: (*Sings.*)

> Only because my son, Sifan, came to my tent to beg on their behalf,
> Have I so easily agreed to spare the lives of those brothers. (*They all exit.*)

LIU QIULAN: (*Enters and weeps.*) My royal father, whom I'll never see again![15] (*Sings.*)

---

15. This is an expression normally used to refer to someone who has already died. Here she is anticipating his death.

I, your daughter, Qiulan, weep out loud in my own tent,
I can't stop my tears from pouring down continuously.
I kneel to my royal father, whose kindness in raising me is as great as a mountain,
Adopting me as a foster daughter, you taught me military skills day and night.
But your child will burn your camp tonight in return for your kindness,
Ending up being both ungrateful and unfilial.
Considering my crime, I don't in the end expect to be spared by Heaven and Earth.
Now that night is approaching, the birds return to roost and clamor,
I will ensure that none of the barbarians will be able to escape alive.

Barbarian Soldier: (*Enters.*) I report: the Yang army has entered our camp.

Liu Qiulan: Report to the main camp. (*The barbarian soldier responds and exits.*) Let me take away all the weapons at the camp. (*Exits.*)

Barbarian Soldier: (*Off stage.*) I report to my lord—the Yang army has entered our camp!

Barbarian King: (*Off stage.*) Bring my horse and pitchfork!

Barbarian Soldier: (*Off stage.*) The pitchfork was stolen by the princess.

Barbarian King: (*Off stage.*) Oh no! Bring my whip! (*He enters with his whip,*[16] *marches across the stage and exits. He then re-enters and fights with Yang Sifan and Liu Yong, who enter from the other side. He defeats Yang Sifan and Liu Yong and chases them off stage. Liu Qiulan and the Barbarian King enter from opposites of the stage and engage in combat. She stabs the Barbarian King, and they exit. Yang Sifan and Liu Yong enter from one side of the stage; Liu Qiulan enters from the opposite side.*)

Liu Qiulan: Are you my brother?

Liu Yong: Are you my good sister? Ah! I thought I'd never see you again!

Yang Sifan: Why are you weeping so hard? What's this about her being your sister?

Liu Yong: Don't ask right now. We'll tell you everything back at the camp. Get back on our horses. (*Sings.*)

16. This signifies that he is on horseback, as in Peking Opera. I did not see any puppets of horses in the marionette theater of Heyang.

Ever since that year when we siblings lost each other at the cemetery,
We can finally rejoice being reunited on the battlefield this very day. (*They exit.*)
(*Four soldiers lead Xu Long on stage.*)

XU LONG: (*Sings.*)

The Yang father and son have exceptional military skills,
The father and son did not boast in vain.
I was really hoping that they'd be killed in battle,
But who would have expected them to attain great merit instead?

(*Speaks.*) Because I arrived late with provisions, the old one wanted to have me executed. Fortunately, I was saved by his son, Sifan. The way I figure it, I'd better return to the court secretly. I'll see my father and concoct something to implicate the old one. Colonels! Let's return to the court! (*Sings.*)

I will now go to the capital in secret,
To see my father and concoct a scheme. (*They exit.*)
(*Four extras lead Yang Bo on stage.*)

YANG BO: (*Sings.*)

We father and son pacified River Yang, our power and fame are illustrious,
Achieving great merit, we relied much on Qiulan of the Liu clan.

SOLDIER: (*Enters.*) I report—the grain provisions officer has escaped!
YANG BO: The villain is returning to the court in secret. When he sees his father, he will invariably make me look bad. Soldier! (*A soldier responds.*) Tell your Fourth Young Lord to return to the court secretly to report the victory to the Emperor and preserve the lives of our family. Leave immediately!
SOLDIER: Yes, sir! (*He exits.*)
YANG BO: (*Sings.*)

The villain Xu Long's escape to Beijing will cause a great calamity,

I only fear that the lives of my entire clan will be in jeopardy.
I've ordered Sifan to return to the court and have an audience with the Emperor,
To announce the victory as well as to protect the safety of the entire family. (*They exit.*)

Scene 3: "Mistaken Beating"

(*The soul of Guan Yu leads the souls of Guan Ping and Zhou Cang on stage.*)
Soul of Guan Yu: (*Sings.*)

We brothers swore an oath at the peach orchard that we will endure disasters together,
Killing a white horse and slaughtering a black ox, we made a great sacrifice to Heaven.
Eldest Brother entrusted his son at the White Emperor City 白帝城 and then left the world,
Third Brother, as the Prince of Langzhong 阆中王, also died and returned to Heaven.
Fourth Brother, reincarnated as Xu Feng, can really do combat and fight,
Later on, he will be shot by myriad arrows and die a pitiful death.
I preside over Mount Jade Spring 玉泉山,[17] where I've been cultivating myself long and hard,
For the sake of the Ming dynasty, I have frequently used my powers to help maintain peace and prosperity. (*Recites.*)
My thoughts remain with the three-way partition of the Han Empire,[18]
My intentions aim solely at the book of the *Spring and Autumn Annals*.[19]

---

17. This is the place where he reveals himself after his death in *Romance of the Three Kingdoms*.

18. Guan Yuan and his sworn brothers established the Kingdom of Shu during the Three Kingdoms Period (220–265) after the fall of the Later Han dynasty.

19. The *Spring and Autumn Annals* is a history of the Spring and Autumn Period (722–484 BCE) from the point of view of the state of Lu 鲁 that has been traditionally attributed to Confucius. Guan Yu is widely known as a fervid reader of this text.

(*Speaks.*) I am Guan of the imperial family of the Han dynasty 汉室汉. When we brothers swore allegiance to each other at the peach orchard, we promised that we would live and die together. Imperial Eldest Brother died at White Emperor City; Third Brother died at Langzhong. I became a god at Mount Jade Spring. Eldest Brother has been reincarnated as the Wanli Emperor. Third Brother has been reincarnated as Yang Sifan, and Fourth Brother has been reincarnated as Xu Feng. Eldest Brother is fated to reign for forty-eight years. I am going to descend to the mortal world for two purposes: one, to report my merits and request enfeoffment; two, to bring the souls of Third and Fourth Brother back to Heaven. Guan Ping, Zhou Chang! (*They respond.*) Bring me my steed, Rouge 胭脂! (*Sings.*)

My trusted steed, Rouge, flashes on the cloud that we're riding,
Guan Ping and Zhou Cang have to restrain its magnificent power. (*They exit.*)
(*Four eunuchs lead the Emperor on stage.*)

EMPEROR: (*Weeps.*) We, the Emperor, are scared to death! (*Sings.*)

We, the Wanli Emperor, leave the throne hall shivering in fear,
The sound of court boots behind our back is so very eerie.
It has always been said that evil spirits cannot appear before the real Son of Heaven,
Could it be that my state is about to collapse that ghosts/ghouls won't leave us?
Shivering and trembling, I now leave the throne hall,
Let Us, the Emperor, inquire of Minister Zhang about it.

EUNUCH: Zhang Jin has arrived for an audience.

ZHANG JIN: (*Enters.*) I, your minister, prostrate myself to Your Majesty. (*He kowtows.*)

EMPEROR: Aihai!

ZHANG JIN: Why is Your Majesty so shocked?

EMPEROR: How would you, our minister, have known? We went to our throne hall this morning and were leaving the palace at night, when all of a sudden we heard a loud clicking of boots behind us. Do you suppose the palace is haunted?

ZHANG JIN: Your Majesty is a real dragon and Son of Heaven. How can any evil spirit even get close to you? It's probably some minister who died wrongfully during the earlier part of the dynasty. Seeing that Your Majesty has ascended the throne at a young age and with such great virtues, he has probably come to ask for enfeoffment. If such a special ghost[20] should indeed arrive, Your Majesty must ask him what he wants and confer a title upon him.

Emperor: Our dear minister—what are you talking about? If a special ghost should arrive, we'd be so scared stiff, how would we be able to enfeoff him?

Zhang Jin: Don't you know that bravery wards off evil?

Emperor: My dear minister, can bravery really ward off evil?

Zhang Jin: Yes, of course.

Emperor: Really?

Zhang Jin: Really.

Emperor: You may leave now.

Zhang Jin: Yes, Your Majesty. (*He exits.*)

Emperor: Minister Zhang has just left. Let us be brave and turn around to take a look. It really has become nice and quiet. Bravery really does ward off evil. I can now return to my palace.

Guan Yu: (*Enters.*) Wait a minute, Eldest Brother!

Emperor: Oh no! Now he's here, here again! (*Sings.*)

Hearing noise, We, the Emperor, are so scared that our souls
scatter and disperse.
It's not far away, it's close by, it's right next to us.
Having no choice, we exert ourselves to be brave,
We will inquire of him what he wants.

(*Speaks.*) There's a loud clatter of boots behind us. Who is it?

Guan Yu: I am your Number Two Younger Brother Guan 二弟关.

Emperor: We, the Emperor, asked who he was. The special ghost answered that he was our Number Two Younger Brother Guan. We think to ourselves, Lord Guan was a man of the Later Han dynasty and the Three Kingdoms period. Could it be that we, the Emperor, are a reincarnation of Liu Bei 刘备? Let us ask him again. So you are my Number Two Younger Brother?

Guan Yu: Yes, you are the Eldest Brother.

Emperor: Where is our Third Younger Brother?

20. *Qigui* 奇鬼. This is not a common concept.

Guan Yu: The Third Younger Brother attained merit. You were so delighted that you just made him overseer of the imperial guards. He has gone to guard the main gate of the harem.

Emperor: Why are you here?

Guan Yu: My dear Eldest Brother: you are destined to reign for forty-eight years. I, your younger brother, have come here to protect you.

Emperor: We don't need you to protect us. From now on, don't surprise us again. We confer upon you the title of Demon-Subduing Great Emperor 伏魔大帝. Go assume your position immediately!

Guan Yu: Thank you very much, dear Eldest Brother. (*He exits.*)

Emperor: Our Second Younger Brother! He was our Second Younger Brother! This is truly funny! (*Sings.*)

> This incident really makes Us, the Emperor, laugh out loud,
> We, the Emperor, are in fact a reincarnation of Liu Xuande 刘玄德[21] in the Ming dynasty.
> Second Brother Guan in the Afterworld has been guarding our safety secretly,
> We entitled him the Demon-Subduing Great Emperor; he has gone to assume his post.
> According to him, our Third Brother Zhang pacified the North and was duly rewarded,
> We've awarded him the high position of overseer of the imperial guards.
> But since he is our brother, then this position would be too low for him,
> We'll have to raise his position tomorrow in order to show the closeness of our brotherhood.

(*Speaks.*) But just wait a minute! (*Sings.*)

> With this matter weighing on our heart, we find it hard to wait until tomorrow.
> We miss Third Brother so much that we truly cannot wait until tomorrow morning.

(*Speaks.*) Ah, we have it! (*Sings.*)

> We merely have to doff our dragon robe and imperial headgear (*he exits, gets changed and re-enters.*)

21. Xuande is Liu Bei's courtesy name.

Secretly, we'll go to the harem gate and take a good look at him.
We have seen the merit ledger but have not seen his face,
Tonight at the harem gate, we'll take a good look at him. (*He exits.*)

Yang Sifan: (*Enters and Sings.*)

We father and son recaptured River Yang, our fame spreads far and wide,
My father ordered me to return to the court to report our achievements.
Tonight for some reason I feel troubled and anxious,
I can neither sit nor stand, my eyes twitch and my body feels uneasy.

(*Speaks.*) I am Yang Sifan. My father and I achieved merit at River Yang. His Majesty was delighted and consequently made me overseer of the palace guards. I now guard the gate of the imperial harem. Tonight I feel troubled and anxious. Let me take my metal whips[22] and stroll around the gate. (*Sings.*)

My father who pacified River Yang is advanced in age,
Avenging a private grudge, the provisions officer escaped overnight. (*Exits.*)

Emperor: (*Enters.*) Third Younger Brother! Don't leave! (*He follows Yang Sifan and exits.*)
Yang Sifan: (*Enters and Sings.*)

Returning to the court, my lord has been most reasonable,
He made me overseer of the imperial guards, my position is high and mighty. (*He exits.*)

Emperor: (*Enters.*) Don't leave, Third Younger Brother! (*Exits.*)
Yang Sifan: (*Enters and Sings.*)

Tonight for some reason I feel ever so anxious,
Holding my metal whips, I will stroll around the gate of the harem. (*He travels around the stage once.*)

Emperor: (*Enters.*) Third Younger Brother! Third Younger Brother!

22. Literally, iron whip. The *tiebian* 铁鞭 is in fact a military weapon. Warriors frequently used a pair of them.

YANG SIFAN: Stop! Who are you? Watch my metal whips! (*He strikes at the Emperor, who falls.*)
EMPEROR: (*Stopping him hurriedly.*) Don't strike, general! We are the Wanli Emperor.
YANG SIFAN: If you are my lord, then show me some proof.
EMPEROR: We have a golden plaque around our neck. Look!
YANG SIFAN: (*Examines the plaque.*) Aiya! Oh, no! (*He runs off stage.*)
EMPEROR: Aiya! Oh, no! (*He chases after him, exits, and re-enters.*) We were so scared! (*He exits.*)
YANG SIFAN: (*Enters and weeps.*) I'm scared to death! (*Sings.*)

I resent the fact that the Wanli Emperor is so young in age,
How can you treat that precious golden body of yours as lightly as a reed?
Please don't blame me, your minister, for being too stubborn and proud,
It was your own fault, being too young, that you made a mess of things.

(*Speaks rapidly.*) How would I have known? The Emperor visited the gate of the imperial harem on his own, incognito, and I hit him by mistake. When he ascends the throne tomorrow, who will guarantee the lives of my entire clan? But although the Wanli Emperor assumed his position at a tender age, he is a reasonable and intelligent emperor. If he should consider the facts that we, father and son, helped preserve the state and that we have been loyal and upright, he would invariably issue an edict of pardon and exonerate my entire clan from blame. (*Sings.*)

I will wait at my residence for the arrival of the pardon,
I only wish that the Emperor would pardon this minister of his. (*He exits.*)

EMPEROR: (*Enters.*) We, the Emperor, were scared to death! (*Sings.*)

Tonight we almost lost the three souls[23] of ours from fright,
If we hadn't shown the golden plaque, we wouldn't have escaped alive.

23. The Chinese believe that each person has a variety of different souls and that these scatter when one is scared, faints, or dies.

We don't blame him for hitting us and being overbearing,
It was in fact the fault of our youth that made us blunder.

(*Speaks.*) What do you know? When we went to the gate of the harem, we were kicked and fell flat on the ground and were beaten by someone before we saw that Third Brother of ours. We hurriedly showed our golden plaque and ran away without seeing his face. We have it! Come tomorrow, we will summon him to the imperial court so that we can examine him carefully. Aiya, oh no! The way we see it, if the one who hit us by mistake was General Yang Sifan, he would invariably commit suicide for what he did. What should we do? We have to issue an edict of pardon right away and absolve him of any blame. The watch drum has just struck the third watch.[24] Here's our writing brush. (*He writes.*) Palace Attendant! (*The head eunuch responds.*) This is a pardon. Send it to Xu Long of the Board of Revenue and Population and have it delivered to the Yang residence. There should be no delay! (*The head eunuch responds and exits; the Emperor Sings.*)

At the third watch, We, the Emperor, issue a pardon,
But We have to wait until dawn to see our Third Brother's face.
(*He exits.*)

Xu Long: (*Enters and Sings.*)

I resent what Yang Bo has done—he was too overbearing,
My neck almost suffered being sliced by a steel blade.
When his army advanced, he did not have the flag raised and cannon fired,
He then blamed me for not performing my military assignment and responsibilities.
(*He sits down.*) I am Xu Long of the Board of Revenue and Population.

Soldier: (*Enters.*) I report: His Highness the eunuch sent over a pardon to be delivered to the Yang residence.

Xu Long: Bring it over! (*The soldier hands him the edict and leaves.*) Let me take a look at it! So the Wanli Emperor visited the gate of the imperial harem incognito and was struck by Yang Sifan. His Majesty issued a

24. The third watch is midnight.

pardon and ordered me to deliver it to the Yang residence immediately. I should go right now. (*He thinks.*) Wait a minute! The way I see it, I was almost executed by his father when the provisions arrived slightly late. Now Yang Sifan hit the emperor by mistake. I should keep the pardon until he has committed suicide before delivering it. (*Sings.*)

This incident today happened quite timely,
I will not deliver the pardon until he is dead. (*He exits.*)

Scene 4: "Suicide"

YANG SIFAN: (*Enters and Sings.*)

Waiting in vain for the longest time for the arrival of the edict,
Unable to stand or sit, I am overtaken by anxiety.

(*Speaks.*) The sun travels so fast! (*Sings.*)

Very soon it will be afternoon, but the imperial edict is still not here,
Does he really intend for this minister to leave this earthly realm?

(*Speaks.*) I'll have to thank His Majesty for this imperial favor then![25] (*Sings.*)

Hurriedly I kneel to thank His Majesty for the imperial favor,
Unwittingly, my tears flow down in a torrent and splatter.
Don't blame this minister of yours for being too proud and overbearing,
Your young age is in fact responsible for the poor way you handled things.

(*Speaks.*) Oh my mom and dad, whom I'll never see again! (*Sings.*)

After showing gratitude for the imperial favor, I now call out to my two parents,
Your son won't be able to serve the two of you during your old age.

---

25. Even if he has been ordered to die, he is supposed to ritually thank the emperor for "the imperial favor" of granting him death.

Pacifying River Yang, my old father is already advanced in age,
How would you have known that your son has caused a great calamity that he won't be able to escape from?

(*Weeps.*) My wife, Madam Wang! Yang Baotong—oh, let me forget it all, son of mine! (*Sings.*)

Husband and wife, father and son are like birds in a forest,
When danger arrives, each makes its own escape.
Suddenly, I hear someone calling from mid-air,
I will cut off my own head and return to the Underworld. (*He commits suicide.*)

Guan Yu: (*Enters.*) Hello Third Younger Brother! (*The soul of Yang Sifan rises out of his body, which changes into Zhang Fei.*)
Yang Sifan's Soul: Hello, Second Elder Brother! (*They exit.*)
Warrior Servant: (*Enters.*) Why does my lord weep so tragically at this time? Aiya, oh no! Grand Dame, oh no!
Lady Yang: (*Enters.*) What happened?
Warrior Servant: My lord has committed suicide in the inner hall.
Lady Yang: Let me take a look! (*Sings.*)

The warrior servant made an announcement to me,
It certainly made old me terribly shocked.
Ordering the warrior servant to hold and support me,
I will go to the inner hall and take a close look at it. (*She tours the stage, sees the corpse and weeps.*)

(*Speaks.*) Yang Sifan—it's finished. Oh, dear son of mine! (*She faints.*)
Warrior Servant: Please wake up, grand dame!
Lady Yang: (*Sings.*)

Seeing the corpse, I was so shocked that my soul floated out of my body,
My son's body lies flat in the inner hall.
Forcing myself to wake up, I lift my head and look,
It is but the warrior servant guarding my son's corpse.

(*Weeps.*) Ah, Yang Sifan, the son this mother of yours will never see again! (*Sings.*)

You, father and son, were most fortunate in having pacified the region of River Yang,
Who told you to return to the court to report on the victory?
I don't know who it was that caused the death of my dear son,
Now that you are dead, how can your mother not be consumed in sorrow?

MADAM WANG: (*Enters.*) My lord, whom I'll never see again! (*The warrior servant exits; Madam Wang Sings.*)

I, Dame Wang, embrace the corpse and weep loudly in sorrow,
I weep that my lord died so bloodily and tragically.
No longer will you be able to advise me, your wife, as to how to serve your parents,
No longer will you be able to teach me, your wife, the *Classic of Filial Piety*.
No longer will you be able to admonish me concerning the ways of the world,
No longer will you be able to teach Baotong the intricacies of military skills.
Today you've become a headless ghost and lost your life under the blade,
Who will send off your parents to their grave when their time is up?

YANG BAOTONG: (*Enters.*) My old dad, who died a wrongful death! (*Sings.*)

Seeing my dead father, my liver and entrails burst,
Embracing his corpse, I can't help but weep until my voice reaches the Heavens.
No longer will you be able to instruct me, your child, to study hard,
No longer will you be able to teach me, your child, how to analyze military texts.
Having pacified River Yang, we don't know if grandfather will be met with fortune or misfortune,
How can you bear to abandon your family and entrust your life to the Yellow Springs?[26]

26. That is, the Underworld.

Warrior Servant: (*Enters.*) I report to My Lady—an edict of pardon has arrived.

Lady Yang: Bring it here! (*Sings.*)

Perusing the edict, I examine the time the edict was dispatched,
The Wanli Emperor was not clear about it when he issued the edict.
My son waited until after noon hour before he committed suicide,
Is it possible that someone dared to go against His Majesty's intention?

(*Speaks.*) Warrior Servant, who delivered the edict of pardon?

Warrior Servant: The President of the Board of Revenue and Population delivered it.

Lady Yang: Could it have been Xu Long of the Board of Revenue and Population?

Warrior Servant: Yes, it was precisely he.

Lady Yang: Oh, what a villain! (*Sings.*)

That villain Xu Long must have delayed the edict and disobeyed the Emperor,
Without a good reason, he caused my son to stain the yellow earth with his blood.
I yell for the warrior servant to prepare a horse outside our gate,
He and I will go to the court and ask the Emperor for justice.

Madam Wang: Mother-in-law, please don't do it! (*Sings.*)

Hurriedly, I lift up my damask skirt and kneel on both knees,
I ask my mother-in-law not to be angry and listen to me carefully.
You'll cause that villain, Xu Long, to shame and laugh at us,
When father-in-law returns, we'll report everything to him.
And make sure that we'll exact revenge from that villain Xu Long.

Lady Yang: My daughter-in-law has a point. You can all rise now. Warrior servant! Move your young lord's corpse to the White Tiger Hall and tell everyone in the residence to wear mourning clothes and attend the funeral. Move the corpse yourself. (*The warrior servant covers the corpse and exits with it.*) Aiya, my dear son Sifan! Don't blame His Majesty for your death; you were victimized by that villain Xu Long! (*Sings.*)

Thinking of the enemy, I weep until my throat is hoarse.

Madam Wang: (*Sings.*)

Suffering this calamity, it was just like rain battering wilted flowers.
In private, I yell and curse the treacherous villain,
If you should ever end up in my hands, I won't let you off lightly.

Baotong: (*Sings.*)

Whenever Xu Long is mentioned, my liver and bile burst in anger,
Someday I will take a treasured sword and destroy this enemy.
(*They exit.*)

Scene 5: "Weeping at the Funeral"

(*Four eunuchs lead the Emperor on stage.*)
Emperor: (*Sings.*)

Last night we visited the gate of the harem on our own,
There we met our Third Brother Zhang, who is now Sifan of the Yang family.
We don't blame him for transgressing the imperial rules in hitting us,
It was really due to our young age that we acted inappropriately.

(*Speaks.*) The general struck us with his metal whips by mistake. We immediately issued an edict of pardon. Why is it that he has not yet come to the imperial court to thank us? This makes us suspicious.

Xu Long: (*Enters and kowtows.*) Your Majesty, your minister is here with the edict.

Emperor: What edict did you bring?

Xu Long: Your Majesty dispatched your minister to deliver the edict of pardon. I was one step too late—the general had already committed suicide.

Emperor: We're so shocked. . . . (*He faints.*)
Xu Long: Wake up, Your Majesty!
Emperor: (*Sings.*)

Hearing of the bad news, We, the Emperor, were so shocked that our souls dispersed,
Shaking and shivering, our body fell upon the golden throne.
Slowly, we raise our head and examine with our eyes,
We see the eunuchs and Xu Long standing at our sides.

(*Weeps.*) Third Brother Zhang! Yang Sifan! Our Third Brother who died in vain! (*Sings.*)

We, the Wanli Emperor, weep incessantly in the Golden Throne Hall,
We cry for our Third Brother Zhang, Sifan of the Yang family.
We only regret that being young, we lack common sense,
At the gate of the harem, you struck us by mistake.
If we had known that you would end up dead,
We would have let you strike us ten times at the gate of the harem.
In the Golden Throne Hall, we cry until Heaven grieves and Earth is dark,
To meet again, it would have to be in the dreamland of Nanke 南柯.[27]

Xu Long: Since the general is already dead, weeping will do no good. What about the overseer of the imperial guards? Who should assume the position now?
Emperor: What would you suggest?
Xu Long: How about Cui Shou? He is loyal and honest. He can take over the position of overseer of the imperial guards.
Emperor: As you suggest—instruct Cui Shou to assume the post right away. After that, tell all the civil and military officials at the court to follow us to the Yang residence to attend his funeral! (*Sings.*)

27. According to "The Biography of the Prefect of Nanke 南柯太守传," a Tang dynasty story by Li Gongzuo 李公佐 (late 8th–early 9th century), the protagonist spent twenty years in the Kingdom of Nanke, a land inhabited by ants, only to wake and find it was all a dream.

We issued an edict for the palace attendants to bring our carriage,
We expect that no one will have any idea as to what's really on my mind.
We are only thinking of our deep love for the brother of the Peach Orchard,
The death of the general has created a grief that struck through our heart and liver.

ZHANG JIN: (*Enters.*) May I inquire as to where Your Majesty is going? (*He kneels and blocks the way.*)
EMPEROR: Our dear minister! (*Sings.*)

We, the Emperor, are taking the ministers to the Yang residence to offer a funerary sacrifice,
Only because, because that Yang Sifan died ever so pitifully.

ZHANG JIN: Ever since Pangu 盤古 separated Heaven and Earth[28] down to our own dynasty, there has only been the case of ministers offering sacrifices to deceased emperors. Who has ever heard of an emperor making a funerary offer to a minister?
EMPEROR: Our dear minister! (*Sings.*)

Only because he pacified the North and achieved astounding merit,
That we want to perform an imperial offering, don't say anything more.
We, the Emperor, will go even if none of you want to join us.

ZHANG JIN: I, your minister, am willing to go.
EMPEROR: If you are willing to go, then get up and go! (*Zhang Jin rises; the Emperor Sings.*)

With tears drenching our dragon robe, we weep and descend from the throne. (*They exit.*)

(*Enter Yang Baotong and Madam Wang.*)
MADAM WANG: (*Sings.*)

28. That is, the beginning of the world.

Suddenly I heard that the Wanli Emperor is coming to the funeral,
It makes me, Madam Wang, feel as if my heart has been pierced by an arrow.
I weep and cry out to my lord—you cared only about severing your own life,
Who will send our parents to their graves when their days are up?

Yang Baotong: (*Sings.*)

Hearing that the Wanli Emperor has come to make offerings at the funeral,
I, Baotong, weep and hurriedly prostrate myself before the coffin.

(*Zhang Jin, four eunuchs, and the head eunuch lead the Emperor onto the stage.*)
Emperor: (*Sings.*)

We, the Wanli Emperor, hurriedly descend from our dragon and phoenix carriage,
We raise our head and see the funerary paper banners hanging above the gate of the Yang residence.
Without announcing our arrival, we enter the courtyard of their residence. (*He enters the residence. Zhang Jin and the head eunuch follow him. The four eunuchs exit by walking backward off stage.*)

Madam Wang: (*Weeps.*) Ah, My Lord!
Emperor: (*Sings.*)

We see the lady and the son kneel before the coffin,
Seeing his spirit tablet, we can't help but feel even more grieved.
Embracing the spirit tablet, we weep until the sounds reach Heaven.

(*Speaks emotionally.*) We cry, we cry for our Third Younger Brother! We regret having visited the rear palace on our own. You, the general, didn't know and struck us with your whip by mistake. We issued an edict of pardon as soon as we returned to our palace. But who could have known that it arrived one step too late and you'd already committed suicide. How this fills us, your Elder Brother, with remorse! Palace Attendant!
Head Eunuch: Your slave is here.

Emperor: Set out the offerings. Let us perform the sacrificial rites.

Zhang Jin: Ever since Pangu separated Heaven and Earth, we've only heard of ministers making offerings at the funerals of deceased emperors, but never of emperors making offerings to ministers. Shall I, your minister, make the offering on behalf of Your Majesty?

Emperor: (*Weeps.*) My dear minister makes sense. So you will perform the sacrifice on our behalf. (*The Head Eunuch sets out the offering. Zhang Jin kneels on behalf of the Emperor. Then the two of them stand sideways facing each other on opposite sides of the stage. The Emperor sings.*)

Remembering how in the past we brothers were born during the Later Han dynasty,
Killing a white horse and slaughtering a black ox, we made a great sacrifice to Heaven.
We defeated the Yellow Turbans, and captured Zhang Jiao 张角 and his mighty army of one million,[29]
At the Pass of Tiger Prison 虎牢关, our three forces took turns fighting Fengxian 奉先.[30]
Who would have thought that we'd be reborn into this present dynasty of the Ming?
We, the Elder Brother, have become its emperor; with the younger brother guarding our gate, we felt uncomfortable.
Our true intention was to bestow upon you a higher title, but we created a calamity instead,
We made a mistake and forced your untimely departure from the world of men.
Seeing this hall filled with glittering funerary paper banners,
We, the Emperor, cannot help but weep and blame the blue Heaven.
Remembering how in the past we brothers swore that we would share all disasters,
But now the rest are all dead, leaving us to live vainly in this mortal world.

29. Zhang Jiao is the patriarch of a Taoist sect known as the Yellow Turbans, who raised a major rebellion during the end of the Later Han dynasty.

30. This refers to an episode in chapter 5 of *Romance of the Three Kingdoms* in which Liu Bei, Guan Yu, and Zhang Fei fight the formidable general, Lü Bu 吕布 (courtesy name Fengxian).

Zhang Jin: His Majesty is going crazy—he's thinking of the Later Han dynasty and the Three Kingdoms Period.

Emperor: (*Sings.*)

We, the Wanli Emperor, weep until Heaven is in sorrow and the
Earth is full of grief,
We don't expect others to know of the complexities of this
secret.
At Yang Bridge 阳桥, you forced a retreat on Cao Cao's 曹操
army of a million,[31]
Traveling across Bazhou 巴州 at night, you released Yan Yan 严
颜.[32]
Back then, you were so glorious that you were admired by all,
At present, we relied on your heroic abilities to subdue the
Western barbarians.
Until now, you've been helping your elder brother preserve the
longevity of our state,
Defending the region of River Yang and killing the barbarians,
your fame spread far and wide.
We regret having visited you at the gate of the rear palace,
This mistake of ours forced you to go to the Yellow Springs
untimely.

Yang Sifan's Soul: (*Enters and Sings.*)

Hualala, a gust of black wind blows through the inner hall,
I call for my Elder Brother—please listen to me carefully.
This event was preordained by fate, I was destined to die,
I implore all of you that you stop weeping and shedding tears.

---

31. In chapter 42 of *Romance of the Three Kingdoms,* Zhao Yun 赵雲 rescued Liu Bei's son at the Slope of Changban 长板坡 while being chased by the forces of their enemy, Cao Cao 曹操. Zhang Fei met them at the Changban Bridge 长坂桥, also known as the Dangyang Bridge 当阳桥 (shortened as the Yang Bridge in this play). Sitting on his horse on the bridge, Zhang Fei gave three such fearful, thunderous roars that Cao's army was scared away.

32. In chapter 63 of *Romance of the Three Kingdoms*, Zhang Fei led an army into Bazhou, where he captured its defending general, Yan Yan. Zhang's personally releasing Yan's bonds and going so far as to kneel before Yan was instrumental in getting Yan to not only turn over the armies under his control, but also to himself decide to fight for Liu Bei.

MADAM WANG: (*Sings.*)

I, Madam Wang, raise my voice and inquire into the air,
I ask, My Lord, why you don't show yourself to us?
Members of the family can at least meet and shed our tears,
How could you bear to leave your parents? How could you be so cruel?

YANG BAOTONG: (*Weeps.*) My dear old dad! (*Sings.*)

I, Yang Baotong, watch the auspicious cloud[33] and can't stop weeping,
I ask you, my dear old dad, why are you are standing there on the cloud?
Only mindful of yourself, you have entered the realm of the deceased,
Did you care how your child would now grow to adulthood?

EMPEROR: (*Speaks.*) We cry, we cry for our Third Younger Brother! Now that your spirit is here, why don't you come down and join us, so that we can meet? Why do you stay on the cloud? We miss you so much we could die!

ZHANG JIN: See how the funerary banners flutter. I think the general's spirit must be here. Why doesn't Your Majesty confer a title upon him?

EMPEROR: (*Weeps.*) Dear Minister Zhang, there's no need for you to say another word. We fully understand. Ah, our Third Younger Brother, who died in vain! (*Sings.*)

Unwittingly, we cannot help but first shed rueful tears,
An unintentional mistake on our part forced you to die—this is the absolute truth.
Here we see a gust of black wind filling the entire hall,
So it is the wronged ghost of our Third Younger Brother Zhang.
Now you hear how we, the Emperor, voice our sorrow and regret,
We, the Emperor, will bestow upon you the title of Messenger God. (*Yang Sifan's spirit exits.*)

ZHANG JIN: The general's spirit has left. Your Majesty, please return to the palace.

---

33. They know that Yang Sifan's spirit is on the cloud.

Emperor: Prepare the carriage to return to the palace. (*Sings.*)

Tear drops drench the dragon robe, our grief is excessive,
Weeping out loud, We, the Emperor, leave the Yang residence.

(*Zhang Jin and the Head Eunuch lead the Emperor out of the residence. Four eunuchs enter.*)
Yang Baotong: We bid farewell to His Majesty!
Emperor: (*Weeps.*) Poor young man! (*Sings.*)

Seeing Baotong, tears flow from our eyes once again,
We pity you for losing your father at such a tender age.
When you see us in the future, do not call us Your Majesty anymore,
From now on, just call us your Imperial Uncle.
So long as you grow to adulthood and serve us loyally,
We will also make you overseer of the palace and have you guard our gates. (*Exits with his entourage.*)

Madam Wang: (*Sings.*)

I don't believe a word of what His Majesty has said,
We will see if any of it will materialize in the future.

Yang Baotong: (*Sings.*)

I should have asked the Son of Heaven for further details,
But I was afraid that I might make him angry instead. (*They exit.*)

Scene 6: "Punishing the Villain"

(*Four soldiers enter with Cui Shou.*)
Cui Shou: (*Recites.*)

I have an imperial edict, I must not be remiss,
As the new overseer of the imperial guards, I now assume my post.

Soldier: I report—we have arrived at the Yang residence.

Cui Shou: There is no need to announce me. Just take the palanquin straight to the main hall.

Soldier: There's a sacred area within the Yang residence where civilian officials have to descend from their palanquins, and military officers have to dismount. Even the Emperor himself had to walk a few steps when he entered the residence.

Cui Shou: We will comply with the rule temporarily then. Lower the palanquin. Order someone to go in and announce that Lord Cui has arrived to assume his new post. Tell them to vacate the residence!

Soldier: Yes, sir. (*Calls toward the gate*) Who's here?

Household Warrior: (*Enters and comes out of the gate.*) What do you want?

Soldier: Lord Cui has come to assume his post. He wants your family to vacate the residence immediately.[34]

Household Warrior: Stay here. I will report to the Young Lord—Cui Shou has come to assume his post. He wants us to vacate the residence immediately.

Yang Baotong: (*Enters.*) Household Warrior, tell him that my father just died and I am still in mourning. We'll vacate the residence in three years after I'm done with the mourning.

Household Warrior: (*Comes out of the gate.*) My Young Lord said that he is still in mourning. We'll vacate after he's done mourning in three years.

Cui Shou: This is rubbish! One of my terms lasts three years! Who will be drawing the salary? I'm going to yell and curse if you don't vacate.

Household Warrior: Stay here. (*He enters the residence.*) Cui Shou is yelling and cursing at the gate.

Yang Baotong: Take me to him. (*He exits the residence with the Household Warrior.*)

Soldier: My Lord, Yang Baotong is here.

Cui Shou: Let me take a look. So you are Yang Baotong. I, your lord, have come to assume my post. Why do you refuse to vacate the residence?

Yang Baotong: Can't you see that my father just died and I'm in mourning? We'll vacate in three years after my mourning.

Cui Shou: This is simply ridiculous. I'm not going to wait even three hours,[35] let alone three years! Even your grandpa Yang Bo would have had to vacate for me!

---

34. While this creates drama it is rather absurd. Cui is acting as if the Yangs are living in the yamen of Yang Sifan's official posting.

35. The original is actually three *shichen* 時辰, each *shichen* being two hours.

Yang Baotong: What a villain! (*Sings.*)

Hearing him, I'm so angered that a terrible flame rises within me,
I curse at the villain, Cui Shou—you are truly raving mad.
You are by nature a jackal and wolf, belonging to packs of foxes and dogs,
How dare you have the gall to rebel at the gate of the Yang residence?
Our two families must have been enemies from a previous incarnation,
In an instant, we'll beat you up and send you to the King of the Underworld.

(Speaks.) Household Warrior! Give him a good beating! (*Yang Baotong and the Household Warrior beat Cui Shou, who exits with the four soldiers.*)

Madam Wang: (*Enters.*) How come the wretch hasn't come back yet![36] (*Yang Baotong runs across the stage, chasing Cui Shou. They exit.*) Oh no! (*She chases after them and exits. Yang Baotong enters, chasing after Cui Shou. He beats Cui Shou, who exits. Madam Wang enters and beats Yang Baotong.*) What a wretch! (*Speaks emotionally.*) I yell, I yell: Baotong—senseless wretch! Your father just died, you're still in mourning, yet you'd go around picking fights. Don't you care if others laugh at you? What am I going to do with you, you wretch!

Yang Baotong: (*Speaks emotionally.*) I yell, I yell: "Mother." Did you know that Cui Shou had arrived to assume this post and wanted us to vacate the residence immediately? Your child went out and tried to negotiate with him with reasonable words, but he brought up my grandfather's name and cursed at him. Don't you think your child should beat him up? (*Sings.*)

I implore my mother not to be angry with me; please listen to the details,
The villain, Cui, is truly exceptionally treacherous and evil.
Cursing my grandfather's name, his language was most excessive,
Calling him a commoner, each sentence was unbearable to your child.
I ask my mother, why don't you consider it yourself?
Who wouldn't agree that we of the Yang family are good and loyal?

Madam Wang: (*Weeps.*) My Lord, who died too early! (*Sings.*)

36. The term his mother uses here to refer to him is *nucai* 奴才, literally, "slave," to show her displeasure with him.

Hearing Baotong explain in detail as to what had transpired,
I can't help but turn away, so full of grief and sorrow.
I weep, My Lord, that you thought only of yourself when you died,
Pacifying River Yang, my old father-in-law has not yet returned.
When the villain, Cui, curses at our gate, who is there to stop him?
Yang Baotong is so young, who is there to make decisions?

(*Speaks.*) I say, my dear child! (*Sings.*)

I turn toward him and tell Baotong to listen to me carefully,
Don't you argue with others, not ever again!
Your father's death is a sky-falling calamity for us,
I will support my child with my own hand—do follow your mother, my child. (*They exit.*)

Scene 7: "Confiscating the Residence"

(*Four eunuchs lead the Emperor on stage.*)
EMPEROR: (*Sings.*)

We regret that we went to the rear palace gate to see him,

It was all because of our youth and lack of common sense.
One mistake forced him to die, his life ended prematurely,
It made Us, the Emperor, full of grief night and day.

XU ZAN: (*Enters.*) Your minister needs to memorialize to Your Majesty!

EMPEROR: Go ahead.

XU ZAN: Your Majesty ordered Cui Shou to assume his post, but he was beaten by Yang Baotong until his head was black and blue and his face was swollen. Please make a decision concerning it, Your Majesty.

EMPEROR: You must have been mistaken. If Cui Shou goes to assume the post, he must have brought a lot of men with him. How could the thirteen-year-old Yang Baotong beat him up? We find this incredible.

XU ZAN: If Your Majesty doesn't believe me, summon him to the court and see for yourself.

EMPEROR: Why don't you leave it? A minor incident like this—do you want us to confiscate the property of the Yang family for it? (*He waves with his sleeve, and the four eunuchs lead him off stage.*)

Xu Zan: I obey the edict! His Majesty has just issued an oral edict. Colonel! (*Four colonels respond and enter.*) Follow me to the Yang family to confiscate their property. (*They exit.*)

Zhang Jin: (Enters.) The villain is going to confiscate the Yang family's property. How can I notify the lady and her son? This . . . oh yes! I'll have to go to them via a shortcut. I'll have to inform the lady and her son immediately. (*Sings.*)

I hate the fact that the villain monopolizes power at the court,
He creates schemes and devises strategies to victimize the loyal and virtuous.
I shouldn't stay here for long,
I have to go inform the lady and her son of this news. (*He exits hurriedly.*)

Madam Wang: (*Enters and Sings.*)

My Lord died and returned to Heaven,
My father-in-law is at River Yang, not yet returned home.
The villain, Cui Shou, is truly too audacious,
How dare he yell and curse at the gate of our residence?

Yang Baotong: (*Enters and sings.*)

This overwhelming anger is truly hard for me to swallow,
Someday I will kill the villain and avenge this enmity.

Zhang Jin: (*Enters and recites.*)

In a great hurry, I rush like an arrow,
Only resenting that my steps are too slow. (*He enters the residence.*)

(*Speaks.*) My Lady and Young Gentleman! I've got bad news!

Yang Baotong: Uncle, what happened?

Zhang Jin: On account of your beating up Cui Shou, Xu Zan memorialized to the throne concerning it and received an oral edict to confiscate your residence.[37] (*Madam Wang faints.*)

37. Confiscating the properties here also implies executing members of the family.

YANG BAOTONG: Wake up, mother!
MADAM WANG: (*Sings.*)

Hearing this, I got so frightened that my soul floated away,
Tottering, my body fell down in the inner hall.
Slowly, I raise my head to take a careful look,
It's only Baotong here guarding his father's corpse.

(*Weeps.*) Ah, My Lord, who died too early! (*Sings.*)

Suddenly, a great calamity descends upon us from Heaven,
Weeping, I call to My Lord, who died too soon.
We of the Yang family have produced loyal generals for generations,
I inquire of Heaven why it hasn't taken any consideration of that.[38]

YANG BAOTONG: (*Sings.*)

My belly is as full of hatred as a mountain,
Should our two families ever meet, we're bound to fight.

ZHANG JIN: You might as well rebel!
YANG BAOTONG: My dear uncle! (*Sings.*)

If Heaven wants me to die,
Which direction should I hide?
If the Emperor wants to execute his minister, who dares to resist?
How can we jump over this wall of contentions?

ZHANG JIN: Escape to River Yang. Let your grandfather decide what to do.
YANG BAOTONG: Uncle, do you think we should rebel?[39]
ZHANG JIN: Yes.
YANG BAOTONG: Mother, what do you think?
MADAM WANG: Aiya, Baotong! Now that things have come to this, your mother can't control you anymore.

38. Heaven refers to the omniscient being that executes justice in the mortal world.

39. Here rebelling refers to refusal to submit to the imperial will (i.e., to be executed).

Zhang Jin: This means your mother wants you to rebel.
Yang Baotong: Household Warrior, what do you think?
Household Warrior: I say you should rebel!
Yang Baotong: I am going to rebel then! (*Sings.*)

Angrily, I give orders to the Household Warrior incessantly,
Open our armory and arrange the swords and spears.
Carry the Grand Dame on your back and mount the horse,
I will use my horse to protect my mother.

Zhang Jin: My dear Young Gentleman! (*Sings.*)

You and your family must escape without any delay,
The soldiers of the villains are coming to your residence.
When you see your grandfather in River Yang region,
Tell him to dispatch an army to avenge yourselves.

(*Yang Baotong exits with Madam Wang, followed by the Household Warrior.*)
Zhang Jin: My dear Young Gentleman, you have to escape right away! Now that I've allowed them to escape, I'd better run back home. (*Yelling and clamoring are heard off stage.*) Oh no! I suddenly hear the clamor of people and horses—the villain's army has already arrived. What shall I do? Oh yes, I heard that the Yang family has a fifteen-acre[40] garden. Why don't I hide in the garden? (*He exits.*)
(*Four colonels lead Xu Zan on stage.*)
Colonel: I report—we have arrived at the gate of the Yang residence.
Xu Zan: Go in, lock everything, and tie everyone up. (*They enter.*)
Colonel: There's no one here.
Xu Zan: Who leaked the news? The Yang family has a fifteen-acre garden. They must have escaped to the garden. Colonel! Search the garden. (*They exit.*)
Zhang Jin: (*Enters.*) Here is the garden. What a large place. Here's a chair. Why don't I sit down and take a short rest before I return home? (*Yelling and clamoring are heard off stage.*) I suddenly hear people yelling. The villain is coming to the garden. Where shall I hide? I see a tablecloth around the table. Let me hide under the table. (*He goes under the table.*)
(*Xu Zan enters with four colonels.*)
Colonel: I report—we've arrived at the garden.

40. This is a one hundred *mou* 亩 garden. Each acre is 6.6 *mou*.

XU ZAN: Search the flower pavilion. (*They search.*)

COLONEL: I don't see anyone from the Yang family, but I found Lord Zhang shivering under a table.

XU ZAN: Get out of my way. Let me take a look. I hear a humming noise under the table? What is it?

ZHANG JIN: It's just I.

XU ZAN: Who are you?

ZHANG JIN: I am just myself.

XU ZAN: Why are you hiding in there?

ZHANG JIN: There's no wind down here. I'm hiding from the wind.

XU ZAN: Come out!

ZHANG JIN: What's so good about the outside? All right, I'll come out. (*He emerges from under the table.*)

XU ZAN: I was wondering who it was. So it is you, Your Excellency Zhang!

ZHANG JIN: I am a first-degree minister at the court—how dare you address me as merely "Your Excellency"!

XU ZAN: So it is Grand Minister Zhang.

ZHANG JIN: I am clearly the Prime Minister. Who dares to say otherwise?

XU ZAN: What a treacherous villain! I received an edict to confiscate the family residence—why did you let them all escape?

ZHANG JIN: (*Aside.*) He is the treacherous villain! (*To Xu Zan.*) You came to confiscate the Yang family's residence—I think you are really the treacherous villain!

XU ZAN: Yes, yes, yes! So I am a treacherous villain. What a lowborn creature you are! Showing your teeth and claws in the garden—do you intend to beat me up as well?

ZHANG JIN: What are you talking about? You are an imperial official of the Board of Civil Service, and I am merely a small prime minister. You scare me to death. How dare I?

XU ZAN: I didn't think you'd dare. Come, touch me!

ZHANG JIN: What a treacherous villain. (*He hits him. Xu Zan runs off stage.*) Leave! (*The four colonels exit.*) Now that the villain has left, I'd better run home. (*He exits.*)

(*The four colonels and Xu Zan run on stage helplessly.*)

XU ZAN: I went to confiscate the Yang residence, but I met that lowborn Zhang Jin, who gave me a good beating. I would like to memorialize to the throne concerning the incident. But confiscating the Yang's residence was my own idea, I should just say . . . oh, yes, I've got an idea. Let me return home and issue a false edict ordering Yang Bo's family to guard the borderland in perpetuity, never to return to court. Colonels! (*The colonels respond.*) We'll all return to my residence. (*They exit.*)

Scene 8: "Ridding the Villain"

(*Four extras, Yang Baotong, and the Household Warrior lead Yang Bo on stage.*)
Yang Bo: (*Sings.*)

> Hearing that my son has lost his life,
> I feel as if a steel knife has stabbed at my heart.
> The whole family has escaped here to the region of River Yang,
> I preside over my yamen to execute my enemies. (*He sits in his military tent.*)

(*Speaks.*) Baotong, do you know who killed your father?
Yang Baotong: Of course I do. Household Warrior, summon Xu Jiao!
Household Warrior: Summon Xu Jiao!
Xu Jiao: (*Enters and kneels.*) Xu Jiao here to serve the commanding general.
Yang Bo: Baotong! Do you happen to know this person?
Yang Baotong: Let me see. Are you Xu Jiao?
Xu Jiao: Yes, I am.
Yang Baotong: Kneel over here. What a villain! (*He kills Xu Jiao.*)
Yang Bo: Drag him away! (*The Household Warrior drags Xu Jiao's corpse off stage and re-enters.*)
Household Warrior: I report—an imperial edict has arrived.
Yang Bo: Let's all go out to receive it. (*He and Yang Baotong exit and re-enter with the imperial messenger. Everyone but the latter kneel.*)
Everyone: Please open the edict, Your Excellency.
Edict Messenger: I open the edict. The imperial edict says, "Although Yang Sifan should have been executed for hitting us, the Emperor, we exonerated him on account of Yang Bo's loyalty and uprightness in preserving our state. We now order Yang Bo to guard the border, never to return to the court.[41] End of the Edict." (*Everyone rises.*) Accept the edict.
Yang Baotong: Edict messenger, where are you from?
Edict Messenger: I'm from the Xu residence.
Yang Baotong: What a villain! (*He kills the Edict Messenger.*)
Yang Bo: Baotong, why did you kill the edict messenger?
Yang Baotong: Grandfather, that was a false edict.
Yang Bo: How do you know?
Yang Baotong: The imperial edict should have been dispatched by either the Military Board or the Penal Board, never the Board of Revenue and Population.

---

41. This is tantamount to being exiled.

YANG BO: You have a point. Drag the body out of here. (*The Household Warrior drags the corpse out.*) Baotong: listen to my order! You will lead the vanguard, Liu Yong will lead the rearguard, Qiulan will be in charge of transporting the provisions. We'll go avenge your daddy's death! (*They exit.*)

XU ZAN: (*Enters and recites.*)

The crows clamor under the eaves,[42]
I, an old man, am filled with anxiety. (*He sits down.*)

SOLDIER: (*Enters.*) I report—Yang Bo has arrived with a great army.

XU ZAN: Oh no! Let me take a brush. (*He writes on a plaque.*) Come here! This is a short letter. Travel both night and day to Nanjing 南京 and ask your Third Young Lord to bring his army. (*He exits.*)

SOLDIER: I've got the letter. (*He exits.*)

(*Four extras and the Household Warrior lead Yang Bo on stage.*)

YANG BO: (*Sings.*)

We amassed our army from the region of River Yang,
We intend to avenge the wrong suffered by my son.
Just as I, the commanding general, am taking off with the army,
Suddenly I see the Household Warrior arrive to make a report.

HOUSEHOLD WARRIOR: I report—we have arrived outside the region of River Yang.

YANG BO: Go to the pass and declare war. (*He exits with his men.*)

HOUSEHOLD WARRIOR: Yes. (*Yells toward the pass.*) Come out and fight!

(*Four soldiers enter with Cui Shou.*)

SOLDIER: My Lord,[43] they are picking a fight out there!

CUI SHOU: Bring me my war mallets and horse! (*He mounts and rides to the outside of the city, and meets Yang Bo leading Liu Yong and four extras entering.*) I have arrived outside the city. Are you Yang Bo on the horse?

YANG BO: The warrior who approaches—please announce your name!

CUI SHOU: I am your lord, Cui Shou.

YANG BO: (*Toward Liu Yong.*) General, why don't you kill him!

LIU YONG: What a villain! (*He kills Cui Shou.*[44] *The four soldiers run off stage.*)

42. Crows' caws were thought to be inauspicious.

43. The title used here is *junma* 郡马, which means husband of a princess.

44. This would entail much fighting between the two, accompanied by drums and gongs, before one of them is killed.

Household Warrior: (*Enters.*) Cui Shou has fallen from his horse. Xu Feng has just arrived with a large army from Nanjing.

Yang Bo: Surround them—do not let them enter the city. (*They exit. Liu Qiulan fights Xu Feng. She is defeated and chased off stage by him. Yang Baotong and Liu Qiulan enter.*)

Yang Baotong: What good killing! What a good fight! Xu Feng is a skilled warrior! Our army can't win—I'm so mad!

Liu Qiulan: Don't be frustrated, general! When Xu Feng comes here again, you can fight him and I'll secretly shoot him with an arrow. We'll win for sure.

Yang Baotong: Xu Feng is famous for his skills as an archer. Aren't you taking a great risk?

Liu Qiulan: Skillful archers are never wary; the wary are never the skillful ones. When he comes here again, I'll shoot him.

Xu Feng: (*Off stage.*) Here I come! (*He enters and fights; Yang Baotong is defeated and exits.*)

Liu Qiulan: Watch my arrow! (*She shoots Xu Feng, who exits with an arrow on him.*[45] *Yang Baotong enters with a soldier.*)

Soldier: Xu Feng has been shot and escaped.

Yang Baotong: Surround the city and attack! (*The soldier responds and exits. Baotong sings.*)

Even if I have to die, I will avenge my father's death,
When will the injustice and enmity ever dissipate? (*He exits with Liu Qiulan.*)

Xu Zan: (*Enters and sings.*)

My son is fighting outside the city wall,
I, an old man, am filled with anxiety. (*He sits down.*)

Xu Long: (*Enters.*) Dad,[46] bad news!

Xu Zan: What happened?

Xu Long: Third Younger Brother is back at the camp—he's been shot.

Xu Zan: Hurry, hurry. Bring him in. (*Xu Feng enters and sits down dazed.*) Xu Feng! (*Aside.*) Now we're finished!

Xu Long: Now our cooking pot has been smashed![47] Xu Feng, wake up!

45. The shooter pretends to shoot, and the shootee suddenly reveals an arrow.

46. He calls his father *laozi* 老子, literally, the old one. The appellation is very informal but not as irreverent as the translation "old man" would suggest.

47. That is, they can no longer survive. The Chinese eat all foods cooked.

XU FENG: (*Sings.*)

In a daze, I am in the midst of fighting with the Yang army,
I wield my pear flower spears until my arms are sore.
I have to force myself to stay awake—I lift my head to look,
Oh, I'm actually sitting in front of my father and my brother.

(*Speaks emotionally.*) I cry, I cry for my daddy! I, your son, returned from Nanjing and was defeating the Yang army, when all of a sudden a woman with a steel prong stabbed me and I almost fell from my horse. When I was in the midst of fighting with Yang Baotong, the woman came up again and shot several arrows at me. Your child has been shot. Baotong has ordered a massive attack of the city from all sides. Daddy, what are we going to do?

XU ZAN: Aiya, my dear son! You're known as the miracle archer. Why didn't you guard against it?

XU FENG: (*Speaks emotionally.*) My muddle-headed old daddy! Don't you remember that although Yang Youji 养由基 was known for his archery,[48] he died from being shot by an arrow? The old general Huang Zhong 黄忠 of the Three Kingdoms period[49] also died from an arrow shot. It has been said that the skilled are not wary, the wary are not skilled. It seems that your child is fated to die this way. Ah, my dear daddy!

XU ZAN: (*Speaks emotionally.*) I ask of Heaven! I, Xu Zan, have never done anything immoral or evil—how can you allow my son to be shot? I could die from the sorrow!

XU FENG: Please sit down. Your child has been shot. Do you weep out of grief for me?

XU ZAN: You are my son. How can I not feel grief?

XU FENG: Well said! (*Speaks emotionally.*) Your child has been shot, and although we don't know if I'll live or die, you weep loudly out of grief for me. Do you remember how you and Elder Brother detained the edict of pardon? Oh, daddy! Did you ask Yang Bo if he was full of grief? Oh, my dear old daddy! (*Sings.*)

48. The characters for Yang Youji should be Yang Youji 养游基, who was a great archer of the state of Chu 楚 during the Spring and Autumn Period (722–484 BCE). He was known to have been able to hit the leaf of a poplar tree from the distance of a hundred paces.

49. Although aged, Huang Zhong was one of the mightiest generals under Liu Bei.

You, father and son, were not righteous in your dealings in the past,
If you disagree with me, just place your hand on your chest and think about it.
Detaining the edict of pardon, you jeopardized Sifan's life,
Could you say that old Yang Bo was not aggrieved?
You forced his whole family to escape to the River Yang region to protect their own lives,
That old Yang Bo surrounds Beijing out of pure anger.
You, father, ordered your child to advance from Nanjing with my army,
Heaven was displeased and caused your son to wear this arrow's feather on my neck.

(*Speaks emotionally.*) I cry, I cry out to my daddy! When your son was returning from Nanjing, I heard everyone say that the Yang family was loyal and that we, the Xus, were treacherous.

Xu Zan: How was the Yang family loyal? How were we treacherous?

Xu Feng: How can you even ask such a question?

Xu Zan: I want to be clear about it.

Xu Feng: (*Speaks emotionally.*) Don't you remember that when the Longqing Emperor died, his heir was very young? The treacherous villain Li Liang 李良 monopolized power at the court and intended to usurp the throne. You, as the leader of the civilian courtiers, urged all the civil and military ministers to put Li Liang on the throne.

Xu Zan: But . . .

Xu Feng: (*Speaks emotionally.*) What are you saying "But . . ." for? You were an old minister who had served through three reigns and an imperial official on the Board of Civil Service. But even these honors were not enough for you. Did you want to wear two official caps on your head at the same time? It was only by relying on the efforts of Xu Yanzhao 徐延昭, the Duke of Dingguo 定国公, and General Yang Bo that Li Liang was ousted and the young emperor got to ascend the throne. According to this, would you consider the father and son of the Yangs loyal or not? Would you consider our family treacherous or not? Oh, my dear old daddy! (*Sings.*)

When the Longqing Emperor died, his heir was young in age,
The villain Li Liang monopolized power and wanted to seize the throne.

Leading the civilian and military officials, father, you wanted to support the villain,
On account of that, the father and son of the Yang family raised arms against you.

(*Speaks emotionally.*) My dear Elder Brother! You and daddy detained the edict of pardon and caused Sifan to die. Yang Bo consequently brought his army to avenge his son's death. Our brother-in-law fought outside and fell from his horse. I, your younger brother, returned with an arrow in my neck. Now that Baotong has ordered an attack on the city from all sides, why don't you lead an army against him?

XU LONG: Oh, my dear Third Younger Brother! Surely you're fully aware of your brother's lack of military abilities!

XU FENG: You must be afraid of dying.

XU LONG: I'm but a chicken feather.

XU FENG: Oh, you villain! (*Weeps.*) You villain who has caused the calamity! (*Sings.*)

You, father and son, planned and schemed within the imperial court,
Detaining the edict of pardon, you caused the death of Yang Sifan.
Now that the army of the Yangs has arrived, why don't you go out and fight?
Could it be that you fear also having a knife or arrow in your neck?
In my ears, I suddenly hear the clamor of people yelling,
To where can our family now escape to find safety?

XU ZAN: Xu Long! Carry your brother and let us escape to the Jinshan Temple 金山寺. (*They exit.*)

YANG BAOTONG: Where did they escape to?

ZHANG JIN: Toward the Jinshan Temple.

YANG BAOTONG: Do you think we can catch up with them?

ZHANG JIN: Yes.

YANG BAOTONG: Household Warrior—chase after them. (*Household Warrior responds and exits. Baotong exits subsequently. Xu Zan enters. Household Warrior enters, captures Xu, and they exit.*)

(*Four extras lead Yang Bo and Yang Baotong on stage.*)

HOUSEHOLD WARRIOR: (*Enters.*) I have captured Xu Zan.

Yang Bo: Tie him up and take him into the capital city. (*They exit.*)
(*Four eunuchs lead the Emperor on stage.*)
Emperor: (*Recites.*)

Battles raged for days,
Today peace finally prevails.

(*He sits down. Yang Bo, Yang Baotong, Liu Yong, and Liu Qiulan enter. They kowtow to the emperor and then stand in a row.*)
(*Speaks.*) Ministers, listen to my conferment of titles!
Everyone: Your ministers are present! (*They all kneel.*)
Emperor: Yang Bo will receive the title of Duke of Yuelao 月老公[50]—you will never have to attend court again. Zhang Jin will be promoted three grades.[51] Baotong will inherit his father's post. Liu Yong will be commander of the army in the capital. Qiulan will marry Baotong and receive the title of Lady of Heroism 英烈夫人. You may rise! (*Everyone responds and rises.*) Summon the guards! (*Four colonels enter.*) Bring in Xu Zan.
Four Colonels: Yes, Your Majesty! (*They exit and return with Xu Zan.*)
Xu Zan: Please spare my life Your Majesty! (*He kowtows.*)
Emperor: What a treacherous villain! We should have executed you for causing the death of Sifan. In consideration of the fact that you served as minister under our imperial father, who had promised that you would never be executed, we will have your flower emblems plucked and your position removed. You can return to your native land and be a commoner. Your descendants will never be allowed to enter the court in the future. Guards, drive him out of the court! (*The four colonels take Xu Zan off stage.*) You ministers have exerted yourselves to preserve our realm. We have ordered a banquet for you at the Guanglu si 光禄寺 to celebrate. We will now return to the palace. (*They exit.*)

END OF PLAY

50. Yuelao sounds like a shortened version of *yuexia laoren* 月下老人, Old Man Under the Moon, a deity in charge of matchmaking. But here Yuelao is most likely the name of a region that is being given to Yang Bo.

51. This is an amazingly high raise in rank. It is also curious that, as prime minister, he does not already occupy the top rank.

Part III

Romance

The White Undershirt and *Pavilion of the Immortals in Exile* are romantic plays. They are also the most sophisticated in this collection of marionette plays in terms of their language and use of literary allusions. *The White Undershirt* is the only play in this collection whose provenance can be traced to a human-actor Ming *chuanqi* play (although the marionette version playwright did not seem to have possessed or seen a copy of the Ming play). *Pavilion of the Immortals in Exile* is a most unusual romantic play. Two beautiful and talented young ladies are allowed to choose their own mates through personally interviewing and administering examinations to eligible young scholars.

26. A maid (Wei Tiancai's puppet). Photo by Fan Pen Li Chen.

27. An old female (Wei Tiancai's puppet). This puppet can be used for Huangfu's mother. Photo by Fan Pen Li Chen.

28. Matchmaker (Wei Tiancai's puppet). Photo by Ingrid Chen.

29. An evil scholar (*jing* 净 role; Wei Tiancai's puppet). This puppet can be used for Han Shizhong. Photo by Ingrid Chen.

30. Official presiding over a court (Wei Tiancai's puppet). This puppet can be used for Li Ruoshui. Photo by Fan Pen Li Chen.

The White Undershirt 白汗衫

Introduction

Based on the Ming dynasty (1368–1644) *chuanqi* 传奇 play *Tale of the Hairpins and Bracelet* 钗钏记,[1] *The White Undershirt* is the only play in this collection that definitely derived from the human operatic tradition. This play, and the *Pavilion of the Immortals in Exile*, are the most sophisticated in terms of their language and use of literary allusions. Like the *Immortals in Exile*, it fulfills both female agency in marriage (i.e., the woman chooses her desired mate) and male fantasy (particularly of destitute scholars, that beautiful girls would choose them and even sacrifice themselves for them). Another typical motif found in this play is the near drowning of the protagonist, who is saved and adopted by a childless high official and his wife, and eventually reunites with her intended. However, this tale is more Confucian than most romantic plays. The protagonist insists on marrying a poor scholar (because of fidelity to a prior parental marriage agreement), rather than straying due to love for a talented young scholar. Because of this superior sense of loyalty and trustworthiness, she is excused for disobeying her parents' plan for her to marry an established, albeit older, official.

Aside from being a romantic story, this play is also a detective tale. Common to traditional Chinese detective stories, the interest lies not in finding out who did what (which is already known), but in the ingenuity with which the wise official, presiding over the court, discovers the truth

1. See Wang Yufeng, 1–163.

and brings about justice. Given its closeness to a *chuanqi* opera[2] and the choice of a romance emphasizing Confucian ideals, it was likely written by one of the many Confucian scholars in Heyang who participated in the development of local puppet plays. Despite its lack of originality (or the fact it was adapted from a *chuanqi* play), *The White Undershirt* is nevertheless a highly entertaining, ingenious play.

Cast of *The White Undershirt*[3]

HUANGFU YIN 黄甫荫: a young scholar
HUANGFU'S MOTHER 黄甫母: mother of Huangfu Yin
XIA SHIQING 夏士清: a young scholar; Huangfu Yin's friend
HAN SIZHONG 韩思忠: a young scholar played as the clown role; Huangfu Yin's friend
WEI GONGLIAN 魏公廉: a bearded gentleman
MATCHMAKER 媒婆
OFFICIAL ATTENDANT 司吏
HAN LI 韩立: Han Sizhong's father
SERVANT 人役
BOATMAN 艄公
SHI ZHI 史直: Emerald Peach's father
MADAM MEI 梅氏: Emerald Peach's mother; Shi Zhi's wife
EMERALD PEACH 碧桃: a young lady
CLOUD FRAGRANCE 云香: Emerald Peach's maid
LI RUOSHUI 李若水: a censor
ZHANG SHU 张恕: an elderly gentleman
LADY ZHANG 张夫人: Zhang Shu's wife
MADAM WEI 魏氏: Han Sizhong's mother; Han Li's wife
COLONEL 校尉

2. This puppet play is, by no means, an exact copy of the *chuanqi* opera (which is longer and slightly more literary). The marionette playwright is obviously very familiar with the opera's story, but does not possess a copy of *Chaichuan ji*. Even the names of the characters are written differently. For example, Huangfu Yin 黄甫荫 is 皇甫吟, Han Sizhong 韩思忠 is 韩时忠, and Xia Shiqing 夏士清 is Xia Shishai 夏时晒 in the *chuanqi* opera.

3. The script for this play is found in Shaanxisheng Wenhuaju, ed., *Heyang xianxi* in *Shaanxisheng chuantong jumu, xianxi*, 965–1001. The original play script belonged to the Chen'guang Marionette Troupe 晨光线戏社.

Scene 1: "Literary Gathering"

Huangfu Yin: (*Enters and recites.*)

> Having spent ten years under the cold window,[4]
> At night, I dream of a flower blooming on my brush.[5]

(*He sits down and speaks.*) I hail from the county of Zhizhou 直州. My family name is Huangfu, my personal name is Yin, and my style is Zhenzhou 真州. My father has passed away, leaving my mother at our home. Every day, I study at the local school. I just heard that a famous teacher is going to give a lecture at the neighboring village. I would like to attend the lecture and am going to discuss this with my mother. Dear mother, your child requests your presence!

Huangfu's Mother: (*Enters.*) Here I come! (*Recites.*)

> One ages of one's own accord, without being rushed by the sun and the moon,[6]
> Unconsciously, my once youthful head has turned completely white.

Huangfu Yin: Here you are, dear mother. Please take a seat.

Huangfu's Mother: What do you want to discuss with your mother at this hour?

Huangfu Yin: You wouldn't have known, dear mother. A famous teacher is going to give a lecture at the neighboring village. I, your child, would like to go to listen to it, and have asked you to come here, mother, to discuss this.

Huangfu's Mother: Lectures by famous teachers represent orthodoxy. Listen to your mother here in our grass hut. (*Sings.*)

> To cross the pool in the Confucian temple—who doesn't long for the dragon gate?[7]

---

4. "Spending time under the cold window" refers to studying.

5. This is an omen for success.

6. The sun and the moon refer to time.

7. *Youpanshui* 游泮水, crossing the pool in the Confucian temple, refers to attaining the first degree in the civil service examination system. The dragon gate refers to the imperial palace.

But it depends on your own willingness to work hard under the lamp and by the window of your study.
Seeing famous teachers and visiting fine friends, listen to their lectures intently,
Your learning has to be exceptional before you'll be able to accompany the emperor.

HUANGFU YIN: (*Sings.*)

I, your child, am diligent, although my learning is limited,
Living in the region of Zhizhou, it being but a tiny county.
Each day, I muster up all my efforts to attend school and listen to lectures;
Without resting during daytime, at night I emulate the scholar who bore a hole in the wall to borrow light.[8] (*Xia Shiqing and Han Sizhong enter together.*)

XIA SHIQING: (*Sings.*)

We brothers are all awaiting success and fame.

HAN SIZHONG: (*Sings.*)

You and I have come here on account of the literary gathering.

XIA SHIQING: I am Xia Shiqing.
HAN SIZHONG: I am Han Sizhong.
XIA SHIQING: After you, Elder Brother.[9] We brothers have come to invite Elder Brother Huangfu to go to a literary gathering. We have just arrived at the gate of his residence.
HAN SIZHONG: Let me knock at the door. Is Elder Brother Huangfu in?
HUANFU'S MOTHER: Oh, my son, someone's at the door. Let me go inside to avoid the visitor.[10] You can open the door and take a look. (*She exits.*)

---

8. Tradition has it that an aspiring student (who could not afford an oil lamp) "borrowed" light from his neighbor by boring a hole in the wall and studied at night using the light that shone through the hole.

9. They address each other as elder brothers out of courtesy.

10. Proper women were not supposed to be seen by unrelated men. "Inside" refers to an inner chamber, most likely her bedroom.

Huangfu Yin: Who's at the door? (*Opens the door.*) So it's my two Elder Brothers. Please come into my humble abode.

Xia and Han: We're entering Elder Brother Huangfu's home. Please accept our greeting!

Huangfu Yin: I return the greeting! Please sit down, Elder Brothers. May I inquire as to what I owe the pleasure of your visit?

Han Sizhong: Elder Brother Huangfu, we've come to invite you to attend a literary gathering at my home tomorrow.

Huangfu Yin: Sorry, but I can't attend the literary gathering. My family is so poor that I can't go anywhere very easily.

Han Sizhong: Aiya, how tragic! I, your Elder Brother, will present you with five taels[11] of silver for your family.

Huangfu Yin: I'm very grateful to Elder Brother Han for your generosity. I will come to your residence shortly.

Han Sizhong: Come early tomorrow. We now bid you farewell.

Xia Shiqing: (*Sings.*)

The Elder Brother is currently in a state of destitution.

Han Sizhong: (*Sings.*)

In the future, he will invariably reach the moon.[12]

Huangfu Yin: (*Sings.*)

Thank you, Elder Brother Han, for treating me with kindness.

Han Sizhong: (*Sings.*)

So that he would not end up being stuck in the mud. (*They exit.*)

Scene 2: "Reneging on the Marriage"

(*Shi Zhi and Madam Mei enter.*)

Shi Zhi: (*Sings.*)

11. A tael of silver is equivalent to an ounce of silver.

12. Literally, *shangong* 蟾宫, toad palace. This is a toad that supposedly lives on the moon.

Thinking of the way of the world, I nod to myself and lament its tragic nature;
Without descendants, what good is it to have fields and gardens aplenty?

MADAM MEI: (*Sings.*)

Our deeply cloistered sixteen-year-old daughter counts with her fingers and wonders,
As to when she will finally unite with her finely matched husband.

SHI ZHI: I, the old one, am Shi Zhi.
MADAM MEI: I, the old one, am Madam Mei.
SHI ZHI: We are residents of Zhizhou. We two old ones have no descendants, having only given birth to a daughter named Emerald Peach. We promised her as wife to Huangfu Yin in the past. But who would have expected him to become as poor as a pauper? I would like to consider reneging on the marriage arrangement. Dear wife, how do you feel about it?
MADAM MEI: Aiya, my dear squire! We have to discuss it with our daughter. (*Calls.*) Come here, Emerald Peach!
EMERALD PEACH: (*Enters.*) Here I am! (*Recites.*)

In pairs, mandarin ducks frolic in the pond,
Using colors, I paint a lone branch of plum flower.

(*Speaks.*) Venerable mother and father—I, your child, greet you!
MADAM MEI: There is no need for formalities.[13] Sit down.
EMERALD PEACH: May I ask what it is mom and dad wish to impart to your child?
MADAM MEI: Your father promised you to Huangfu Yin in the past, but he's now as poor as a pauper! Your father is considering reneging on the marriage and would like to discuss it with you.
EMERALD PEACH: Mom and dad, you've got to be joking!
SHI ZHI: Marriage is a serious event—why would we joke about it?

13. She either bows or kowtows at this point.

Emerald Peach: My dear muddle-headed parents! (*Sings.*)

Poverty is a very common situation, why blame him for it?
Since you've promised me to him, why renege on the marriage and seek another?

Shi Zhi: My dear child! (*Sings.*)

Huangfu Yin is as poor as a pauper and resides in a shabby lane,
He and you, my dear child, do not match in the way a phoenix and a luan-bird[14] should.

Madam Mei: (*Sings.*)

You are a proper young lady skilled in the art of embroidery;
In terms of scholarship, you are also superior to scholars and famous intellectuals.

Emerald Peach: (*Sings.*)

The words of my parents defy logic!
I, your child, have something to say; please listen to me.
Since you've already promised me to him in the past,
Why complain of his being poor right now?
Don't even think of persuading your child to marry another,
It would be tantamount to the sun rising in the west and the water flowing upstream. (*She exits.*)

Shi Zhi: Idiot child! (*Sings.*)

The silly child is stubborn and refuses to submit.

Madam Mei: (*Sings.*)

Pressing her hands against her chest, she understands the situation her own way.

---

14. Both the phoenix and luan-birds are exquisite, superior birds.

Scene 3: "Sending for a Matchmaker"

WEI GONGLIAN: (*Enters and sings.*)

Having admonished the emperor through a memorial, I have been sent into exile;
Having lost my high official position, I was to return to my native home to retire as a hermit.
But the imperial favor is magnanimous and I received a reprieve;
I will be a censor at Hongzhou 洪州; it's a token position without worries.

(*Speaks.*) I am an official surnamed Wei. My name is Xiang 象, and my style is Gonglian. I was a minister at the Song court and occupied the position of a censor. On account of presenting a memorial admonishing the emperor, I have been exiled to Hongzhou. My wife just passed away unexpectedly. I would like to take another wife. Yamen runner, bring a matchmaker here to see me.

YAMEN RUNNER: (*Enters.*) A matchmaker has arrived!

MATCHMAKER: (*Enters and recites.*)

Relying on my three-inch tongue,[15]
I manage to arrange good marriages.

(*Speaks.*) I, the matchmaker, kowtow to my lord.

WEI GONGLIAN: Rise.

MATCHMAKER: My lord, may I ask what you sent me here for?

WEI GONGLIAN: Matchmaker, I just arrived at my post at Hongzhou, and unexpectedly lost my wife. I'd like to take another wife. Is there someone available right now?

MATCHMAKER: There just happens to be one right now.

WEI GONGLIAN: Which family is it?

MATCHMAKER: There is a Shi Zhi in our city with a daughter by the name of Emerald Peach. She is so beautiful that, upon seeing her, birds will fall and fish will sink, the moon will disappear and flowers will be put to shame. Let me go and talk to him about the marriage. He'll agree to it for sure.

---

15. She makes up tales to get such a long tongue.

Wei Gonglian: If this is the case, go ahead and make the marriage proposal. A big reward awaits you if you succeed.
Matchmaker: I obey your command. (*She exits.*)
Wei Gonglian: (*Sings.*)

Dispatching the matchmaker to make the marriage proposal for me,
If she succeeds, the concern in my heart will be relieved. (*He exits.*)

Scene 4: "Accepting the Marriage Proposal"

(*Enter Shi Zhi and Madam Mei.*)
Shi Zhi: (*Sings.*)

Advanced in age but still high spirited and healthy,
I only regret that I do not have a filial son.

Madam Mei: (*Sings.*)

Our daughter of sixteen years of age is fully grown,
When will she get married and be paired like the mandarin ducks?

Major Domo: (*Enters.*) I report to the squire. A matchmaker requests to see you.
Shi Zhi: Tell her to come in.
Major Domo: Matchmaker, you're told to go in.
Matchmaker: (*Enters and recites.*)

Matchmaker, matchmaker, matches I make,
For gold and silver, for drinks and food, everything I take.

(*Speaks.*) I, the matchmaker, kowtow to the Squire.
Shi Zhi: Stand up. What do you wish to see me for?
Matchmaker: I've come here to arrange a match for the young lady.
Shi Zhi: Which family are you representing?
Matchmaker: I'm sent by Wei Gonglian, from west of the city. What do you think of his proposal?
Shi Zhi: Wife, how do you feel about our daughter marrying Wei Gonglian?
Madam Mei: I'm all right with it. But what if Huangfu Yin objects?

SHI ZHI: Huangfu Yin is as poor as a pauper. If he objects, we'll return the betrothal gift.

MATCHMAKER: Squire, why promise your daughter to another if you've already accepted a betrothal gift?

SHI ZHI: Ah, matchmaker! (*Sings.*)

Huangfu Yin is as poor as a pauper and lives in a shabby lane,
In no way is he a match for my child, like Liang Hong 梁鸿 or
Meng Guang 孟光.[16]
A thin weakling, he looks like a wreck,
How can a crow like him aspire to pair with a phoenix?

MATCHMAKER: Squire, there's no need to say anymore. I understand completely. (*Sings.*)

The beauty and the talent match each other perfectly.[17]

SHI ZHI: (*Sings.*)

All on account of the matchmaker's arrangements.

MADAM MEI: (*Sings.*)

Even if a cold wind is unable to move anything,

MATCHMAKER: (*Sings.*)

I can make the Weaving Girl[18] marry the Cowherd. (*They exit.*)

(*Enter Emerald Peach and Cloud Fragrance.*)

---

16. Liang Hong and Meng Guang were considered a perfect couple from the Later Han dynasty (25–220). The wife, Meng Guang, was so reverent toward her husband that she would lift the tray to the level of her eyebrows when serving food to her husband (*ju'an qimei* 举案齐眉).

17. The beauty here refers to Emerald Peach; the talent refers to the established intellectual, Wei Gonglian.

18. The Weaving Girl and the Cowherd are two celestial stars who fell in love with each other. When Jade Emperor, father of Weaving Girl, found out about their affair, he was so incensed that he banished them to opposite sides of the Milky Way. But once a year, on the seventh day of the Seventh Month, they are allowed to meet by crossing a bridge formed by flying magpies. Despite their plight, they symbolize perpetual conjugal love.

Emerald Peach: (*Sings.*)

Summer days are gone, the cold wind blows, moonlight shines through the gauzy window pane,
In my boudoir, it is truly hard for me to withstand the coldness of my damask quilt.
I watch the sojourning wild geese forming double rows at the edge of the sky,
And the mandarin ducks in the pond, sporting in pairs.

(*Speaks.*) Cloud Fragrance, my parents despise the poor and love the rich. They've promised me to another. What should I do?

Cloud Fragrance: Miss, it's *your* marriage—you have to do something about it.

Emerald Peach: Why don't you go to Huangfu Yin's home and tell him to proceed with the wedding right away?

Cloud Fragrance: Miss, the gentleman is as poor as a pauper. He won't be able to afford the wedding anyway.

Emerald Peach: If that's the case, why don't you go to his home and invite him to come to our garden the night of the fifteenth of the Eighth Month? I'll present him with some gold and silver so that he'll be able to proceed with the wedding.

Cloud Fragrance: I'll go there right now. (*She exits.*)

Emerald Peach: Yes, hurry! (*Sings.*)

The autumnal wind is always different from the spring eastern wind,
It blows when cassia flowers bloom and permeate their fragrance.
Hearing the clear pounding sounds of washer women beating on clothes,
The heart and entrails of this maiden are worried sick in her secluded boudoir. (*She exits.*)

Scene 5: "Arranging a Rendezvous"

Huangfu Yin's Mother: (*Enters and sings.*)

Although poor, my son is replete with ambitious aspirations,
I only hope that he will succeed in order to assist the imperial family.

Someday the thunder will clap during the spring, and the fish will transform into a dragon,[19]
At that juncture, I the old one, will be thrilled with utter delight.

CLOUD FRAGRANCE: (*Enters and sings.*)

One can't help but feel shy about a woman seeking a man about marital matters,
A girl fears people's laughter when we leave our house.
People say that he lives in the Qingong 芹宫 district,
But who knows how many families live in the Qingong district?

(*Speaks.*) I see an old lady sitting there. Let me go and ask her. Greetings, Madam!

HUANGFU'S MOTHER: Why do you bow to me, Miss?

CLOUD FRAGRANCE: Please madam, could you tell me where Mister Huangfu lives?

HUANGFU'S MOTHER: Huangfu is my son. Why do you ask?

CLOUD FRAGRANCE: So you are his venerable mother?[20]

HUANGFU'S MOTHER: Yes.

CLOUD FRAGRANCE: Can we go to your home? I have something to report to you.

HUANGFU'S MOTHER: All right, please go in.

CLOUD FRAGRANCE: Please accept my greetings again, Madam.

HUANGFU'S MOTHER: Don't stand on formalities, Miss. Please take a seat. Which family are you from?

CLOUD FRAGRANCE: Madam, you wouldn't have known me. I'm from the Shi family.

HUANGFU'S MOTHER: Why are you here?

CLOUD FRAGRANCE: Actually . . .

HUANGFU'S MOTHER: Actually what?

CLOUD FRAGRANCE: (*Sings.*)

---

19. The belief that carp (which sometimes leap up waterfalls) may transform into a dragon alludes to the mother's hope that her son will succeed in the examinations and become an official.

20. The term used here is *laoanren* 老安人.

My Miss sent me here with a private message,
I can't talk about it until I see the young gentleman.

Huangfu's Mother: My son is not at home. You can speak to me about it.

Cloud Fragrance: (*Sings.*)

You, mother and son, are obviously of the same mind,
But I'm bound by my Miss's bidding and hesitate to speak too openly.

Huangfu's Mother: Why do you hesitate?

Cloud Fragrance: Is there anyone else at your home?

Huangfu's Mother: Since my son isn't home, I'm the only one here. You can speak the truth.

Cloud Fragrance: (*Sings.*)

My Miss is now sixteen and fully grown,
The squire despises your poverty and has promised her to a Wei family.

Huangfu's Mother: I can die from anger! (*Sings.*)

Hearing this, my throat clogs from anger,
Unwittingly, my teeth chatter from fear.
Unsympathetic to our plight, In-Law Shi harbors an evil intention,
But I wonder which family your Miss would like to marry?

Cloud Fragrance: (*Sings.*)

My Miss is not at all afraid of living in destitution,
She does not at all desire to live the life of luxury enjoyed by Wei Gonglian.
According to her, ethical behavior has been of the utmost importance since antiquity,
When one follows one's destined fate, even poverty will likely lead to prosperity.

Huangfu's Mother: What a wise young lady! I'd die happy if I could just meet her once. But I'm afraid that a serious affair like marriage is not up to her.

Cloud Fragrance: You wouldn't have known, Madam, but my Miss has asked for the young gentleman to come to our garden to meet her on the night of the fifteenth of the Eighth Month. She'll give him some gold and silver so that he can arrange for the wedding.

Huangfu's Mother: If that's the case, I'll tell my son about it after he comes home.

Cloud Fragrance: (*Sings.*)

My Miss awaits me anxiously in her embroidery boudoir,
She won't be able to rest in peace until she sees me.

Huangfu's Mother: Let me make a cup of tea for you.

Cloud Fragrance: (*Sings.*)

A girl is afraid of being seen whenever she ventures beyond her own house,
I will have tea at your home another day.

Huangfu's Mother: Let me ask you—what is your name?

Cloud Fragrance: It is . . .

Huangfu's Mother: What?

Cloud Fragrance: (*Sings.*)

I feel so shy that I lower my head.

(*Speaks.*) My name is Cloud Fragrance Shi—please don't laugh at it.

Huangfu's Mother: What an elegant name. Let me see you off. (*Cloud Fragrance exits. Huangfu's mother sings.*)

How true is the saying that the slave of a wealthy home is like the maiden of a poor household,
She is not only intelligent and quick, but also well-behaved and proper.
After my son returns home from attending the lecture,
I will relate to him everything she has said to me, from the beginning to the end. (*She exits.*)

Scene 6: "Returning and Reporting"

Emerald Peach: (*Sings.*)

Silently, I feel lonely, chilly, and sad,
Confusingly, my wondering thoughts clutter like unsorted hemp.
Totally alone, I have no news of Cloud Fragrance,
It is already dusk, but she has not yet returned.

Cloud Fragrance: (*Enters and sings.*)

Wise and proper, my Miss refuses to marry another,
She had sent me to help her secretly.

Emerald Peach: Here's Cloud Fragrance. So you're back.
Cloud Fragrance: Yes, I'm back.
Emerald Peach: Did you see Mister Huangfu at his place?
Cloud Fragrance: You wouldn't have known, my dear Miss, but the gentleman wasn't at home. I told his elderly mother about it. His mother said (referring to you): what a wise and virtuous young lady; I'd die happy if I could meet her even once.
Emerald Peach: (*Sings.*)

Hearing the words, I can't help but shed tears like the rain,
Who is there to pity my hoary, aged mother-in-law?

Cloud Fragrance: My dear young Miss! (*Sings.*)

The way I see it, you are too good for them.

Emerald Peach: My dear Cloud Fragrance! (*Sings.*)

How would you know how badly I want this to work out?

Cloud Fragrance: It's too late. Let's go to bed.
Emerald Peach: My dear scholar![21] (*Sings.*)

I can't wait for you to come and build a bridge of magpies,[22]
To relieve my sorrow, you must have your name engraved in the wild goose pagoda.

21. She addresses him as *xiucai* 秀才, licentiate. I translate *xiucai* as "scholar" in this play because "licentiate" sounds too similar to "licentious."

22. See footnote 18.

On the drum tower, the drum beats the watches so rapidly,[23]
Hanging at the edge of the sky, the moonlight does not shine upon me. (*They exit.*)

Scene 7: "Taking Advantage of the Friend"

(*Enter Huangfu Yin and Han Sizhong.*)
HUANGFU YIN: (*Recites.*)

A hundred years travel as fast as a horse,

HAN SIZHONG: (*Recites.*)

A youth who does not study won't be able to in old age.

HUANGFU YIN: Ai . . .
HAN SIZHONG: Elder Brother Huangfu, you're here for a literary meeting at my home. Why are you so unhappy?
HUANGFU YIN: Elder Brother Han, you wouldn't have known. My father-in-law despises the poor and loves the rich. He has promised my wife to another. That's why I'm stricken by grief.
HAN SIZHONG: Elder Brother Huangfu. I think your father-in-law did it to hasten your arranging the wedding.
HUANGFU YIN: Elder Brother Han, you wouldn't have known. He has already promised his daughter to Wei Gonglian.
HAN SIZHONG: How can that be? Did he really promise her to Wei Gonglian?
HUANGFU YIN: Yes, he did.
HAN SIZHONG: Do you know how your wife feels about it?
HUANGFU YIN: My wife sent her maid to my home to tell me to meet her in their back garden the night of the fifteenth of the Eighth Month. She will present me with silver to arrange for the wedding.
HAN SIZHONG: What is her maid's name?
HUANGFU YIN: She's called Cloud Fragrance.
HAN SIZHONG: Who did Cloud Fragrance speak to?
HUANGFU YIN: She spoke to my mom.

23. The drum announces time.

Han Sizhong: Who told you about it? Do you know this Cloud Fragrance?

Huangfu Yin: No, I don't know her.

Han Sizhong: Have you ever met your wife?

Huangfu Yin: No, I've never met her either.

Han Sizhong: Ah? So you don't know either Cloud Fragrance or her Miss?

Huangfu Yin: I really don't know either of them.

Han Sizhong: If such is the case, let me think about it. (*He gestures thinking.*) Elder Brother Huangfu, the way I, your younger brother, see it—this is not a gesture of goodwill on the part of your wife. I'm truly afraid that this was a deceptive scheme.

Huangfu Yin: Why do you think that it was a scheme?

Han Sizhong: Elder Brother Huangfu, if your wife had meant well, she should have sent someone to give the silver to you during the day. Why did she ask you to go to her the night of the fifteenth of the Eighth Month to get it? It is commonly said that intruders at night are either thieves or rapists; one can kill them with impunity!

Huangfu Yin: Elder Brother Han, what enmity is there between her and me that she'd want to see me dead?

Han Sizhong: My Elder Brother Huangfu, don't you understand? He was afraid that you'd sue him because he promised his daughter to someone else, so he concocted this scheme to get you killed to protect himself.

Huangfu Yin: Thanks Elder Brother Han for clarifying the situation for your younger brother. When will I ever be able to avenge myself!

Han Sizhong: Concentrate on your studies right now. When you become successful and famous, then you can go after them and avenge yourself.

Huangfu Yin: I'm so mad! (*Sings.*)

Good thing Elder Brother Han clarified the situation for me,
I'm going to make sure that he will grieve from the failure of his scheme.
Thinking of Shi Zhi, I cannot help but be consumed with anger.

Han Sizhong: Elder Brother Huangfu, are you going there tonight or not?

Huangfu Yin: (*Sings.*)

Why would I be willing to enter the lion's den and bring catastrophe upon myself? (*He exits.*)

HAN SIZHONG: It is verily a case in which a poor man lacks common sense just as a thin horse has long hair. Since he is afraid of going to the garden tonight, I'll use his name and meet Emerald Peach there myself! (*Sings.*)

Emerald Peach is as beautiful as a painting,
I love her just from thinking about her.
Just to be able to exchange a few words with her in the garden,
Would have made it worthwhile for me to have lived under this
Heaven. (*He exits.*)

Scene 8: "Presenting the Hairpins and the Bracelet"

The moon is full, the flowers are blooming, the clouds are dispersing.

CLOUD FRAGRANCE: (*Enters and sings.*)

It looks just like a caltrop-flower mirror[24] hanging at the edge of the sky.

EMERALD PEACH: (*Sings.*)

I long for the meeting of the Cowherd and the Weaving Girl.[25]

CLOUD FRAGRANCE: (*Sings.*)

Chillingly, the full moon moves across the railings.

HAN SIZHONG: (*Enters and sings.*)

I walk along fearing that I might be seen,
The garden door is locked from the inside, from the inside.

(*Speaks.*) Please open the door, Miss! Please open the door, Cloud Fragrance!
EMERALD PEACH: (*Sings.*)

24. A mirror in the shape of a water-chestnut flower.

25. See footnote 18.

Suddenly, I hear someone calling softly at the garden door,
It is most likely the intended gentleman of the appointment.
I call for Cloud Fragrance to open the door and see who it is,
Ask him what his name is and who told him to come here.

Han Sizhong: Cloud Fragrance, please open the door!
Cloud Fragrance: Who's knocking at the door?
Han Sizhong: I'm Han . . .
Cloud Fragrance: Han what? Your name is Han what?
Han Sizhong: I'm the *han*-Confucian,[26] Huangfu Yin.
Cloud Fragrance: Who told you to come here?
Han Sizhong: Cloud Fragrance talked to my mother at my home yesterday. My mother told me to come here.
Cloud Fragrance: So the scholar is here. Let me open the door for you. The door is open; please come in.
Han Sizhong: Please accept my bow, dear Miss.
Cloud Fragrance: Are you blind? I'm not the Miss.[27]
Han Sizhong: Ai, I didn't look carefully. So you are Cloud Fragrance. Where is the Miss? Let's go see the Miss!
Cloud Fragrance: Follow me! Miss, the scholar is here.
Emerald Peach: So my scholar is here. Please sit down.
Han Sizhong: Thank you.
Emerald Peach: May I ask the scholar, why you are not marrying me although we are already engaged?
Han Sizhong: I'm too poor to arrange for the wedding. Do you think I don't want to marry you?
Emerald Peach: (*Sings.*)

I will ask the scholar not to stain his face with tears,
If you marry me early, I can take care of my aged mother-in-law.

Cloud Fragrance: (*Sings.*)

The chastity of my Miss is as enduring as the pines and firs during winter,
She is not at all like the whimsical willow trees of Zhangtai 章台.[28]

26. *Hanru* 寒儒 means poor Confucian.

27. He should have been able to tell from her hairdo, ornaments, and clothing.

28. The willows of Zhangtai refer to courtesans.

EMERALD PEACH: Cloud Fragrance, bring my hairpins and bracelet and the silver.

CLOUD FRAGRANCE: Miss, I leave you with the scholar. Conduct yourself with propriety. (*She exits.*)

HAN SIZHONG: (*Sings.*)

> I see that Cloud Fragrance has left to make it more convenient for us,
> I ask the Miss, please let's consummate our marriage right now.

EMERALD PEACH: (*Sings.*)

> I will tell the scholar that our wedding date is already within reach,
> We will then become husband and wife and share mandarin-duck pillows 'til a hundred years of age.

HAN SIZHONG: (*Sings.*)

> Ever since antiquity, only parentally approved marriages are legal,
> Why do you, my dear Miss, continue to resist?

EMERALD PEACH: Cloud Fragrance, come here immediately!

CLOUD FRAGRANCE: (*Enters and sings.*)

> I, Cloud Fragrance, hear the call and hurry like an arrow,
> In an instant, I've rushed from there to here.

HAN SIZHONG: Who told you to come?

CLOUD FRAGRANCE: Miss, here are the hairpins and bracelet and silver.

EMERALD PEACH: Give them to the scholar, and tell him to leave immediately.

CLOUD FRAGRANCE: Scholar, here are a pair of hairpins, a bracelet, and fifty taels of silver. Take them.

HAN SIZHONG: Bring them here. Let me thank the Miss personally.

EMERALD PEACH: It's all right. Cloud Fragrance, tell him to leave.

CLOUD FRAGRANCE: Scholar, my Miss wants you to leave.

HAN SIZHONG: I'm not ready to leave yet.

CLOUD FRAGRANCE: What do you want to do?

HAN SIZHONG: I have a few words I want to say to the Miss.

Cloud Fragrance: You can tell me. I'll tell them to her.

Han Sizhong: How thick can you be, Cloud Fragrance? How can I tell you my innermost feelings?

Cloud Fragrance: Leave! (*She closes the door and exits with Emerald Peach.*)

Han Sizhong: Cloud Fragrance, don't you tease me! I want to talk to the Miss some more. How come you've shut the door on me! Ai! I really had hoped that I'd be able to do such and such here. Who would have known that I didn't get to do any such thing! If I had known that I wouldn't be able to do anything, I wouldn't have bothered with such and such. Ai! (*Sings.*)

I truly had wished that we could be a luan-bird and phoenix tonight,
Who would have known that the expectation was all in vain?

Huangfu's Mother: (*Enters and sings.*)

I am so mad!
Fortunately, a good friend clarified the situation for us,
The dreamers were woken up by words of medicinal wisdom.
I didn't know until now that that Cloud Fragrance was in fact a spy,
It is truly a case of old age destroying a person's common sense.

Cloud Fragrance: (*Enters and sings.*)

Last night, the husband and wife met at the garden,
Like Liang Hong 梁鸿 and Meng Guang 孟光,[29] the wife was most reverent.
Presenting him with hairpins and bracelet and silver, she was like a lifelong friend,
Not at all like Bai Lixi 百里溪, who forgot the spouse in poverty.[30]

---

29. See footnote 13.

30. This line literally says, "Unlike Bai Lixi who forgot *yanyi* 扊扅." *Yanyi* is a bar used to bolt doors. Bai Lixi was a minister during the Qin dynasty (221–206 BCE). During a party, one of the hired entertainers sang a song about how Bai Lixi had only five sheepskins and was so poor that he used door bolts as fuel. The singer then asked whether he had forgotten her now that he was wealthy. Bai Lixi thereupon discovered that the woman was his wife when he was destitute and took her in as wife again. *Yanyi* has since been used to refer to extreme poverty.

(*Speaks.*) Madam, please accept my greetings.
HUANGFU'S MOTHER: Don't you come bothering me again. What do you want, Cloud Fragrance?
CLOUD FRAGRANCE: (*Sings.*)

> My Miss sent me here to ask about the wedding,
> Her parents are forcing her to marry another as urgently as fire is burning one's eyebrows.

HUANGFU'S MOTHER: Cloud Fragrance! (*Sings.*)

> Our family is too poor, we are unable to prepare for the wedding,
> She will have to wait until my son wears a purple court gown.

CLOUD FRAGRANCE: (*Sings.*)

> I came here the other day precisely on account of this,
> That was why I asked the gentleman to go to our garden.

HUANGFU'S MOTHER: Don't speak rubbish again. My son didn't go.
CLOUD FRAGRANCE: (*Sings.*)

> Clearly, he did go, why would I deceive you?
> Old madam, how could you go against your own conscience?
> My Miss gave him her hairpins and bracelet and silver,
> He said that he will arrange for the wedding as soon as he returned home.
> Now her goodwill has been turned into ill intentions,
> My virtuous Miss is being wronged and will suffer injustice.

HUANGFU'S MOTHER: Virtuous or not, I'm not marrying her to my son.
CLOUD FRAGRANCE: (*Sings.*)

> I don't care if you will marry her to your son or not,
> But my Miss has certainly labored in vain to preserve her chastity.

HUANGFU'S MOTHER: What a joke about her preserving her chastity!
CLOUD FRAGRANCE: (*Sings.*)

Old madam, you act against your conscience, you are totally devoid of reason,
Cheating by taking another's money and tricking others, you are pretending wrong is right.

Huangfu's Mother: (*Sings.*)

Let me tell you, Cloud Fragrance, you with a wolf's heart and a dog's lungs,
Just because you are rich and we are widowed and orphaned, you came to take advantage of us.
Miss Shi is marrying another and got you to act as a spy,
So that you can trick my son to your garden and jeopardize his life.
We, mother and son, are good people; we abide by the laws of Heaven,
We refuse to be victimized innocently—we intend to protect ourselves.

Cloud Fragrance: (*Sings.*)

I don't care if you accept her favor or not,
But today I want you to return to me the things we gave you.

Huangfu's Mother: What things? What?

Cloud Fragrance: A pair of hairpins, a bracelet, and fifty taels of silver.

Huangfu's Mother: Aren't you spitting blood at innocent people who've never seen those hairpins and bracelet and silver of yours? You're full of rubbish!

Cloud Fragrance: Wait a minute! I'll leave as soon as I get the hairpins and bracelet and silver. Without them, I'll die here before I leave!

Huangfu's Mother: You little slut.[31] You can't blame me—leave at once!

Cloud Fragrance: Madam, don't you call me names again. I can call you names, too, if you continue.

Huangfu's Mother: What sort of name can you call me?

Cloud Fragrance: What did you call me?

Huangfu's Mother: I called you a little slut.

Cloud Fragrance: I'm going to call you an old . . .

31. Literally, *jianren* 贱人, lowborn, is a term frequently used to refer to prostitutes.

HUANGFU'S MOTHER: An old what?
CLOUD FRAGRANCE: An old madam.
HUANGFU'S MOTHER: I didn't think you'd be capable of calling names.
CLOUD FRAGRANCE: You're a stupid old thing!
HUANGFU'S MOTHER: Leave! (*She pushes Cloud Fragrance out of the gate and shuts it.*) Doesn't the child fear anything anymore? She even called me names. (*She exits.*)
CLOUD FRAGRANCE: Stupid old thing—open the door! Open the door! My Miss has such a poor fate! (*Sings.*)

The fallen flower would like to follow the flowing water,
But the flowing water has no love for the fallen flower. (*She exits.*)

Scene 9: "Writing on the Shirt"

EMERALD PEACH: (*Enters and sings.*)

Ever since Cloud Fragrance left, I cannot stop thinking,
Unable to neither stand nor sit, my heart feels so anxious.

CLOUD FRAGRANCE: (*Enters and sings.*)

Huangfu Yin turned her good intentions into malice,
It was truly the encounter of a gentle woman with an inferior man.

EMERALD PEACH: Are you back, Cloud Fragrance?
CLOUD FRAGRANCE: Yes, I'm back.
EMERALD PEACH: Why do you look so angry?
CLOUD FRAGRANCE: My dear Miss! (*Sings.*)

Huangfu Yin turned your good intentions into malice,
His old mother says that you wanted to marry the wealthy suitor.
She accused me, Cloud Fragrance, of being a spy running between you two,
She also said that you despised his poverty and acted with evil intentions.

Emerald Peach: Didn't she say anything about our hairpins, bracelet, and silver?

Cloud Fragrance: (*Sings.*)

She didn't say anything about the hairpins, bracelet, and silver
you gave him,
I was so embarrassed by her tirade that I didn't know where to hide.

Emerald Peach: (*Sings.*)

Hearing this, I cannot help but start to weep,
Unwittingly, the tears shed, and I call to Heaven.
How could one treat so lightly the marriage of a proper maiden?
This is the result of loving wealth and turning against ethics.

Cloud Fragrance: (*Sings.*)

I urge you, dear Miss, not to blame your parents anymore,
This really is caused by the malice of the scholar.

Emerald Peach: Cloud Fragrance, bring me my white undershirt.

Cloud Fragrance: What do you want the undershirt for?

Emerald Peach: The scholar is inhumane and unrighteous. But if I marry another, I'm afraid that my reputation will be ruined. Bring me my white undershirt. I'm going to write a poem on it for the ungrateful man to see, if I should enter the Wei household.

Cloud Fragrance: I'll bring it right away! (*Exits and re-enters.*) Miss, here is the undershirt.

Emerald Peach: How cruel the scholar is! (*Sings.*)

I, the beauty, am ill-fated—there's no way to save me.
To die from drowning, it's truly sad.
Faithful women are usually valorous,
Unfaithful men are devoid of ethics.

(*Speaks.*) My dear mom and dad!

Your child will unfortunately jump into the river and die,
Upon the grass hut, I will abandon my mom and dad. (*They exit*).

Scene 10: "Rescuing the Girl"

(*Zhang Shu, Lady Zhang, and the Boatman enter.*)
ZHANG SHU: (*Recites.*)

Looking afar, I see the winding stone steps of the Southern Mountain,
And in the midst of the willow forests, scattered houses.

(*Speaks.*) I am old Zhang Shu, a minister of the Song dynasty court. I received an imperial edict to go to my post. I am presently traveling in a boat in the middle of the river. Boatman, move along! (*Sings.*)

Having received an imperial edict, who dares to dally?
To my official post, I now proceed. (*He exits.*)

EMERALD PEACH: (*Enters and sings.*)

Suddenly I hear the drums at the watch tower strike three,[32]
Teary-eyed, I call for my mother; my mother does not answer.
Without any worries, mommy sleeps soundly in her bed.
Full of anxiety, I, your child, can neither sit nor sleep.
Sorrowfully, I open the side door, tears flowing unceasingly,
In the dark night, without telling mom and dad, I leave my home. (*She exits, re-enters, and sings.*)
I resent the fact that my mom and dad are short-sighted in their dealings,
Reneging on the marriage without any reasons, they are in the wrong.
I will only bring resentment upon myself if I should marry into the Wei family,
I intend to become a woman of chastity, known for my virtue and filial piety.[33]
Hurriedly, I arrive at the bank of the river,
I must jump into the river and lose my life to the Yellow Spring.[34]

---

32. The third watch denotes midnight.

33. Here she is obviously considering herself the daughter-in-law of the Huangfu family and being filial to her mother-in-law.

34. The Yellow Spring refers to the underworld.

(*Speaks.*) Forget it all! (*She gestures jumping into the water.*)

Boatman: (*Enters.*) Fish out the person! (*He gestures saving her. Zhang Shu and Lady Zhang enter.*)

Zhang Shu: (*Recites.*)

Suddenly, I hear a splash in the river,
Hurriedly, I arrive at the front of the boat.

Boatman: I report to my lord. We rescued a girl from the river.

Lady Zhang: Let me take a look. Her eyes and eyebrows are so pretty; she must not be the child of a poor family.

Zhang Shu: If that's the case, take her to the back of the boat. Wake her up and talk to her. The Boatman achieved merit for rescuing a person. Reward him with five ounces of silver. Put up the sail and go. (*Sings.*)

I thought we would end up old and childless,
Then a bright pearl is brought to our boat. (*They exit.*)

Scene 11: "Lawsuit"

Cloud Fragrance: (*Off stage.*) Miss! Miss! (*Enters.*) Oh no! (*Sings.*)

Not seeing the Miss, I am scared stiff,
Let me talk to the Squire about it all from the very beginning.

(*Speaks.*) Squire and Madam, please come here quickly!

Shi Zhi: (*Enters with Madam Mei.*) Why are you so flustered, Cloud Fragrance?

Cloud Fragrance: The Miss cried for half of the night and then disappeared.

Shi Zhi: She must have escaped to Huangfu Yin's home. Go there and take a look, Cloud Fragrance. If she is at his home, we will not let his family rest.

Cloud Fragrance: The Miss could not have gone to his home.

Shi Zhi: How did you know that she could not have gone to his home?

Cloud Fragrance: Last night, the Miss said the scholar is neither humane nor righteous. But she said that if she married another, her name would be ruined. She asked for her white undershirt to write a poem for the ungrateful man to see if she should end up at the Wei household.

SHI ZHI: If that's the case, bring me the white undershirt.

CLOUD FRAGRANCE: (*Exits and re-enters.*) Here's the undershirt.

SHI ZHI: There's a poem on it. Let me take a look. So my daughter drowned herself in the river. Oh my strong-willed child! (*Sings.*)

Jumping into the river, my daughter has given up her life,
Seething in pain, the nine intestines of my entrails are bursting.
You have always been known for virtue and filial piety,
How could this happen to you before you died?

CLOUD FRAGRANCE: You wouldn't have known, Squire. But after the matchmaker came here, the Miss sent me to Huangfu Yin's home to ask him to come to our garden on the fifteenth of the Eighth Month to give him hairpins, a bracelet, and silver to help him arrange the wedding. Who would have known that he wouldn't arrange for the wedding after he received these things? That's why the Miss drowned herself.

MADAM MEI: Why didn't you tell us sooner? My dear child, who died untimely! (*Sings.*)

This is all caused by the treachery of the poor Confucian scholar,
He has forced my own dear daughter to stain her blood on the yellow sand.[35]
He has cheated us two old ones of having descendants—how could we let him get away with it?
I ask the Squire to file a murder charge against him at the official yamen.

SHI ZHI: Madam, I would like to file a lawsuit against him, but we don't have any witnesses.

CLOUD FRAGRANCE: If the Squire wants to file a charge against him, I'm willing to serve as witness at the court.

SHI ZHI: Then I'll take Cloud Fragrance with me and file a lawsuit against him. Cloud Fragrance! (*Sings.*)

I want you to insist without wavering,

CLOUD FRAGRANCE: (*Sings.*)

That he caused her death through rape. (*They exit.*)

---

35. A reference to death.

Scene 12: "The Trial"

(*Li Ruoshui enters with a colonel.*)
Li Ruoshui: (*Sings.*)

Receiving the imperial edict, I have left the capital city,
To examine corruption and the desires of the people.
I travel in a palanquin carried by eight men.[36]
Above me hang a pair of treasured swords.[37]

Messenger: (*Enters.*) The local officials have come to pay their respects at an audience.

Li Ruoshui: Tell them that there is no need for them to pay their respects.

Messenger: The Office Attendant of Zhizhou Prefecture has arrived to pay his respects at an audience.

Li Ruoshui: Ask him to attend me at the court. (*He exits, re-enters, and sings.*)

The cannon has been fired three times, I preside over the court,
The prefectural and county magistrates all hurry over.
I give the order that I will not meet with any of them,
Lest the common citizens suspect my integrity.

(*Speaks.*) I am Minister Li Ruoshui, a courtier of the Song dynasty. I am an Official Scholar of the Literary Court (*wenhuadian daxueshi* 文华殿大学士). I received an imperial edict to leave the capital to review the court cases of criminals condemned to be executed. I am presently presiding over the court of Zhizhou Prefecture.

Colonel: The Office Attendant has brought the files of all the cases.

Office Attendant: I pay my respects to your Excellency.

Li Ruoshui: Office Attendant, how many cases are there?

Office Attendant: There are twenty-four cases.

Li Ruoshui: Open them and let me take a look at them. The first case: a famous robber named Sun Zitu 孙子图 murdered a man for his money. He should be executed. The second case: a man by the name of Chen

---

36. A palanquin carried by eight people indicates extremely high-ranking status (the third rank or higher) of the official.

37. This seems to also indicate his superior power. The swords may have been conferred upon him by the emperor.

Yu 陈余 threw a brick outside of his wall and hit a pedestrian. This is an unintentional hit. He should be given thirty lashes and set free. The third case: a man named Huangfu Yin caused the death of a person because of rape. Shi Zhi has a daughter named Emerald Peach who was promised to Huangfu Yin as wife. However, despising poverty and loving wealth, Shi Zhi subsequently promised his daughter to a Wei family. Emerald Peach was unwilling to submit. She sent Cloud Fragrance to Huangfu Yin's home to ask him to go to her garden the night of the fifteenth of the Eighth Month, to present him with hairpins, a bracelet, and silver to help him fund the wedding. Huangfu Yin, however, did not arrange for the wedding after he obtained the hairpins, bracelet, and silver, leading to Emerald Peach drowning herself in the river in despair. Aiya! The way I see it, since he is her husband, he should not be charged with rape. This case needs examination. Office Attendant, arrange for a hearing of the case on rape leading to drowning. Summon the plaintiff, Shi Zhi!

COLONEL: Summon Shi Zhi!

SHI ZHI: (*Enters.*) At your service, my Lord.[38]

LI RUOSHUI: Summon the defendant, Huangfu Yin.

COLONEL: Summon Huangfu Yin!

HUANGFU YIN: (*Enters.*) At your service, my Lord.

LI RUOSHUI: Summon the witness, Cloud Fragrance.

COLONEL: Summon Cloud Fragrance!

CLOUD FRAGRANCE: (*Enters.*) At your service, my Lord.

LI RUOSHUI: Shi Zhi and Cloud Fragrance can kneel down there. Huangfu Yin, kneel up here first. Now, Shi Zhi is suing you because you caused a death through rape. Do you have a written defense or are you going to defend yourself orally?

HUANGFU YIN: I have in fact a written defense. Please read this, my Lord.

LI RUOSHUI: If such is the case, bring the defense to me, Colonel, and let me read it. (*Reads.*)

"Presented by Huangfu Yin concerning the trumped-up charge due to reneging on a marriage. Shi Zhi has a daughter named Emerald Peach who was arranged to be married to me before my father died. My family became poor subsequent to my father's death. Despising poverty and loving wealth, Shi Zhi promised his daughter to the Wei household. Emerald Peach refused to submit and committed

38. He should kneel at this point.

suicide through drowning in the river. Fearing ensuing problems, Shi Zhi had Cloud Fragrance make up a tale about presenting hairpins, a bracelet, and silver to frame Yin. Fearing neither the law nor Heaven, Shi Zhi sues unjustly an innocent man. Sorrowfully, I beg my Lord to execute justice."

Huangfu Yin, Shi Zhi charged you with murder through rape, but your defense tried to deny everything.

Huangfu Yin: I, your inferior, do not dare.

Li Ruoshui: Then tell the truth according to your written defense.

Huangfu Yin: Please allow me to report, my Lord! (*Sings.*)

Venerable Lord sitting above, you will execute justice with integrity.
I don't know how to lie craftily—all my words are true.
When my father was alive, he arranged a marriage for me with the daughter of the Shi family,
Because he died and left us, our household fell into destitution.
The wedding was not arranged due to our poverty, it was not an intentional delay,
I spent all my days at the school studying the books of the sages.

Li Ruoshui: How advanced are you with your studies?

Huangfu Yin: (*Sings.*)

Not yet selected by the attendant of the God of Literature,[39]
But I am nevertheless a scholar of local renown.
My father-in-law disdains my poverty and chose another son-in-law.

Li Ruoshui: Whom else did he promise her to?

Huangfu Yin: (*Sings.*)

He promised her to Wei Gonglian of the Imperial Privy Council.
Without reason, he also tried to set a trap to trick me
And sent Cloud Fragrance to my home as a spy.

Li Ruoshui: What did she go to your home for?

Huangfu Yin: (*Sings.*)

39. That is, not yet successful in passing the metropolitan civil service examination.

She invited me to meet like the Weaving Girl and the Cowherd
the night of the Moon Festival,
Fearing falling into the trap, I did not dare to go.

LI RUOSHUI: Wait down there. Summon Cloud Fragrance. (*Huangfu Yin exits.*)

CLOUD FRAGRANCE: (*Enters.*) At my Lord's service.

LI RUOSHUI: Since you are the witness, you must be familiar with what went on. Tell the truth.

CLOUD FRAGRANCE: (*Sings.*)

Venerable Lord sitting above, you will execute justice with integrity,
I, a young maid, do not lie; I will tell the truth.
My Miss did send me to his home to visit,
In order to invite him to our garden the night of the Autumn
Festival.

LI RUOSHUI: So did he come?

CLOUD FRAGRANCE: (*Sings.*)

He did come to the garden that night to meet with her,
I, the maid, personally gave him silver, hairpins, and bracelet.
He said that he would arrange for the wedding as soon as he got
home.
Who would have known that, although he was a gentleman, he
had the heart and liver of an inferior man?

LI RUOSHUI: Wait down below. Summon Huangfu Yin. (*Cloud Fragrance exits.*)

HUANGFU YIN: (*Enters.*) At my Lord's service.

LI RUOSHUI: Huangfu Yin, your wife presented you with hairpins, a bracelet, and silver the night of the fifteenth of the Eighth Month. Why did you not arrange for the wedding after you received the things? How dare you defend yourself with false words?

HUANGFU YIN: My father-in-law had Cloud Fragrance concoct a trumped-up charge to frame me.

LI RUOSHUI: Even if your father-in-law tried to frame you, the truth was that you were presented with hairpins, a bracelet, and silver.

HUANGFU YIN: I didn't even go to their place. How could I have seen her hairpins and bracelet and silver?

Li Ruoshui: Get back down there and wait. Summon Shi Zhi. (*Huangfu Yin exits.*)

Shi Zhi: (*Enters.*) At your service, my Lord.

Li Ruoshui: Ho! What is the reason for selling your daughter twice?

Shi Zhi: Before my daughter died, she left a white undershirt. Please take a look at it, my Lord.

Li Ruoshui: Colonel, bring me the undershirt. There is a poem on it. Let me read it. (*Recites.*)

The beauty is ill-fated, there's no way to save me.
To die from drowning, 'tis truly sad.
Faithful women are usually valorous,
Unfaithful men are devoid of ethics.

(*Speaks.*) What a pity! She was indeed a woman of talent. Shi Zhi, was this poem really written by your daughter?

Shi Zhi: Yes, it was.

Li Ruoshui: Go back down and wait. Summon Huangfu Yin. (*Shi Zhi exits.*)

Huangfu Yin: (*Enters.*) At your service, my Lord.

Li Ruoshui: Huangfu Yin, you did receive the hairpins and bracelet and silver. Why did you insist that you didn't go there?

Huangfu Yin: I truly did not go there.

Li Ruoshui: The poem on the white undershirt left by your wife, before she died, says clearly, "Faithful women are usually valorous; unfaithful men are devoid of ethics." She described you as unfaithful to indicate her despair with you. How can you claim that you didn't go there?

Huangfu Yin: I can explain the poem on the undershirt.

Li Ruoshui: Elucidate me.

Huangfu Yin: Emerald Peach is a young girl living in a secluded boudoir. Who could have recognized her handwriting?

Li Ruoshui: You are full of rubbish! Even if this poem is not valid as evidence, her presenting you with hairpins, a bracelet, and silver is a fact.

Huangfu Yin: I never went there. How could I have seen the hairpins, bracelet, and silver?

Li Ruoshui: Go back down there and wait. Summon Cloud Fragrance. (*Huangfu Yin exits.*)

Cloud Fragrance: (*Enters.*) At my Lord's service.

Li Ruoshui: Was it Huangfu Yin who came to your garden that night?

Cloud Fragrance: My Lord, it was indeed Huangfu Yin who came that night.

LI RUOSHUI: I, the judge, see through this case now.

CLOUD FRAGRANCE: What have you seen through?

LI RUOSHUI: I think, as a maid, you had an affair and secretly shared the hairpins, bracelet, and silver with your lover. You then insisted that it was Huangfu Yin to extricate yourself, in total disregard of his life. Am I right or not?

CLOUD FRAGRANCE: My Squire runs a very strict household. I do not dare do anything wayward.

LI RUOSHUI: Tell me—who was it that came to your garden that night? I'll have him executed. You will not be implicated.

CLOUD FRAGRANCE: It really was Huangfu Yin.

LI RUOSHUI: Ho! I expect that you won't confess without torture. Colonel! Have this maid's fingers pressed!

COLONEL: Yes, sir! (*He has her fingers pressed in the torture equipment.*)

CLOUD FRAGRANCE: Oh no! (*Sings.*)

> Even since childhood, I have only sewed and embroidered with my Miss,
> How could I have ever known the excruciating pain of the finger press?
> Ten fingers bleeding, my whole body sweats from the agony,
> I expect that most likely my life will not be spared, either.

COLONEL: She will not confess!

LI RUOSHUI: Release the press. Take her back down. (*Sings.*)

> Unexpectedly, the girl is as tough as a stubborn man,
> Enduring beatings and the five tortures, she remained steadfast.
> Interrogating Cloud Fragrance is leading nowhere,
> I will have to summon Shi Zhi and question him again.

(*Speaks.*) Summon Shi Zhi.

SHI ZHI: (*Enters.*) At my Lord's service.

LI RUOSHUI: Shi Zhi, did Cloud Fragrance come to your home as a child, or did she just arrive?

SHI ZHI: She came as a child.

LI RUOSHUI: Are her parents and relatives around?

SHI ZHI: No.

LI RUOSHUI: Are there others around the age of her and your daughter?

SHI ZHI: There's no one else.

Li Ruoshui: Go back down and wait there. Summon Cloud Fragrance. (*Shi Zhi exits.*)

Cloud Fragrance: (*Enters.*) At my Lord's service.

Li Ruoshui: Cloud Fragrance, did you join the Zhi family as a child or did you enter their service recently?

Cloud Fragrance: I came since I was a child.

Li Ruoshui: Are your parents and relatives around?

Cloud Fragrance: No.

Li Ruoshui: Are there others around your age?

Cloud Fragrance: No.

Li Ruoshui: The answers tally. Go back down and wait there. Summon Huangfu Yin. (*Cloud Fragrance exits.*)

Huangfu Yin: (*Enters.*) At my Lord's service.

Li Ruoshui: When Cloud Fragrance delivered the invitation, were you at home?

Huangfu Yin: No, I was not at home.

Li Ruoshui: Whom did she talk to?

Huangfu Yin: She talked to my mother.

Li Ruoshui: Who told you about it?

Huangfu Yin: My mother told me about it.

Li Ruoshui: Was there anyone else at your home?

Huangfu Yin: No, no one else.

Li Ruoshui: Go back down and wait there. Summon Cloud Fragrance. (*Huangfu Yin exits.*)

Cloud Fragrance: (*Enters.*) At my Lord's service.

Li Ruoshui: Cloud Fragrance, when you delivered the invitation, was Huangfu Yin at home?

Cloud Fragrance: No, he was not at home.

Li Ruoshui: To whom did you talk to?

Cloud Fragrance: I told his mother about it.

Li Ruoshui: Was there anyone else at his home?

Cloud Fragrance: No, there was no one else.

Li Ruoshui: The answers tally. Go back down and wait there. Summon Huangfu Yin. (*Cloud Fragrance exits.*)

Huangfu Yin: (*Enters.*) At my Lord's service.

Li Ruoshui: Huangfu Yin, your wife wanted you to go to her garden the night of the fifteenth of the Eighth Month to give you hairpins, a bracelet, and silver to assist with preparations for the wedding. I feel that she was the most righteous woman in the world. But you did not go to meet her. Who told you not to go?

HUANGFU YIN: My Lord, an old friend stopped me.
LI RUOSHUI: What's the name of your old friend?
HUANGFU YIN: His name is Han Sizhong.
LI RUOSHUI: What is his profession?
HUANGFU YIN: He's a scholar.
LI RUOSHUI: How did he persuade you not to go? Tell the truth.
HUANGFU YIN: I went to his home for a literary meeting that day. He saw me unhappy and asked me about it. I told him the truth. He said that intruders at night are either thieves or rapists, that one can kill them with impunity. Therefore, I was afraid to go there.
LI RUOSHUI: So that's how it was! Ha-ha! This explains it! Summon the jailer.
JAILER: (*Enters.*) At your service, my Lord.
LI RUOSHUI: Put Huangfu Yin in the jail temporarily. Do not give him a hard time. Take him away. Tell Shi Zhi and Cloud Fragrance to post bail and leave. Official Attendant!
OFFICIAL ATTENDANT: At your service, my Lord.
LI RUOSHUI: Official Attendant, I have an errand for you. Go to the school in Zhizhou. Tell them that His Excellency Li is looking for some talented students to be his protégées, and that I want all the scholars of Zhizhou to come here. Anyone missing will forfeit his eligibility to attend school and take the examination. (*The Official Attendant responds and exits. Li sings.*)

Today, I will be questioning him,
Huangfu Yin could not have performed the rape that night. (*He exits.*)

Scene 13: "A Literary Examination"

(*Enter Xia Shiqing and Han Sizhong.*)
XIA SHIQING: (*Recites.*)

For more than ten years, we've stuffed ourselves with the Confucian classics.

HAN SIZHONG: (*Recites.*)

To pluck cassia in the moon palace,[40] we'll see who gets there first.

40. This refers to passing the metropolitan civil service examination.

Xia Shiqing: I am Scholar Xia Shiqing.
Han Sizhong: I am Scholar Han Sizhong.
Xia Shiqing: Greetings, Elder Brother Han. His Excellency Scholar Li is seeking talented students to be his protégés. Let's go together to his court. (*Sings.*)

The main examiner wants to test our talent.

Han Sizhong: (*Sings.*)

You and I will leave for there immediately without further ado.
(*They exit.*)

Li Ruoshui: (*Enters and sings.*)

The judge hurriedly presides over the court,
A bright mirror[41] hangs over the front hall.

Colonel: The scholars have all arrived.
Li Ruoshui: Tell them to come in. (*Xia Shiqing, Han Sizhong, and other scholars enter.*)
Xia Shiqing: The scholars kowtow to Your Excellency.
Li Ruoshui: Please rise, scholars. I will give a standard test today. Report your names first.
Xia Shiqing: I am Scholar Xia Shiqing.
Han Sizhong: I am Scholar Han Sizhong.
Li Ruoshui: Oh, so you are Han Sizhong.
Han Sizhong: Yes.
Li Ruoshui: I've already heard of your name in the capital.
Han Sizhong: I'm most honored. Ever since I started to take the examinations, I have been ranked among the top third and, consequently, my fame thunders through regions beyond.
Li Ruoshui: Oh good! What a fame that thunders through regions beyond! Stand aside for a minute. Come here, Scholar Xia. I have a literary concept that I want you to explain.
Xia Shiqing: Yes, please.
Li Ruoshui: That which leads to central harmony; Heaven and earth are located therein; myriad things are nurtured therein.

41. Mirrors are known to ward off evil.

Xia Shiqing: Only the virtue that was original to the human heart, contemplation of which will lead to understanding of the wonders of all transformations.

Li Ruoshui: Well explained. Stand aside. Come over here, Scholar Han. I have a line for you to match. "Yin Gongchuo 尹公绰 desires Meng Jiangnü 孟姜女 and enters the house of Zhang Zifang 张子房; it's either to rape or to rob."

Han Sizhong: "Min Zijian 闵子骞 takes Ran Boniu's 冉伯牛 cattle and plows Zheng Zichan's 郑子产 field; he is rich but not righteous."

Li Ruoshui: What a great line—"rich but not righteous"! You two are talents with such quick minds! Colonel, see to his reward and send Scholar Xia on his way. Scholar Han should go to a back room here, and I would like to speak with him some more there.

Han Sizhong: Was my Lord impressed with me as a person, or with my literary abilities?

Li Ruoshui: I was impressed with both.

Han Sizhong: So it was important that I studied and have knowledge in me! (*He exits.*)

Li Ruoshui: Summon the Official Attendant.

Official Attendant: (*Enters.*) At your service, my Lord.

Li Ruoshui: Official Attendant, I'm dispatching you to go to Han Sizhong's home to get some hairpins and a bracelet. Deal with his parents as you see fit. Bend over,[42] secrecy is of the utmost importance.

Official Attendant: I understand. (*He exits.*)

Li Ruoshui: (*Sings.*)

Entering the court, I examine his appearance,
If I find the hairpins and bracelet, he will be sure to die. (*He exits.*)

Scene 14: "Obtaining the Hairpins and Bracelet"

(*Han Li and Madam Wei enter.*)
Han Li: (*Recites.*)

My son went to take an examination and has not yet returned.

Madam Wei: (*Recites.*)

It makes old me rather worried.

42. This indicates that he will whisper instructions to the Official Attendant.

Han Li: I am Han Li.
Madam Wei: I am Madam Wei.
Han Li: His scholarly Lordship wanted to find a talented scholar. Our son went to his examination. Why hasn't he returned yet?
Madam Wei: That son of mine has always been good at studying. He will be sure to be selected. Why worry? Let's wait for good news.
Official Attendant: (*Enters and recites.*)

Filled with secrets and concerns,
None should be revealed.

(*Speaks.*) I have come to the gate of the Han household. Let me knock at the door. Old Brother Han,[43] open the door.
Han Li: Wife, there's someone at the door. Why don't you go inside for a while[44] and let me open it? (*Madam Wei exits.*)
Official Attendant: Old Brother Han, open the door!
Han Li: I open the door. Ai! Where is this honored guest from? Did my son emerge at the top at the examination?
Official Attendant: You must be Old Brother Han. Congratulations!
Han Li: What are you congratulating me for?
Official Attendant: Old Brother Han, you wouldn't have known. His Excellency Scholar Li was seeking a talented scholar because he has a daughter whom he would like to marry to your son. Your son said he had nothing to give as a gift, but that he has a pair of hairpins and a bracelet at home and wanted me to fetch them. Let me ask you, Old Brother Han, do you have them or not?
Han Li: Well . . .
Official Attendant: So, do you have them or not?
Han Li: Could you wait a minute? Let me go ask his mom.
Official Attendant: Please.
Han Li: Wife, come over quickly.
Madam Wei: I'm here. I'm here. What do you want me for?
Han Li: Ha, ha! Congratulations, Wife!
Madam Wei: What for?
Han Li: Our son went to the examination. His Excellency Scholar Li said that he has a daughter whom he wants our son to marry, but he had no gift to give to the girl. Our son said that he has a pair of hairpins

43. As an officer, he feels superior to the commoners he visits. Here he addresses Han Li in a familiar manner most likely in order to put the latter at ease.

44. It is improper for women to be seen by strangers.

and a bracelet at home, and sent someone here to fetch them. Let me ask you, do we have them or not?

MADAM WEI: Oh yes, we do have them.

HAN LI: How come I know nothing about it?

MADAM WEI: They were hidden by the boy.

HAN LI: Go get them right away. What a smart boy!

MADAM WEI: (*Enters with the hairpins and the bracelet.*) Aren't these the hairpins and bracelet?

HAN LI: Give them to me. These are fine stuff.

OFFICIAL ATTENDANT: Old Brother Han, do you have them or not?

HAN LI: We do have a pair of hairpins and a bracelet. Why don't you take them?

OFFICIAL ATTENDANT: Give them to me. Old Brother Han, you are so blessed and fortunate! Farewell! (*They exit.*)

Scene 15: "The Indictment"

LI RUOSHUI: (*Enters and sings.*)

> I've sent someone to the Han household to get the hairpins and bracelet,
> Why has he not yet returned?

OFFICIAL ATTENDANT: (*Enters.*) I report to my Lord. I have obtained the hairpins and bracelet.

LI RUOSHUI: Bring them here for me to take a look. This case has been solved. Who gave them to you?

OFFICIAL ATTENDANT: His parents gave them to me.

LI RUOSHUI: Go down there and rest. (*The Official Attendant exits.*) Colonel, summon Shi Zhi and Huangfu Yin.

SHI ZHI AND HUANGFU YIN: (*Enter.*) At the service of my Lord.

LI RUOSHUI: Shi Zhi, do you recognize your daughter's hairpins and bracelet?

SHI ZHI: If they belong to my household, I'd recognize them for sure.

LI RUOSHUI: This is of utmost importance. Do not make any mistakes. Take a look at these.

SHI ZHI: Let me take a look. They are indeed my daughter's hairpins and bracelet.

LI RUOSHUI: Huangfu Yin is truly innocent. Colonel, unshackle him. You two stand aside. Summon Han Sizhong!

Colonel: Scholar Han, his Lordship summons you!
Han Sizhong: (*Enters.*) Thank you, my Lord, for treating me to a meal.
Li Ruoshui: Scholar Han. You have been sued.
Han Sizhong: I, a scholar, who studies at home all day. I've never done anything wrong. Why would anyone sue me?
Li Ruoshui: Shi Zhi sues you for rape leading to death. It concerns the Huangfu Yin case.
Han Sizhong: You wouldn't have known, my Lord. Huangfu Yin is a close friend of mine. I frequently render assistance to him because of his poverty. He has wrongly implicated me in this case.
Li Ruoshui: This is not what I understand. Huangfu Yin is over there right now. I want the two of you to sort it out.
Han Sizhong: Yes, we must sort this out.
Li Ruoshui: Summon Cloud Fragrance.
Cloud Fragrance: (*Enters.*) At your service, my Lord.
Li Ruoshui: Cloud Fragrance, there are two Huangfu Yins over there. Go identify him. This is of utmost importance. You must not make a mistake.
Cloud Fragrance: I understand.
Han Sizhong: Huangfu Yin, this is your murder case. Why implicate me?
Cloud Fragrance: (*Tugs at Han Sizhong.*) My Lord, this is he!
Han Sizhong: Hey, what is this maid tugging at me for?
Cloud Fragrance: You came to the garden the other night to get the hairpins, bracelet, and silver. Who was it, if it wasn't you?
Li Ruoshui: Wait down there, Cloud Fragrance. Scholar Han, the evidence against you is right here. How dare you not confess!
Han Sizhong: What evidence? Tell me.
Li Ruoshui: Open your eyes and tell me what these are?
Han Sizhong: Who gave them to you?
Li Ruoshui: Your parents did.
Han Sizhong: What a Ma and Pa—you've sent your kid into a dead-end!
Li Ruoshui: What kind of behavior is this? Colonel, slap his mouth!
Han Sizhong: My Lord, you're going to kill me!
Li Ruoshui: Let me ask you. Since these hairpins and bracelet didn't belong to you, why didn't you return them?
Han Sizhong: I was drunk from drinking that night—that's why I didn't return the hairpins and bracelet.
Li Ruoshui: Now that Emerald Peach is dead, who will pay for her life?
Han Sizhong: I can say nothing else. I am willing to pay for her life.
Li Ruoshui: Summon the jailer.
Jailer: (*Enters.*) At your service, my Lord.

LI RUOSHUI: Incarcerate Han Sizhong to be executed in the autumn!
HAN SIZHONG: Ai! What a waste of all my learning!
LI RUOSHUI: Come over here, Shi Zhi.
SHI ZHI: At your service, my Lord.
LI RUOSHUI: Your case has been solved. Take the hairpins and bracelet, and go home with Cloud Fragrance.
SHI ZHI: Thank you, my Lord. (*He exits with Cloud Fragrance.*)
LI RUOSHUI: Come back! I want you to help Huangfu Yin when he goes to the capital to take the civil service examination. Huangfu Yin, I want you to study hard at the school. The emperor will conduct a civil service examination soon. You will go to the capital to take the examination. I will be your sponsor.
HUANGFU YIN: Thank you, dear Master.[45]
LI RUOSHUI: You're welcome. Go home now. (*Huangfu Yin exits.*) Fire the cannon three times and close the gate. (*Sings.*)

Today I have cleared an unsolvable case,
Tomorrow I memorialize to the emperor concerning it. (*He exits.*)

Scene 16: "Living Together"

HUANGFU'S MOTHER: (*Enters and sings.*)

Daily I guard my door, vexed and grieved,
The moss on the walls is green and damp, it's so pitiful.
Imprisoned, my son has been struck with an evil fate,
Causing old me to be plagued by anxiety, day in and day out.

HUANGFU YIN: (*Enters and sings.*)

His Excellency Li managed to extricate me from the engulfing net,
Without noticing, I've now arrived at my old home.
I see my mom waiting for me in front of our door,
I step forward, kowtow to her, and ask how she has been faring.

HUANGFU'S MOTHER: Oh, you're back, my son! Good, good, good. Rise!

45. Huangfu Yin is now considered Li Ruoshui's protégé and student.

Huangfu Yin: Thank you, Mother!
Huangfu's Mother: My dear son. How did you manage to escape?
Huangfu Yin: (*Sings.*)

His Excellency Li examined the case, and used deduction to find out the evil party.
Han Sizhong dressed himself as your child and went as an imposter.

Huangfu's Mother: So what's happening to Han Sizhong?
Huangfu Yin: Han Sizhong will be executed in the autumn. His Excellency Li also ordered your child to go to the capital to take the civil service examination.
Huangfu's Mother: He is truly a judge with great integrity and wisdom.
Cloud Fragrance: (*Sings.*)

Wearing a beautiful, colorful silk outfit and
Scented and fragrant, I arrive to welcome the bridegroom.

(*Speaks.*) Greetings, Old Madam.
Huangfu's Mother: Is it you again, Cloud Fragrance? I will have no more of your nonsense. When you were at the court, you insisted that my son forced your Miss to die. Why do you come here again?
Huangfu Yin: Mother, it was all the fault of that treacherous man. Don't blame Cloud Fragrance.
Huangfu's Mother: Did I blame her wrongly?
Huangfu Yin: Yes.
Huangfu's Mother: Why did you come here, Cloud Fragrance?
Cloud Fragrance: Our Squire has ordered me to come to invite Madam and the scholar to come live at our house, so that the licentiate may go to the capital to take the examinations later.
Huangfu Yin: What do you think, Mother?
Huangfu's Mother: Since your father-in-law invited us, I think we should go.
Huangfu Yin: Help with the packing, Cloud Fragrance, and we'll go with you.
Huangfu's Mother: (*Recites.*)

Let us speak no more of what has transpired in the past,

CLOUD FRAGRANCE: (*Recites.*)

It is commonly said that people live long just as Heaven does. (*They exit.*)

Scene 17: "Visiting the Master"

LI RUOSHUI: (*Enters and recites.*)

Returning to the imperial court, I saw the emperor and was given an edict,
I was personally appointed by the imperial brush to be the chief examiner.

(*Speaks.*) I am Li Ruoshui. After I returned from reviewing the case at Zhizhou, I memorialized to the emperor and was personally appointed by His Majesty to be the chief examiner. Yesterday, I saw Huangfu Yin's name on the list of successful candidates. I'm sure my fine protégé ranked first. Today is the propitious date when the results will be published. Colonel, let me know as soon as the top candidate arrives.[46] (*Sings.*)

The name Huangfu emerges prominently as the top candidate,[47]
I am so delighted that my fine protégé has attained first place. (*He exits.*)

HUANGFU YIN: (*Enters and sings.*)

I am so delighted that I managed to climb the immortal cassia upon arriving at the capital.
In one stroke, I have become famous, known to the entire world.

---

46. As the chief examiner, he is considered to be the teacher of all the successful candidates. The top ranking candidate is expected to visit him and thank him.

47. Since all the test papers were anonymous (they were all recopied without the names of the examinees), Li Ruoshui selected the top candidate without knowing the name until he saw the results.

I am Huangfu Yin. I am so delighted that the gracious Master selected me as the top candidate. I have already sent to have my family moved here and have just received an imperial edict to visit the Li residence. Attendants, take me to the Li residence in a palanquin and report my arrival. (*Sings.*)

So delighted that I've been fortunate to emerge as top candidate at the capital,
It is but natural that I should go pay my respects to my gracious teacher. (*Exits.*)

Li Ruoshui: (*Enters and sings.*)

The examinations are done, my body feels tired,
This morning I will play a happy tune on my zither.

Attendant: (*Enter.*) The new Gentleman of Honor has arrived!
Li Ruoshui: Tell him to come in.
Attendant: You have been invited to come in, new Gentleman of Honor.
Huangfu Yin: (*Enters.*) Here I am. Please assume a position of honor so that I, your student, can pay my respects properly.
Li Ruoshui: You don't need to kowtow.
Huangfu Yin: But I really should.
Li Ruoshui: Please sit down. When I saw the name Huangfu on the imperial list yesterday, I knew my fine protégé had attained first place. Congratulations!
Huangfu Yin: I relied on the assistance of my gracious teacher.
Attendant: His Excellency Zhang requests a meeting.
Li Ruoshui: Invite him in.
Attendant: His Excellency Zhang is invited in.
Zhang Shu: (*Enters.*) Here I am, your Excellency Li.
Li Ruoshui: Please sit down, your Excellency Zhang. New Gentleman of Honor, come and meet his Excellency Zhang.
Huangfu Yin: Please come closer, Excellency Zhang, let this minor official pay my respects.
Zhang Shu: Please sit down, new Gentleman of Honor. May I inquire of the native land you hail from and of your honorable name?
Huangfu Yin: I am from Zhizhou, and am named Huangfu Yin.
Zhang Shu: I've heard of a Huangfu Yin at Zhizhou who was incarcerated. How did he become a top candidate?

LI RUOSHUI: You wouldn't have known, your Excellency Zhang. He was imprisoned, but fortunately, I tried his case and saved him. It was also I who selected him as top candidate of the examination.

ZHANG SHU: So he was Excellency Li's student.

LI RUOSHUI: You flatter me.

ZHANG SHU: Could the new Gentleman of Honor tell us the story of your imprisonment?

HUANGFU YIN: Since your Excellency Zhang has asked, please listen to me. (*Sings.*)

The splitting of Zhu 朱 and Chen 陈, and Qin 秦 and Jin 晋 was not expected.[48]
My father-in-law is named Shi Zhi; he loved the rich and despised the poor.
My wife, named Emerald Peach, was unwilling in her own heart to give up our betrothal to marry wealth.
She therefore invited me to her garden on the night of the Moon Festival to present me with money to arrange our wedding.
Puzzled and suspicious, I discussed this invitation with a friend,
But who would have known that Han Sizhong had a human face, but the heart of a beast?
He pretended to be a deer, but was a horse and went to the garden to fool my bride.
Under the moonlight, she could not tell whether he was the real groom or not.
Presenting the hairpins and bracelet, she truly expected the *qin* 琴 and *se* 瑟 musical instruments to harmonize,[49]
But that Emerald Peach waited for our wedding, but received no news.
Urgently, her parents forced her to marry another,
The strong-willed girl refused to submit and drowned in the river.

---

48. Zhu Chen refers to Bo Juyi's 白居易 (773–846) poem "The Village of Zhu Chen" 朱陈村, in which two clans surnamed Zhu and Chen always intermarried. Qin and Jin also referred to the custom of intermarriage among the ruling families of the states of Qin and Jin during the Warring States period (475–221 BCE). Here Huangfu is referring to the fact that he and Emerald Peach should have been married.

49. The harmonizing of these two zither-like instruments denotes conjugal bliss.

Her father sued me for obtaining the money and causing her death,
I owed it to my gracious teacher to have saved me from that calamity.
This year, I arrived at the capital and advanced with one leap,
Through the assistance of my gracious teacher, glories were piled upon me.

Zhang Shu: Now that the Gentleman of Honor has become an official, you should take another wife.
Huangfu Yin: (*Sings.*)

I carry the hairpins and bracelet with me on account of our love as husband and wife,
I will not forget my deceased wife; the hairpins and bracelet will always be a reminder.

Zhang Shu: I want to make a pair of hairpins and bracelet just like these for my daughter. Can I borrow them from you?
Huangfu Yin: My dear Excellency Zhang! (*Sings.*)

These hairpins and bracelet represent our love as husband and wife.
Please don't break them and ruin what I owed my wife.

Zhang Shu: (*Sings.*)

I will let my daughter see these hairpins and bracelet and be particularly careful with them,
I will return them to you as soon as a similar pair has been made. (*He exits.*)

Li Ruoshui: Let me see His Excellency off. (*Sings.*)

It is most peculiar that he should have borrowed the hairpins and bracelet,
It really makes me, the old one, highly suspicious. (*They exit.*)

Scene 18: "Seeing the Hairpins and Bracelet"

Emerald Peach: (*Enters and sings.*)

Too lazy to face the caltrop-flower mirror, I am afraid to
perform toiletry,
It is not a case of longing for the lover, it is rather a case of
hating him.

Lady Zhang: (*Enters and sings.*)

Your dad went to the Li residence to pay a visit,
He will be back very shortly.

Zhang Shu: (*Enters and sings.*)

Having borrowed the hairpins and bracelet, I am full of delight,
Let me tell the tale to the mother and daughter.

Lady Zhang: Your Lordship is back. Please sit down.
Emerald Peach: You're back, daddy. Please accept a bow from your child.
Lady Zhang: How was the new Gentleman of Honor at the Li residence?
Zhang Shu: Your Ladyship wouldn't have known. I asked carefully and found out that he was none other than Huangfu Yin. I've borrowed his hairpins and bracelet to show our daughter.
Lady Zhang: Come my child, see if you recognize these.
Emerald Peach: Oh my hairpins and bracelet! (*Sings.*)

My liver and entrails are torn, as soon as I see the hairpins and
bracelet,
My tears flow torrentially, they cannot be dried.
For you, I jumped into the river and committed suicide,
How come you are now here?

Lady Zhang: (*Sings.*)

My daughter was so eager to preserve her chastity,
Why does she now weep upon seeing these hairpins and
bracelet?

Zhang Shu: (*Sings.*)

Don't fill your face with tears, my dear child,
I will effect a reunion between you and your husband.

(*Speaks.*) Groom our daughter, my Lady. I will present her. (*Sings.*)

> If fated to meet, one will meet, even if one lived a thousand miles apart,
> If not fated to meet, one will not meet, even if one comes face to face. (*They exit.*)

Scene 19: "Drinking the Nuptial Cup"

Huangfu Yin: (*Enters and sings.*)

> The hairpins and bracelet I lent have not been returned,
> I cannot help but being very concerned.

Servant: (*Enters.*) I report to my lord—your family has arrived.
Huangfu Yin: Take the palanquins to the inner hall.
Servant: Excellency Zhang wishes to see you.
Huangfu Yin: Invite him in.
Zhang Shu: (*Enters.*) Greetings, Gentleman of Honor. I heard that your in-laws have just moved to the capital?
Huangfu Yin: Yes, they have.
Zhang Shu: Ask your father-in-law to come here. I'd like to meet him.
Huangfu Yin: Please come here, father-in-law.
Shi Zhi: (*Enters.*) Here I am.
Huangfu Yin: Please meet his Excellency Zhang.
Zhang Shu: Greetings, father-in-law.
Shi Zhi: I am so greatly honored.
Zhang Shu: Ho! In the past, you despised the poor and loved the rich, and sold your daughter twice. If it weren't for His Excellency Li trying the case and extricating him, Huangfu couldn't have become the top candidate now. If I were trying the case, I would have given you forty lashes.
Shi Zhi: I know I was wrong.
Zhang Shu: Since you have acknowledged that you were wrong, you can stand up now. Gentleman of Honor, I have brought your wife to you. You can kowtow to the elders together and get married. (*They kowtow and everyone exits.*)

END OF PLAY

31. A young male. Fully dressed with the headgear of a prize candidate (Wei Tiancai's puppet). Photo by Fan Pen Li Chen.

32. A young mistress (Wei Tiancai's puppet). Photo by Ingrid Chen.

33. A young man (Wei Tiancai's puppet). Photo by Ingrid Chen.

Pavilion of the Immortals in Exile 谪仙楼

Introduction

Pavilion of the Immortals in Exile (hereafter *Immortals in Exile*) is one of the longest and most popular plays[1] of Heyang's marionette theater repertoire. Entirely fictional and refreshingly unusual, this tale reflects superbly the subconscious desires of young men and women of traditional society. Although female agency (that also benefits the desires of young men) is common in Chinese drama, *Immortals in Exile* requires even more suspension of disbelief than usual. In this story, two heroines get to interview and select their own husbands; and a woman warrior marries the warrior of her dreams. Scholars who have not yet proven themselves through obtaining the Third Degree (the highest Presented Scholar [*jinshi* 进士] degree) can be selected for marriage by exquisitely beautiful, intellectual, and intelligent young ladies from an upper-class family. A young Chinese warrior is similarly chosen by a highly eligible female, and gains both an easy victory over invaders and the hand of a foreign princess through the agency of the warrior princess.

The name of this play, *Pavilion of the Immortals in Exile*, is based on the pavilion built by the mother of Wonder Immortal (*Xu Miaoxian* 许妙仙) as the site where she and her cousin, Jade Immortal (*Xie Yaoxian* 谢瑶仙), will interview and select their husbands. Although women in Chinese operas frequently scheme to elope with or marry poor, handsome scholars without parental consent, this marital selection arrangement is quite exceptional, even for a play. These young ladies get the best of both worlds. They get to choose their own mates, with the approval of their mother and guardian.

1. The script for this play is found in Shaanxisheng Wenhuaju, ed., *Heyang xianxi* in *Shaanxisheng chuantong jumu, xianxi*, 767–809. The play script was collected by Ma Jingxian 马静轩.

And despite the unconventional atmosphere, a sense of decorum is maintained throughout the interactions between the young men and women. The maid serves as a go-between, handing the men writing implements to prevent direct contact between them.

The world of this pavilion is dominated by young women. Even the maid shows her clout before allowing the scholar Li Zhen 李珍 to present his poem to her mistresses. The young ladies are in total control of the criteria for their selections. Handsomeness and intellectual abilities discerned through poetic talent are required, but Jade Immortal further desires a savvy romantic scholar, while Wonder Immortal seeks a gentleman of honesty and integrity. Once they make their decisions, Lady Xu, Wonder Immortal's mother, is asked to come and grant her approval. The fathers play absolutely no role in this process. Anxious for her mother to give consent and legitimize their selections immediately, Wonder Immortal forthrightly tells her mother to decide right away and reminds her that "It is commonly said that grown-up daughters should not be kept at home." Lady Xu abidingly queries Li Zhen and gives her consent for Wonder Immortal to wed Li, and for Jade Immortal to marry her beau, Bai Rui 白瑞.

Female agency prevails throughout the play. Wonder Immortal and Jade Immortal are smart and proactive in every scene. When the villain, Jiang Shangyou 江上游, and his housekeeper abduct the girls, they manage to extricate themselves and escape. Jade Immortal tricks the housekeeper into putting down his broadsword, and then hacks him with it. Wonder Immortal realizes immediately the power of her abductor's shrewish wife, Madam Hai 海氏, and convinces the latter to release her. When Bai Rui marries a prominent minister's daughter and reneges on his marital pact with Jade Immortal, the latter attempts to travel to the capital cross-dressed as a man. Eventually, both she and Wonder Immortal almost give Bai a beating.

Despite her ugliness, Madam Hai controls Jiang by yelling at him and beating him. His renowned fear of her is reflected in his nickname, *Chaozong* 朝宗, worshipping one's origin or ancestor, coined by his friends in reference to his surname Jiang 江 (which means river). Hai 海's surname means sea, and there was a common belief that rivers originated in the sea. The couple's interactions provide comic relief. Hai eventually forces Jiang to bed her as punishment for attempting to stray.

Jiang Yulian 江玉莲 and Wang Youqiang 王又嫱, daughters of prominent ministers (and Bai Rui and Li Zhen's other matches), are also extremely beautiful and proactive. Typical of evil minister's daughters who nevertheless wed "good" heroes, Jiang Yulian becomes a "good" character by assisting the heroes and denouncing her own father. She aids both Li and Bai. Wang

Youqiang is determined to marry Li the minute she sees him. When he escapes from their bedchamber to remain faithful to Wonder Immortal, she vows to enter a convent to show her chastity. All the beautiful women deserve the handsome, young scholars. Ultimately, they all get to marry the men they want. In this polygamous society, each scholar ends with two beauties as his wives (with the unusual arrangement of having both as formal wives of equal status). Indeed, despite female agency and the proactive roles played by heroines, this fantasy play is ultimately patriarchal (promoting polygamy to the benefit of the heroes).

The case of Princess Myriad Flowers 万花公主, the foreign or "barbarian" female warrior, exemplifies another key element of the Chinese patriarchal imagination. This fictional world is not only male-centered, but also Sino-centric, with advantage to the Chinese state as a central concern. Like the typical foreign princess in Chinese novels and plays, Princess Myriad Flowers falls in love with a young Chinese warrior and persuades him to marry her by offering assistance in his fight against her own state. Although this part of the tale is cursorily enacted in *Immortals in Exile*—the princess proposes to the Chinese warrior, Hua Tianbiao 花天彪, with the promise to aid him, and he readily accepts[2]—the main motif is clearly followed. The princess kills her own relative (in this case, her brother, the Black Demon King 黑魔王) so that the young general wins an immediate victory, and the Chinese state is saved from foreign invasion. The desire for a foreign warrior princess to aid the Chinese is so prevalent that this theme is also found in two other plays translated here: *Short Version of River Yang* and *Yang Wenguang*.

The foils in *Immortals in Exile* also display uncharacteristic features that add a sense of freshness and variety to the play. As a foil, Jiang Shangyou is typical since he is ugly and lascivious and lacks intellectual abilities. A wayward scion of an evil minister, his sole attributes are his family position and wealth. Unlike the typical villain, however, Jiang is not only already married but also hopelessly henpecked. Also atypically, when Jiang fails to win the hand of a beauty, he abducts her by force in a scheme masterminded by an equally lascivious housekeeper. Bai Rui's infidelity is foreshadowed in

---

2. A web page that featured "The Heyang Marionette Theatre in Shaanxi" listed *Immortals in Exile* as one of three most frequently performed plays. The other two were *Romance of the Western Chamber* and *The Golden Bowl Hairpin*. Unfortunately, the web page, http://www.ccnt.com.cn/show/chwindow/culture/qyzjmopy/ohter/mo2-3.htm, is no longer in operation.

the first part of the play when Wonder Immortal emphasizes the importance of honesty and integrity (which Jade Immortal does not take into consideration when selecting Bai). An unusual scholar-hero, Bai is unfaithful and weak, but is clearly not an evil character. He reneges on his marital promise only because he lied about it to the minister and his daughter, and does not know how to get out of it. He ultimately reunites with Jade Immortal, and his infidelity merely provides a contrast to the perfect scholar-hero, Li Zhen, thereby adding more twists to the plot.

Like many shadow and marionette plays, factionalism within the imperial court forms the backdrop to the plot and informs the tensions between "evil" and "good" ministers. Marionette and shadow plays tend to side with the military—victimized generals who rebel and recruit peasants, probably very much like those among the audience. The prime minister is typically the evil one who victimizes a prominent general, reflecting the perpetual tension between civil officials who issued orders at court, and military commanders who held "real" power through control of the armies. In *Immortals in Exile*, Jiang Bin 江彬 (who is accused of monopolizing power within the imperial court) has victimized Chief Commander Hua, Hua Tianbiao's father. Jiang is a "bad" minister, while Hua is a "good" minister. Hua is a relative of Li Dongyang 李东阳 (i.e., Li Zhen's father), and Li is consequently also a "good" minister. Through the feuds, Gao Gu 高固 is Jiang's accomplice, making him another "bad" minister, while Li is assisted by Wang Ao 王鏊, another "good" minister. Military personnel often display the same animosity toward "evil" ministers. In this case, Marshal Yang Yiqing 杨一清 hates Jiang Bin so much that he vows to have Jiang's son, Shangyou, executed, even before the latter is proven guilty. The scions of victimized generals typically escape and raise rebellions, until they become so powerful the emperor grants them amnesty and bestows upon them rank and wealth. In *Immortals in Exile*, Hua Tianbiao is invited back into the imperial fold and sent to fight the invading Black Demon King. This motif of factionalism is also the backbone of the plays, *River Yang* and *Yang Wenguang*.

Immortals in Exile is based on the unconventional fantasy of talented girls selecting their own husbands. The concept is so incredible, however, that even within the context of the play, Wonder Immortal claims (more traditionally) that she had been promised to Li Zhen since childhood, when she introduces herself at Yang Yiqing's military court. Still another practice in this play similarly flouts convention in favor of wishful thinking. When Jiang Bin selects Bai Rui to marry his daughter, he sends Li Zhen (whom he thought was Bai), directly to his daughter's bedchamber—without fulfilling any of the required marital protocols (gifts, matchmaker, etc.) or the wedding ceremony (the kowtow to the ancestors, banquet, etc.). The same happens with the marriage between Li Zhen and Wang Youqiang. When Li's father tells Wang's father that he does not have time to prepare the bridal gifts, the latter declares it unnecessary, and promptly forces the reluctant Li Zhen to his daughter's bedroom.

However, the ending of the play is not unconventional for Shaanxi's shadow and marionette plays. Enfeoffments, or a wedding and/or banquet, end the show. In *Immortals in Exile*, an imperial decree bestows titles on all the heroes and heroines, and orders two women to marry each of the men. Even Hua Tianbiao is to wed both Princess Myriad Flower and Pretty Plum for having assisted him, although the play itself does not reveal Pretty Plum's role in his military exploits.[3] This is, after all, a happy world that returns to patriarchal dominance and reabsorbs all the dissident elements. All the fantasies are fulfilled: everyone marries his or her beloved, with two women for each man—an acceptable practice so long as the women like each other—the rebel joins the imperial ranks, and the foreign invasion is quelled.

Cast of *Pavilion of the Immortals in Exile*[4]

Li Zhen 李珍: a young scholar; styled[5] Zhaoxian 兆先; also known as Jieyuan Li 李解元[6]

Madam Hua 花氏: Li Zhen's mother

Bai Rui 白瑞: a young scholar; styled Yutang 玉堂

Hua Tianbiao 花天彪: Li Zhen's cousin; a warrior

Wonder Immortal 许妙仙: a young lady

Lady Xu 许夫人: Wonder Immortal's mother

Jade Immortal 谢瑶仙: a young lady; Wonder Immortal's cousin

3. In most women warrior tales, the foreign princess is initially despised and rejected by the Chinese warrior, and she has to prove her power and indispensability before she is accepted as wife by the Chinese warrior and his family.

4. The original version of the play may have been longer. The present version (which can be traced to a hand-copied play script dated to 1852) is considered to be different from the original (Huang 1999, 69).

5. The style is a type of name scholars gave themselves at around the age of twenty.

6. *Jieyuan* was the title given to the top candidate of the prefectural examination. But after the Song and Yuan dynasties, it became a title for scholars in general.

PRETTY PLUM 秀梅: maid of Wonder Immortal and Jade Immortal
LI DONGYANG 李东阳: a good minister
WANG AO 王鏊: a good minister
WANG YOUQIANG 王又嫱: daughter of Wang Ao
JIANG YULIAN 江玉莲: daughter of Jiang Bin; sister of Jiang Shangyou
JIANG BIN 江彬: an evil minister; father of Jiang Shangyou
JIANG SHANGYOU 江上游: a clown role; an ugly scholar
GAO GU 高固: a bad minister
YANG YIQING 杨一清: a general
BLACK DEMON KING 黑魔王: a barbarian king
PRINCESS MYRIAD FLOWERS 万花公主: a foreign/barbarian princess
MAJORDOMO JIANG 江管家: Majordomo of Jing Shangyou's family
MADAM HAI 海氏: Jiang Shangyou's wife
EMPEROR ZHENGDE 正德王 (r. 1506–1522): an emperor of the Ming dynasty
MAID 丫头
COLONEL 校尉
FOUR SOLDIERS 四兵
FOUR BARBARIAN SOLDIERS 四番卒
FOUR LOWLY SOLDIERS 四喽卒
FOUR HITMEN 四打手
FOUR YAMEN RUNNERS 四人役
FOUR EUNUCHS 四内侍
HEAD EUNUCH 大太监
HOUSEHOLD SERVANT 家院
WEDDING ASSISTANTS 傧相

Scene 1: "Leaving Home"

LI ZHEN: (*Enters and recites.*)

Studying for more than ten years,
I'm frequently accompanied by a lamp and aged volumes.
At the provincial examination, I wrote seven embroidered essays;[7]
And fortunately got to attend the celebratory banquet for the
Second Degree.

7. *Qiuwei* 秋闱 refers to the triennial examination mentioned in note 6.

(*Speaks.*) I am surnamed Li with the personal name of Zhen and the style of Zhaoxian 兆先. I hail from Chaling 茶陵 of Hunan. I have just received my Second Degree and am unmarried. My father serves at the imperial court as president of the Board of Rites. Now, the treacherous Jiang Bin monopolizes the power within the imperial court and has gotten my maternal uncle executed. Having received no news concerning the whereabouts of my cousin, I would like to find him. I have to ask my Mother to come out of the inner chambers to discuss this with her. Venerable Mother, I, your child, request your presence!

Madam Hua: (*Enters and recites.*)

Beautiful flowers look the same year after year,
Old people look differently age after age.

Li Zhen: My dear venerable Mother, I, your child, bow to you.

Madam Hua: There is no need for formalities. Sit down my child.

Li Zhen: Your son will take a seat.

Madam Hua: For what did my child ask me to come to the hall?

Li Zhen: It's solely because my maternal uncle has been victimized by the treacherous villain, and we have lost the whereabouts of my cousin. Your child would like to go find him. How do you, Mother, feel about it?

Madam Hua: I, your Mother, also had this in mind. Since you are going to leave, listen to the following advice from Mother. (*Sings.*)

Since you, my child, will travel afar,
Listen to your Mother and keep it in your heart.
Retire to an inn as soon as the sun sets,
Under no circumstances board a boat when the wind is high.
As soon as you meet and see your cousin,
Come home with him straight away.

(*Speaks.*) Ai, my dear child! (*Sings.*)

It is commonly said of the clothes of a traveler,
That he should remember the sewing threads of his loving Mother.[8]

Li Zhen: Your child bids farewell now! (*Sings.*)

8. This alludes to the two famous lines of Bo Juyi's 白居易 poem "*Youzi yin*" 游子吟.

Hurriedly, I kowtow to my venerable parent,
I bid farewell to my Mother to whom I owe so much love.
Your son could not possibly be like that Cai Zhonglang 蔡中郎,
Who abandoned his mother and never returned home![9]
But the fact that the hoary one will always lean against the door looking for me,
Will always cause me, the son, to be filled with sadness privately.

(*Speaks.*) Please stay, dear Mother. Your son will now leave. (*They exit separately from opposite sides of the stage.*)

Scene 2: "Raising Arms"

(*Four barbarian soldiers enter with Princess Myriad Flowers.*)
PRINCESS MYRIAD FLOWERS: (*Recites.*)

Highest-ranked in the Palace of Wu 吴宫[10] in the hundred military arts,[11]
I am in charge of the entire army at the Sea and Cloud Pass 海云关.
Among women warriors, I am the best,
Aspiring to emulate Mu Guiying 穆桂英[12] of yesteryear.

I am Princess Myriad Flowers, younger sister of the Black Demon King. I am in charge of the Sea and Cloud Pass at the orders of my brother. I have heard that there is a man named Hua Tianbiao in China who

9. Cai Zhonglang is formally named Cai Yong 蔡邕 (132—192), styled Bo Jie 伯喈. A talented scholar of the Han dynasty, he is transformed in the Ming *chuanqi* drama, *Pipaji* 琵琶记 (Tale of the Lute) into a heartless top candidate of the civil service examinations who neglects the impoverished wife and family of his native home and remarries the daughter of a high-ranking minister.

10. The Wu region refers to the vicinities of Jiangsu and Zhejiang. Here it seems to refer to a state outside the control of the Chinese government, along the coast of southeast China.

11. The use of various military weapons.

12. A famous fictional foreign warrior princess who married a Chinese general of the renowned Yang family during the Song dynasty.

is the most heroic man on earth. I would like to have him join our state and marry me. The four mountains are bright and clear today. Barbarian soldier!

Barbarian Soldier: Here I am!

Princess Myriad Flowers: Get the men and horses ready. We will advance toward Jiangnan 江南![13]

Barbarian Soldier: I received the order! (*He exits.*)

Princess Myriad Flowers: (*Sings.*)

For the purpose of finding my man, I leave my palace in the borderland,
And emulate Mulan 木兰[14] through participating in a military expedition.
I only wish that the Old Man Under the Moon will expedite the process,
By secretly tying for me those red threads of marriage.[15] (*She exits.*)

Scene 3: "Attending the Selection"

Jiang Shangyou: (*Enters and recites.*)

Dreadful to look at ever since infancy, I have always been ugly,
Eyes awry, mouth crooked, my whole face is filled with pockmarks.
(*He sits down.*) When it comes to studying, I am not at all good,
I can only roam and wander, or simply fool around.
The few essays ever written by me,
Were considered as fart by my teacher.

I am none other than Jiang Shangyou, styled Langxian 浪仙. I hail from Xuanhua Prefecture 宣化府. I presently live in Jiangnan. My Father serves at the imperial court and has received the title of Marquis of

13. The area that covers the provinces of Jiangsu and Anhui.

14. A fictional woman warrior who became popular through a ballad of the Six Dynasties.

15. Preordained marriages are supposed to have been matched by an old man found under the moon who uses red threads to tie together the ankles of intended couples.

Pingbei 平北侯. He has taken my younger sister to the capital in order to select a handsome husband for her. This is beside the point. What I want to say right now is that I am surnamed Jiang, meaning river, but I happen to have married a wife surnamed Hai 海, meaning sea. This lowborn is such a shrew that my fellow classmates have awarded me the nickname of Chaozong 朝宗, to refer to the river paying reverence to its origin.[16] Yesterday, I arranged with my friend, Old Bai,[17] to go to the Pavilion of the Immortals in Exile to meet the beauties there. It's getting late—why hasn't he arrived yet?

Bai Duan: (*Enters and recites.*)

Having studied at the local school since childhood,
I am skilled at composing poetry, lyrics, songs, and rhyme prose.
When will I finally meet an incomparable beauty?
I lack but a fair lady in my life.

I am named Bai Duan, with the style of Yutang 玉堂. Yesterday, I arranged with my friend Jiang to go to the Pavilion of the Immortals in Exile today. I've just arrived at the door of the school. Let me go in. Is Elder Brother Jiang here?

Jiang Shangyou: How come you're so late Old Bai?

Bai Duan: We're not late yet. Let's go right now! (*Sings.*)

Don't be too rushed, dear Elder Brother Jiang,
It's the quality of our literary works that will count there.
You, Elder Brother, are Liu Lang 刘郎; I, the Younger Brother, am Ruan Lang 阮郎.[18]
You and I, together we will ascend Mount Heavenly Terrace 天台.

---

16. *Chaozong* literally means "worshipping one's ancestor." The implication here is based on the belief that rivers originated in the seas; hence Jiang, the river must worship, Hai, the sea.

17. Adding "Old" to Bai's surname makes it an appellation denoting familiarity and informality. Here it also suggests Jiang's lack of civility when compared to the courteous way Bai addresses him.

18. Liu Lang and Ruan Lang refer to Liu Chen 刘晨 and Ruan Zhao 阮肇. According to legend, they went to Mount Heavenly Terrace during the beginning of the Eastern Han dynasty to collect medicinal herbs, and were invited to live with two beautiful immortals. When they returned home half a year later, they discovered that seven generations had passed.

Jiang Shangyou: (*Sings.*)

What's all this business about Liu Lang and Ruan Lang?
It all depends on the amount of luck each of us has.
While there's no question who will win when judged from the exterior,
I'm afraid you might not "cut it" when judged from the interior.
(*They exit together.*)

Scene 4: "Pavilion of the Immortals in Exile"

(*Pretty Plum enters with Wonder Immortal.*)
Wonder Immortal: (*Recites.*)

I leave my embroidery in the inner chamber after rising from bed,
There is so much spring outdoors! So heartless is the eastern wind,
Filling the courtyard with petals of fallen flowers.

I am none other than Wonder Immortal Xu. I was raised by my father to be skilled in the literary arts since childhood, along with Younger Sister, Jade Immortal.[19] Hence, my parents are reluctant to marry me off to just anybody. My mother built for my sister and me a building called the Pavilion of the Immortals in Exile, where we can select talented young men for ourselves. Pretty Plum, ask the young lady to join me.
Pretty Plum: Young Lady Xie, your presence has been requested.
Jade Immortal: (*Enters and sings.*)

Suddenly I hear the maid calling urgently for me,
Awaking me from my spring dream of Nanke 南柯.[20]
Before I can even tidy up my black cloud hairdo,
I see the red sun setting in the west.

(*Speaks.*) I am none other than Jade Immortal Xie. I've lived at my maternal uncle's home since childhood. My sister has just sent for me. I'd better go to see her. Greetings, Elder Sister!

---

19. She calls her cousin "younger sister" to denote intimacy.

20. Nanke refers to a dream. The reference originated from Li Gongzuo's 李公佐 Tang dynasty short story, "Tale of Nanke" 南柯记, in which the protagonist dreamt of becoming a notable in the Kingdom of Nanke.

WONDER IMMORTAL: Greetings! Please sit down, Younger Sister.
JADE IMMORTAL: I will take a seat.
WONDER IMMORTAL: May I ask you, Younger Sister, what type of man you plan to select?
JADE IMMORTAL: Please listen to me, Elder Sister! (*Sings.*)

Sly creatures tend to be obnoxious,
Mature ones tend to be crude.
I want to pick a handsome, romantic one like Zhang Junrui 张君瑞,
With the manners of Pan An 潘安 and the talents of Zijian 子建.[21]
It would be great to marry a savvy, romantic guy!

WONDER IMMORTAL: I, your Elder Sister, feel differently about it.
JADE IMMORTAL: Pray tell me, Elder Sister.
WONDER IMMORTAL: Please listen to me, Younger Sister! (*Sings.*)

Don't admire the romantic ones, dear Younger Sister,
The romantic ones don't last long.
Don't you remember the tale of Liang Hong 梁鸿 and Meng Guang 孟光?[22]
Holding the tray above her eyebrows, their love endured.
It is better to marry a gentleman of honesty and integrity,
It is better to be in a situation where the husband sings and the wife harmonizes.

(*Speaks.*) Pretty Plum, go to the gate of the pavilion and report right away if you see anyone arrive.
PRETTY PLUM: Yes! (*Sings.*)

---

21. Zhang Junrui is the handsome hero of the Yuan play, *Romance of the Western Chamber* (*xixiang ji* 西厢记). Pan An is a Six Dynasties scholar who was so handsome that women tossed flowers at him in the street. Zijian refers to Cao Zijian 曹子建 (192–232), who was known as an exceptional poetic talent.

22. Liang Hong and Meng Guang were considered a perfect couple from the Eastern Han dynasty (25–220 CE). The wife, Meng Guang, was so reverent toward her husband that she would lift the tray to the level of her eyebrows when serving food to her husband.

A pair of Yingying 莺莺 orioles have arrived at the Western Chamber,[23]
But they ask the maid to wait for Master Zhang 张郎.
The dew on the green moss soaks through my shoes,
But I am willing to emulate the little Hongniang 红娘.[24]

(*Enter Bai Rui and Jiang Shangyou.*)
Bai Rui: (*Sings.*)

In order to seek Xishi 西施,[25] we have come to Gusu 姑苏,
We have now arrived within the Village of Zhuluo 苎萝村.

Jiang Shangyou: (*Sings.*)

I know how to play the flute to attract the phoenix,
Xiao Shi 萧史 will ascend the Qin Pavilion 秦楼 today.[26]

Bai Rui: Listen, maid at the pavilion. Please tell your young mistresses that two gentlemen have arrived to play a poetry matching game with them.
Wonder Immortal and Jade Immortal: Tell them to come in.
Pretty Plum: Yes. Gentlemen, you've been invited to go in.
Bai Rui: (*Recites.*)

---

23. Yingying, a name that means "oriole" refers to the heroine of the aforementioned Yuan play, *Romance of the Western Chamber*, in which she falls in love with a scholar named Zhang at the Western Chamber of a monastery.

24. See above. Hongniang is Yingying's maid who helped to effect the rendezvous between her mistress and Zhang in *Romance of the Western Chamber*.

25. One of the most beautiful women in Chinese history, Xishi lived during the end of the Spring and Autumn period (722–481 BCE). She was used by the ruler of one state to seduce and bring to ruin the head of another state.

26. Xiao Shi was a renowned flute-playing immortal of the Spring and Autumn period (722–481 BCE). According to *Taiping Guangji* 太平广记 of the Song dynasty, Duke Mu of Qin 秦穆公 married his daughter, Nongyu 弄玉, to Xiao Shi. The duke built a pavilion in which the couple resided until one day the two flew away with Nongyu riding on a phoenix and Xiao Shi riding on a dragon (see Guo Wei 2000, 419–420).

Before the male and female trees unite,[27]
We first get to see the pair of sister flowers.[28]

(*Speaks.*) Tell the young mistresses that we bow to them.
XIU MEI: Young Lady, the gentlemen bow to you.
BAI RUI: (*Sings.*)

Before entering Pujiu Monastery 普救寺,[29]
I suddenly chanced upon Cui Yingying 崔莺莺.
Without the clever assistance of Hongniang,
How can Zhang Junrui convey his love?

JADE IMMORTAL: Oh, wonderful! (*Sings.*)

I, Jade Immortal, arrive and display a smile,
Today I see the young scholar of my dreams.
So handsome and attractive are his deportment and appearance,
Paintings would fail to portray his romantic elegance.
If only I could be with him as the luan-bird and the phoenix,[30]
Couldn't it make one be filled with utter delight?

JIANG SHANGYOU: Let me take a look first! (*Sings.*)

Let me, Old Jiang, gaze first with my eyes,
I see before me beauty of the famed West Lake.[31]
Their eyebrows are so well defined, their eyes so beautiful,
Their cheeks are so delicate, their lips so red.
Verily, they are a pair of E'huang 娥皇 and Nüying 女英,[32]
In an instant, I have contracted love sickness.

---

27. A footnote in this version of the play says that according to *Jinluan miji* 金銮密记, the "male and female trees *xiongcishu* 雄雌树," refer to two entwining pear trees at the well of the Hall of Nine Immortals (*jiuxian xian*九仙殿) at the imperial palace. Here it refers to getting married.

28. Beautiful sisters are frequently referred to as a pair of sister-flowers, *jiemeihua* 姐妹花.

29. In the Yuan play, *Romance of the Western Chamber*, Zhang met Cui Yingying at the Pujiu Monastery.

30. Here marriage is inferred.

31. The West Lake is known as the most beautiful lake in China. Here the speaker compares the young ladies to the lake.

32. E'huang and Nüying are daughters of the legendary emperor 尧 Yao and wives of the legendary emperor Shun 舜.

Wonder Immortal: Ask them to sit down, Pretty Plum. May I ask where you two gentlemen are from?

Bai Rui: (*Sings.*)

I am named Bai Rui; my style is Yutang 玉堂.
My native home is outside of the city of Suzhou 苏州.
I lost my parents during my infancy; I have no other hopes
    other than advancing myself,
Since childhood, I have attended school and composed literature.
Presently eighteen years of age, I am at the height of my youth;
I have taken the civil service exams and attained the First
    Degree.
I present my resume without a shred of falsehood,
Please, dear ladies, examine all the details most carefully.
I hope that you beauties will deign to critique one of my works.

Jiang Shangyou: Listen to me, ladies! (*Sings.*)

I am a student who lives at the City of Suzhou,
My name is none other than Jiang Shangyou.
My style is Langxian, my nickname is Chaozong,
Vainly, I have passed through ten and eight years.
Speaking of achievements, I surpass the rest,
The Imperial College, I aim to be my future.
The Marquis of Pingbei within the Imperial Court
Is none other than my father and your father-in-law—your
    father-in-law!

Wonder Immortal: What a brute! Pretty Plum, chase out that ugly thing for me!

Pretty Plum: Get out, you ugly worm!

Jiang Shangyou: I haven't composed my poem yet. How can I leave now?

Pretty Plum: Get out right now before you make a fool of yourself!

Jiang Shangyou: Somebody must have ruined this marital prospect for me. Well, I, your lord, am not going to let this go. I'm so mad! (*He exits.*)

Bai Rui: I'm here on account of my admiration for your talents. Please don't blame me, ladies.

Wonder Immortal: Pretty Plum, bring the writing implements to the young scholar. (*Pretty Plum hands Bai Rui paper and brush.*)

Bai Rui: Let me write something! (*Recites as he writes.*)

A piece of music on the Rainbow Robe[33] celebrates the immortals,
The waving brush lands on the paper like cloud and smoke.
So delighted is this person to find himself in the immortal realm,[34]
In the Jade Pavilion, I am drunk from a sky full of apricot blossoms. (Bai Rui hands the poem to Pretty Plum, who gives it to Wonder Immortal, who looks at the poem.)

WONDER IMMORTAL: How romantic and elegant—he is indeed a talent. But his display of talent seems rather arrogant. Younger Sister, why don't you compose a poem to harmonize with it?

JADE IMMORTAL: (*Sings.*)

The lines in his poem displays the beauty of a mountain during spring,
This amount of talent and emotions seem so very rare.
Let me fill half of this sheet of paper with red leaf imprints,[35]
So that we can form a pair of root-joining water lilies.[36] (*Recites.*)
Two parts of spring with a sky full of apricot blossoms,
Apricot blossoms and spring showers permeate the clouds and mist.
The feeling of spring exudes in the red flowers on the branch,
Let me just pluck one to accompany the fairy in the immortal realm.[37]

PRETTY PLUM: Here, look!

BAI RUI: So she used the same rhyme scheme as mine and developed the poem by rolling my motif backward—how different and refreshing. This marriage is eighty to ninety percent set. I only wonder about the scholarly talents of the Young Lady Xu.

---

33. The original tune of Rainbow Feathered Robe was danced by Yang Guifei 杨贵妃, the celebrated consort of Xuanzong 玄宗 (r. 713–756; more commonly known as Tang Minghuang 唐明皇) of the Tang dynasty. Here Bai Rui seems to refer to his own poem as a song that applauds the immortals/fairies, a euphemism for beautiful women (i.e., Wonder Immortal and Jade Immortal).

34. The "*xian*" 仙 in the names of both Wonder Immortal and Jade Immortal literally means immortal, celestial, or fairy.

35. This seems to refer to a decorated sheet of paper typically used for writing letters.

36. The implication is that she wants to marry him.

37. *Yaoxian*, fairy, immortal, or celestial in an immortal realm of jade, is also Xie's name.

Wonder Immortal: Honorable young scholar, please return to your venerable residence. I will await your instructions another day.
Bai Rui: If such is the case, I will bid you farewell. (*Sings.*)

Her moving eyes convey discreetly her love,
Which youth is not fond of the joining of fish with water?
This propitious union, I figure, is eighty to ninety percent done,
When the marriage consummates, we will ascend the phoenix pavilion. (*He exits.*)

Jade Immortal: (*Sings.*)

I tell you, Elder Sister, you are really too practical,
Let me, your Younger Sister, tell you what's on my mind.
Why do you let go of that man from your hand ever so easily?
Do you really intend to marry a duke or a marquis?

Wonder Immortal: (*Sings.*)

One can't rush with a matter as important as marriage,
A bright pearl should never be tossed away blindly in the dark.
Although that man was very elegant and romantic,
I fear that he might not be romantic enough for me.

Scene 5: "Court Discussion"

(*Four eunuchs and the Chief Eunuch lead Emperor Zhengde on stage.*)
Emperor Zhengde: (*Recites.*)

The gate of the nine-leveled Forbidden City opens,
The brilliant light of the candles shines upon the platform.
The golden bell strikes thrice for the Emperor to ascend the throne,
Slowly and leisurely appears the ruler, We, the Emperor.

We are Emperor Zhengde of the great Ming dynasty. We have just received an urgent report that the Black Demon King has raised a rebellion. We are presiding over the morning court. Attendant!

CHIEF EUNUCH: Yes, Your Majesty!

EMPEROR ZHENGDE: Issue our edict—the civil and military ministers can now enter the court.

CHIEF EUNUCH: The civil and military ministers should enter the court! (*Off stage.*) We accept the edict. (*Enter Jiang Bin, Li Dongyang, Wang Ao, and Gao Gu.*)

JIANG BIN, LI DONGYANG, WANG AO, GAO GU: How is the imperial-dragon bearing of our lord, Your Majesty?

EMPEROR ZHENGDE: Thanks to the immense blessings from Heaven, we are fine. How are you, our ministers?

JIANG BIN, LI DONGYANG, WANG AO, GAO GU: Thanks to the imperial blessings, we are fine. For what has Your Majesty summoned us to the court?

EMPEROR ZHENGDE: We just received an urgent report that the Black Demon King has raised a rebellion. Should we organize an expedition to quell him?

JIANG BIN: I, your minister Jiang Bin, would like to present a memorial.

EMPEROR ZHENGDE: Yes, you may present it.

JIANG BIN: Li Dongyang is skilled in both civil and military affairs. I recommend that he lead the military expedition.

LI DONGYANG: Aiya, Your Majesty! I, your minister, am just a civil minister. What if I fail this vital national mission?

GAO GU: Your Majesty, Li Dongyang covets life and fears death. What kind of punishment should he receive?

WANG AO: Your Majesty, Li Dongyang is a vital minister within the imperial cabinet. He should not leave the capital. We have so many talented generals. I hope Your Majesty will dispatch another.

EMPEROR ZHENGDE: Please rise, my ministers. We have an idea ourselves. Attendant!

CHIEF EUNUCH: Yes, Your Majesty.

EMPEROR ZHENGDE: Summon Yang Yiqing to the court.

CHIEF EUNUCH: His Majesty has issued an edict. Yang Yiqing should enter the court!

YANG YIQING: (*Off stage.*) I accept the edict. (*Enters.*) Your minister, Yang Yiqing prostrates to Your Majesty.

EMPEROR ZHENGDE: The Black Demon King has raised a rebellion. We bestow upon you, our minister, an army of a hundred thousand. Leave the capital tomorrow!

YANG YIQING: I accept the edict!

Emperor Zhengde: You may all leave, our ministers. Raise the curtain[38] and conclude the court audience.

Jiang Bin, Li Dongyang, Wang Ao, Gao Gu: Farewell, Your Majesty! (*They exit.*)

Scene 6: "Assassination"

Hua Tianbiao: (*Enters and sings.*)

> I grind my teeth in anger, but the hatred does not diminish,
> Without a valid reason, the treacherous villain victimized his colleague.

My name is Hua Tianbiao. My father served as the marshal at the imperial court; but the treacherous villain Jiang Bin devised a devious scheme and had him victimized. I have come to the capital to avenge my father's death. I'm waiting for the old villain to return from court audience to assassinate him. Here comes the old villain as I speak.

(*Four colonels lead Jiang Bin on stage. Gao Gu follows.*)

Jiang Bin: (*Sings.*)

> Above, I deceive the Son of Heaven;[39] below, I lord over the officials,
> All the civil and military ministers cower when they see me.

(*Hua Tianbiao attempts assassination and is blocked by the colonels.*)

Hua Tianbiao: Don't you leave, you old villain!

Jiang Bin: Oh no! There's an assassin! Surround him, colonels! Don't let him get away! (*Hua Tianbiao and the colonels fight. Hua is captured.*)

Colonels: We've captured the assassin.

Jiang Bin: Bring him here! (*Sings.*)

---

38. This may have been a misunderstanding of court protocol by the playwright. While empress dowagers who ruled traditionally held audience behind a curtain, emperors faced the ministers directly.

39. The Son of Heaven is the emperor.

Encountering an assassin, my three souls fled from fright,
Now that you're in my hands, I'll never let you go.

(*Speaks.*) Colonels, tie the assassin up and bring him over! You were unsuccessful in your attempt at assassination. Why don't you confess now!

HUA TIANBIAO: Listen to me, you treacherous villain! (*Sings.*)

I, your young lord, hail from Shandong,
My father was the Commander-in-chief, Marshal Hua.
Now that I have failed in my attempt at assassination,
I'll let you skin me or have me fried.

JAING BIN: Take him away and kill him!

GAO GU: Don't do that Your Excellency! I heard that the rebel Black Demon King in Jiangnan wanted to kill Hua Tianbiao. Why don't you send him there, and then have him killed? This would also deter the invasion and earn credit for Your Excellency.

JIANG BIN: Colonels—take the fellow to Jiangnan, have him executed there by one of the local officials, and then give him to the barbarian.[40]

HUA TIANBIAO: What a villain! (*The colonels escort Hua Tianbiao off stage.*)

JIANG BIN: (*Sings.*)

The Shilang's 侍郎[41] scheme is truly incomparable,
It's even better than the "liuchuqi" 六出歧 of Nanyang 南阳.[42]

GAO GU: A banquet has been prepared in the inner hall to help calm Your Excellency's nerves. If you please! (*They exit.*)

Scene 7: "Befriended"

LI CHEN: (*Enters and sings.*)

I have come to Suzhou to seek my cousin,
Man and horse, both exhausted, we take a break.

---

40. That is, the Black Demon King.

41. *Shilang* is vice president of one of the Six Boards at the imperial court.

42. The "liuchuqi" refers to "liuchu qishan" 六出岐山, "departing from Mount Qi six times" of Zhuge Liang 诸葛亮, the renowned strategist of the popular novel, *Romance of the Three Kingdoms* (*Sanguo yanyi* 三国演义).

Bai Rui: (*Enters and sings.*)

At leisure, I leave my home and wonder around,
Passing over dikes both short and long.
I see over there a man of elegant appearance,
By the road, I greet him and inquire of him.

(*Speaks.*) May I inquire of Elder Brother as to where you hail from?
Bai Rui: (*Sings.*)

My name is none other than Bai Yutang,
My native home is right within this very region.
Having earned a bachelor's degree and its associated benefits,[43]
I hope to be able to inscribe my name on the Wild Goose Pagoda.[44]

(*Speaks.*) What fortune it is for me to meet Elder Brother today. It must have been the result of an affinity from three lives ago! I, your Younger Brother, would like to become your sworn brother, but I don't know your honorable opinion concerning this. . . .
Li Zhen: I would be more than honored.
Bai Rui: What is your honorable age?
Li Zhen: I, your Younger Brother, have vainly lived for eighteen years. May I ask what the honorable age of Elder Brother is?
Bai Rui: I, your Younger Brother, am sixteen years old.
Li Zhen: Why don't we make a mound with the earth and burn some sticks of incense right here.[45] (*Sings.*)

The two brothers prostrate ourselves to the ground.

Bai Rui: (*Sings.*)

We address the gods in the air—pray listen to us.

---

43. Literally, "having crossed the *panshui* 游泮水 (the pool at a Confucian temple), I still have on me fragrant mud from it." To cross the above-referenced pool implies having completed the first degree.

44. This seems to imply his desire to pass the metropolitan civil service examinations.

45. This refers to the ritual of sworn brotherhood that involves performing prayers to Heaven.

LI ZHEN: (*Sings.*)

We would like to emulate Lian 廉 and Lin 藺, who committed suicide to be with each other.[46]

BAI RUI: (*Sings.*)

And not be like Hua Xin 华歆 and Guan Ning 管宁.[47]

LI ZHEN: My dear Younger Brother, I hear that there's a place called the Pavilion of the Immortals in Exile where two talented women are seeking talented men for marriage. Is this true?

BAI RUI: I, your Younger Brother, was just there yesterday. If Elder Brother wishes to go, I can take you there.

LI ZHEN: Yes, please. This truly is a case of . . . (*Recites.*)

In order to visit the two Qiao 乔, we both cross the river.

BAI RUI: (*Recites.*)

So that they would marry Sun Ce 孙策 and Zhou Lang 周郎.[48]

Scene 8: "Plotting"

(*The Majordomo of the Jiang family leads Jiang Shangyou on stage.*)
JIANG SHANGYOU: (*Recites.*)

46. Lian stands for Lian Po 廉颇, and Lin stands for Lin Xiangru 藺相如, a mighty general and civil minister of the State of Zhao whose cooperation enabled their own minor State of Zhao 赵国 to withstand the powerful State of Qin 秦国 during the end of the Warring States period (403–221 BCE).

47. According to the "Dexing 德行" chapter in Liu Yiqing's 刘义庆 (403–444) *Shishuo xinyu* 世说新语, Guan Ning was so disappointed by Hua Xin when the latter went out of their study to watch the procession of a nobility passing by rather than concentrating on studying, that he cut the mat on which the two were seated and renounced his friendship with Hua.

48. The two Qiao refers to Da Qiao 大乔 (the Older Qiao) and Xiao Qiao 小乔 (the Younger Qiao), two ravishing beauties in *Romance of the Three Kingdoms*. They married two heroes, Sun Ce and Zhou You 周瑜 (Zhou Lang).

The beauties did not seek after me,
I worry about it, day and night.

I am Student Jiang Shangyou.[49] Ever since I saw the two beauties the other day, I have not been able to sit or lie down with ease. That Wonder Immortal was particularly exceptional. I intend to trick her into my hands, but I don't have a scheme.

Majordomo Jiang: I, your servant, have a scheme. . . . The Black Demon King has rebelled recently. Why don't I and our henchmen dress up as demons and kidnap the woman during the middle of the night? Who would know the difference?

Jiang Shangyou: Wonderful, wonderful, wonderful!

Majordomo Jiang: My lord—if I kidnap both women, that Jade Immortal should be mine.

Jiang Shangyou: Certainly. Come here, hitmen! (*Four hitmen enter.*)

Four Hitmen: Our lord—what job do you have for us?

Jiang Shangyou: I want you to kidnap a bride for me. Don't let the mistress know about this, no matter what. Change your outfits immediately.

Four Hitmen: Yes, Sir. (*They exit and re-enter with Majordomo Jiang, all outfitted and made up to resemble demon soldiers.*)

Majordomo Jiang: (*Sings.*)

The servants and I have all made ourselves up,
So that we may capture Xishi and E'huang.[50]

Jiang Shangyou: (*Sings.*)

I am dispatching a few ghosts and goblins,
And adding to them the assistance of an infernal judge.

Majordomo Jiang: (*Sings.*)

Master Ghost Valley (*guiguzi* 鬼谷子) will serve as the matchmaker,
So that King Yama here will become a bridegroom.[51] (*They exit.*)

---

49. He has not even passed the examinations for the First Degree.

50. See footnotes 25 and 32.

51. King Yama is the head of the Underworld, with control over all the ghost and demon guards. Here he is referring to their master, Jiang Shangyou.

Scene 9: "Chosen"

(*Enter Li Zhen and Bai Rui.*)
LI ZHEN: (*Sings.*)

> Uninterested in visiting the flower streets and willow lanes,[52]
> I seek for a natural beauty of heavenly demeanor.

BAI RUI: (*Sings.*)

> Suddenly I look up and see a vermilion gate and green windows,
> We have already arrived at the Pavilion of the Immortals in
> Exile.

(*Speaks.*) Elder Brother—a maid approaches. Speak to her when she arrives.
PRETTY PLUM: (*Enters and sings.*)

> Having served the two immortals since childhood,
> I also learned how to compose essays and poems
> When I ground ink and held the inkwell for them,
> I also inhaled the fragrances of the brushes and ink.[53]
> Outside the pavilion stand two talented scholars,
> I have no idea as to from where they hailed.
> I hurry over with my golden lotus feet and turn to one side,[54]
> Let me see what it is that they want.

LI ZHEN: Elder Sister Maid,[55] are your young ladies at the pavilion?
PRETTY PLUM: (*Sings.*)

> The man asks a question, but hasn't said anything,
> Would it be that you are also here to present a poem?
> This pavilion belongs to two immortals in exile,
> My ladies are here in order to select their husbands.

---

52. That is, brothels.

53. That is, she can also read, write, and appreciate literature.

54. The golden lotus feet refer to her small, bound feet. She turns to one side to indicate decorum and modesty.

55. He calls her "Elder Sister" as a sign of respect.

Countless romantic and elegant scholars have already come,
But not even one of them was chosen by the young ladies.

Li Zhen: Would the two of us be allowed to see them?

Pretty Plum: I, a humble one, cannot compare myself to the talented, literary maid of Kangcheng 康成,[56] since I have but a sketchy knowledge of the literary arts. But it is I who report to my ladies as to the caliber of your scholarship. You'll have to be passed by the resident official (*luofang guan* 落房官) before you get to see the main examiner. There is, in fact, also an examination by the eunuch.[57] You must abide by the procedures of the three examinations. If you don't, you will invariably fare worse than Sun Shan 孙山.[58] Before I see all of your talents, first give me an introductory poem. Let me assume the position of an assistant examiner.

Li Zhen: (*Laughs.*) Well! Ha, ha, ha . . . ! So she wants to test me first. Since such is the case, let me give the brush a try.

Pretty Maid: Let me bring it to you. (*She obtains a paper and brush and hands them to Li Zhen.*)

Li Zhen: Let me write a poem. (*Recites.*)

Desiring to obtain the foremost flower of the Jiangnan region,
The poet takes a brush, filled with boundless thoughts.
Where can one find the fragrant beauty? I ask for the ford in
order to reach her,
Alone tumbles the solitary sun, next to the colorful clouds.

(*Speaks.*) Take a look at this, Elder Sister Maid.

Pretty Maid: (*Sings.*)

So many good poems have I seen,
But this one is quite exceptional.
Although it consists of only a few words,

56. Zheng Kangcheng 郑康成 (127–200) was such a great scholar that even his maids had a high level of literary training.

57. She assumes the position of an important underling in the official imperial examination.

58. Sun Shan was at the end of a list of successful candidates. Hence, the phrase, "faring worse than Sun Shan" has been used to refer to unsuccessful examinees.

The proverb says that one word can be worth a thousand ounces of gold. (*She exits.*)

BAI RUI: (*Sings.*)

With that poem of yours, Elder Brother,
You will invariably be selected by the chief examiner.
The head of the examination hall must be highly discerning,
Just wait for the announcement of your attainment of the top prize.

PRETTY MAID: (*Enters and sings.*)

The poem has struck the fancy of the chief examiner,
You definitely did not fare worse than Sun Shan.
I step forward and present the invitation,
You have been invited to attend the celebratory banquet of the successful candidates.

LI ZHEN: Please lead the way, Elder Sister Maid. It truly is a case of . . . (*Recites.*)

Today being the date my Elder Brother will attain a top grade.

Scene 10: "Engagement"

(*Enter Lady Xu, Wonder Immortal, and Jade Immortal.*)
LADY XU: (*Recites.*)

I await the arrival of a son-in-law on the eastern bed,
Here finally arrives Wang Youjun 王右军, lying there with his belly exposed.[59]

59. Wang Youjun is more commonly known by the name of Wang Xizhi 王羲之 (321–379), one of the most renowned calligraphers. When the Grand Tutor of the Crown Prince wanted to select a son-in-law from the Wang family, all the eligible young men tried to impress the messenger dispatched by the Grand Tutor. Wang Xizhi, however, lay nonchalantly on his bed with his belly exposed. When the messenger described the various young men to the Grand Tutor, Xizhi was the one chosen to be his son-in-law. "The one lying on the eastern bed with exposed belly" has come to refer to son-in-law.

(*Enter Li Zhen and Bai Rui.*)
Li Zhen: (*Recites.*)

Today the friends, Liu 刘 and Ruan 阮,

Bai Rui: (*Recites.*)

Get to climb Mount Heavenly Terrace.[60]

Li Zhen and Bai Rui: Greetings, venerable lady. We two young scholars bow to you.
Lady Xu: You have come from afar, honored scholars. Excuse me for not meeting you at the gate.
Li Zhen and Bai Rui: Young ladies, please accept our greetings.
Wonder Immortal and Jade Immortal: We return the greeting. Pretty Plum, ask the guests to be seated.
Wonder Immortal: Ai, how lovely! (*Sings.*)

Having read that fine poem of his,
One can consider him the most talented on earth.
Who would have expected him to be so handsome as well,
He is verily comparable to Pan An 潘安 and Song Yu 宋玉.[61]

Li Zhen: (*Sings.*)

I, Li Zhen, gaze at her with my eyes,
I am dazzled by this lovely countenance of hers,
Her elegant demeanor will truly sink fish and wild geese.[62]
She is no less than the stunning Diao Chan 貂婵[63] of yesteryear.

Bai Rui: (*Sings.*)

I, Bai Yutang, judge the situation with scrutiny,
The marriage of these two seems completely set.

60. See footnote 18.

61. Pan An (247–300) and Song Yu (a Warring States period figure) have been acclaimed as the two most handsome men in Chinese history.

62. The implication is that she is so beautiful that even fish and birds will hide in shame.

63. A famous beauty in the popular novel, *Romance of the Three Kingdoms*.

That darling of mine is standing on the side,
I intend to bring up the union between this luan-bird and phoenix today.

WONDER IMMORTAL: (*Sings.*)

I walk up to my mother and speak to her,
I, Wonder Immortal, will make it very clear to you.
Over here, the mandarin ducks are gathered as a pair,
Over there, the butterflies are flying as a couple.
You'll need to make a decision, fast and quick,
It is commonly said that grown-up daughters should not be kept at home.

LADY XU: You may all sit down. I, the mother, have it all figured out. The girls have already met scholar Bai yesterday. (*Turns toward Li Zhen.*) This scholar—from where do you hail?

LI ZHEN: (*Sings.*)

My home is in Hunan, near Wuxi 五溪.
I am a son of a minister of the Board of Rites.

LADY XU: What is your honorable name?

LI ZHEN: (*Sings.*)

A descendant of Taibai 太白,[64] my surname is Li,
My personal name is what one serves at elaborate banquets.[65]

LADY XU: So the scholar's name is Li Zhen. Are you a student at a local school or at the imperial academy?

LI ZHEN: (*Sings.*)

I am neither a student of a local school nor of the imperial academy,
I placed first at the celebratory banquet of the second-degree candidates.

---

64. Li Bai 李白 (701–762), or Li Taibai, of the Tang dynasty, is one of the most famous poets in China.

65. He is referring to the word "*zhen*" in *shanzhen haiwei* 山珍海味, literally, "treasures from the mountains and flavors from the seas."

Lady Xu: So you are a top candidate of the second degree. What is your honorable age?

Li Zhen: (*Sings.*)

Not daring to announce myself as a scholar of eighteen,
I am but two years short of being capped.[66]

Lady Xu: I have a mind to marry these two daughters to the two of you. How do you feel about it?

Li Zhen: I am most honored by the offer. How dare I not obey your command? But I have not yet achieved fame and fortune. I will need to report to my parents before I can get married.

Lady Xu: How many years do you expect it to take?

Li Zhen: It should take no more than ten years.

Lady Xu: Ten years seems too long. What do you think, my daughter?

Wonder Immortal: I don't mind waiting.

Lady Xu: Scholar Bai—when can you get married?

Bai Rui: I'm going to the capital right now. If I can obtain an official post, I will send for her immediately.

Jade Immortal: My dear scholar! (*Sings.*)

Hearing that you, the scholar, will be leaving for the capital,
I, Jade Immortal, have a few words of advice for you.
When you get to wear the brocade robe, return immediately,
Do not forget me and never mention me again.

Bai Rui: (*Sings.*)

My dear young lady, please do not worry,
I, the young scholar, am a truly devoted lover.
If I should pass the examinations in the capital,
I will definitely send for you to join me.
How could I have you become a Madam Shu 苏氏,
Forever weaving a love-sick poem into a crossword puzzle?[67]

Li Zhen: I bid you farewell.

---

66. The capping age was twenty.

67. Madam Su refers to Su Hui 苏蕙, also named Su Ruolan 苏若兰 (b. 357). When her husband was exiled to a desert area in western China, she wove for him a brocade with a love poem consisting of 840 characters that can be read both vertically and horizontally.

LADY LI: We hereby see you off.
LI ZHEN: This is truly a case of . . . (*Recites.*)

This morning, we have joined the trees with interlocking branches,

BAI RUI: (*Recites.*)

Another day, we will paint the pictures of loving unions. (*Li Zhen and Bai Rui exit.*)

LADY LI: Ai, this is wonderful! (*She sings.*)

I rejoice having obtained two sons-in-law in one day,
The pairs of mandarin ducks will fly off on their own.

(*Speaks*) Jade Immortal, go back to your embroidery chamber. Wonder Immortal, come and sleep with Mom. (*They exit.*)

Scene 11: "Abducting a Bride"

(*Majordomo Jiang enters with four hitmen.*)
MAJORDOMO JIANG: (*Recites.*)

Outfitted and made up as soul-snatching demons,
We are in fact Jade-stealing bandits.

(*Speaks.*) We have arrived at the gate of the Pavilion of the Immortals in Exile. Let's barge in. Ho! I am inside! Let me go and separate the two girls from the others. Don't you leave, my darlings! Here we come! (*They run off stage.*)
PRETTY PLUM: (*Enters flustered and recites.*)

When great calamities descend from Heaven,
Most often it is during the midst of a dream.[68]

68. The original says 在黄梁 *zaihuangliang*, literally, "at the yellow millet," referring to a Tang dynasty short story about the dream of a man who experienced an entire life when a monk was cooking yellow millet.

(*Speaks.*) Come here quickly, Young Lady!
Jade Immortal: (*Enters and recites.*)

> About to take off my make-up and get ready for bed,
> I hear a great clamor and commotion of battle cries.

(*Speaks.*) Pretty Plum, what are you yelling about?

Pretty Plum: Haven't you heard yet, Young Mistress? A whole group of horrible demons just barged into the front courtyard, threatening to kill people and set fire to our place. Let's escape through the back door!

Jade Immortal: Follow me, Pretty Plum! (*They run off stage. Four hitmen enter with Wonder Immortal on one of their backs. They are followed by Majordomo Jiang.*)

Majordomo Jiang: Did you abduct only one of them? Carry her back to our residence. Let me find the other beauty. (*The four hitmen exit with Wonder Immortal. Majordomo Jiang searches inside the door.*) Ho! Why is it so quiet in here? She must have escaped through the back door. Let me chase after her there. Truly this is a case of . . . (*Recites.*)

> With my life-threatening broadsword in hand,
> I intend to catch the fish that escaped the net. (*He exits.*)

Jade Immortal: (*Enters disheveled and sings.*)

> Having left home in the dark night, I do not recognize the way,
> The maid and I, the two of us, got separated going east and west.
> I am now totally flustered, my mind wavers like a compass needle,
> Let me listen carefully and watch out for traces of the maid.
> (*She exits.*)

Pretty Plum: (*Sings back stage.*)

> Leaving the back door, Young Mistress and I got separated.

(*Enters and speaks.*) Just now Young Mistress and I made our escape through the back door. Suddenly we heard the bandits chasing after us, so I ducked and hid until the bandits passed. Now I don't know where Young Mistress is. What shall I do?

Jade Immortal: (*Off stage.*) Wait for me, Pretty Plum, here I come.

PRETTY PLUM: Aiya! I seem to hear Young Mistress's voice. Let me hide here and listen more carefully. (*She hides.*)

JADE IMMORTAL: (*Enters and sings.*)

My tears stream down incessantly like threads of hemp,
My legs are sore, my feet are in pain, how can I struggle any longer?
Furthermore, my three-inch lotus feet[69] and my curved shoes are tiny,
I so fear encountering those bandits and bringing disaster upon myself.

Aiya! I just heard Pretty Plum's voice, but why has it become so quiet all of a sudden? Fortunately, there's no one here. Let me risk finding out. Pretty Plum, where are you?

PRETTY PLUM: (*Enters.*) Here I am.

MAJORDOMO JIANG: (*Enters quietly with a broadsword in one hand and squeezing his nose with his other hand to imitate a woman's voice.*) Young Lady, here I am.

PRETTY PLUM: (*Enters.*) Here I am. (*She walks forward and collides with Majordomo Jiang.*) Where are you, Young Lady? Where . . .

MAJORDOMO JIANG: Watch my broadsword! (*Pretty Plum runs away, but Jiang grabs hold of Jade Immortal.*) Where do you think you are going, girl? Come, come and marry Old Number Three here. I'll kill you otherwise!

IMMORTAL JADE: Ai! What a bandit! (*Sings.*)

I am in fact a woman of heroic chastity,
How would I be willing to marry a bandit?

MAJORDOMO JIANG: See how dark it is. There's no one around. You'd better obey me.

JADE IMMORTAL: (*Sings.*)

I curse the bandit, damned by Heaven,
How would a phoenix be willing to marry a pheasant?

MAJORDOMO JIANG: If you are not willing to obey me, I'll hack you.

69. This refers to her small, bound feet.

Jade Immortal: Kill me if you wish! Who's going to obey you?

Majordomo Jiang: Let me kill the slave girl!

Jade Immortal: Go ahead and kill me! Kill, kill, kill!

Majordomo Jiang: (*Laughs.*) How can I kill someone so beautiful? What to do? I've got it! I'll have to grab her hair and force her to the ground. See if you can refuse me then! (*He steps on her. She tries to run away but is unable to. He sings.*)

Seeing her exceptionally beautiful face under the moonlight,
I, Majordomo Jiang, am so aroused that I cannot refrain myself.
I have a mind to force myself upon her in this wilderness,
But I fear that I might destroy her frail body and charming face.
Let me pull out my broadsword and scare her with threats,
Who's worried that she would still refuse with a heart of iron?

Jade Immortal: (*Nodding and pretending to agree and looks at the broadsword.*) My lord—please put the sword away. I'll . . .

Majordomo Jiang: You'll what?

Jade Immortal: I'll go along with you.

Majordomo Jiang: Since you're willing. Let me put the sword away. (*He puts the broadsword in its sheath.*) Let's consummate our marriage right now.

Jade Immortal: My lord—you don't look like a ruffian to me. How is it that you do not know the rites?

Majordomo Jiang: My dearest—what do you mean by the rites?

Jade Immortal: Look at the strange hills and rocks around here. How can this be an appropriate place for marriage? Besides, a marriage without a matchmaker not only defiles Heaven and Earth but also prevents performance of the rites. Since my lord is a gentleman knowledgeable of the laws and rites, how could you carry out such an unrighteous act?

Majordomo Jiang: Aiya! She does have a point! She even knows that a marriage without a matchmaker prevents performance of the rites. (*He looks to the left and right.*) Ho! I got it! Yes, my dearest—look, there's an old shrine over there. How about if the two of us ask a god to be our matchmaker so that we can consummate our marriage right now and live happily hereafter? What do you think?

Jade Immortal: (*Looks at the broadsword.*) This would work. My Lord—better leave your sword out here before you go into the shrine to pray to the god.

MAJORDOMO JIANG: (*Leaves the broadsword and goes into the shrine. Jade Immortal picks up the broadsword.*) Come here quickly, my dearest—look how clean this old shrine is. Let me take my clothes off first. (*He disrobes. Jade Immortal hacks him with the broadsword.*)
JADE IMMORTAL: Here, bandit! (*Sings.*)

I yell, "Bandit, don't you behave barbarically!"

(*Speaks.*) Watch my sword!
MAJORDOMO JIANG: Aiya, oh no! (*He is injured.*) What to do? I'm empty handed and empty fisted. I'd better run away! (*He exits.*)
JADE IMMORTAL: (*Continues to sing.*)

I have no fear of your steel sword,
I, your lady, am a virgin of integrity.
How would I let an ugly bandit trample over me?
Let me wrap the sword in my skirt here,
And voice the injustice I suffered at the local court.

(*Speaks.*) Ai, oh Heaven! (*She exits.*)

Scene 12: "Rescued"

JIANG SHANGYOU: (*Enters and recites.*)

Dispatching the imposter demons on their way,
I hope to have them abduct the beauty for me.

THE HITMEN: (*Enter.*) We report to our lord—we've brought the beauty.
JIANG SHANGYOU: Bring her in. (*The four hitmen carry Wonder Immortal on stage.*)
THE HITMEN: Congratulations, our lord!
JIANG SHANGYOU: Go get your reward down there. (*They exit.*) Let me lock the door. Wake up, Young Lady!
WONDER IMMORTAL: (*Sings.*)

Seeing those horrible demons, my souls[70] were scared so stiff that they flew away,

70. The Chinese believe that a variety of souls, mainly the *hun* 魂 and the *po* 魄, reside within each person.

Suddenly, I hear someone calling me beside my ear.
I lift my head and gaze with my two eyes,
How is it that a monster now stands before me?

Jiang Shangyou: Young Lady, do you still recognize me, your lord?
Wonder Immortal: (*Sings.*)

I curse at the bandit who tried to deceive one with trickery,
If marrying me is your intention, you can forget it right now.

Jiang Shangyou: (*Sings.*)

I ask you, dear Young Lady, not to argue,
Diao Chan 貂婵 is destined to marry Fengxian 奉先.
This "interlocking strategy" (*lianhuan ji* 连环计) has been
designed for quite sometime,[71]
Let's wait and see the planting of the beautiful jade in Lantian 兰田.[72]

Wonder Immortal: (*Sings.*)

I curse you, you shameless villain,
There's no question that I would ever consider marrying you.
If Jieyuan Li should find out about this,
He would invariably fry you, you beast, in scalding oil.

Madam Hai: (*Enters quietly, listens and calls.*) Open the door, robber![73]
Jiang Shangyou: Please lower your voice, Young Lady. The female tiger[74] is here. Oh, no! I'm in trouble! (*Sings.*)

I was just about to consummate my marriage with the girl,
Who should arrive but the Yaksha deity demon?[75]

---

71. The "Interlocking Strategy" usually refers to the scheme described in *Romance of the Three Kingdoms* in which Diao Chan is promised to two men, one of them being Lü Fengxian (also known as Lü Bu 吕布), to create animosity between them.

72. Lantian in Shaanxi produced beautiful jade. Here, however, Jiang Shangyou seems to be suggesting that the girl—that is, the beautiful jade—will be planted in Lantian (literally, Orchid Field), which may refer to himself.

73. In Shaanxi plays, women who are not trying to show respect or to endear themselves to their husbands typically referred to their husbands as robbers.

74. Shrewish women are popularly called female tigers.

75. Demons that fly like meteors; messengers from Hell.

I have a mind not to open the door,
But how dare a minor ghost resist the might of King Yama?[76]
Yet, if I should open this door,
What am I going to do with this girl?

MADAM HAI: Robber! Are you not going to open the door?
JIANG SHANGYOU: (*Sings.*)

I have no choice but to let her in. (He opens the door. Madam Hai enters and beats him.)

MADAM HAI: (*Sings.*)

I'm going to ensure an untimely meeting with King Yama for you!

(*Speaks.*) Hm! Why don't we do something else instead? Now that you've done this, robber, why don't you kneel down first? (*He kneels.*)
WONDER IMMORTAL: Please save me, Elder Sister-in-Law![77]
MADAM HAI: Where is this girl from? Get out immediately!
WONDER IMMORTAL: I'm most grateful to you, Elder Sister-in-Law! (*She exits.*)
MADAM HAI: (*Sings.*)

I curse you, robber, how dare you misbehave?
Without any reason, you act without restraint.
You must think I'm too old for you
And wish to find another to be "luan-bird and phoenix" with.
This extra job of yours you truly schemed well,
Now that I've caught you in the act, I'll never let you off the hook.
Today you were caught as a womanizing robber,
Ignoring imperial regulations, you have transgressed the law.[78] (*She hits him.*)

---

76. He is so terrified of his wife that he refers to her as the king of the Underworld while he is but a minion of that realm.

77. This is a polite and endearing address for older women of the same generation.

78. There was no law against taking concubines in imperial China; she was probably referring to her own rules as imperial.

Jiang Shangyou: Darling wife, please spare my life! I won't dare to do it again!
Madam Hai: Since you've admitted your crime, just kowtow to me!
Jiang Shangyou: (*Prostrates and kowtows.*) Darling wife, I am grateful to you for your graciousness!
Madam Hai: (*Sings.*)

Now that I have exonerated you from your crime today,
Let's enter the bed curtains and sort out this court case of ours.

Jiang Shangyou: (*Sings.*)

I was born with a red face without any luck,
Just now I've lost the job I've already had in hand.

(*Speaks.*) Ai! I've already goofed up this time. This truly is a case of . . . (*Recites.*)

I had hoped to steal a beauty and obtain an extra source of fun,

Madam Hai: (*Sings.*)

This Dongshi 东施 is certainly able to emulate the charming frown.[79]

Scene 13: "Combat"

(*Four barbarian soldiers enter with the Demon King and Princess Myriad Flowers.*)
Demon King: (*Recites.*)

Having learned and practiced sorcery since childhood,

Princess Myriad Flowers: (*Recites.*)

We can create armies out of scattered beans.

79. This refers to the popular tale about the incomparable beauty, Xishi (see footnote 25), known for her charming frown that was induced by a persistent heartache. The ugly Dongshi tried to make herself more attractive by emulating Xishi's frown, but ended up looking even worse.

DEMON KING: We are the Black Demon King.[80]

PRINCESS MYRIAD FLOWERS: I am none other than the Princess of Myriad Flowers.

DEMON KING: We, the great king, have learnt and practiced sorcery since childhood. We use soldiers of ghosts and demons to win. Yang Yiqing has just arrived with an army. Barbarian soldiers, charge! (*Chinese soldiers enter from the exit side,*[81] *followed by Yang Yiqing. He combats the Black Demon King and Princess Myriad Flowers. The latter brother and sister are defeated, and they exit. Yang Yiqing chases after them and exits. The Black Demon King enters dressed as a demon. Yang Yiqing enters and chases after him. They fight. Yang Yiqing is defeated and exits.*)

BARBARIAN SOLDIERS: Yang Yiqing has escaped.

BLACK DEMON KING: Don't chase after the defeated army! Ai! Let's return to our camp. (*Sings.*)

> We fought until the Chinese army ran for their lives,

PRINCESS MYRIAD FLOWERS: (*Sings.*)

> The brother and sister will now return to camp with our soldiers. (*They exit.*)

Scene 14: "Escape from Danger"

(*Two prisoner escorts enter with Hua Tianbiao.*)

HUA TIANBIAO: (*Sings.*)

> I regret only that I haven't avenged my father's grievance,
> Who would have thought that I would incur a disaster instead?
> Facing Heaven, I cannot help but call upon it.

(*Speaks.*) Oh, Heaven! (*Sings.*)

> When will this grief and enmity ever dissipate?

---

80. Although only the emperor was supposed to use the "royal we" (*gujia* 孤家, the Lone One), the Demon King refers to himself as *gujia*, indicating that he considers himself an equal to the Chinese emperor.

81. Like the human actors' theater, the puppets typically enter from the left and exit to the right, unless a party is definitely arriving from a different direction.

Li Zhen: (*Enters and sings.*)

> Traveling along, I now arrive at a main highway,
> I see a few guards escorting a prisoner.
> Carefully, I take a good look at the criminal,
> Who would have thought that it would be my cousin, Hua Tianbiao?

(*Speaks.*) Ai, my suffering cousin!

Hua Tianbiao: Cousin, what are you doing here?

Li Zhen: I came here to look for you at Mother's bidding. What happened to you, cousin?

Hua Tianbiao: You wouldn't have known, cousin, but I, your Elder Brother, went to the capital intending to kill the treacherous villain. But I ended up being captured by him instead. I expect that this will be the end of my life.

Li Zhen: Ai! My dear cousin, whom I can't help! (*Barbarian soldiers yell backstage.*) Barbarian soldiers are coming—what are we going to do? I've got it! Elder Brother Escorts, why don't you release my cousin so that he can fight the barbarian soldiers and save our lives?

Guards: Warrior[82]—we are going to unlock you right now. But if the barbarian soldiers are defeated, you'll have to put the cangue back on again.

Hua Tianbiao: Of course.

Guard: Let me release you.

Hua Tianbiao: Here's the cangue, let me fight with it. (*He exits with Li Zhen and the guards. Princess Myriad Flowers and Hua Tianbiao enter from opposite sides of the stage, followed by Li Zhen and the guards.*)

Princess Myriad Flowers: Announce your name, warrior!

Hua Tianbiao: The name of your lord here is Hua Tianbiao. I'm accompanied by my cousin, Li Zhen. Don't go away, little girl! (*They fight.*)

Princess Myriad Flowers: What a fine warrior! (*She exits.*)

Li Zhen: The bandits have left. There's no need to provoke them further.

Hua Tianbiao: We were too easy on her.

Guards: Warrior—please come here and put the cangue back on.

Hua Tianbiao: Who's going to wear that thing again?

Guards: Are you eating your words?

Hua Tianbiao: I don't think you dare to go home anyway. Why don't you follow me to Mount Tiger Hill (*huqiu shan* 虎邱山) and raise a rebel-

82. The literal appellation used here is *jieshi* 杰士, meaning "hero."

lion with me there? When we succeed in the future, you'll all become rich and famous.

GUARDS: Yes, we have no choice but to follow you now, warrior.

HUA TIANBIAO: My dear cousin, let's bid each other farewell now. This is precisely a case of . . . (*Recites.*)

Two hands separated life from death,

LI ZHEN: (*Recites.*)

One foot jumps out of the pit of scandal. (*They exit.*)

Scene 15: "Assumed Identity"

BAI RUI: (*Enters and recites.*)

Harboring the ambition to ride the clouds,
I intend to return with the banner of a champion.[83]

(*Speaks.*) I am Bai Rui. The metropolitan civil service examination is held this year, and I am on my way to the capital to sit for it. (*Someone yells, "Take him! Take him!" off stage.*) Aiya! Oh no! (*Two barbarian soldiers enter and capture Bai Rui.*)

BARBARIAN SOLDIERS: We've got him. Let's tie him up and take him to the Princess. (*They exit with Bai Rui.*)

(*Four barbarian soldiers enter with Princess Myriad Flowers.*)

PRINCESS MYRIAD FLOWERS: (*Recites.*)

Yesterday, I met the young Master Hua,
I would like to capture and keep him as mate.

I am Princess Myriad Flowers. Yesterday, I got to meet Hua Tianbiao. Although we didn't talk, we had a great bout of combat. He was so skillful that I could hardly keep up. I would like to keep him, but he disappeared. What shall I do?

BARBARIAN SOLDIER: I report to the Princess—we've captured a scholar.

PRINCESS MYRIAD FLOWERS: Bring him over! (*The soldier responds: "Yes."*)

83. One of the prize candidates.

Bai Rui: (*Enters.*) Princess, please spare my life.
Princess Myriad Flowers: Hello, scholar—are you Li Zhen?
Bai Rui: (*Aside.*) She seems to like Li Zhen. She must not want to kill Li Zhen. I know what to do now. (*Speaks.*) Yes, I am Li Zhen.
Princess Myriad Flowers: Is Hua Tianbiao your cousin?
Bai Rui: Yes, he is my cousin.
Princess Myriad Flowers: I, the Princess, would like for him to marry me. I implore you to be the matchmaker and persuade him. Barbarian soldiers—escort him to search for Hua Tianbiao! (*She exits.*)
Barbarian Soldiers: Let's go!
Bai Rui: (*Sings.*)

I assumed an identity without thinking,
How could I have done such a thing?
I have never met this man surnamed Hua,
And I've been asked to be his matchmaker.
A careful reflection indicates that I was mistaken,
I shouldn't have agreed to it without any thought.
The fact that I was bound in ropes before I agreed
Made it easier for her to persuade me to be an Old Man Under the Moon.[84]
This really is a turn of fate for the worse; unfortunately,
I have no choice but to take a trip and go with them. (*They exit.*)

Scene 16: "Meeting on the Road"

Jade Immortal: (*Enters and sings.*)

I met a bandit during the middle of that other night,
Heading for the court, I intend to voice my grievances.
Moving my golden lotus feet, I travel forward,
I see a woman out there, back there behind me.

(*Speaks.*) Let me rest for a while and wait for her.
Wonder Immortal: (*Enters.*) I'm walking. (*Sings.*)

Behind my back I curse resentfully that Jiang Chaozong,
Who dared to get the demons to commit acts of violence.

---

84. That is, matchmaker.

As I walked, I look up to take a look,
I see Younger Sister Jade Immortal sitting by the road.

(*Speaking.*) My dear sister—what happened to you?
JADE IMMORTAL: Please listen to me, dear Elder Sister! (*Sings.*)

When the evil demons arrived at our front court,
I escaped through the back door to save my life.
But unfortunately, I met a bandit on my way,
The knave tried to force me into marrying him,
But I secretly tricked his broadsword from him,
And hacked his right arm until red blood spurted.
Now I have a piece of real evidence from the bandit,
I'm going to lodge a suit against him with General Yang.

(*Speaks.*) Dear Elder Sister, what happened to you?
WONDER IMMORTAL: Ah, my dear Younger Sister! (*Sings.*)

When the watch tower struck midnight that other night,
Innumerable ghosts and goblins arrived at our home.
They kidnapped me and took me to the Jiang residence,
The main instigator behind it all was Jiang Chaozong.
He tried to force me into agreeing to marry him,
And then suddenly a savior appeared at the scene.
It turned out that this Chaozong was a henpecked fellow,
And his wife rescued me from the prison cage.
I will now sue him for forming an alliance with the demon bandits,
This is no ordinary accusation that he will have to deal with.

JADE IMMORTAL: According to Elder Sister's story, the bandit I met that night must have been someone from the Jiang residence as well. The sword here has a name on it. Let's sue them for forming an alliance with the demon bandits and get them nailed. This is precisely a case of . . . (*Recites.*)

You and I will go to the military tent to lodge our suit,

WONDER IMMORTAL: (*Recites.*)

Let's go there immediately without further delay. (*They exit.*)

Scene 17: "Official Search"

(*Yamen runners enter with Gao Gu.*)
Gao Gu: (*Sings.*)

> When cutting grass, one must pull it up by the root,
> Don't let the sprout grow and proliferate once again.

I am an official by the name of Gao Gu. Li Zhen, the son of Li Dongyang, made an alliance with the barbarians and had Hua Tianbiao released. His Excellency Jiang memorialized to the throne and had Old Li put in jail. He also ordered me to search all over for Li Zhen to bring him to the capital to be indicted. Before I left, His Excellency also told me that he wants to marry his daughter to Bai Rui and wants me to seek Bai's whereabouts. Yamen runners, get the horses moving! (*Sings.*)

> I have to search for a son-in-law as well as a criminal,
> I am truly worried that I can do both adequately.
> Having to carry out both tasks simultaneously,
> This lowly official cannot help but sweat nervously. (*They exit.*)

Scene 18: "Lodging a Suit"

(*Four soldiers enter with Yang Yiqing.*)
Yang Yiqing: (*Sings.*)

> The other day I suffered defeat in combat; I am most annoyed;
> I cannot help but heave and sigh while sitting in my precious tent.

(*Speaks.*) I am Marshal Yang Yiqing. Yesterday I fought with the barbarians and was defeated. I am so upset.

Soldier: I report to the Marshal—two civilian girls are yelling that they have been wronged.

Yang Yiqing: Tell them to go to the front of the tent.

Soldier: The Marshal ordered you to go to the front of the tent.

Wonder Immortal and Jade Immortal: (*Enter.*) Your Excellency—we have been wronged! We have been wronged!

Yang Yiqing: Present your case.

Wonder Immortal: (*Sings.*)

I, Wonder Immortal Xu, kneel before the tent and make my report,
I have been engaged to Jieyuan Li ever since childhood.
But the bandit Jiang Shangyou tried to create trouble,
Taking his household servants, he entered my home during the dark night.
A quarrel broke out at his residence, and I was able to escape the trap,
Therefore I am now able to come to your military court to lodge a suit.

YANG YIQING: The other girl—present your case, too.
JADE IMMORTAL: (*Sings.*)

I have been engaged to become luan-bird and phoenix with Bai Rui,
In the middle of the night, I left the seclusion of my residence to escape invaders.
I happened to run into the bandit after he had her kidnapped,
In a shrine, he tried to force me into marrying him.
Using a ruse, I tricked this weapon from the knave,
Using force, I hacked at him and was able to escape.
This very sword here bears the name of the bandit,
This is the true evidence of the criminal bandit.

YANG YIQING: It turns out that both of them are suing Jiang Shangyou. Colonel, take the two girls back to their homes. Arrest Jiang Shangyou and bring him here to see me. (*The colonel responds and exits with Wonder Immortal and Jade Immortal.*) What a treacherous villain! You monopolize the power at the imperial court, and your son is also full of wickedness. I'm not a human being, if I, your old Lord Yang, don't have your son killed when I return to the imperial court.
COLONEL: (*Enter.*) I've arrested Master Jiang.
YANG YIQING: Bring him up here! (*The colonel responds.*)
JIANG SHANGYOU: (*Enters.*) What is this about, Uncle?[85]

---

85. Although Yang and Jiang's father obviously belong to different factions, they are both high ministers at the imperial court, and Jiang Shangyou knows him as a colleague of his father.

Yang Yiqing: What a beast! You made an alliance with the demon bandits and kidnapped civilian girls. Tear off the dog's hide of his and give him forty lashes!

Jiang Shangyou: Please spare my life, Uncle!

Yang Yiqing: Colonels! (*The colonels respond.*) Keep the fellow imprisoned at the back of the camp. When I, Your Lord, return from pacifying the barbarians, I'll present a memorial to His Majesty and get rid of both the father and the son together. This is precisely a case of . . . (*The colonels take Jiang Shangyou off stage. Yang recites.*)

Wait until I attain success and sing the song of victory,
I will surely get rid of the treacherous demons when I return to the capital. (*They exit.*)

Scene 19: "Finding a Son-in-Law"

(*A household servant enters with Jiang Bin.*)
Jiang Bin: (*Sings.*)

I have been worried about my daughter's marriage,
But today I will tie the knot of the luan-bird and the phoenix.

(*Speaks.*) Boy, ask Scholar Bai to come here. (*The servant responds.*)
Li Zhen: (*Enters and sings.*)

Due to my assuming a false identity the other day,
The yamen runners have sent me to the Jiang residence.
Facing the old villain, I make a deep bow,
And stand to one side without uttering a word.

Jiang Bin: (*Sings.*)

Bestowing upon you a chair so that you can sit down,
I require of the scholar when you've arrived in the capital?

Li Zhen: (*Sings.*)

You and I are neither relatives nor friends,
What do you care if I arrived in the capital or not?

JIANG BIN: (*Sings.*)

This old man has a beautiful young daughter,
To date, she has not been joined in a union of the luan-bird and phoenix.
I have heard for a long time about your talent and fame,
Concerning this marriage, I expect that you will accept.

LI ZHEN: (*Sings.*)

I've never learned the celestial tune to attract the phoenix,
Xiao Shi 萧史 dares not climb the Qin Pavilion (*qinlou* 秦楼).[86]

JIANG BIN: I've already made the offer—why resist? Boy, take Scholar Bai to the wedding chamber. (*The household servant responds.*)
YAMEN RUNNER: (*Enters.*) We've captured Li Zhen. He's at the gate waiting for trial.
JIANG BIN: Beat the drum and open the court room! (*Exits.*)
LI ZHEN: I can die from fright! (*Sings.*)

Hearing this, my souls are so frightened that they fly and disperse,
Suddenly they report that they have captured Jieyuan Li.
I am clearly just sitting here chatting with the old villain,
Could it be that someone else is here to extricate me from trouble?
I think of what happened before and after, and I am totally confused,
This event is completely inexplicable and incomprehensible to me.

HOUSEHOLD SERVANT: Scholar, please enter the bridal chamber.
LI ZHEN: Ai! (*Sings.*)

I assumed another identity only to escape the tiger's den,
Who would have thought that I would end up with this karmic fate?
I have no intention of having a candlelit night in a bridal chamber,
How could I be willing to be part of the joining of the entwining trees?

86. See footnote 26.

They wanted me to participate in the harmonizing of the luan-bird and phoenix,
But I wonder for whom I am substituting in this marriage?
I would very much like to refuse this offer of marital union,
But how could I explain the truth about assuming another identity?

(*Speaks.*) Ai! Let's let it be! (*Sings.*)

Since I've got to be here temporarily, let it be temporary.
It is commonly said that one shouldn't brake abruptly when the carriage stops. (*They exit.*)

Scene 20: "Trial"

(*A colonel enters with Jiang Bin.*)
Jiang Bin: (*Sings.*)

Angrily I preside over the court, where I exude power and awe,
Now that I have captured the traitor, I will force him to confess.
A Fifth King of the Underworld (*wuyan jun* 五闫君) meditating at his Luosen 罗森 Court,
I will make sure of your demise now that you're in my hands.

(*Speaks.*) Colonel, tie him up and bring him up here! (*The colonel responds.*)
Bai Rui: (*Enters and kneels.*) Your Excellency, I have been wronged! I have been wronged!
Jiang Bin: What a Li Zhen! You made alliances with the barbarians and Hua Tianbiao. How dare you not confess!
Bai Rui: Please allow me to explain! (*Sings.*)

I am Bai Rui, my style is Yutang,
My native home is outside the city of Suzhou.
I was coming to the capital the other day,
But unexpectedly ran into barbarian soldiers on the way.
The identity of Li Zhen, I did assume,
And hence brought about this disaster by mistake.
I know not the whereabouts of Jieyuan Li,
I am in fact the scholar Bai Yutang.

JIANG BIN: Ho! Bai Rui is my son-in-law. He's at my residence right now. I see you obviously won't confess without torture. Colonel, put him on the rack!

HEAD EUNUCH: (*Enters.*) Greetings, Your Excellency Jiang!

JIANG BIN: Greetings. What is Your Excellency here for?

HEAD EUNUCH: His Majesty is watching the light displays at the light pavilion. He has ordered for Your Excellency to go there and accompany him. You should proceed there immediately. I bid you farewell right now. (*He exits.*)

JIANG BIN: I will see you off. What an unfortunate interruption. Oh, well—lock the slave in the small room. I'll take care of him when I return. This is precisely a case of . . . (*Recites.*)

When I return from accompanying His Majesty,
I will make sure of your trip to the Yellow Springs.[87] (*He exits.*)

COLONEL: Scholar Li, let's go to the small room.

BAI RUI: Ai! (*Sings.*)

Although I escaped the tiger's mouth, I ended up in the net of a villain,
The problems of Elder Brother Li, I now have to shoulder.
These must be the result of my karma from a previous life,
Imprisoned, I have now become a Gongye Chang 公冶长.[88]
(*They exit.*)

Scene 21: "The Bridal Chamber"

(*The scenery of a bridal chamber; Jiang Yulian enters.*)

JIANG YULIAN: (*Sings.*)

In the bridal chamber, the candles are lit as brightly as daylight,
The water-chestnut mirror and the fairyland flower pillow are most delicate.

---

87. The ancient Chinese believed that the deceased went to the Yellow Springs in the Underworld; hence, the speaker is saying that he will make sure of Li's demise.

88. Gong Yechang (dates unknown) was imprisoned unjustly. Confucius (551–479 BCE), however, sympathized with him and gave him his daughter's hand.

So delighted that tonight the two surnames will be joined,
In the sky, toward the east, glitter three or five stars.

(*Speaks.*) I am Jiang Yulian. My father has invited Scholar Bai here and told us to get married tonight. How come he is not here yet?

Maid: (*Enters.*) Please walk faster, Master Scholar.

Li Zhen (*Enters and sings.*)

Loudly, the little maid continuously asks me to hurry,
She invites me to go to the bridal chamber to consummate the marriage.
Although a scholar, I am now involved in a scandalous situation,
Let me sit outside the door and be dumb, as someone without voice.

Maid: Young Lady, the scholar won't come in. He just sits there.

Jiang Yulian: Let me take a look! (*Sings.*)

I, Jiang Yulian, take a look at the bridegroom,
Why is he just sitting outside the bridal chamber?
Could it be that he considers me ugly and despises me?
Could it be that he considers me lacking in decorum and dislikes me?
I walk up to him, full of smiles, and greet him graciously,
I ask, Scholar, what grief has locked the tips of your eyebrows?
(*Li Zhen refuses to speak.*)

(*Speaks.*) Please come here, dear Scholar. Accept my greetings. (*Li Zhen ignores her. She sings.*)

Well intentioned, I greeted the bridegroom over and over,
Why does he remain totally silent and dumb?
He must despise me because my father monopolizes power,
Having victimized the Hua family and now Jieyuan Li.
I implore the scholar not to despise me and treat me with disdain,
I am in fact a boat of merciful salvation within the sea of sorrow.

Li Zhen: (*Sings.*)

I thought that I would have nothing to say at the bridal chamber,
Who would have known that his daughter would be so wise and upright?
I walk up to her, greet her with a bow, and tell her everything:
My name is Li Zhen, and my father is none other than Dongyang.
Assuming a false identity, I ended up meeting your father, an enemy of my family.
I, Li Zhaoxian, should not have been identified as Yutang of the Bai clan.

JIANG YULIAN: Since you are Li Zhen, why did you pretend to be Bai Rui?
LI ZHEN: Bai Rui is my sworn younger brother. I used his identity to prevent trouble.
JIANG YULIAN: (*Sings.*)

According to the explanations of the Jieyuan,
I am in fact the wife of your sworn younger brother.
Releasing you tonight and setting you free,
I will rely upon you as matchmaker for my marriage.[89]

LI ZHEN: Since the Young Lady is so kind, I will be happy to ensure the success of your marriage.
MAID: Follow me.
LI ZHEN: (*Recites.*)

Once the carp is extricated from the golden hook,
It will leave without looking back. (*The maid exits with Li Zhen and then returns.*)

JIANG YULIAN: Maid, go get a cup of tea for me.
MAID: Yes. (*Exits and returns in a hurry.*) Oh no, Young Lady! I sent the young man to the middle courtyard. But just now I met a servant boy who told me that Jieyuan Li was caught and locked in the small room.
JIANG YULIAN: (*Sings.*)

I resent that the scholar was so lacking in skills,
To save you, I had the back door opened.

89. That is, Li Zhen will help persuade Bai Rui to marry her.

Why did you go to the front and get into trouble?
And have now created a disaster all of a sudden?

(*Speaks.*) Maid, what are we going to do now?

Maid: Young Lady, I heard that your father, the Old Lord, has gone to accompany His Majesty the Emperor. Let's go to the small room while there's no one around and see what we can do. What do you think?

Jiang Yulian: (*Sings.*)

Lightly, I move my golden lotus feet to the front court,
There are no servant boys inside or outside this court.
The maid and I listen carefully outside the window,
We hear grievous weeping inside the small room.

Bai Rui: (*Off stage.*) I'm being wronged to death! (*Enters from the exit side and sings.*)

Now that I have landed in the hands of a villain,
To whom can I relieve my chest full of sorrow?
Soaked in tears without any rescuers,

This small room will be my City of Wronged Deaths.

Jiang Yulian: (*Sings.*)

I cock my ear and listen outside the small room,
He has indeed re-entered the fire pit once again.
I released you to escape through the back door,
How did you get to be locked in the small room?

Bai Rui: (*Sings.*)

Who released me to escape through the back door?
Of which family are you its beautiful daughter?

Jiang Yulian: (*Sings.*)

Do you not remember me, Jieyuan?
My name is none other than Jiang Yulian.

Bai Rui: (*Sings.*)

Since the Young Lady of the family is here,
Please rescue me and save my life immediately.

JIANG YULIAN: (*Sings.*)

Jiang Yulian arrives and comes up with a scheme,
Quickly I tell the maid to keep an eye out for me.
Grabbing a brick with this hand of mine,
Let me smash the golden lock and open the prison. (*Jiang Yulian smashes the lock. She acts as if she has hurt her hand, and Bai Rui exits from the door.*)

(*Speaks.*) Aiyoyo! (*To Bai Rui.*) Quickly, follow me to the back door to escape!

BAI RUI: Thank you, Young Lady, for saving my life. I bid you farewell now. (*He is about to leave.*)

JIANG YULIAN: (*Pulls at him.*) Wait a minute! Just wait a minute! (*Sings.*)

I ask the Jieyuan to wait but a minute,
Your sister-in-law has something to say.
Twice I have saved you from the tiger's mouth,
You have to promise to seek news of your sworn brother.

BAI RUI: (*Sings.*)

What's this sworn brotherhood thing about?
I, Bai Rui, have no idea what you are saying.

JIANG YULIAN: (*Sings.*)

Scholar, how could you act so immaturely?
How could you pretend to be confused with me?
Previously you said that you were surnamed Li,
How come now you pretend to be surnamed Bai?

BAI RUI: I am originally surnamed Bai. I pretended to be Li Zhen the other day because of barbarian troops. Your father had me captured and brought here by mistake. According to what you said, did you meet a Jieyuan Li?

JIANG YULIAN: (*To the maid.*) Bring the lamp, Maid. Let me take a look personally to see who he is. (*She looks at him.*) Aiya! How strange! (*Sings.*)

At the Western Chamber, Zhang Junrui 张君瑞 managed to escape,
Could it be that Yingying 莺莺 was unable to recognize him?[90]
Although the maid Hongniang 红娘 identified him clearly,[91]
How could he suddenly become a knight on a white horse, a knight on a white horse?

Bai Rui: What are you talking about?
Jiang Yulian: Ai, my dear Scholar! (*Sings.*)

Just now when it was early evening,
My father mistook Elder Brother Li as you.
The fact was he assumed your name and identity,
And my father did not verify it at the time.
He was sent to the bridal chamber to get married,
But the scholar was stubborn and refused to enter the door.
I then questioned him in detail and with care,
And ordered the maid to see him off through the back door.
Then all of a sudden some bad news arrived,
And we heard that Li Zhen had been captured once again.
I therefore came here to assist him a second time,
Who would have thought that this time it's the real Master Bai?

Bai Rui: According to the Young Lady, Elder Brother Li is alive! Now you can let me go.
Jiang Yulian: Wait—wait just a minute! (*Sings.*)

Please be patient, my dear Scholar,
I will take care of everything cleverly.
I will hide you in my embroidery boudoir,
This marriage is something he already knew about.
If my father still comes to inquire about you,
I will say that you caught a cold and are indisposed.
Come—come with your wife to go through the rituals,
We will go to the bed as a couple and become husband and wife. (*They exit.*)

---

90. Zhang Junrui and Cui Yingying are protagonists of *Romance of the Western Chamber*. See footnote 29.

91. Hongniang is Cui Yingying's maid, who acted as go-between for the illicit relationship between Zhang Junrui and Yingying.

Scene 22: "Visit"

(*Wang Ao enters with his daughter, Wang Youqiang.*)
Wang Ao: (*Sings.*)

I resent the fact that his Majesty has a soft ear and believed slander,
My poor colleague Li was consequently imprisoned in the jail.
To this date, we have absolutely no news of the son of Li,
Causing old me to worry constantly, I worry constantly.

Wang Youqiang: (*Sings.*)

My Daddy is old, but his heart is completely loyal,
Concerning that case of the Li family, he is very worried.
I hope Heaven will protect them and all will be well eventually,
Then the loyal and the treacherous will become clear to all.

Wang Ao: I, the old one, am Wang Ao.
Wang Youqiang: I am his daughter, Youqiang.
Household Servant: (*Enters.*) I report to My Lord—the son of the Li family is here.
Wang Ao: Ask him to come in immediately!
Household Servant: Yes!
Wang Ao: Go inside, my daughter.
Wang Youqiang: Your child knows. (*She exits.*)
Li Zhen: (*Enters and recites.*)

When will the injustice ever be cleared?
Let me first visit the honorable scholar.

(*Speaks.*) Dear Uncle, please allow your nephew to greet you.
Wang Ao: Just do the normal bow.[92] Please take a seat.
Li Zhen: Thank you.
Wang Ao: Dear Nephew, the treacherous villain memorialized to the throne, accusing you of establishing an alliance with the barbarians and Hua Tianbiao. Was this true?

92. He is telling Li not to perform the elaborate, formal kowtow.

LI ZHEN: Please listen to me, Uncle! (*Sings.*)

Consider the facts that your nephew is a scholar and scion of a clan of renown,
How would I dare to ally with the barbarians and act recklessly?
Last year in my native home, I received an order from my mother,
I rushed to Jiangnan in search of my cousin from the Hua family.
Fortuitously, we met in the middle of a road while traveling,
But suddenly, barbarian soldiers appeared on the plain.
The prison guards released him in order to fight the bandits,
He then thought why would a free bird return to the cage?
The treacherous villain accused me of allying with the demon bandits.
To avoid problems, I had no recourse but to change my name.
As soon as I met Jiang Bin, he called me his son-in-law—a most unusual occurrence.
Fortunately, I met his daughter, who was extremely wise and virtuous.
After finding out the truth, she released me through the back door,
Only after the escape was I finally able to come to Uncle's residence.
I hope Uncle will memorialize all of this to the throne in detail,
To have the injustice rectified will be like rebirth—I will be forever indebted.

WANG AO: So that's what happened. Don't worry, dear Nephew. Come with me to see His Majesty. (*He exits with Li Zhen.*)
WANG YOUQIANG: (*Enters and sings.*)

Watching the young gentleman from behind the screen, I'm impressed by his gracefulness,
He is every bit as handsome as Pan Anren 潘安仁 of yesteryear,[93]
Causing me to be so aroused that I cannot restrain the monkey and horse of my mind,[94]
When Daddy returns, I want to marry the man, to marry the man. (*Exits.*)

93. Pan Anren is also known as Pan An. See footnote 21.

94. In Buddhism, the uncontrollable impulses of the mind are symbolized by the monkey and horse.

Scene 23: "Escaping from Marriage"

(*Enter Li Dongyang, Wang Ao, and Li Zhen.*)
LI DONGYANG: (*Recites.*)

> I am sincerely grateful to you for giving me back my life.

WANG AO: (*Recites.*)

> The pleadings of an orphaned rabbit[95] were difficult to refuse.

LI ZHEN: (*Recites.*)

> Although the father and son were victimized by the slandering minister,
> The creator saved us by sending us a propitious rescuer.

(*Speaks.*) Ah, Daddy, who has suffered so much!
LI DONGYANG: This was all predestined by fate.
WANG AO: Elder Brother Colleague has suffered much injustice.
LI DONGYANG: Thank you for worrying about old me. His Majesty has ordered me to transport provisions for the military expedition. I would like for my young son to study at your residence.
WANG AO: Actually, Elder Brother Colleague, this Younger Brother of yours has a daughter who is not yet engaged. I would like for her to marry your son. Please do not refuse.
LI DONGYANG: The only problem is that I, your Younger Brother, have to leave the capital immediately; I won't have the time to prepare for the betrothal gifts.
WANG AO: Let's dispense with the betrothal gifts. Come with me! Ha, ha, ha! (*They exit. The maid enters with Wang Ao and Li Zhen.*)
LI ZHEN: Uncle—concerning the marriage, your Nephew does not dare to obey your wishes.
WANG AO: Don't refuse. Maid, get your Young Lady ready for the wedding rituals.
MAID: Yes. (*She exits and re-enters supporting Wang Youqiang. Wang Youqiang and Li Zhen bow to each other.*)
WANG AO: Take them to the bridal chamber. Ha, ha, ha! (*He exits.*)

---

95. Li Zhen was compared to an orphaned rabbit when his father was imprisoned.

Maid: Let me take the bride's bridal veil off.

Wang Youqiang: Maid, there's no need for you to wait on us.

Maid: Yes. (*Facing Li Zhen.*) New Young Master, please be gentle with our Young Lady. Don't scare her. (*She exits.*)

Wang Youqiang: Let me close the door. (*She locks the door. Li Zhen stamps his feet and acts unhappy.*) Jieyuan, please accept my greeting! (*Li Zhen does not respond to her.*) Jieyuan, I greet you! (*She looks at Li Zhen.*) Aiyo! Aiyo! Lord Heaven! Look at the way he behaves! Ai, Jieyuan! (*Sings.*)

Walking up to him, I am full of smiles,
I have something to tell, please listen to me.
Although you are the son of a Secretary of State,
I am nonetheless the daughter of a Prime Minister.
If you don't consider this a perfect match,
Do you intend to marry an immortal from a realm of the fairies?
If we try to take you beyond the clouds to that realm,
I'm afraid that your body of flesh and blood will pose a
problem—it will pose a problem. (*Li Zhen ignores her and pretends to sleep.*)

(*Speaks.*) Jieyuan, who are you worried about and who are you angry at? Are you deaf, or are you dumb? Ai, ai, ai! How come you've fallen asleep? (*Li Zhen pretends to sleep. She sings.*)

I say, Jieyuan, that you are too lacking in talent,
Where did all this sleepiness come from?
This moment of a precious night is worth a thousand pieces of
gold and hard to buy,
If you miss this moment, it will never come by again.
Don't you know anything about this at all?
You truly are a blockhead who knows only about studying!

(*Speaks.*) Ah, yes. I guess scholars tend to be shy, and he is a scholar. Even so, I'm not going to let him snore away by himself. Why don't I take a nap too? I'll perform the scheme of hooking the carp when he comes after me. Ai, ai, ai! I'll let you be dumb, dumb, dumb! (*Sings.*)

I'm going to dream all the way to the Pavilion of the Sun,
And then you can act dumb with me.

I'm going to enter inside the brocade bed curtains,
Even if you cry, I'm not going to wake up. (*She sleeps and Li Zhen awakes.*)

LI ZHEN: (*Sings.*)

Her figure inside the brocade curtains is so slight and delicate,
In an instant, the fire in my heart surges up aroused.
Walking to the bed, I open the curtains and gaze at the silver sea,
She looks like a living Guanyin 观音[96] sleeping on her lotus platform.
The fairy jade flower pillow is covered by her slanting hairdo of black clouds.
The fairy flower blanket reveals her embroidered shoes with phoenix heads.
Uncovering the brocade blanket, her fragrance and charm are fully revealed—
With willow leaf eyebrows, pear flower face, almond eyes, and peach cheeks.
Her panties are embroidered with mandarin ducks; her knees are totally naked,
In the middle of it all, I spy a bit of red—a peony flower half-opened.
I have to restrain myself and be absolutely patient,
To regard her as a saintly deity, not to be encroached.

(*Speaks.*) The Young Lady is sound asleep. Let me go to the bed and sleep too. Wait a minute—I made a pact with Wonder Immortal that I will marry her after I pass the palace examinations. It would be unrighteous of me if I forget the old when I see the new. If I now sleep with Young Lady Wang, people will invariably gossip about it. Why don't I escape from the Wang residence right now when no one is around? I will then be relieved of this affair. Let me leave! This is precisely a case of . . . (*Recites.*)

Tonight I will escape from the stockade of amour,

96. Guanyin, the Chinese version of Avalokitesvera, also known as the Goddess of Mercy, is a Bodhisattva known for her beauty.

I shake my head, swing my tail,[97] and vow to never come back again. (*He exits.*)

(*The cock crows and Wang Youqiang wakes up.*)

Wang Youqiang: Jieyuan, listen to the cock announcing the morn. Are you still standing there? Jieyuan, Jieyuan! Aiya, oh no! (*Sings.*)

By mistake I entered the land of darkness and sweetness,
And Mt. Wu 巫山 has lost its Duke Xiang of the Chu 楚襄王[98] state.
Hurriedly, I call for my father.

Wang Ao: (*Enters.*) What happened, child?

Wang Youqiang: Oh, Daddy! (*Sings.*)

Listen to what your child has to say from her heart,
You picked a talent for your child,
But he had the heart of a jackal and wolf.

Wang Ao: Why do you say that?

Wang Youqiang: Ai, Daddy! (*Sings.*)

Your child and he were in the bridal chamber,
I greeted him several times, but he refused to speak.
Not half a word did he say, not a noise did he make,
Pretending to be deaf and dumb, he sat to one side.
Your child went to bed and slept by myself,
When I woke up, I know not where he had gone.
Bring me a knife to end my life right now and here,
I'll make myself an example for others of my gender.
Or enter a monastery to spend the rest of my life on meditation,
Your child would rather shave her head, become a nun, meditate alone with the Buddhist lamps, chant the sutra, and sleep on a cold bed!

Wang Ao: Ai, my child! Don't cry. Daddy will dispatch people to search for him immediately. Come with Daddy! (*They exit.*)

97. To walk in a confident and swaggering manner.

98. Duke Xiang was supposed to have made love to a goddess on Mt. Wu.

Scene 24: "Opening the Letter"

(*Yamen runners enter with Bai Rui.*)
BAI RUI: (*Recites.*)

Ten years of studying, under the cold window, totally anonymous,
One successful final exam, fame and fortune, the entire world knows.

I am the Official Bai Rui. Elder Brother Li was the top candidate, and I came in third for the final examinations. Previously, when the Jiang residence invited me to marry their daughter, I made the mistake of telling them that I was not engaged in my home town. If I should bring Jade Immortal to the capital now, His Excellency Jiang would invariably be upset with me. Hence, I have just written a parting letter to her to ask her to marry someone else. Come, someone! (*A yamen runner responds.*) Be sure to deliver this letter to the Pavilion of the Immortals in Exile. (*Sings.*)

I regret that I made a mistake when I spoke,
I should not have said that I have not yet been married.
A letter of parting, I now dispatch a runner to deliver,
Fearing that the girl might come to the capital to seek for me. (*They exit. Pretty Plum carries a lamp and leads Wonder Immortal and Jade Immortal on stage.*)

WONDER IMMORTAL: (*Sings.*)

After we lodged the suit at the military court,
The sisters have returned to our old nest.

JADE IMMORTAL: (*Sings.*)

Having heard of the success of both of the brothers,
We await for the arrival of the sealed golden letter tonight.

(*Speaks.*) Pretty Plum, put the lamp down. You can leave.
PRETTY PLUM: Yes.
JADE IMMORTAL: Elder Sister, I heard that brother-in-law was top candidate in the examinations and Master Bai came in third. How come we haven't received any letters from them yet?

Wonder Immortal: Younger Sister, congratulations! (*Sings.*)

When you and Master Bai made a pact between yourselves,
He said that he will move you to the capital city.
My side made a pact with me for ten whole years,
Counting on my fingers, there are still eight left,
Until he arrives, I am willing to remain chaste,
I expect to wait a while before hearing from him.

(*Speaks.*) The night is deep, let's go to bed.

Jade Immortal: You go on ahead, Elder Sister. I'm going to sit by myself for a while.

Wonder Immortal: My dear Younger Sister! (*Sings.*)

Younger Sister, there really is no need to think so much,
Why do you want to sit alone and not go to sleep?
I'm going to go right to sleep to dream and enter Nanke,[99]
People without worries are always sleepy.

Jade Immortal: (*Sings.*)

Seeing Elder Sister sleeping on her bed,
The immortal of the jade realm sits by herself longing for her Master Bai.
When will we be a pair of mandarin ducks inside golden bed curtains?
When will we be a pair of luan-birds and phoenix leaning against each other in a jade hall?
When will we be able to paint the eyebrows and emulate Zhang Chang 张敞?[100]
When will I become the fairy who serves rice with sesame seeds to Ruanlang 阮郎?[101]

99. Nanke is the name of a country in a Tang tale about a dream. See footnote 20.

100. Zhang Chang (d. 48 BCE), mayor of the capital, had such a loving relationship with his wife that he was known for helping his wife paint her eyebrows.

101. See footnote 18.

How can I evade the curtain of love and romance?[102]
I will have to move my steps and leave my boudoir.

(*Speaks.*) Aiya! How lovely! (*Sings.*)

I, Jade Immortal Xie, gaze up at Heaven
And see the Weaving Maid and the Cowherd constellations.[103]
One of them is in the east; the other lies in the west,
When will the seventh day of the Seventh Month ever arrive?
This silvery river of the Milky Way separates you,
That red wall over here is hard to remove.
Without the flying magpies forming a bridge,
The Weaving Maid can only sit alone on the washer stone.[104]

(*Speaks.*) It's so late now—let me go to my small room and sit by myself for a while. (*Sings.*)

I am delighted—I am only delighted by the fact that Master Bai passed the examinations with flying colors.
I am worried—I am only worried by the fact that his letter is arriving so late.
I am upset—I am only upset by the fact that I am sitting in my boudoir all alone,
I resent—I only resent the fact that I cannot reach Liaoxi 辽西[105] through dream. (*She goes backstage and reappears in the guise of a soul in dream.*)

---

102. *Fengliuzhang* 风流帐 is a double entendre, meaning either a curtain or tent of romantic love, or an account on the gains and losses of romantic love. Both meanings are implied here. I chose the former in the translation to correlate better with the following line.

103. The Weaving Maid is a daughter of the Jade Emperor in Heaven. When he found out about her love affair with a mere Cowherd, he was so furious that he separated the lovers on opposite banks of the Heavenly River, the Milky Way. Eventually feeling sorry for the pair, he relented by allowing them to meet once a year on the seventh day of the Seventh Month via a bridge formed by flying magpies. The Weaving Maid is the star Vega in the constellation of Lyra.

104. This stone, known as *zhijishi* 支机石, is the name of the stone which the Weaving Maid uses to pound silk when she washes it in the Milky Way.

105. *Liao* means "distant" and might also refer to northeastern China once occupied by the Khitans; and *xi* means "west." Hence, *liaoxi* may mean a distant land to the west, or west of the Liao region.

Jade Immortal: A familiar looking official is coming this way.
Bai Rui: Young Lady, please accept my greetings.
Jade Immortal: Did the scholar really become an official?
Bai Rui: Yes, I've become an official and am here to take you to the capital. Get your luggage ready.
Jade Immortal: I obey your command. (*A cock crow is heard, and Bai Rui's soul exits. Jade Immortal awakes.*) How wonderful! (*Sings.*)

Just now my sleepy eyes were in a daze,
I dreamt that my darling Bai greeted me.
I love his smart outfit and handsome new cap.
Just as Duke Xiang and I were dreaming of Mt. Wu,[106]
The heartless cock gave a big loud crow.
Waking up in a shock, there is not a trace of him,
And, suddenly, I realize how bright it had become on the east.

Pretty Plum: (*Enters.*) Young Lady, congratulations!
Jade Immortal: What is the good news?
Pretty Plum: The Third Prize Candidate has sent a letter.
Jade Immortal: Let me take a look at it. (*Sings.*)

I, Jade Immortal Xie, am all in smiles,
Scholar Bai's name is on the envelope.
I call for Elder Sister to wake up quickly,
My dear Bai's letter has finally arrived.

Wonder Immortal: Did you say that the letter has arrived? Read it to me.
Jade Immortal: My dear Elder Sister! I don't think we need to read it at all! (*Sings.*)

I'm sure he is asking me to hire help for traveling,
If not, he must be asking me to prepare the dowry.
I'm sure he is asking me to bid farewell to the relatives,
If not, he must be asking me to take along two maids.
Let me open the letter and read with my eyes. (*She reads and shows disappointment.*)
How is it possible that a puff of smoke appeared in this letter!

106. See footnote 98.

WONDER IMMORTAL: Why don't you read it out loud, Younger Sister?
JADE IMMORTAL: (*In a deep and sorrowful voice.*) You wouldn't have known, Elder Sister, that robber got married in the capital and sent a parting letter to me. He wants me to marry someone else. Here is his letter. Go ahead and read it.
WONDER IMMORTAL: Ai! My dear Younger Sister! (*Sings.*)

When he wrote the poem at the pavilion the other year,
I knew he was the unfaithful type.
But back then you were so stubborn,
Now you regret it, but it is too late.

JADE IMMORTAL: Now that this has happened, I have a mind to go search for him in the capital. What do you think?
WONDER IMMORTAL: Don't do it, Younger Sister. You are an unmarried young maiden—it would not be convenient for you to travel. Since Li has become the prize candidate, he will invariably come for me. Let's tell the top candidate about this, and we'll go from there. (*Sings.*)

Romantic men tend to be unfaithful,

JADE IMMORTAL: (*Sings.*)

This turn of events could be the death of me. (*They exit.*)

Scene 25: "Amnesty"

(*Yamen runners enter with Li Zhen outfitted as the top candidate.*)
LI ZHEN: (*Recites.*)

One success, I am famous, my name is on the golden roster,
After ten years, I have finally arrived at the Phoenix Pool.

(*Speaks.*) I am Li Zhen, top candidate of the palace examination this year. I have brought an edict from the emperor to come to Mount Tiger Hill to proclaim amnesty. When I have done this, I will return to bring Young Lady Xu to the capital. Come! Spur the horses on. (*They exit. Jade Immortal enters dressed as a man.*)

Jade Immortal: (*Sings.*)

Leaving during dark night, heaven and earth are a blur,
On the road, I have no idea as to the four directions.
Wearing a scholar's clothes and head scarf, I feel most awkward,
I can't help but stand in the middle of the road, flowing in tears.

(*Speaking rapidly.*) I, Jade Immortal Xie, am so ill-fated. Ever since the robber sent the letter saying that he was invited to be married to the Jiang household and wanted me to marry someone else, I put on men's clothes and ran out of the house in the middle of the night without letting Elder Sister know about it. I'm going to the capital to find the robber. The way is far, however. I don't know the directions at all, and I'm lost! (*Sings.*)

Behind his back, I curse and complain about the robber,
Now that you have become a high official, you renege upon
your promise.
For you, I have endured an attack in the middle of the night,
For you, I have gone to a military court and lodged a suit.
Now you want to break the strings of the zither with me,
You act without conscience, but azure Heaven lies above you.
(*She exits. Four soldiers enter with Hua Tianbiao.*)

Hua Tianbiao: Brothers, surround the enemy! (*Sings.*)

Anger and hatred press upon my chest, all because of a feud,
In front of Mount Tiger Hill, I now train jackals and wolves.
When I will eventually attain the road to fame and success,
I won't rest until I have finally killed that knave Jiang Bin.

Soldier: (*Enters.*) I report to the Great King. An official has arrived at the foot of the mountain claiming to be your cousin.
Hua Tianbiao: That's your Lord Li. Invite him up.
Soldier: Lord Li, you have been invited to go in.
Li Zhen: (*Enters and recites.*)

I received an order to search for my cousin,
Today we finally get to meet.

(*Speaks.*) Cousin, please come here and accept my bow.

HUA TIANBIAO: Dispense with the formalities. I have just heard that you, my brother, took the top prize among all under Heaven. Congratulations to you! What are you here for?

LI ZHEN: I, your younger brother, memorialized to the throne and had you pardoned. You have been ordered to go attain merit in the military. If you return victorious, you could exact revenge upon your enemy.

HUA TIANBIAO: I obey Younger Brother's command.

SOLDIER: I report to the Great King. We captured a scholar.

HUA TIANBIAO: Tie him up and bring him here!

JADE IMMORTAL: Please spare my life, Great King!

LI ZHEN: Where are you from, scholar?

JADE IMMORTAL: Allow me to report, Great King! (*Sings.*)

> I am a scholar named Bai Rui, I hail from the province of Suzhou,
> On my way to the capital, I passed by the front of Mount Tiger Hill.
> I hope Your Excellency will be generous and take pity on me,
> In the future, if I succeed, I'll "tie a grass loop and bring bracelets" for you.[107]

LI ZHEN: This is pure rubbish. Bai Rui is my sworn brother. He is now in the capital—what kind of rubbish are you talking about?

JADE IMMORTAL: My dear Elder Brother!

LI ZHEN: There you go again!

---

107. To "tie a grass loop and bring bracelets" refer to payment for favors received. According to *Zuozhuan* 左传, during 654 BCE, General Wei Ke 魏颗 of the State of Jin was fighting a general from the State of Qin, when an old man unbalanced the latter using a grass-tied loop and enabled the former to win. That night the old man appeared in Wei Ke's dream to inform him that he was none other than the father of a concubine of Wei's father whom Wei Ke decided to allow to remarry rather than being buried with his deceased father. The bracelets refer to another numinous tale found in a historical record. According to a note in the biography of Yang Zheng 杨震 (54–124 BCE) in the dynastic history of the Later Han dynasty, Yang's father saved and nursed an injured yellow bird. After the bird healed and flew away, a boy wearing a yellow robe visited him in his dream explaining that he was in fact a messenger of Mother Goddess of the West. To thank Yang's father for saving his life, he presented him with four white bracelets that he claimed would ensure the officialdom and integrity of his descendants. Yang Zheng, his son, grandson, and great grandson were all famous officials known for their integrity.

Jade Immortal: (*Sings.*)

Remember how Bai Rui and I had a marriage pact in the past,
Who would have known that he was a man devoid of faith.
In the capital, he gained fame and found another partner.
The robber reneged on our marriage and his prior promise.
Dispatching a messenger, he had a parting letter sent to me,
He told me to remarry, to wear the brocade skirt inside out.[108]
It was inconvenient for me to travel to find my husband,
Therefore I left my home, dressed as a man.
If you don't believe me, look at these locks under the head scarf,
I am the wife of your sworn brother—Jade Immortal of the Xie clan.

Hua Tianbiao: Ha, ha, ha! This is so strange!

Li Zhen: What a Bai Rui! How unfaithful of you! Please get up, Young Lady. I was just going to fetch your sister, Wonder Immortal. The two of you can go to the capital with me. You can leave your marriage in my hands. Come, yamen runners! Find a palanquin for the Young Lady, and bring me my horse. Cousin, your Younger Brother bids you farewell. (*The yamen runners respond. Li Zhen and Jade Immortal leave with the yamen runners.*)

Hua Tianbiao: Let me see you off. Soldiers, march toward the imperial camp! (*Sings.*)

Having received the imperial edict today,
I rush to join the imperial army to attain great merit. (*They exit.*)

Scene 26: "Bestowing Entitlements"

(*Four barbarian soldiers enter with Princess Myriad Flowers.*)

Princess Myriad Flowers: I am Princess Myriad Flowers. Hua Tianbiao has arrived with an army. Let me charge and fight him! (*Exits. Soldiers enter with Hua Tianbiao. Princess Myriad Flowers enters with soldiers from the opposite side. They fight.*)

Princess Myriad Flowers: What is the name of the charging warrior?

108. The implication is that the right side of the skirt is already used; hence she is being asked to marry again as a used object.

HUA TIANBIAO: I am your lord, Hua Tianbiao.

PRINCESS MYRIAD FLOWERS: Wait a minute. If you are willing to marry me, I will show you the way within my camp and you can win by attacking from both within and without.

HUA TIANBIAO: All right, I will marry you. Lead the way. (*They go around the stage. Black Demon King enters and fights with Hua Tianbiao. Princess Myriad Flowers kills Black Demon King.*) I'm so delighted that I gained victory after just one battle. Follow me to meet with the marshal. (*They exit.*)

LI ZHEN: (*Enters and recites.*)

Having designed a perfect scheme,
I am going to match a good marriage.

(*Speaks.*) I am Official Li Zhen. I have dispatched a yamen runner to invite my sworn brother over. How come he hasn't arrived yet?

YAMEN RUNNER: (*Enters.*) Lord Bai is here.

LI ZHEN: Tell him to come in. (*The yamen runner responds. Bai Rui and Jiang Yulian enter.*) Get the family settled at the residence in the back. (*Bai Rui and Jiang Yulian greet Li Zhen. Jiang exits.*) I didn't know that Younger Brother had acquired a concubine. We should celebrate!

BAI RUI: I wouldn't presume to trouble Elder Brother.

LI ZHEN: I assume that your first wife is also in the capital?

BAI RUI: You wouldn't have known, Elder Brother, that after I came to the capital, that lowborn woman married someone else.

LI ZHEN: That's terribly unrighteous of her. She obviously didn't have the good fortune of becoming a lady of the First Rank. I bid you farewell. (*Exits. Enter Wonder Immortal and Jade Immortal, holding rods.*)

JADE IMMORTAL: (*Recites.*)

Arriving prepared with unfeeling rods,

WONDER IMMORTAL: (*Recites.*)

With which to beat up the unfaithful lover.

JADE IMMORTAL: Who is that official standing there?

BAI RUI: (*Surprised.*) I just heard that you, the Young Lady, have arrived in the capital, and hence I've come to welcome you.

JADE IMMORTAL: What a robber! (*Sings.*)

You already said that you had no more love for me,
Otherwise where would the parting letter have come from?
How could you still try to deny it right now?
I'll make sure that your skin and flesh will tear from a good beating.

Bai Rui: (*Toward Wonder Immortal.*) Please plead forgiveness for me, dear sister-in-law!

Wonder Immortal: (*Sings.*)

Considering the talent in unfaithfulness you have exhibited,
Who is willing to speak for you on your behalf now?
You have created this karmic debt yourself without help,
You'll have to stay there and endure it in your own good time.

Li Zhen: (*Enters.*) Dear Sister, please spare him for my sake. Younger Brother, you have endured much injustice.

Bai Rui: You jest! (*Off stage: "an imperial edict has arrived!"*)

Li Zhen: Go to the residence at the back. (*Wonder Immortal and Jade Immortal exit. Li Dongyang, Hua Tianbiao, and Wang Ao enter to accept the edict. Music proceeds the arrival of the Head Eunuch bearing the edict.*)

Head Eunuch: The imperial edict pronounces: Jiang Bin has monopolized the power and treads above his rights at the court. Envious of the capable and mistreating the loyal and upright, he has ignored the laws and overstepped his role with pretensions. In fact, he lacked the talents of Mang 莽 and Zhuo 卓, but possessed the treachery of Cao 操 and Yi 懿.[109] In consideration of the fact that he was one of the original ministers of our reign, we will release him from office with leniency. Commanding General Hua was wrongly victimized, and the event was most unfortunate. We will bestow upon him posthumously the First Rank title of Marquis of Righteousness and Bravery (*yiyong hou* 义勇侯) along with ten thousand taels[110] of gold. We will have him reburied and commemorated immediately. His son, Hua Tianbiao, annihilated the Black Demon King and brought about the surrender of the Princess of Myriad Flowers. He cannot be considered lacking in attaining great merit, and deserving of being son of a warrior clan. We will grant him

109. Cao Cao 曹操 (155–220).

110. A tael is equivalent to an ounce.

the title General of Wisdom and Bravery (*zhiyong jiangjun* 智勇将军), and allow him to inherit his father's title and fief. Ministers Wang Ao and Li Dongyang have been loyal and reliable. They can truly be considered pillars of the state. We bestow upon both of them purple gowns. The new prize candidate, Li Zhen, memorialized concerning the treachery and pretensions of Jiang Bin and his son, as well as the merits attained by Hua Tianbiao. He has demonstrated responsibility and loyalty. Upon him we bestow a plaque inscribed with our personally written characters, "The First Prize Candidate (*zhuangyuan jidi* 状元及第)." The Third Prize candidate, Bai Rui, will be retained at the Board to demonstrate his talents. Li Zhen has also memorialized concerning the ability of Wonder Immortal Xu of the Pavilion of the Immortals in Exile to preserve her chastity after being trapped at the Jiang residence. Jade Immortal Xie, too, met with an assassin en route, but was even able to wrest away his broadsword and sue him. The two young ladies were able to preserve their chastity during moments of extreme crises; they can be considered pure jades without blemish! We bestow upon both of them the title of Lady of Righteous Chivalry (*xiayi furen* 侠义夫人) of the first rank. Wonder Immortal Xu and Wang Youqiang will emulate Ying and Huang of the past and serve Li Zhen simultaneously.[111] Jade Immortal Xie and Jiang Yulian will both marry Bai Rui without distinguishing seniority in position. Relying on his father's position, Jiang Shangyou has been ruthless and pretentious. We will allow the local official of his territory to banish him according to his crimes in accordance with the laws of the state. Both Princess Myriad Flowers and Pretty Plum[112] assisted a meritorious subject. We decree that Ministers Wang and Li assume the role of matchmaker so that the two ladies may marry General Hua Tianbiao. Today is a propitious date;[113] we decree that all the newly appointed nobles go through the wedding ritual. This is the end of the edict. Express your gratitude to his Majesty. Hail three times!

---

111. Ying and Huang refer to Nüying and E'huang, who both married the legendary Emperor Shun 舜 (see footnote 32). The implication here is that the two wives will have equal status as formal wives.

112. It is possible that in a more extensive version of this play, Pretty Plum was also involved in Hua Tianbiao's military exploits and that a romance also developed between them.

113. An almanac called the Yellow Calendar indicates all the propitious and unpropitious dates for important activities such as performing specific ritual ceremonies, building houses, and traveling.

Everyone: Ten Thousand Years, Ten Thousand Years, Ten Thousand Ten Thousand Years![114]

Wang Ao: Excellencies!

Everyone: Yes, Your Excellency!

Wang Ao: According to the edict of his Majesty, today is a propitious date, and you have been ordained to get married. Wedding assistants, throw petals to form a carpet of flowers. (*Wedding assistants enter and respond to Wang. Wonder Immortal Xu, Jade Immortal Xie, Jiang Yulian, Wang Youqiang, Princess Myriad Flowers, and Pretty Plum enter. They bow to each other with Li Zhen, Bai Rui, and Hua Tianbiao and then exit.*)

Wang Ao: Excellencies, let's attend the banquet!

Everyone: Please! (*They exit.*)

END OF PLAY

114. The emperor is addressed by all as Wansui 万岁, ten thousand years, implying that he will live forever.

Works Cited and Bibliography of Chinese Puppet Theater

Baird, Bill. 1973. *The Art of the Puppet.* New York: The Macmillan Co., a Ridge Press Book.

Breton, M. 1824. "Puppet-show." In *China: Its Costume, Arts, Manufactures*, vol. IV, 127–132. London: Howlett and Brimmer.

Caituan Faren Zhonghua Minsu Yishu Jijinhui 财团法人中华民俗艺术基金会. 2005. *Taiwan budaixi yu chuantong wenhua chuangyi chanye yantaohui wenji* 台湾布袋戏与传统文化创意产业研讨会文集 [Collected essays from the Taiwan Budaixi and Traditional Culture Creative Industries Symposium]. Yilan County: Guoli Chuantong Yishu Zhongxin.

Cai Wenting 蔡文婷. 2004. "Xuansi qianqi, kuilei chusha 悬丝牵起, 傀儡出煞 [Taiwanese puppetry: pulling strings to dispel a myriad of demons]." In Cai Wenting, ed., *Xiange buchuo: Taiwan xiqu gushi* 弦歌不辍 台湾戏曲故事 [Hold that note!—stories from Taiwan's stage], 290–307. Taibei: Guanghua zazhi. (This book is bilingual.)

———. 2004. "Dada butongkuan—nanbei kuileixi 大大不同款一南北傀儡戏 [Puppet theater north and south]." In Cai Wenting, ed., *Xiange buchuo: Taiwan xiqu gushi.* 弦歌不辍: 台湾戏曲故事 [Hold that note!—stories from Taiwan's stage], 308–311. Taibei: Guanghua zazhi. (This book is bilingual.)

———. 2004. "Zhenzuoxi jiachusha 真做戏 假出煞 [Too theatrical for the ghosts?]." In Cai Wenting, ed., *Xiange buchuo: Taiwan xiqu gushi* 弦歌不辍: 台湾戏曲故事 [Hold that note!—stories from Taiwan's stage], 312–315. Taibei: Guanghua zazhi. (This book is bilingual.)

———. 1993. "Tianshang renjian liang xiaoyao—Tainan Pujidian songshen 天上人间两逍遥一台南普济殿送神 [When the gods go home for the holidays]." *Guanghua* 光华 (*Sinorama*) 29.4: 90–95. (This article is bilingual.)

This bibliography does not include the Chinese shadow theater, for which please see the bibliography in Fan Pen Chen, *Chinese Shadow Theatre: History, Popular Religion, and Women Warriors.*

Cao Lusheng 曹路生. 1998. "Qingdian xiju yishi—yindu luomuoju, xizang zangxi, quanzhou mu'ou mulianxi bijiao 庆典与戏剧仪式—印度罗摩剧, 西藏藏戏, 泉州木偶目连戏比较 [Festivities, drama, and rituals—a comparison of the Indian Ramayana, the Tibetan dramas, and the Mulian drama of the Quanzhou Marionette Theatre]." *Xiju yishu* 3: 4–8.

Cao Ping 曹萍. 1991. "Tuanjie mu'ou jutuan jiankuang 团结木偶剧团简况 [On United Puppetry Troupe]." In Zhongguo xiquzhi Jiangsu juan Nantong fenjuan bianjishi 中国戏曲志江苏卷南通分卷编辑室, ed., *Dantongshi xiqu ziliao xuanbian* 南通市戏曲资料选编 [Selected works on the traditional operas of the city of Nantong], vol. 5, 98. Nantong: Nantongshi wenhuaju xiquzhi bianjishi.

Cao Zhanmei 曹占梅. 1993. "Xin faxian de gudai beifang mu'ou yingxi shiliao 新发现的古代北方木偶影戏史料 [Recent discoveries of historical sources on puppetry and shadow puppetry in Northern China during antiquity]." *Minsu quyi* 民俗曲艺 81: 121–135.

Chang Renxia 常任侠. 1955 (1984 reprint). "Tan kuileixi he piyingxi 谈傀儡戏和皮影戏 [On puppetry and shadow theater]." In *Chang Renxia yishu kaogu lunwen xuanji* 常任侠艺术考古论文选集 [A selected collection of Chang Renxia's essays on art and archeology], 137–143. Beijing: wenwu chubanshe.

———. 1954. "Yindu kuileixi yu zhongguo kuileixi 印度傀儡戏与中国傀儡戏 [The puppet theaters of India and China]." In *Zhongguo gudian yishu* 中国古典艺术 [Chinese traditional arts], 104–117. Shanghai: Shanghai chuban gongsi.

———. 1951 (1984 reprint). "Woguo kuileixi de fazhan yu yong de guanxi 我国傀儡戏的发展与俑的关系 [The relationship between the development of Chinese puppetry and burial statues]." In *Chang Renxia yishu kaogu lunwen xuanji* 常任侠艺术考古论文选集 [A selected collection of Chang Renxia's essays on art and archaeology], 113–136. Beijing: Wenwu chubanshe. Also in *Zhongguo gudian yishu* 中国古典艺术 [Chinese traditional arts], 82–119. Shanghai: Shanghai chuban gongsi, 1954.

Chen Dexin 陈德馨. 1986. "Quanzhou tixian mu'ou de chuanru yu fazhan 泉州提线木偶的传入与发展 [Transmission and development of the marionette theater in Quanzhou]." In Chen Ruitong 陈瑞统, ed., *Quanzhou mu'ou yishu* 泉州木偶艺术 [The art of puppetry in Quanzhou], 6–26. Xiamen: Lujiang chubanshe.

Chen, Fan Pen (Chen Fanping 陈凡平). 2011. "Baldy's Wedding Night: A Post-Midnight Marionette Play." *Chinoperl Papers* 29: 133–141.

———. 2011. "Baishazhen Shuizhu'yangcun Tiangonghui de luantan kuileixi, *Mu Guiying zhaoqin* 白沙镇水竹洋村田公会的乱弹傀儡戏穆桂英招亲 [*Mu Guiying Finds Herself a Husband*: A Luantan Marionette Play Performed at the Tiangong Festival at the Shuizhuyang Village of Baishazhen, Western Fujian]." In Ye Mingsheng and Liang Lunyong, eds., *Shanghang mu'ouxi yu Baisha Tiangonghui yanjiu wenji* 上杭木偶戏与白沙田公会研究文集 [Research collection on the Tiangong Festival of Baisha and the Marionette Theatre of Shanghang], 29–36. Fuzhou: Haichao sheying yishu chubanshe.

———. 2011. "*All Three Fear Their Wives (Sanpaqi):* A Post-Midnight Shadow Play." *Asian Theatre Journal* 26.2: 197–214. This play is also published as "A Postmidnight Shadow Play from Shaanxi: *All Three Fear Their Wives.*" In Victor H. Mair and Mark Bender, eds., *Chinese Folk and Popular Literature*, 288–295. New York: Columbia University Press.

———. 2007. *Chinese Shadow Theatre: History, Popular Religion, and Women Warriors.* Montreal: McGill-Queen's University Press.

———. 2004. *Visions for the Masses: Chinese Shadow Plays from Shaanxi and Shanxi.* Ithaca: Cornell East Asia Series.

———. 1992. "Female Warriors, Magic and the Supernatural in Traditional Chinese Novels." In Arvind Sharma and Katherine K. Young, eds., *The Annual Review of Women in World Religions, Volume II: Heroic Women*, 91–109. Albany: State University of New York Press.

Chen, Fan Pen, and Bradford Clark. 2010. "A Survey of Puppetry in China." *Asian Theatre Journal* 27.2: 333–365.

Chen Geng 陈耕. 1986. "Quanzhou mu'ou yishu zai Beijing 泉州木偶艺术在北京 [The art of Quanzhou puppetry in Beijing]." In Chen Ruitong 陈瑞统, ed., *Quanzhou mu'ou yishu* [The art of puppetry in Quanzhou], 222. Xiamen: Lujiang chubanshe.

Chen Hanguang 陈汉光. 1971. "Kuileixi yu minjian zongjiao xinyang 傀儡戏与民间宗教信仰 [The marionette theater and popular religion]." *Taiwan fengwu* 台湾风物 21: 58–59.

Chen Lingling 陈玲玲. 1978. *Ba Xian zai Yuan Ming zaju he Taiwan ban xian xi zhong de zhuang kuang* 八仙在元明杂剧和台湾扮仙戏中的状况 [The eight immortals in the immortal plays in Taiwan]. M.A. thesis. Taiwan: Zhongguo wenhua xueyuan yishu yanjiusuo [College of Chinese culture]. (Pp. 46–47 are on the marionette theater.)

Chen Longting 陈龙廷. 2007. *Taiwan budaixi fazhanshi* 台湾布袋戏发展史 [A history of glove puppetry in Taiwan]. Taibei: Qianwei chubanshe.

———. 1999. *Huang Junxiong Dianshi Budaixi Yanjiu* 黄俊雄电视布袋戏研究 [Research on Huang Junxiong's Television Po-te-hi]. M.A. thesis. Department of Art, Chinese Culture University, Taiwan.

Chen Mei 陈枚. 1986. "Minnan kuileixi yinyue 闽南傀儡戏音乐 [Music of the marionette theater in Minnan]." In Chen Ruitong 陈瑞统, ed., *Quanzhou mu'ou yishu* [The art of puppetry in Quanzhou], 182–187. Xiamen: Lujiang chubanshe.

Chen Mushan 陈木山. 2000. *Yunlin xian budaixi fazhan shi ji budaixi zongshi Huang Haidai chuanqi* 云林县布袋戏发展史及布袋戏宗师黄海岱 [History of the development of Budaixi in Yunlin County and the legend of puppetmaster Huang Haidai]. Taipei: Taiwan Xuesheng.

Chen Pingyuan 陈平原. 1995. *Qiangu wenren xiake meng: wuxia xiaoshuo leixing yanjiu* 千古文人侠客梦: 武侠小说类型研究 [The eternal swordsman dream of the literati: genre research on Wuxia fiction]. Taipei: Maitian.

Chen Ruitong 陈瑞统. 1986. *Quanzhou mu'ou yishu* 泉州木偶艺术 [The art of Quanzhou puppetry]. Xiamen: Lujiang chubanshe.

Chen Ruxing 陈儒行 and Jiang Wuchang 江武昌. 1985. "Taiwan difang xishen chuanshuo (1) 台湾地方戏神传说 (一) [Legends of the patron gods of local theaters in Taiwan]." *Minsu quyi* 民俗曲艺 34: 21–36.

Chen Tianbao 陈天保 and Cai Junchao 蔡俊抄. 1986. "'*Dachusu*' Quanzhou difang xiqu' 大出苏'泉州地方戏曲 [The local play 'Dachushu' of Quanzhou]." In *Quanzhou tixian mu'ou chuantong qupai* 泉州提线木偶传统曲牌 [Traditional melodies and scores of the Quanzhou String-Puppet Theatre], 136–160. Quanzhou: Quanzhou difang xiqu yanjiushe yu Quanzhou mu'ou jutuan.

Chen Xiaogao 陈啸高, and Gu Manzhuang 顾曼庄. 1955. "Fujian de Puxianxi 福建的莆仙戏 [The Puxian Opera of Fujian]." In *Huadong xiqu juzhong jieshao dierji* 华东戏曲剧种介绍第二集 [On the operatic traditions in Eastern China, vol. 2], 90–105. Shanghai: Xinwenyi chubanshe.

Chen Zhengzhi 陈正之. 1991. *Zhangzhong gongming: Taiwan de chuantong ouxi* 掌中功名: 台湾的传统偶戏 [Fame from the hands: traditional puppetry in Taiwan], 17–80. Taibei: Taiwan shengzhengfu xinwenju bianyin.

Chen Zhicheng 陈志诚. 1986. "Yishuang shou caozong sanshiliu tiao xian 一双手操纵三十六条线 [Manipulating thirty-six strings with two hands]." In Chen Ruitong 陈瑞统, ed., *Quanzhou mu'ou yishu* [The art of puppetry in Quanzhou], 247. Xiamen: Lujiang chubanshe.

Cohen, Alvis P. 1981. "A Taiwanese Puppeteer and His Theatre." *Asian Folklore Studies* (Nagoya) 40.1: 33–49.

Dang Qingfan 党晴梵. N.d. "Huayun zaji: Shaanxi minjian xiju zhiyi—tixianxi 华云杂记: 陕西民间戏剧之一—提线戏 [A miscellany by Huayun: on a folk opera of Shaanxi, the marionette theater)." [Article mailed to me without citation.]

Dang Zhengqian 党正千. 1988. "Xianqiang yinyue xingcheng chutan 线腔音乐形成初探 [A preliminary investigation into formation of the marionette music]." *Xiyue yiyuan* 3: 43–64.

Dean, Kenneth. 1995. "The Revival of the Spiritual Tradition: The God of the Theater." In Deborah Sommer, ed., *Chinese Religion: An Anthology of Sources*, 317–325. New York and Oxford: Oxford University Press.

———. 1994. "Comic Inversion and Cosmic Renewal: The God of the Theater in the Ritual Traditions of Putian." In *Proceedings of International Conference on Popular Beliefs and Chinese Culture* (II), Center for Chinese Studies Research Series no. 4, 683–732.

———. 1993. *Taoist Ritual and Popular Cults of Southeast China*. Princeton: Princeton University Press.

———. 1989. "Lei Yu-sheng (Thunder Is Noisy) and Mu-lien in the Theatrical and Funerary Traditions of Fukien." In David Johnson, ed., *Ritual Opera Operatic Ritual: "Mu-lien Rescues His Mother" in Chinese Popular Culture*, 46–104. Berkeley: Publication of the Chinese Popular Culture Project. (Pp. 82–87 are on the marionette theater.)

Ding Yanzhao丁言昭. 1991. *Zhongguo mu'oushi* 中国木偶史 [History of the Chinese puppet theaters). Shanghai: Xuelin chubanshe.

———. 1980. "Zhongguo mu'ouxi fazhan jianjie 中国木偶戏发展简介 [A short essay on the history of Chinese puppetry]." *Xiju yishu* 戏剧艺术 1.

Dolby, William. 1981. "The Origins of Chinese Puppetry." *Journal of the School of Oriental and African Studies* 41.1: 97–120.

Dong Fu 董复. 1983. "Kemu qiansi nong kuilei: cong kuilei yishu yanxihui tanqi 刻木牵丝弄傀儡—从傀儡艺术研习会谈起 [Carving wood and pulling strings to manipulate marionette puppets—starting with a workshop on the art of the marionettes]." *Xianghuo* 16: 46–49.

Dong Meikan 董每戡. 1983. "Shuo 'kuilei' 说傀儡 [On the puppet theaters]." In *Shuoju* 说剧 [On operas], 19–41. Beijing: Renmin wenxue chubanshe.

———. 1983. "Shuo 'kuilei' bushuo 说傀儡补说 [An addendum to *On the Puppet Theaters*]." In *Shuoju* 说剧 [On operas], 42–55. Beijing: Renmin wenxue chubanshe.

———. 1983. "Shuo 'guolang' wei 'pai'er zhishou' 说郭郎为俳儿之首 [On Guolang as the leading actor]." In *Shuoju* 说剧 [On operas], 56–67. Beijing: Renmin wenxue chubanshe.

Doolittle, Justus. 1895 (1986 reprint). *Social Life of the Chinese*. Singapore: Graham Brash. (Pp. 297–298 of vol. 2 are on marionette and glove puppet theater performances in Fuzhou.)

Dschi, Hian-Lin. 季羡林. 1950. "Lieh-tzu and Buddhist Sutras: A Note on the Author of Lieh-tzu and the Date of Its Composition." *Studia Serica* 9.1: 18–32. (Pp. 23–28 are on possibly the earliest literary mention of a performing puppet.)

Du Deqiao 杜德桥. 1999. "Guanyin xiuxing—Qingdai kuileixi chaoben 观音修行—清代傀儡戏抄本 [*Guanyin Attains Buddhahood*—a Qing dynasty marionette play script]." *Minsu quyi* 民俗曲艺 121: 167–201.

Du Jianhua 杜建华. 1993. "Muou, Piyingxi zhongde mulianxi jumu 木偶、皮影戏中的目连戏剧目 [Mulian drama in puppet and shadow theaters]." In *Bashu mulian xiju wenhua gailun* 巴蜀目连戏剧文化概论 [The culture of Mulian drama in the Ba and Shu regions], 254–265. Beijing: Wenhua yishi chubanshe.

Duan Anjie 段安节. 1982 (reprint). *Yuefu zalu* 乐府杂录 [Miscellany on the Music Bureau]. In Zhongguo xiqu yanjiuyuan 中国戏曲研究院, ed., *Zhongguo gudian xiqu lunzhu jicheng* 中国古典戏曲论著集成 [Collections of articles on Chinese operas], vol. 1. Zhongguo xiqu chubanshe.

Einstein, Susan. 1979. *Asian Puppets: Wall of the World*. Los Angeles: Museum of Cultural History, UCLA.

Feng Shuxiang 冯书祥. 1986. "Zhanxin de sixiang neirong, xianming de difang secai—kan Quanzhou tixian mu'ouxi 崭新的思想内容，鲜明的地方色彩—看泉州提线木偶戏 [New thought contents and brilliant local flavors—watching a Quanzhou marionette play]." In Chen Ruitong 陈瑞统, ed., *Quanzhou mu'ou yishu* [The art of puppetry in Quanzhou], 214–215. Xiamen: Lujiang chubanshe.

Feuchtwang, Stephan. 2001. "An Gong, or the Truth of Puppets." In *Popular Religion in China: The Imperial Metaphor*, chapter 7. Surrey: Curzon Press.

Finnane, Antonia. 2016. "Folding Fans and Early Modern Mirrors." In Martin J. Powers and Katherine R. Tsiang, eds., *A Companion to Chinese Art*, 392–409. West Sussex: John Wiley and Sons Ltd.

Fu Zhengling 傅正玲. 1986. "Taiwan difang xishen chuanshuo (5) 台湾地方戏神传说 (五) [Legends on the patron gods of the local operas of Taiwan]." In *Minsu quyi* 民俗曲艺 39: 174–180.

Gao Sichun 高思春. 2003. "Tixian mu'ou zai fa xinsheng—guan Quanzhou mu'ou jutuan xinzuo *Qinchai Dachen* 提线木偶再发新声一观泉州木偶剧团新作《钦差大臣》 [Another fresh voice in the marionette Theater—watching the new play *Imperially Appointed Minister* by the Quanzhou Puppet Theatre)." *FujianYishu* 5: 39–40.

Goodrich, L. Carrington, ed., 1976. *Dictionary of Ming Biography 1368–1644*. New York and London: Columbia University Press.

Genju neibu ziliao zhengli. 1991. "Liupai tixian mu'ou de xingcheng he fazhan 刘派提线木偶的形成和发展 [Creation and development of the Liu style marionette puppetry]." In Zhongguo xiquzhi Jiangsu juan Nantong fenjuan bianjishi 中国戏曲志江苏卷南通分卷编辑室, ed., *Nantongshi xiqu ziliao xuanbian* 南通市戏曲资料选编 [Selected works on the traditional operas of the city of Nantong], vol. 5, 96–97. Nantong: Nantongshi wenhuaju xiquzhi bianjishi.

Guan Jinyan 关金炎. 2007. "Pucheng zhuanzi mu'ou 浦城传子木偶 [The Zhuanzi Marionette Theatre of Pucheng]." In Ji Wenai 季文爱, ed., *Pucheng xiqu* 浦城戏曲 [Traditional operas of Pucheng], 66–70. Published as *neibu ziliao* by Zhengxie Fujiansheng Puchengxian Weiyuanhui 政协福建省浦城县委员会 and Xuexi Wenshi Weiyuanhui 学习文史委员会.

Guo Duanzhen 郭端镇. 1983. "Jiekai kuilei xi'ou de waiyi: tan kuilei de gouzao 揭开傀儡戏偶的外衣: 谈傀儡的构造 [Derobing the marionettes: a discussion of the construction of marionettes]." *Minsu quyi* 民俗曲艺 23–24: 34–47.

Guo Qihong 郭启宏. 2001. "Jueyi qishilu—Quanzhou tixian mu'ou guanhou 绝艺启示录一泉州提线木偶观后 [A manifestation of fabulous art—after watching the marionette puppetry of Quanzhou]." *Zhonguo Xiju* 3: 48–49.

Guoli lishi bowuguan bianji weiyuanhui 国立历史博物馆编辑, ed., 2007. *Ouxi zhimei* 偶戏之美 [The beauty of Taiwanese puppetry]. Taibei: Shiboguan.

Guo Wei 郭伟. 2000. *Zhongguo nüshen* 中国女神 [Chinese goddesses]. Nanning: Guangxi jiaoyu chubanshe.

Hansen, Valerie. 1990. *Changing Gods in Medieval China, 1127–1276*. Princeton: Princeton University Press. (P. 74 is on marionettes.)

Hatchelder, Marjorie H. 1947. *Rod-Puppets and the Human Theatre*. Columbus: The Ohio State University Press. (Chapter 3.)

He Bingyun 何秉昀. 1983. "Toukui de zhizuo 头盔的制作 [How to make puppet headgear]." *Minsu quyi* 民俗曲艺 23–24: 48–57.

———. 1983. "Kemu qiansi zuo laoweng—Lin Zancheng yu kuileixi 刻木牵丝作老翁—林赞成与傀儡戏 [Carving wood and pulling strings to make the puppet of an elderly man—Lin Zancheng and the marionette theater]." *Minsu quyi* 民俗曲艺 26: 167–171.

———. 1983. "Kuilei xi de guoqu, xianzai, weilai 傀儡戏的过去，现在，未来 [The past, present, and future of the marionette theater]." *Ziyou qingnian* 自由青年 70: 34–37.

He Guanhuan 何冠环. 2003. "Chuanren Yang Wenguang (?–1074) shiji xinkao 传人杨文广 (?–1074) 事迹新考 [New study of the historical figure, Yang Wenguang]." In *Bei Song wujiang yanjiu* 北宋武将研究 [The generals of northern Song]. Hong Kong: Zhonghua shuju.

Heyangxian Wenhuaguan 合阳县文化馆. n.d. "Heyang xianqiangxi gaishu 合阳线腔戏概述 [An overview of the marionette opera at Heyang]." Heyang: Heyangxian wenhuaguan.

Heyangxian Xinyi Xian'ou'tuan 合阳县新艺线偶团. 2002. *Luohanshan* 罗汗衫 [The brocade undershirt]. VCD of a marionette play produced by Xi'an dianying zhipianchang luyin chubanshe 西安电影制片厂录音出版社.

———. 2002. *Heyangxian tixian mu'ouxi jingcui* 合阳县提线木偶戏精粹 [Choice selections from the marionette theater of Heyang]. A VCD produced by Xi'an dianying zhipianchang luyin chubanshe 西安电影制片厂录音出版社.

———. 2002. "Zhongxiaoxian 忠孝贤 [Loyalty, filial Piety, and sagacity]." VCD of a marionette play produced by Xi'an dianying zhipianchang luyin chubanshe 西安电影制片厂录音出版社.

Hou Yi 侯仪. 1988. "Mu'ouxi suotan 木偶戏琐谈 [A chat on puppetry]." *Xiyue yiyuan* 西岳艺苑 3: 39–42.

Hou Yihong 侯怡泓. 1983. "Minjian chuantong yineng yu jiyi yanjiu: yi kuileixi yu huzhi weili 民间传统艺能与技艺研究—以傀儡戏与糊纸为例 [The marionette theater and paper crafts: examples of research on traditional Chinese folk performing arts and crafts]." In Taiwan Daxue Renleixuexi 台湾大学人类学系, ed., *Zhongguo minjian chuantong jiyi yu yineng diaocha yanjiu di sannian baogaoshu* 中国民间传统技艺与艺能调查研究第三年报告书 [The third annual report on traditional Chinese folk performing arts and crafts], 89–98.

Hsiao Li-ling. 2001. *The Eternal Present of the Past: Performance, Illustration, and Reading in the Drama Culture of the Wanli Period (1573–1619)*. Ph.D. dissertation. St. Anne's College, University of Oxford.

Hsieh, Chun-Pai. 1991. *The Taiwanese Hand-Puppet Theatre: A Search for Its Meaning*. Ph.D. dissertation. Brown University. Dissertations & Theses: A&I. (Publication No. AAT 9204882).

Huang Chun-ming. 黄春明 1972. "The Forbidden Puppets." *Echo Magazine* 2.9: 26–29.

Huang Huajie 黄华节. 1967. "Kuileixi 傀儡戏 [Puppetry]." In *Zhongguo gujin minjian baixi* 中国古今民间百戏 No. 8 [The various Chinese folk shows from antiquity to the present], 48–59. Taibei: Taiwan Shangwu yinshuguan.

Huang Qianghua 黄强华, director. 2001. *Shengshi chuanshuo* 圣石传说 [Legend of the sacred stone]. 119 min. Pili International Multimedia Company. Taipei.

Huang Renjian 黄仁健. 2010. "Taiwan budaixi shangchangxi yanjiu 台湾布袋戏上场戏研究 [The Shangchang glove puppetry in Taiwan]." M.A. thesis. Taiwan: Guoli zhongyang daxue.

Huang Shaolong 黄少龙 and Wang Jingxian 王景贤. 2007. *Quanzhou tixian mu'ouxi* 泉州提线木偶戏 [String puppetry in Quanzhou]. Hangzhou: Zhejiang renmin chubanshe.

Huang Shaolong 黄少龙, Wang Jingxian 王景贤, and Guo Enlong 郭恩龙. 1987. "Quanzhou mu'ou jutuan jianjie 泉州木偶剧团简介 [Introduction to the Puppetry Troupe of Quanzhou]." *Minsu quyi* 民俗曲艺 50: 10–14.

Huang Shaolong 黄少龙. 1987. "Quanzhou Jiali *Dou Tao* xikao 泉州嘉礼窦淘析考 [Research on *Dou Tao* of the Quanzhou Marionette Theatre]." In *Quanzhou difang xiqu* 2: 78–85.

Huang Shengwen 黄笙闻. 1999. *Xianhu jianshi* 线戏简史 [Short history of the marionette theater]. Xi'an: Renwen zazhi she.

Huang Xijun 黄锡钧. 1988. "Quanzhou tixian mu'ou xishen xianggongye 泉州提线木偶戏神相公爷 [Xianggongye, patron god of the String Puppet Theatre of Quanzhou]." In *Nanxi lunji* 南戏论集 [Collected works on southern dramas], 469–480. Beijing: Zhongguo xiju chubanshe.

———. 1986. "Quanzhou jiali gujin tan 泉州嘉礼古今谈 [Past and present of the Quanzhou Marionette Theatre]." In Chen Ruitong 陈瑞统, ed., *Quanzhou mu'ou yishu* 泉州木偶艺术 [The art of puppetry in Quanzhou], 27–50. Xiamen: Lujiang chubanshe.

———. 1986. "Quanzhou tixian mu'ou xishen xianggongye 泉州提线木偶戏神相公爷 [The patron deity of the Quanzhou Marionette Theatre]." In *Quanzhou difang xiqu* 1: 130–135.

Huang Xiujin 黄秀錦 and Fu Zhengling 傅正玲. 1986. "Taiwan difang xishen chuanshuo (4) 台湾地方戏神传说 (四) [Legends of patron deities of the local operas of Taiwan]." *Minsu quyi* 民俗曲艺 38: 123–126.

Idema, Wilt. 2013. *The Generals of the Yang Family: Four Early Plays*. Hackensack: World Scientific.

Ji Lin 季林. 1991. "Rugaoxian mu'ou jutuan shi 如皋县木偶剧团史 [History of the Rugao County Puppet Troupe]." In Zhongguo Xiquzhi Jiangsu Juan Nantong Fenjuan Bianjishi 中国戏曲志江苏卷南通分卷编辑室, ed., *Nantongshi xiqu ziliao xuanbian* 南通市戏曲资料选编 [Selected works on the traditional operas of the city of Nantong], vol. 5, 87–95. Nantong: Nantongshi wenhuaju xiquzhi bianjishi.

———. 1991. "Nantongxian mu'ou jutuan shi 南通县木偶剧团史 [History of the Puppetry Troupe of Nantong]." In Zhongguo Xiquzhi Jiangsu Juan Nantong Fenjuan Bianjishi 中国戏曲志江苏卷南通分卷编辑室, ed., *Dantongshi xiqu ziliao xuanbian* 南通市戏曲资料选编 [Selected works on the traditional operas of the city of Nantong], vol. 5, 97–98. Nantong: Nantongshi wenhuaju xiquzhi bianjishi.

Ji Xianlin 季羡林. 1957. "*Liezi* yu fuodian 列子与佛典 [*Liezi* and Buddhist scriptures]." In *Zhong Yin wenhua guanxishi luncong* 中印文化关系史论丛 [Cultural relationships between China and India], 75–86. Beijing: Renmin chubanshe.

Jiang Wuchang 江武昌. 1992. "Taimin kuileixi xintan—ji kuileixi Dou Tao, Zhao Tu zhi kaolue yu bijiao 台闽傀儡戏新探—及傀儡戏窦涛. 赵土之考略与

比较 [A new exploration of the marionette theater in Taiwan—and findings on and comparisons of Dou Tao and Zhao Tu]." In *Yishu pinglun* 4: 179–212.

———. 1990. *Xuansi qiandong wanbanqing: Taiwan de kuileixi* 县丝牵动万般情—台湾的傀儡戏 [The myriad emotions created by moving strings: the marionette theater of Taiwan]. Taibei: Taiyuan chubanshe.

———. 1990. *Budaixi jian shi* 布袋戏简史 [A brief history of glove puppet theater]. *Minsu quyi* 民俗曲艺 67–68: 66–126.

———. 1986. "Wan li kan kuilei chusha 万里看傀儡《出煞》[Watching a marionette exorcist ritual at Wanli]." *Minsu quyi* 民俗曲艺 42: 26–37.

———. 1986. "Zhongguo chuantong juchang zhi guiju yu jinji: kuileixi 中国剧场之规矩与禁忌—傀儡戏 [Regulations and taboos in Chinese theaters: the marionette theater]." *Minsu quyi* 民俗曲艺 40: 84–87.

———. 1983. "Xiaoxiao xuansiren: mantan kuileixi 小小悬丝人—漫谈傀儡戏 [Small stringed people: a chat about the marionette theater]." *Zhongguo xiju jikan* 中国戏剧集刊 4: 103–110.

Jiang Wuchang 江武昌 and Wang Lijia 王丽嘉. 1983. "Kuilei de biaoyan dongzuo 傀儡的表演动作 [How to manipulate marionettes]." *Minsu quyi* 民俗曲艺 23–24: 58–98.

Jiang Xiaoqin 蒋萧琴. 1988. "Fangxiang yu kuilei 方相与傀儡 [Sorcerers and puppets]." In *Da'nuokao* 大傩考 [A study on the *Da'nuo*], 63–68. Taibei: Lanting shudian.

Jin Qinghai 金清海. 2003.*Taimin diqu kuileixi yanjiu* 台闽地区傀儡戏研究 [Research on the marionette theater of the Min region of Taiwan]. Taibei: Xuehai chubanshe.

———. 2000. "Taiwan kuileixi zongjiao, yule, yishu gongneng zhi xiaozhang yanjiu 台湾傀儡戏宗教,娱乐,艺术功能之消长研究 [On religion, entertainment, and art of the Taiwanese marionette theater]." In *Kuashiji yanjiusheng hanxue guoji xueshu yantaohui.*

Kagan, Alan Llyod. 1978. *Cantonese Puppet Theater: An Operatic Tradition and Its Role in the Chinese Religious Belief System.* Ph.D. dissertation. Indiana University.

Ke Ziming 柯子铭. 1990. "Quanzhou kuilei mulian de dutexing yu kaoyuan qianxi 泉州傀儡目连的独特性与考源浅析 [An exploratory analysis of the characteristics and roots of the Mulian marionette play of Quanzhou]." *Fujian Xiju* 4: 28–32.

Lai Honglin. 2001. "Pili budaixi zhi huanxiang zhuti piping 霹雳布袋戏之幻想主题批评 [Critical analysis of the theme of fantasy in Pili glove puppetry]." M.A. thesis, Mass Communication Department, Fu Jen University.

Laufer, Berthhold. 1923. *Oriental Theatricals.* Chicago: Field Museum of Natural History.

Leyssenne, Monique. 1977. "Recherches sur le Theatre de Marionettes Chinoises." M.A. thesis. Universite de Paris I—Pantheon—Sorbonne: Faculte de Lettres et Sciences Humaines. (Based mainly on secondary sources in French.)

Lee, Wei-Ping. 2004. "Puppet in a New Age: The Reflection of Social Change in Taiwan." M.A. thesis. Bowling Green: Bowling Green State University.

Li Changmin 李昌敏. 1989. *Zhongguo minjian kuilei yishu* 中国民间傀儡艺术 [The art of Chinese puppetry]. Nanchang: Jiangxi jiaoyu chubanshe.

———. 1984. *Hunan mu'ouxi* 湖南木偶戏 [Puppet theaters in Hunan]. Changsha: Hunan renmin chubanshe.

Li Huaisun 李怀荪. 1996. *Hunansheng Qianyangxian wanxixiang de guanyinjiao he chenhe mu'ouxi xiangshan* 湖南省黔阳县湾溪乡的观音醮和辰河木偶戏香山 [The Chenhe puppet play *Xiangshan* and the Guanyin rituals of Wanxixiang of Qianyang County in Henan]. Taibei: Shihezheng jijin.

———. 1992. "Chenhexi *Mulian* chutan 辰河戏《目连》初探 [A initial exploration of the *Mulian* drama in Chenhe opera]." In *Mulianxi xueshu zuotanhui lunwen xuan* 目连戏学术座谈会论文选 [Selected essays from the Conference on Mulian Drama), 42–64. Hunansheng xiqu yanjiusuo 湖南省戏曲研究所 and Zhongguo yishu yanjiuyuan *xiqu yanjiu* bianjibu 中国艺术研究院《戏曲研究》编辑部.

Li Jianyong 李健永. 1996. "Xuansi qianqing—nan Taiwan kuilei jishi 悬丝牵情—南台湾傀儡纪实 [Love produced by dangling strings—field report of the marionette theater in southern Taiwan]." *Xiangcheng shenghuo zazhi* 35.

Li Jiarui 李家瑞. 1934 (1982 reprint). "Kuileixi xiaoshi 傀儡戏小史 [A short history of the puppet theater]." In Wang Qiugui 王秋桂, ed., *Li Jiarui xiansheng tongsu wenxue lunwenji* 李家瑞先生通俗文学论文集 [Collected works on popular literature by Mr. Li Jiarui], 1–16. Taibei: Taiwan Xuesheng shuju. Originally published in *Wenxue jikan* 1934: 4.

Li Jingci 李静慈. N.d. "Heyang xian'ouxi jilue 合阳县偶戏记略 [Jottings on the marionette opera in Heyang]." (Photocopy given to me without citation.)

Li Kemin 李克民 et al., eds. 1999. *Heyang xian'ouxi changduan jijin* 合阳线偶戏唱段集锦 [Excerpts of the best songs from the Marionette Theatrical Troupe of Heyang]. Heyang: Shaanxisheng Heyangxian wenhuaju and Shaanxisheng Heyangxian heqiang tixian mu'ou jutuan.

Li Ko-jan.1960. "Chinese Puppet Plays." In *Puppet Theatre Around the World*, 120–123. New Delhi: Bharatiya Natya Sangh.

Li Shengsen 李声森. 2007. "Mu'ouxi (Wenzhouban) 木偶戏 (温州班) [Puppetry of the Wenzhou Troupe]." In Ji Wen'ai 季文爱, ed., *Pucheng xiqu* 浦城戏曲 [Traditional operas of Pucheng], 82–86. Published as *neibu ziliao* by Zhengxie Fujiansheng Puchengxian Weiyuanhui 政协福建省浦城县委员会 and Xuexi Eenshi Weiyuanhui 学习文史委员会.

Li Shengsen 李声森 (recited) and Xie Yunhan 谢云憾, ed., 2007. "Mu'ouxi (Wenzhouban) geyao changqiang xuanlu (san shou) 木偶戏 (温州班) 歌谣唱腔选录 (三首) [Three selected musical pieces from the Wenzhou Troupe of Puppetry]." In Ji Wen'ai 季文爱, ed., *Pucheng xiqu* 浦城戏曲 [Traditional operas of Pucheng], 87–89. Published as *neibu ziliao* by Zhengxie Fujiansheng Puchengxian Weiyuanhui 政协福建省浦城县委员会 and Xuexi Eenshi Weiyuanhui 学习文史委员会.

Li Xiaocang 李啸苍. 1953. *Song Yuan jiyi zakao* 宋元技艺杂考 [A miscellany on the performing arts of the Song and Yuan dynasties]. Shanghai: Shangza chubanshe.

Liao Ben 廖奔 and Liu Yanjun 刘彦君. 2003. *Zhongguo xiqu fazhan shi* 中国戏曲发展史 [History of Chinese operas]. Taiyuan: Shanxi jiaoyu chubanshe.

Liao Ben. 1996. "Kuileixi lueshi 傀儡戏略史 [A short history of puppetry]." *Minzu yishu* (Nanning) 4: 87–105.

———. 1989. "Kuileixi 傀儡戏 [Puppetry]." In *Song Yuan xiqu wenwu yu minsu* 宋元戏曲与民俗 [Popular culture and artifacts from the Song and Yuan related to the performing arts], 72–84. Beijing: Wenhua yishu chubanshe.

Lin Chunqing 林春晴. 1986. "Mantan Quanzhou tixian mu'ouxi yinyue 漫谈泉州提线木偶戏音乐 [On the music of Quanzhou Marionette Theatre]." In Chen Ruitong 陈瑞统, ed., *Quanzhou mu'ou yishu* [The art of puppetry in Quanzhou], 171–181. Xiamen: Lujiang chubanshe.

Lin Chunxiang 林春祥. 2006. "Fujian Pinnan zhangtou kuilei diaocha zhaji 福建屏南杖头傀儡调查札记 [Research notes on the rod puppet theater of Pingnan, Fujain]." In Wang Pingzhang 王评章 and Ye Mingsheng 叶明生, eds., *Zhongguo sipingqiang yanjiu lunwenji* 中国四平腔研究论文集 [Research articles on the Siping opera of China], vol. 2: 845–857. Beijing: Zhongguo xijuchubanshe.

Lin Fengxiong 林锋雄. 1990. "Taiwan xuansi kuileixi Taohuanü tanyan 台湾悬丝傀儡戏《桃花女》探研 [A study on the Taiwanese marionette play, *Peach Blossom Girl*]." *Hanxue yanjiu* (Taiwan) 8.1: 523–534.

Lin Maoxian 林茂贤. 1986. "Taiwan difang xishen chuanshuo (4) 台湾地方戏神传说 (四) [Legends of the patron deities of the local operas of Taiwan]." In *Minsu quyi* 民俗曲艺 40: 135–139.

Lin Mingde 林明德. 1999. "Taiwan diqu sifeng de xishen zhiyi—Tiandu yuanshuai 台湾地区祀奉的戏神之一田都元帅 [Marshal Tiandu—a theater deity in Taiwan]." In *Chuantong yishu shuangyue kan*, 3.

Lin Mingde 林明德 et al., eds. (also Fujian sheng xiqu yanjiusuo 福建省戏曲研究所编). 1983.
Fujian xishilu 福建戏史录 [History of the theaters in Fujian]. Fuzhou: Fujian renmin chubanshe.

Liu Haoran 刘浩然. 1987. "Xiaoliyuanxi yu tixian mu'ou—kuilei de guanxi 小梨园戏与提线木偶—傀儡的关系 [The relationship between Xiao Liyuan opera and the marionette theater]." *Quanzhou difang xiqu* 2: 88–92.

Liu Ji 刘霁 and Jiang Shangli 姜尚礼, eds. 1993. *Zhongguo mu'ou yishu* 中国木偶艺术 [The art of Chinese puppetry]. Beijing: Zhongguo shijieyu chubanshe.

Liu Nianci 刘念兹. 1986. *Nanxi xinzheng* 南戏新证 [New evidential interpretation of Nanxi]. Beijing: Zhonghua shuju.

Liu Quansheng 刘泉生. 1992. "Zhongguo xiju yuanliu bian 中国戏剧源流辨 [Debates on the origins of Chinese drama]." In Qu Liuyi 曲六乙 and Li Xiaobin 李肖冰, eds., *Xiyu xiju yu xiju de fasheng* 西域戏剧与戏剧的发生 [Central Asian drama and the inception of Chinese drama], 283–287. Wulumuqi: Xinjiang renmin chubanshe.

Liu Xiaoying 刘晓迎. 2002. "Yong'anshi Huangjingshan Wanfutang daqiang kuileixi yu huanyuan yishi 永安市黄景山万福 堂大腔傀儡戏与还愿仪式 [The Daqiang Marionette Theatre and the ritual for vow-fulfillment by the

Troupe of Ten Thousand Felicities at Huangjingshan in the city of Yong'an]." *Minsu quyi* 民俗曲艺 135: 97–166.

Liu Yuan 刘远. 2002. "Minxi mu'ouxi de kuilei jishu 闽西木偶戏的傀儡技术 [The art of puppetry in Western Fujian]." *Minsu quyi* 民俗曲艺 135: 167–258.

Long Bide 龙彼得 (Piet van der Loon) and Fu Xizhan 傅希瞻. 1992. "Guanyu Zhang Quan mulianxi 关于漳泉目连戏 [On the Mulian drama in Zhangzhou and Quanzhou]." *Minsu quyi* 民俗曲艺 78: 53–60.

Lu Zeqi 陆则起. 2006. "Pingnan siping kuileixi diaocha zhaji 屏南四平傀儡戏调查札记 [Field notes on the Siping String Puppet Theatre of Pingnan]." In Wang Pingzhang 王评章 and Ye Mingsheng 叶明生, eds., *Zhongguo sipingqiang yanjiu lunwenji* [Research articles on the Siping Opera of China], vol. 2: 768–794. Beijing: Zhongguo xijuchubanshe.

Lu Zhihong 陆志宏. 2001. *Gansu minjian mu'ou yishu* 甘肃民间木偶艺术 [Art of the folk puppet theaters of Gansu]. Harbin: Heilongjiang meishu chubanshe faxing.

Luo Bin 罗斌. 1995. "Quanzhou kuileixi (tixian mu'ouxi): difang shehui fazhan de chuangkou 泉州傀儡戏 (提线木偶戏): 地方社会发展的窗口 [The Marionette Theatre of Quanzhou: a window to developments in society]." In *Yishu jiaoyu* 97.

Luo Jintang 罗锦堂. 1971. "Kuileixi de youlai 傀儡戏的由来 [The origins of puppetry]." *Dalu zazhi* 41.12: 367–369.

Lü Aihui. 吕爱辉 2006. "Huang Jia San Xiongdi: Chuangzao Wenhua Qiji 黄家三兄弟: 创造文化奇迹 [The three Huang brothers: creation of a cultural miracle)." *Feifan Xinwen he Zhoukan* [UNB weekly] 27 (October 22–28): 58–61.

Lü Sushang 吕诉上. 1961. "Taiwan kuileixi shi 台湾傀儡戏史 [A history of the marionette theater in Taiwan]." In Lü Sushang 吕诉上, ed., *Taiwan dianying xiju shi* 台湾电影戏剧史 [A history of the films and theaters in Taiwan], 461–472. Taibeishi: Yinhua chubanbu.

———. 1955. "Taiwan de jialixi 台湾的加礼戏 [The marionette theater of Taiwan]." *Zhongguo Yizhou* 281: 11.

———. 1952. "Taiwan kuileixi jishalu 台湾傀儡戏祭煞录 [A record of the exorcist rituals of the Taiwanese marionette theater]." *Taiwan fengwu* 2.6: 7–11.

———. 1946. "Taiwan kuileixi he tade jisha 台湾傀儡戏和它的祭煞 [The Taiwanese marionette theater and its exorcist rituals]." *Taiwan wenhua* 1: 12–15.

Lü Wenjun 吕文俊. 1987. "Quanzhou tixian mu'ou yishu chuxi—jiantan jicheng yu chuangxin 泉州提线木偶艺术初析—兼谈继承与创新 [An exploratory analysis of the art of the Quanzhou Marionette Theatre and a discussion on its succession and creativity]." *Quanzhou difang xiqu* 2: 67–77.

Ma Jianghua 马建华. 2006. "Nanxi *Liu Xi Chenxiang Taizi* zai Fujian yichuan de xinfaxian—shilun minxi kuileixi 'Baodaiji' de xingtai tezheng he chansheng niandai 南戏《刘锡沉香太子》在福建遗传的发现—试论闽西傀儡戏《宝带记》的形态特征和产生年代 [Discovery of a legacy of the Nanxi, *Liu Xi Chenxiang Taizi*—an attempt at analyzing the characteristics and dates of 'Baodaiji,' a Western Fujian puppet play]." In Wang Pingzhang 王评章 and

Ye Mingsheng 叶明生, eds., *Zhongguo sipingqiang yanjiu lunwenji*, vol. 1: 392–432. Beijing: Zhongguo xijuchubanshe.

Ma Ye 马也. 1986. "Miaoqu hengsheng de tixian mu'ouxi—Quanzhou mu'ou jutuan biaoyan yishujia tan *Huoyanshan* chuangzuo 妙趣横生的提线木偶戏—泉州木偶剧团表演艺术家谈《火焰山》创作 [A fascinating marionette play—the performing artists of the Quanzhou Puppetry Troupe discuss the creation of *The Mountain of Fire*]." In Chen Ruitong 陈瑞统, ed., *Quanzhou mu'ou yishu* [The art of puppetry in Quanzhou], 160–163. Xiamen: Lujiang chubanshe.

March, Benjamin. 1930. "A Chinese Puppetman." *Puppetry: A Yearbook of Puppets and Marionettes*, 36–42.

Mills, Winifred H. 1937. *Marionettes, Masks and Shadows*. New York: Doubleday, Doran and Co.

Minsu quyi, ed. (Special issue). 1982. *Kuilei xi zhuan ji* 傀儡戏专辑 [A special issue on the marionette theater). *Minsu quyi* 民俗曲艺, 23–24.

——— (Special issue). 2002. *Fujian minjian kuileixi zhuanji* 福建民间傀儡戏专辑 1 [A special issue on the folk marionette theater in Fujian, vol. 1]. *Minsu quyi* 民俗曲艺, 135.

——— (Special issue). 2002. *Fujian minjian kuileixi zhuanji* 福建民间傀儡戏专辑 2 [A special issue on the folk marionette theater in Fujian, vol. 2]. *Minsu quyi* 民俗曲艺, 136.

——— (Special issue). 1983. *Kueileixi zhuanji* 傀儡戏专辑 [A special issue on the marionette theater]. *Minsu quyi* 民俗曲艺, 23–24.

Miyahara Tachio 宫原大刀夫. 1986. "Fujian de mu'ouxi 福建的木偶戏 [Puppetry in Fujian]," translated by Xu Jingliang 许敬良. In Chen Ruitong 陈瑞统, ed., *Quanzhou mu'ou yishu* [The art of puppetry in Quanzhou], 228–230. Xiamen: Lujiang chubanshe.

Nienhauser, William H., Jr., ed. 2002. *The Grand Scribe's Records, Volume II: The Basic Annals of Han China*. Bloomington and Indianapolis: Indiana University Press.

Obraztsov, Sergei. 1961. *The Chinese Puppet Theatre*. Translated by J.T. MacDermott. London: Faber and Faber.

Pili International Multimedia Company. 2006. Pili Multimedia. (Publicity pamphlet.)

———. 2003. Nine Dragon Throne Plot Summary. Pili International Multimedia Company Web Site. Electronic document, http://drama.pili.com.tw/pili/series.php?did=1067504416.

———. 2000. Introduction to Pili International Multimedia Enterprise. (Publicity pamphlet.)

Peng Zhigong 彭植功. 1988. "Cong Saersibao dao Yilan—tan liangdi de xuansi kuileixi 从萨尔斯堡到宜兰—谈两地的悬丝傀儡戏 [From Saltzburg to Yilan—the marionette theaters of two localities]." In *Yinyue yu yinxiang* 179: 84–95.

Qiu Kunliang 邱坤良. 1983. "Taiwan de kuileixi 台湾的傀儡戏 [The marionette theaters of Taiwan]." *Minsu quyi* 民俗曲艺 23–24: 1–24.

———. 1979. "Wai'ao yucun de kuileixi biaoyan 外澳渔村的傀儡表演 [A marionette performance at a village in Wai'ao]." In *Minjian xiqu sanji* 民间戏曲

散记 [A collection of articles on folk operas], 42–50. Taibei: Shibao wenhua chuban shiye youxian gongsi.

Quanzhou difang xiqu yanjiushe 泉州地方戏曲研究社, ed. 1999. *Quanzhou chuantong xiqu congshu* 泉州传统戏曲丛书 [Collection of traditional Quanzhou operas]. Beijing: Zhongguo xiju chubanshe.

Ransome, Grace Greenleaf. 1931. *Puppets and Shadows: A Bibliography*. Boston: F.W. Faxon Co.

Ren Bantang 任半塘 (Ren Erbei 任二北). 1958. *Tangxinong* 唐戏弄 [Tang dynasty performances]. Beijing: Beijing zuojia chubanshe.

———. 1958. "Bo woguo xiju chuyu kuileixi yingxi shuo 驳我国戏剧出于傀儡戏影戏说 [Refuting the theory that Chinese theater originated from the puppet and shadow theaters]." *Xiju luncong* 1: 177–215.

Ren Guangwei 任光伟. 1989. *Yiye zhijian lu* 艺野知见录 [On the arts]. Shengyang: Chunfeng wenyi chubanshe.

Renmin meishu chubanshe 人民美术出版社, ed. 1996. *Zhongguo minjian meishu: mu'ou piying* 中国民间美术—木偶皮影 [Chinese folk art: puppets and shadow figures]. A CD produced jointly by Renmin meishu chubanshe and Beijing yinguan dianzi keji gongsi.

Ridgeway, William. 1964. *The Dramas and Dramatic Dances of Non-European Races*. New York: Benjamin Bloom.

Rong Shicheng (Yung Sai-shing) 容世诚. 1997. "Beidouxi de shenhua he yishi 北斗戏的神话和仪式 [Legend and ritual of the marionette play, *The Northern Dipper*]." In Yung Sai-shing 容世诚, ed., *Xiqu renleixue chutan: yishi, juchang yu shequn* 戏曲人类学初探: 艺术, 剧场与社群 [Anthropology of drama: ritual, theater, and community], 99–131. Taibei: Maitian chubanshe.

———. 1997. "Beidouxi de tianye guancha 北斗戏的田野观察 (Field Report on the Marionette Play, *The Northern Dipper*)." In Yung Sai-shing 容世诚, ed, *Xiqu renleixue chutan: yishi, juchang yu shequn* 戏曲人类学初探: 艺术, 剧场与社群 [Anthropology of drama: ritual, theater, and community], 59–97. Taibei: Maitian chubanshe.

———. 1997. "Guangongxi de quxie yiyi 关公戏的驱邪意义 [Exorcism in Lord Guan plays]." In *Xiqu renleixue chutan: yishi, juchang yu shequn* 戏曲人类学初探: 艺术, 剧场与社群 [Anthropology of drama: art, venue, and social groups), 25–57. Taibei: Maitian chubanshe.

Ruizendaal, Robin. 2006. *Marionette Theatre in Quanzhou*. Leiden: Brill. (Based on his Ph.D. dissertation at the University of Leiden, 1999.)

———. 2000. "Ritual Text and Performance in the Marionette Theatre of Southern Fujian and Taiwan." In Jan A.M. de Meyer and Peter M. Engelfriet, eds., *Linked Faiths: Essays on Chinese Religion and Traditional Culture in Honor of Kristofer Schipper*, 336–361. Leidon, Boston, and Köln: Brill.

———. 1994. "Performance as a Ritual: The Performance Practice of the Marionette Theatre of Southern Taiwan." In Göran Aijmer and Åsa Boholm, eds., *Images and Enactments: Possible Worlds in Dramatic Performance*, 134–189.

Göteborg, Sweden: The Institute for Advanced Studies in Social Anthropology (IASSA) at the University of Gothenberg.

Sanmenxia shi wenhuaju 三门峡市文化局, ed. 1993. *Sanmenxia shi quyi zhi* 三门峡市曲艺志 [Gazetteer of the performing arts of the city of Sanmenxia]. Zhenzhou: Henan renmin chubanshe.

Schipper, K.M. 1966. "The Divine Jester: Some Remarks on the Gods of the Chinese Marionette Theatre." *Bulletin of the Institute of Ethnology* 21: 81–96.

Shaaxi Heyangxian Heqiang tixian mu'ou jutuan 陕西合阳县提线木偶剧团. 1999. *Shaaxi Heyangxian Heqiang tixian mu'ouxi* 陕西合阳县合腔提线木偶戏 [Heqiang marionette plays of the county of Heyang in Shaanxi]. A VCD published by Shaanxi Wenhua Yinxiang chubanshe 陕西文化音像出版社.

Shaanxisheng Wenhuaju 陕西省文化局, ed. 1962. *Heyang xianxi* 合阳线戏 in the *Shaanxisheng chuantong jumu* 陕西省传统剧目 series. Xi'an: Shaanxisheng wenhuaju neibu ziliao.

Shaanxisheng yishuguan 陕西省艺术馆, ed. n.d. *Heyang xian'ouxi yinyue* 合阳县偶戏音乐 [Music of the Heyang marionette theater].

Shanxisheng xiju yanjiusuo Lüliangshi xiju chuangzuo yanjiushi 山西省戏剧研究所吕梁市戏剧创作研究室, ed. 2004. *Shanxi difang xiqu huibian 20: Xiaoyi piqiang, wanwanqiang, piyingxi zhuanji* 山西省地方戏曲汇编 20: 孝义皮腔, 碗碗腔, 皮影戏专辑 [Collection of the local operas of Shanxi, vol. 20: the Piqiang and Wanwanqiang styles of shadow plays in Xiaoyi]. Taiyuan: Shanxi caijing daxue yinshuachang.

Shen Jisheng 沈继生. 1992. "Mulian kuilei zhong de mulianxi 目连傀儡中的目连戏 [The Mulianxi in the Mulian marionette theater]." *Misu quyi* 78: 39–51.

———. 1987. "Quanzhou kuileixi zhong de laolilian—nanxi xishenzhou tanyuan 泉州傀儡戏中的唠哩连－南戏戏神咒探源 [The Laolilian chant in the Quanzhou Marionette Theatre—an Exploration of an origin of the ritual incantations of Nanxi opera]." In *Quanzhou difang xiqu* 2: 93–96.

———. 1986. "Mulian kuilei zhong de mulianxi 目连傀儡中的目连戏 [The Mulianxi in the Mulian Marionette Theatre]." In Chen Ruitong 陈瑞统, ed., *Quanzhou mu'ou yishu* [The art of puppetry in Quanzhou], 144–156. Xiamen: Lujiang chubanshe.

———. 1985. "Mulian kuilei zhong de mulianxi 目连傀儡中的目连戏 [The Mulianxi in the Mulian Marionette Theatre]." In *Mulianxi xueshu zuotanhui lunwen xuan* 目连戏学术座谈会论文选 [Selected essays from the Conference on Mulian Drama], 120–131. Published by Hunansheng Xiqu Yanjiusuo 湖南省戏曲研究所 and Zhongguo Yishu Yanjiuyuan *Xiqu Yanjiu* Bianjibu 中国艺术研究院《戏曲研究》编辑部.

Shi Jizu 师继祖, Cao Guanmin 曹冠敏, and Liu Xingzhao 刘星照, 1989. "Xianqiang de laojia zai Heyang 线腔的老家在合阳 [Heyang is the native home of string-puppetry]." In Weinan Diqu Wenhuaju 渭南地区文化局, ed., *Qindong xiju lunwenji* 秦东戏剧论文集 [Collected works on traditional operas in Eastern Shaanxi], 23–30. Xian: Xibei daxue chubanshe.

———. 1989. "Xianqiang gaige zhi wojian 线腔改革之我见 [My thoughts on revolutionizing string puppetry]." In Weinan Diqu Wenhuaju 渭南地区文化局, ed., *Qindong xiju lunwenji* 秦东戏剧论文集 [Collected works on traditional operas in eastern Shaanxi], 38–45. Xian: Xibei daxue chubanshe.

———. 1989. "Mu'ouxi suotan 木偶戏琐谈 [Cursory thoughts on the puppet theater]." In Weinan Diqu Wenhuaju 渭南地区文化局, ed., *Qindong xiju lunwenji* 秦东戏剧论文集 [Collected works on traditional operas in eastern Shaanxi], 77–82. Xian: Xibei daxue chubanshe.

———. 1989. "Xianqiang yinyue xingcheng chutan 线腔音乐形成初探 [A preliminary discussion on the formation of string puppetry]." In Weinan Diqu Wenhuaju 渭南地区文化局, ed., *Qindong xiju lunwenji* 秦东戏剧论文集 [Collected works on traditional operas in eastern Shaanxi], 92–110. Xi'an: Xibei daxue chubanshe.

Shi Yaozeng 史耀增. 2008. *Heyang tixian mu'ouxi* 合阳提线木偶戏 [Heyang marionette theater). In *Diyipi Shaanxi feiwuzhi wenhua yichan tulu 4: difang xiqu lei, quxi lei* 第一批陕西非物质文化遗产图录 (第四辑) 地方戏曲类, 曲艺类 [The First Group of Intangible Cultural Heritage from Shaanxi: local operas and performing arts], 177–196. Xi'an: Shaanxi renmin chubanshe.

———. 2008. "Wei 'heqiang' zhengming 为合腔正名 [The correct name for Heyang string puppetry]." In *Xinyuan shisui* 莘原拾穗 [Gleanings from the plains of Xin], 78–80. Hong Kong: Tianma chuban youxian gongsi.

———. 2008. "Qingmo minchu heyang xianxi de zhuyao banshe 清末民初合阳线戏的主要班社 [The main string-puppetry troupes in Heyang from the end of the Qing to the Early Republican periods]." In *Xinyuan shisui* 莘原拾穗 [Gleanings from the plains of Xin], 81–84. Hong Kong: Tianma chuban youxian gongsi.

———. 2008. "Li Guan guli de 'Xiangruo jushe' 李灌故里的 '向若剧社' [The Xiangruo Troupe of the native land of Li Guan]." In *Xinyuan shisui* 莘原拾穗 [Gleanings from the plains of Xin], 85–86. Hong Kong: Tianma chuban youxian gongsi.

———. 2008. "Xianxi yishu zhi xiang—Guojiapo 线戏艺术之乡—郭家坡 [Guojiapo—the land of string puppetry]." In *Xinyuan shisui* 莘原拾穗 [Gleanings from the plains of Xin], 87–89. Hong Kong: Tianma chuban youxian gongsi.

———. 2008. "Huanghe kuilei yishu—mu'ou 黄河傀儡艺术一木偶 [Puppetry—an art form of (the region of) the Yellow River]." In *Xinyuan shisui* 莘原拾穗 [Gleanings from the plains of Xin], 316–343. Hong Kong: Tianma chuban youxian gongsi.

———. 2008. "Dui heyang xianxi 'shaoxi'de sikao 对合阳线戏捎戏的思考 [Thoughts on the 'Extra Playlets' of the marionette plays of Heyang]." In *Xinyuan shisui* 莘原拾穗 [Gleanings from the plains of Xin], 344–354. Hong Kong: Tianma chuban youxian gongsi.

———. 2008. "Shitan heyang xinxi zhong de linsegui xingxiang 试谈合阳线戏中的吝啬鬼形象 [The miser in the string-puppet plays of Heyang]." In *Xinyuan shisui* 莘原拾穗 [Gleanings from the plains of Xin], 355–365. Hong Kong: Tianma chuban youxian gongsi.

———. 1999. “Xianqiang yinggai jiao heqiang 线腔应该叫合腔 [‘String puppet/marionette opera’ should be called ‘Heyang opera’].” *Xiyue yisui* 2–3: 59–60.

———. 1998. *Zoujin gu Xin* 走近古莘 [Traveling to the ancient land of Xin], 93–101. Beijing: Dongfang chubanshe.

———. 1998. “Xianqiangxi de laojia zai Heyang 线腔戏的老家在合阳 [Home of the Chinese marionettes is in Heyang].” In *Zoujin gu Xin* 走近古莘 [Traveling to the ancient land of Xin], 93–101. Beijing: Dongfang chubanshe.

———. 1998. “Qian an Heyang xianqiangxi de tixian yishu 浅谈合阳线腔戏的提线艺术 [On the art of manipulating marionettes in the marionette theater of Heyang].” In *Zoujin gu Xin* 走近古莘 [Traveling to the Ancient Land of Xin], 102–110. Beijing: Dongfang chubanshe.

Simmen, René. 1972. *The World of Puppets*. New York: Thomas Y. Crowell Co.

Song Jinxiu 宋锦秀. 1994. *Kuilei, chusha yu xiangzheng* 傀儡, 除煞与象征 [Marionettes, exorcism, and symbolism]. Taibei: Daoxiang chubanshe.

———. 1990. “Guanyu kuileixi de chucha yishi yongfu—jieshi yu shuoming 关于傀儡戏的除煞仪式用符: 解释与说明 [Explanations of the charms and phylacteries in the exorcist rituals of the marionette theater].” In *Taiwanshi tianye yanjiu tongxun* [Newsletter of Taiwan history field research] 15: 19–32.

———. 1988. “Kuileixi jidian yishi zhi yanchu—jianshuo lanyang diqu kuileixi de chucha yishi 傀儡戏祭奠仪式之演出—简说兰阳地区傀儡戏的除煞仪式 [Ritual performances in the marionette theater—a short exposition of the exorcist ritual in the marionette theater of the Lanyang region].” In *Taiwan wenxian* 39.4: 43–60.

———. 1986. “Lanyang diqu kuilei chusha yishi: yige zongjiao renleixue de yanjiu 兰阳地区傀儡除煞仪式—一个宗教人类学的研究 [An anthropological religious study of the exorcist rituals of the marionette theater in the Lanyang region).” M.A. thesis. Guoli Taiwan daxue renleixue yanjiusuo 国立台湾大学人类学研究所.

———. 1985. “Kuileixi de zongjiao yishi 傀儡戏的宗教仪式 [Religious rituals in the marionette theater].” *Minsu quyi* 民俗曲艺 38: 88–112.

Stalberg, Roberta H. 1984. *Puppetry of China.* Catalogue of exhibition with the Center of Puppetry Arts.

———. 1984. *China's Puppets.* San Francisco: China Books.

Suda Kantaro 须田轮太郎. 1998. “Yinggezhen Erqiaoli de kuileixi kao 莺歌镇二桥里的傀儡戏考 [The marionette theater at Erqiaoli in the town of Yingge].” In Lin Chuanfu 林川夫, ed., *Minsu Taiwan* 2, 296–304. Taibei wuling chuban youxiangongsi.

Sun Jianjun 孙建君. 1995. “Gaishu 概述 [A general introduction].” In Wang Zhaowen 王朝文, ed., *Zhongguo minjian meishu quanji 12: youyibian—mu'ou yingxi juan* 中國民間美術全集 12: 游艺篇—木偶影戲卷 [The complete collection of Chinese folk art: entertainment 12—the volume on puppet and shadow theaters), 1–17. Jinan: Shandong jiaoyu chubanshe.

———. 1995. “Mu'ou yu piying yanjiu de wenhuaxue yiyi 木偶与皮影研究的文化意义 [The cultural significance of research in puppet and shadow theaters].” In Wang Zhaowen, ed., *Zhongguo minjian meishu quanji 12: youyibian—*

mu'ou yingxi juan [The complete collection of Chinese folk art: entertainment 12—the volume on puppet and shadow Theaters], 297–303. Jinan: Shandong jiaoyu chubanshe.

Sun Kaidi 孙楷第. 1965. "Jinshi xiqu de changyan xingshi chuzi kuileixi yingxi kao 近世戏曲的唱演形式出自傀儡戏影戏考 [Study of the derivation of the style of performance of Chinese operas from the puppet and shadow theaters]." In *Cangzhou ji* 沧州集 [A collection of Cangzhou] 3, 238–307. Beijing: Zhonghua shuju.

———. 1965. "Kuileixi yingxi buzai 傀儡戏影戏补载 [Addendum to (my study on) the puppet and shadow theaters]." In *Cangzhou ji* 沧州集 [A collection of Cangzhou] 1, 308–316. Beijing: Zhonghua shuju.

———. 1952. *Kuileixi kaoyuan* 傀儡戏考源 [A study of the origins of the puppet theater]. Shanghai: Shanza chubanshe. Also reprinted in *Minsu quyi* 民俗曲艺 23–24 (1983): 141–214.

Sun Shiwen 孙世文. 1980. "Kuileixi qiyuan yu yong kao 傀儡戏起源于俑考 [An investigation of the origin of puppetry in funerary statues]." *Jilin shida xuebao* 1: 40 and 52–57.

Szonyi, Michael. 1997. "The Illusion of Standardizing the Gods: The Cult of the Five Emperors in Late Imperial China." *The Journal of Asian Studies* 56.1: 113–135. (Pp. 124–125 mention a marionette theater play script.)

Taishunxian Zhengxie Wenshiziliao Weiyuanhui 泰顺县政协文史资料委员会, ed. 2000. *Taishun mu'ouxi* 泰顺木偶戏 [The puppet theater in Taishun]. Neibu ziliao.

Taiwan's Government Information Office. n.d. "Puppetry"; "Puppetry—Glove-Puppet Theater"; "Puppetry—Marionette Theater." At http://www.roc-taiwan.org/info/culture/cultur30.html.

Tajima Fumio 田岛义雄. 1998. "Taiwan Renxingju jianwenlu 台湾人形剧见闻录 (Puppetry in Taiwan)." In Lin Chuanfu 林川夫, ed., *Minsu Taiwan* 2, 305–311. Taibei: Wuling chuban youxiangongsi.

Takahashi Noriko 高桥典子. 1994. "Wo suo jian de Taiwan renxingju 我所见的台湾人形剧 [The puppetry theaters I saw in Taiwan]." In Lin Chuanfu 林川夫, ed., *Minsu Taiwan* 4, 116–120. Taibeishi: Wuling chuban youxian gongsi.

Tan Daxian 谭达先. 1982. *Zhongguo minjian xiju yanjiu* 中国民间戏剧研究 [A study on Chinese local operas], 16–17. Taipei: Muduo chubanshe.

Tang Wenbiao 唐文标. 1985. "Kuileixi yu yingxi 傀儡戏与影戏 [Puppetry and the shadow theater]." In *Zhongguo gudai xijushi* 中国古代戏剧史 [A history of ancient Chinese dramas], 48–51. Beijing: Zhongguo xiju chubanshe.

Thompson, Lawrence. 1979. *Chinese Religion: An Introduction*. Belmont: Wadsworth.

Tian Shilin 田士林. 1983. *Zhongguo xiju yanjiu* 中国戏剧研究 [Studies on Chinese drama]. In Lou Tsu-kuang and Wolfram Eberhard, eds., *Asian Folklore and Social Life Monographs*, vol. 165. Taibei: The Chinese Association for Folklore. (Pp. 63–68 list different types of puppet theaters in various localities of China.)

Ting, Yen-chao 丁言昭. 1991. *Zhongguo mu'ou shi* 中国木偶史 [A history of Chinese puppetry]. Shanghai: Xuelin chubanshe.

Tong Jingxin 佟晶心. 1934. "Zhongguo kuileixi kao 中国傀儡剧考 [Research on Chinese puppetry]." *Juxue yuekan* 3.10: 1–12.

Tsao Pen-yeh (Cao Benye) 曹本冶, ed. 1987. *Xianggang de mu'ou piyingxi jiqi yuanliu* 香港的木偶皮影戏及其源流 [The puppet and shadow theaters in Hong Kong and their origins]. Hong Kong: The Museum of Hong Kong.

Uno Kojiro 宇野小四郎. 1995. "Taiwan ren xing ju kao 台湾人形剧考 [A study on the puppet theaters of Taiwan]." In Lin Chuanfu 林川夫, ed., *Minsu Taiwan* 5, 156–232. Taibei: Wuling chuban youxian gongsi.

Wang, Betty. 1982. "In Imitation of Man: The Traditional World of String Puppets." *Free China Review* 32.10: 31–36.

Wang, Georgette. 1984. "Televised Puppetry in Taiwan: An Example of the Marriage between a Modern Medium and a Folk Medium." In G. Wang and W. Dissanayake, eds., *Continuity and Change in Communication Systems: An Asian Perspective.* Norwood: Ablex.

Wang Guowei 王国维. 1915. *Song Yuan xiqushi* 宋元戏曲史 [History of drama in Song and Yuan]. Shanghai: Commercial Press.

Wang Hongsheng 王宏声 and Shi Yaozeng 史耀增, eds. 2004. *Heyang wenshi ziliao 8—Heyang xiqu zhuanji* 合阳文史资料 8—合阳戏曲专集 [Historical and literary sources on Heyang, Volume 8—the volume on the operas of Heyang]. Internal publication by the Zhongguo renmin zhengzhi xieshang huiyi heyangxian weiyuanhui.

Wang Lianhai 王连海. 1995. "Zhongguo mu'ou yuanliukao 中国木偶源流考 [A study of the origin of Chinese puppetry]." In Wang Zhaowen, ed., *Zhongguo minjian meishu quanji 12: youyibian—mu'ou yingxi juan* [The complete collection of Chinese Folk Art: Entertainment 12—the volume on puppet and shadow Theaters], 275–279. Jinan: Shandong jiaoyu chubanshe.

Wanglu Juyuan 网路剧院, ed. 2001. "Taiwan kuileixi 台湾傀儡戏 [The marionette theater of Taiwan]." http://theater.cca.gov.tw/story/folkarts_c/hand/.

Wang Qinzhi 王钦之, and Wang Yuxin 王毓新. 1986. "Mantan Quanzhou tixian mu'ou 漫谈泉州提线木偶 [A cursory discussion on the Quanzhou Marionette Theatre]." In Chen Ruitong 陈瑞统, ed., *Quanzhou mu'ou yishu* [The art of puppetry in Quanzhou], 51–55. Xiamen: Lujiang chubanshe.

Wang Yufeng 王玉峰 (Ming dynasty figure). 2004 (reprint). *Chaichuanji* 钗钏记 [Tale of the hairpin and bracelet]. In Wu Shuyin 吴书荫, ed., *Suizhong Wushi cangchaoben gaoben xiqu congkan* 绥中吴氏藏抄本稿本戏曲丛刊, vol. 8, 1–163. Beijing: Xueyuan chubanshe.

Wang Zhaowen 王朝文, ed. 1995. *Zhongguo minjian meishu quanji 12: youyibian—mu'ou yingxi juan* 中国民间美术全集 12: 游艺篇—木偶影戏卷 [The complete collection of Chinese folk art: entertainment 12—the volume on puppet and shadow theaters). Jinan: Shandong jiaoyu chubanshe.

Wang Zizheng 王子政. 1981. "Yidai kuileiwang Zhang Guocai 一代傀儡王张国才 [Zhang Guocai: king of the Marionette theater]." *Minsu quyi* 民俗曲艺 5: 12–19.

Watson, Burton, trans. 1989. *The Tso Chuan: Selection from China's Oldest Narrative History.* New York: Columbia University Press.

———. 1961. *"Records of the Grand Historian of China" Translated from the "Shih Chi of Ssu-ma Ch'ien," Volume 1*. New York and London: Columbia University Press.

Wei Pingfu 卫平复. 1981. "Liangjian Song sancaizhen 两件三彩枕 (Two Tricolored Ceramic Pillows of the Song Dynasty)." *Wenwu*: 81–82.

Weng Minhua 温敏华. 1999. "Kuileixi sanbian 傀儡戏三辨 [Three debates on puppetry]." In Hu Ji 胡忌, ed., *Xishi bian* 戏史辨 [Debates on the history of theater]. Beijing: Zhongguo xiju chubanshe.

———. 1997. *Zhongguo xiju yu minsu* 中国戏剧与民俗 [Chinese theatre and popular culture], 413. Taipei: Xuehai chubanshe.

Wu Chengji 吴承基. 1986. "Zai Quanzhou kan mu'ouxi 在泉州看木偶戏 [Watching puppet operas in Quanzhou]." In Chen Ruitong 陈瑞统, ed., *Quanzhou mu'ou yishu* [The art of puppetry in Quanzhou], 208–210. Xiamen: Lujiang chubanshe.

Wu Lilan 吴丽兰. 1978. "Taiwan Yilan diqu xuansi kuilei yanjiu 台湾宜兰地区悬丝傀儡研究 [Research on the marionettes in the Yilan region of Taiwan]." M.A. thesis. Zhongguo wenhua daxue yishu yanjiusuo xijuzu 中国文化大学艺术研究所戏剧组.

Wu Lingling 吴玲玲. 1981. "Jilong kan kuileixi jisha 基隆看傀儡戏《祭煞》[Observing a marionette exorcist ritual in Jilong]." *Minsu quyi* 民俗曲艺 9: 51–58.

Wu Mingde 吴明德. 2005. *Taiwan budaixi biaoyan yishu zhimei* 台湾布袋戏表演艺术之美 [The art of Taiwan glove puppet theater]. Taibei: Taiwan xuezhe.

Xi Dejin 席德进. 1973. "Taiwan de minjian yishu 台湾的民间艺术 [Popular arts in Taiwan]." *Xiongshi meishu* 25: 76–85.

Xia Zhulin 厦竹林. 1985. "Taiwan difang xishen chuanshuo (4) 台湾地方戏神传说 (四) [Legends of the patron gods of the local theaters of Taiwan]." *Minsu quyi* 民俗曲艺 35, 108–113.

Xiao Bing 萧兵. 1992. "Kuilei yu gui: tade qiyuan he yingxiang 傀儡与鬼: 它的起源和影响 [Puppetry and ghosts: origins and influences]." In *Nuozha zhifeng: Changjiang liuyu zongjiao xiju wenhua* 傩蜡之风: 长江流域宗教戏剧文化 [The customs of Nuo and Zha: the religious and dramatic cultures of the Changjiang River regions], 773–817. Nanjing: Jiangsu renmin chubanshe.

Xiao Wenping 肖文评 et al. 2002. "Raopingxian Guayuanshe Kengqiancun de chuantong xisu 饶平县瓜园社坑前村的传统习俗 [Traditional popular culture in Kengqiancun, Guayuanshe of Raoping County]." In *Minjian wenhua yu xiangtu shehui: yuedong diqu de minsu yu difang shehui* 民间文化与乡土社会: 粤东地区的民俗与地方社会 [Popular culture and local society in Eastern Canton Province], 52–68. Guangzhou: Huacheng chubanshe. (See "diaoxianxi 吊线戏," p. 68.)

Xiao Yaotian 萧遥天. 1957. "Kuileixi 傀儡戏 [Puppetry]." In *Minjian xiju congkao* 民间戏剧丛考 [Studies of popular dramas], 162–177. Hong Kong: Nanguo chubanshe.

Xie Jiaqun 谢家群. 1957. "Fujian nanbu de minjian xiaoxi 福建南部的民间小戏 [The minor operas in southern Fujian]." *Xiju luncong* 戏剧论丛 3: 197–201.

Xie Songhui 谢松辉. 1983. "Kuileixi xinchuan youren—Lin Zancheng xishang meishao 傀儡戏薪传有人—林赞成喜上眉梢 [Lin Zhancheng is very pleased—he had found a successor to the marionette theater]." *Minsu quyi* 民俗曲艺 23–24: 31–33.

Xu Dishan 许地山. 1925. "Fanju tili jiqi zai hanju shangdi diandian didi 梵剧体例及其在汉剧上底点点滴滴 [The format of Indian drama and its influences on Chinese drama)." Reprinted in Li Xiaobing, ed., *Zhongguo xiju qiyuan* 中国戏剧起源 [The origins of Chinese of drama], 86–118. Shanghai: Zhishi chubanshe.

Xu Jingzhi 徐静之. 1977. "Zhangzhongxi yu kuileixi zhi yan'ge 掌中戏与傀儡戏之沿革 [The spread of the glove and marionette theaters]." *Huagang bo'wuguan guankan* 4: 111–112.

Xu Zhaoge 徐兆格. 2005. *Pingyang mu'ouxi* 平阳木偶戏 [The puppet theater in Pingyang]. Hong Kong: Tianma tushu youxian gongsi.

Yan Fuchang 严福昌, ed. 2004. "Quan maoren 劝茅人. *Sichuan nuoxizhi* 四川傩戏志 [The Nuo dramas of Sichuan]. Chengdu: Sichuan wenyi chubanshe.

Yan Zhitui 颜之推 (531–ca. 591). 1993 (reprint). *Yanshi Jiaxun* 颜氏家训 [Admonitions for the Yan clan: a Chinese classic on household management]. Guiyang: Guizhou renmin chubanshe.

Yan Zhitui 颜之推 and Zong Fuchang, trans. 2004. *Yanshi Jiaxun* 颜氏家训 [Admonitions for the Yan clan: a Chinese classic on household management]. Beijing: Foreign Languages Press.

Yang Hui 杨辉. 1994. "Qiyang mu'ouxi yu nuoji 祁陽木偶戏与傩祭 [The puppet theater of Qiyang and Nuo rituals]." In Hu Jianguo 胡建国, ed., *Hunan nuoxi yanjiu lunwenji* 湖南傩戏研究论文集 [Research articles on the Nuo dramas of Hunan], 191–208. Hong Kong: Shijie chuban gongsi.

Yang Junqian 杨钧千 and Shi Yaozeng 史耀增. 1988. "Qiantan Heyang xianqiangxi de tixian yishu 浅谈合阳线腔戏的提线艺术 [A cursory discussion on the art of manipulation of the Heyang marionette theater)." *Xiyue yishu* 1: 22–26.

Yang Lian 扬琏. 1974. "Kuileixi yu yingxi zongshu 傀儡戏与影戏综述 [On the shadow and marionette theaters]." *Zhonghua wenhua fuxing yuekan* 7.4: 55–61.

Yang Rong 杨榕. 2002. "Putian kuileixi yu luxi, beidouxi zhi tantao 莆田傀儡戏与庐戏北斗戏之探讨 [A discussion on string puppetry in Putian and the plays *Luxi* and *the Northern Dipper*]." *Minsu quyi* 民俗曲艺 136: 41–112.

Yang Xiangping 杨翔平. 1998. "Yan Yu dui mu'ou jiyi de fazhan 颜育对木偶技艺的发展 [Yan Yu's development of the artistry of puppetry]." *Zhongguo xiju* 9: 34–35.

Ye Lüqiu 叶绿秋. 1986. "Tan xianxi de biaoyan yishu 谈线戏的表演艺术 [On the art of performance of the marionette theater]." In Chen Ruitong 陈瑞统, ed., *Quanzhou mu'ou yishu* [The art of puppetry in Quanzhou], 157–159. Xiamen: Lujiang chubanshe.

Ye Mingsheng 叶明生 and Liang Lunyong 梁伦拥. 2010. *Shanghang mu'ouxi yu Baisha Tian'gonghui yanjiu wenji* 上杭木偶戏与白砂田公会研究文集 [Studies on the puppet theater in Shanghang and the festival of Marshal Tian in Baisha]. Fuzhou: Haichao shying yishu chubanshe.

Ye Mingsheng 叶明生. 2007. *Puxian xiju wenhua shengtai yanjiu* 莆仙戏剧文化生态研究 [Cultural ecology of Puxian theater]. Xiamen: Xiamen daxue chubanshe.

———. 2005. *Guyuan kuilei* 古愿傀儡 [Ancient vow-repayment string puppet theaters]. Fuzhou: Haichao sheying yishu chubanshe.

———. 2004. *Fujian kuileixi shilun* 福建傀儡戏史论 [History of the string puppet theaters of Fujian]. Two volumes. Beijing: Zhongguo xiju chubanshe.

———. 2002. "Fu'anshi beibu shanqu xiayangcun de manzhangxi" 福安市北部山区下洋村的幔帐戏 [The Manzhang opera of Xiayang Village of the mountainous region north of Fu'an]. *Minsu quyi* 民俗曲艺 136: 1–39.

———. 2001. "Gudai roukuilei xingtai jiyu Fujian nanxi guanxi tantao 古代肉傀儡形态及与福建南戏关系探讨 [A study on the relationship between the flesh marionette of antiquity and the Nanxi of Fujian]." In Wenzhoushi Wenhuaju 温州市文化局, ed., *Nanxi guoji xueshu yantaohui lunwenji* 南戏国际学术研讨会论文集 [Collected works of an international scholarly conference on Nanxi], 283–297. Beijing: Zhonghua shuju.

———. 2000. *Fujian Shouning siping kuileixi Huaguangzhuan* 福建寿宁四平傀儡戏华光传 [*The Biography of Huaguang*, a Siping tradition marionette play from Shouning, Fujian]. *Minsu quyi series*, no. 79. Taibei: Shihezheng jijinhui.

———. 2000. "Shouningxian Daiyangcun de yuanxiaofu yu liyuanjiao zhi kuileixi *Huaguangzhuan* 寿宁县岱阳村的元宵福与梨园教之傀儡戏《华光传》 [The relationship between the Yuanxiaofu of the village of Daiyang in Shouning County and the marionette play *Biography of Huaguang* of the Liyuan Sect]." *Minsu quyi* 民俗曲艺 122–123: 101–191.

———. 1999. "Liyuanjiao, yige jieshi gudai kuilei yu zongjiao guanxi de dianxing lizheng—yi mindong liyuanjiao zhi fashi kuileixi weili 梨园教，一个揭示古代傀儡与宗教关系的典型例证 [String puppets in the Liyuan rituals of eastern Fukian and the relationship between string puppets and religion]." In Caituan Faren Zhonghua Minsu Yishu Jijinhui 财团法人中华民俗艺术基金会, ed., *Guoji ouxi xueshu yantaohui lunwenji* 国际偶戏学术研讨会论文集 [Collected works of the International Conference on Puppet Theaters], 110–135.

———, ed. Transcribed by Wu Naiyu 吴乃宇. 1997. Ye Mingsheng 叶明生 and Li Yingsuo. 李应梭. 2002. "Zhao'anxian minjian kuilei tiezhixi 诏安县民间傀儡铁枝戏 [The Iron Stick Puppet Theatre of Zhao'an County]." *Minsu quyi* 民俗曲艺 136: 113–160.

Ye Mingsheng 叶明生 and Yang Muzhen 杨慕震. 2002. "Nanpingshi Yanpingqu Hushan daqiang kuileixi 南平市延平区虎山大腔傀儡戏 [The Daqiang Kuileixi of Hushan in Yanpingqu of Nanpingshi]." *Minsu quyi* 民俗曲艺 135: 7–96.

Fujian Shouning siping kuileixi Nainiangzhuan 福建寿宁四平傀儡戏奶娘传 [*Biography of Goddess Nainiang* (Chen Jinggu), a marionette play of the Siping tradition from Shouning County, Fujian]. *Minsu quyi series*, no. 60. Taibei: Shihezheng jijinhui.

——— and Yuan Hongliang 袁洪亮. 1996. *Fujian Shanghang luantan kuileixi furenzhuan* 福建上杭乱弹傀儡戏夫人传 [*Biography of the Lady* (Chen Jinggu), a Luantan marionette play of Shanghang in Fujian]. *Minsu quyi series*, no. 44. Taibei: Shihezheng jijinhui.

———. 1995. "*Minxi Shanghang gaoqiang kuilei yu furenxi* 闽西上杭高腔傀儡与夫人戏 [The Gaoqiang marionette tradition and the play *Biography of the Lady* (Chen Jinggu) in Shanghang of Western Fujian]." *Minsu quyi series*, no. 33. Taibei: Shihezheng jijinhui.

———. 1995. "Fujian Shanghang Chen Jinggu xinyang yu kuileixi furenzhuan shugai 福建上杭陈靖姑信仰与傀儡戏夫人传述概 [A description of the relationship between the worship of Chen Jinggu in Shanghang and the marionette play *Biography of the Lady* (Chen Jinggu)]." *Minsu quyi* 民俗曲艺 94–95: 47–83.

Ye Yangzhong 叶杨忠 (recited by) and Xie Yunhan 谢云憾, ed. 2007. "Zhuanzi mu'ou geyao changqiang xuanlu (si'shou) 传子木偶歌谣唱腔选录 (四首) [Four selected musical pieces from Zhuanzi Marionette Puppet Theatre]." In Ji Wen'ai 季文爱, ed., *Pucheng xiqu* 浦城戏曲 [Traditional operas of Pucheng], 71–74. Published as *neibu ziliao* by Zhengxie Fujiansheng Puchengxian Weiyuanhui 政协福建省浦城县委员会 and Xuexi Wenshi Weiyuanhui 学习文史委员会.

Yeung, Tuen Wai Mary. 2008. *To Entertain and Renew: Operas, Puppet Plays and Ritual in South China*. Ph.D. dissertation. The University of British Columbia (Canada). Dissertations & Theses: A&I. (Publication No. AAT NR31964).

Youmei 幼梅 and Bingyun 秉昀. 1983. "Kuileixi jiehe xiandai qingnian de chuhang 傀儡戏结合现代青年的初航 [First sailing of the collaboration between marionettes and contemporary youths]." *Minsu quyi* 民俗曲艺 23–24: 25–29.

Yu Zheguang 虞哲光. 1957. *Mu'ouxi yishu* 木偶戏艺术 [The art of puppetry], 66–77. Shanghai: Shanghai wenhua chubanshe.

Zeng Jinzheng 曾金铮 and Long Bide 龙彼得 (Piet van der Loon). 1999. "Guanyin xiuxing: qingdai kuileixi chaoben 观音修行一清代傀儡戏抄本 [*Guanyin Attains Buddhahood*: a Qing dynasty hand-copied marionette play script]." *Minsu quyi* 民俗曲艺 121: 167–201.

Zeng Yongyi 曾永义. 2005. "Zhongguo ouxi kaoshu 中国偶戏考述 [Origins of Chinese puppetry]." http://www.sishu.cn/bbs/read.php?tid=2889.

Zhan Huideng 詹惠登. 1985. "Cong lidai kuileixi fazhan yu Zhongguo chuantong xiju de guanxi tan budaixi 从历代傀儡戏发展与中国传统戏剧的关系谈布袋戏 [The glove puppet theater from the perspective of the development of the puppet theaters and its relationship to the traditional Chinese theaters)." *Minsu quyi* 民俗曲艺 35: 39–54.

———. 1979. "Gudian budaixi yanchu xingshi zhi yanjiu 古典布袋戏演出形式之研究 [Types of performance of traditional glove theater]." M.A. thesis. Wenhua yishu yanjiusuo.

Zhang Chengfang 张呈芳. 1982. "Tan Quanzhou fucheng zhi kuileixi 谈泉州府城之傀儡戏 [On the puppet theater of the city of Quanzhou]." *Minsu quyi* 民俗曲艺 21: 45–50.

Zhang Fasheng 张发生. 1998. "Shanghang mu'ouxi qingqian liang'anyuan 上杭木偶戏情牵两岸缘 [The Shanghang Marionette Troupe strings together the bond across the straits]." *Jingji cankaobao* September 27: 2.

Zhang Lei 张耒 (11th century). 1985 (reprint). "Mingdao zazhi 明道杂志 [Miscellany to clarify the way; 1032–1033]." In *Congshu jicheng xinbian* 丛书集成新编 [A new compendium of collected works] 86: 626–632. Taibei: Xinwenfeng chuaban gongsi.

Zhang Qionghui 张琼辉, ed. 2003. *Huang Qianghua, Huang Wenze yu pili budaixi* 黄强华, 黄文泽与霹雳布袋戏 [Huang Qianghua, Huang Wenze, and Pili Glove Puppet Theatre]. Taipei: Shenghuo meixueguan.

Zhang Weinuo 张维诺 and Li Yuchun 李遇春. 1976. "Zhang Xiong fufu muyong yu chuTang kuileixi 张雄夫妇墓俑与初唐傀儡戏 [The relationship between the burial puppets in the tombs of Zhang Xiong and his wife, and puppetry during early Tang)." *Wenwu* 12: 44–50.

Zhang Xinfang 张新芳. 1979. "Qiantan piyingxi yu kuileixi 浅淡皮影戏与傀儡戏 [Cursory discussion of the shadow and marionette theaters]." *Guoli lishi bowuguan* 10: 8–12.

Zhao Shanlin 赵山林. 1990. *Zhongguo xiqu guanzhong xue* 中国戏曲观众学 [Audience of traditional Chinese theater], 14–15 and 23. Shanghai: Huadong shifan daxue chubanshe.

Zheng Guoquan 郑国权. 1995. "Huang Yique de tixian mu'ou biaoyan yishu 黄奕缺的提线木偶表演艺术 [The artistry of Huang Yique's performance of marionettes]." *Zhongwai wenhua jiaoliu* 6: 36–39.

Zheng Mingli 郑明利. 1972. "Zhongguo kuileixi de yanjin ji xiandai zhanwang 中国傀儡戏的演进及现代展望 [Evolution of the Chinese marionette theater and its contemporary outlook]." *Youshi* 35: 4–10.

Zheng Qingshui 郑清水 et al., eds. 1983. *Fujian xishilu* 福建戏史录 [Historical records on the theaters in Fujian]. Fuzhou: Fujiansheng renmin chubanshe.

Zheng Zhenghao 郑正浩. Wu Wenli 吴文理 tr. 1983. "Caishen yikao—Taiwan de tiandu yuanshuai yu xiqin wangye xinyang 财神一考—台湾的田都元帅与西秦王爷信仰 [A study of the god of wealth—Marshal Tiandu and the cult of Prince Xiqin in Taiwan]." *Minsu quyi* 民俗曲艺 23–24: 118–140.

Zhongguo shibao fushihui 中国世宝浮世绘. 1997. *Pili yingxiong dabutie: zui xi'ai de budaixi renwu* 霹雳英雄大布贴: 最喜爱的布袋戏人物 [Pili heroes' roster: favorite puppet characters]. Taipei: Shibao wenhua.

Zhongguo Xiquzhi Weiyuanhui 中国戏曲志编委会, ed. 1990. "Qianxi 线戏 [Marionette theater]." In *Zhongguo xiquzhi Shaanxi juan* 中国戏曲志. 陕

西卷 [Compendia of traditional Chinese operas—the volume on Shaanxi]. Beijing: Wenhua yishu chubanshe.

Zhonghua Minsu Yishu Jijinhui. 中华民俗艺术基金会. 2005. *Taiwan budaixi yu chuantong wenhua chuangyi chanye yantaohui wenji* 台湾布袋戏与传统文化创意产业研讨会文集 [Collected essays from the Taiwan Budaixi and Traditional Culture Creative Industries Symposium]. Yilan County: Guoli chuantong yishu zhongxin.

Zhou Yibai 周贻白. 1983 (reprint). "Zhongguo xiqu yu kuileixi yingxi—dui Sun Kaidi xiansheng *Kuileixi kaoyuan* yishu zhi shangque 中国戏曲与傀戏影戏—对孙楷第先生傀儡戏考源一书之商榷 [Traditional Chinese operas and the puppet and shadow theaters: an evaluation of Mr. Sun Kaidi's *Origins of the Puppet Theatres*]." *Minsu quyi* 民俗曲艺 23–24: 215–255.

———. 1977 (reprint). *Zhongguo xiju fazhan shi* 中国戏剧发展史 [A history of Chinese drama]. Taipei: Xueyi chubanshe.

———. 1979. *Zhongguo xiqu fazhanshi gangyao* 中国戏曲发展史钢要 [Outline of the historical development of the Chinese opera]. Shanghai: Guji chubanshe.

———. 1953. "Kuileixi yu yingxi 傀儡戏与影戏 [Puppetry and shadow theaters]." In *Zhongguo xijushi* 中国戏剧史 [A history of Chinese drama], 124–140. Shanghai: Zhonghua shuju.

www.ingramcontent.com/pod-product-compliance
Lightning Source LLC
Chambersburg PA
CBHW061031100726
47911CB00006B/150